Teaching Music through Performance in Orchestra

G-5565

Teaching Music through Performance in Orchestra

Michael Allen
Louis Bergonzi
Jacquelyn Dillon
Robert Gillespie
James Kjelland
Dorothy Straub

Compiled and Edited by David Littrell
and Laura Reed Racin

GIA Publications, Inc.
Chicago

G-5565

Table of Contents

ACKNOWLEDGEMENTS

The following research associates are gratefully acknowledged for outstanding scholarly contributions to the "Teacher Resource Guides":

Michael Allard
Porterville Unified School District and Porterville Community College
Porterville, California

Gail V. Barnes
University of South Carolina • Columbia, South Carolina

Margaret Haefner Berg
University of Colorado • Boulder, Colorado

Louis Bergonzi
Eastman School of Music
University of Rochester • Rochester, New York

Jeffrey Bishop
Shawnee Mission Northwest High School • Shawnee Mission, Kansas

Glenn Block
Illinois State University • Bloomington, Illinois

Susan Brown
Cabrillo College and University of California at Santa Cruz
Santa Cruz, California

Todd Coleman
Eastman School of Music • Rochester, New York

Andrew H. Dabczynski
Brigham Young University • Provo, Utah

Sandra Dackow
Ridgewood Symphony, New Jersey
Hershey Symphony, Pennsylvania

M. L. Daniels
Abilene Christian University • Abilene, Texas

Kathleen DeBerry-Brungard
Plano Senior High School • Plano, Texas

Rachel Dirks
USD #373 • Newton, Kansas

William Dyson
Atlanta Public Schools • Atlanta, Georgia

Ian Edlund
Retired Music Director/Conductor • Olympia, Washington
Retired Orchestra Director • Lacey, Washington

Janet E. Elliott
Friends University • Wichita, Kansas

Victor Ellsworth
University of Arkansas at Little Rock • Little Rock, Arkansas

Joanne Erwin
Oberlin College • Oberlin, Ohio

Judy Evans
Pine Ridge Middle School • Naples, Florida

Amy Fear-Bishop
Prairie Star Middle School and Stanley Elementary
Shawnee Mission, Kansas

Harry Fisher
Composer/Arranger, Retired Educator • Cherry Hill, New Jersey

Robert S. Frost
Composer/Arranger, Author, Conductor • Smithfield, Utah

Robert Gardner
Eastman School of Music
University of Rochester • Rochester, New York

Doris Gazda
Composer, Retired Teacher/Professor • Tempe, Arizona

Robert Gillespie
The Ohio State University • Columbus, Ohio

Kathlene Goodrich
The Hartt School, University of Hartford • Hartford, Connecticut

James D. Hainlen
Stillwater Area High School • Stillwater, Minnesota

Kathleen A. Horvath
University of Illinois • Urbana, Illinois

C. Gregory Hurley
University of Northern Colorado • Greeley, Colorado

Janet L. Jensen
University of Wisconsin–Madison • Madison, Wisconsin

Mary Lou Jones
Shawnee Mission South High School • Shawnee Mission, Kansas

Scott Laird
Eleanor Roosevelt High School • Greenbelt, Maryland

Jonathan D. Lane
Shawnee Mission East High School and Indian Hills Middle School
Shawnee Mission, Kansas

David Littrell
Kansas State University • Manhattan, Kansas

E. Daniel Long
Slauson Middle School and Ann Arbor Public Schools
Ann Arbor, Michigan

Sheila Morris
Las Vegas, Nevada

Kirt Mosier
Lee's Summit High School and Pleasant Lee Junior High
Lee's Summit, Missouri

Acknowledgements

Liz Murray
Parkway Southwest Middle School • Ballwin, Missouri

David O'Fallon
Composer and Percussion Teacher • Wheaton, Illinois

Ray E. Ostwald
York Community High School • Elmhurst, Illinois

Judy Palac
Michigan State University • East Lansing, Michigan

Phil Peters
Valley High School • West Des Moines, Iowa

Joseph Phillips
Carmel Central School District • Patterson, New York

Gregg Porter
Conductor, String Teacher, Composer • Olympia Fields, Illinois

Selma Pyles
Hilliard City Schools • Hilliard, Ohio

Mary Rudzinski
Marie Murphy School • Wilmette, Illinois

Marsha Chusmir Shapiro
Ormond Beach Middle School • Ormond Beach, Florida

Bret P. Smith
University of Maryland • College Park, Maryland

Dr. Camille M. Smith
University of Florida–Gainesville • Gainesville, Florida

Christa Speed
Grand Island Public Schools • Grand Island, Nebraska

Ida Steadman
Morehead Middle School/ Coronado High School • El Paso, Texas

xiv

Richard Stephan
Crane School of Music
State University of New York at Potsdam • Potsdam, New York

Kristin Turner
Arizona State University • Tempe, Arizona

Mary L. Wagner
Fairfax County Public Schools • Fairfax, Virginia

Robert Washburn
Crane School of Music
State University of New York at Potsdam • Potsdam, New York

Michele Winter
Lowell High School • San Francisco, California

Arlene Witte
Atlanta Public Schools • Atlanta, Georgia

Gary Wolfman
Appleton North and West High Schools • Appleton, Wisconsin

PART I

THE TEACHING
OF MUSIC

CHAPTER 1

Building Well-Rounded Orchestral Musicians in a Performance Setting

Jacquelyn Dillon

The Need for Teaching "About the Music"

Teaching Music through Performance in Orchestra was written primarily to assist string and orchestra conductors in teaching student musicians "about the music" that has been chosen for performance—while they actually participate in learning to play the music.

Orchestra conductors must never forget that school administrators often view them primarily as teachers of music—not as orchestra conductors. Consequently, the orchestra program needs to always be presented as an educational pursuit as well as a performance-based activity. Instrumental ensembles will be viewed on par with academic courses *if* students in these groups are trained as comprehensive musicians, i.e., they play well and also understand the music that they play. This means understanding such things as historical background of the composer and the composition, the form and style of the music, and stylistic considerations for playing the music, to name a few.

Quality orchestra conductors have always tried to make sure their students understand the music to be learned. Yet, in reality, most conductors today simply do not have the time to study and research the performance music thoroughly enough to be able to help the students learn very much about the music they are learning for performance. Others want and intend to teach students to understand the music, but they simply can't spare the time in rehearsal to really be able to accomplish this.

This book is intended to save orchestra conductors time in preparing to teach new compositions to ensembles. For each composition included in this book, the conductor will find helpful information to be used in teaching students to know about and understand the music. Also included are practical guidelines for the teacher's use in helping the students to learn to play the music.

Another important aspect of the book is that information is included for each composition so conductors can ensure that the National Standards for teaching a piece of music are followed. Upon completion of any compositions listed in this volume, conductors should be able to more easily assess if the students actually learned and understood the music performed.

Source for High-Quality Repertoire

The need has long existed for a dependable and easily accessible source from which to find high-quality repertoire for orchestras at all levels. The authors believe that this book offers to string teachers and orchestra conductors of all levels a dependable source of high-quality repertoire for performance ensembles.

The musical selections covered in this book range from Grade 1 to Grade 6 and were especially selected by the six co-authors. They are all compositions of the highest quality that have stood the "test of time" with many successful orchestra conductors. Many of these compositions are found on recommended or required state lists of high-quality orchestra repertoire.

The Music IS the Curriculum

Conductors of secondary-level instrumental groups agree that the repertoire chosen for performance actually IS the curriculum for the ensembles. Thus, it is critical to choose music for an orchestra that will inherently challenge and upgrade the overall technical abilities of the ensemble.

Equally important when considering repertoire for performance is to ensure that the compositions are musically satisfying and interesting to the students. If students don't care for the music, teaching it will be difficult—if not impossible.

Also essential is to choose music for performance that will have lasting value and contribute positively to the students' overall understanding and appreciation of music. The music should also have a direct relationship to what students in the group need to learn. Consequently, the planning of repertoire for groups is perhaps the single most important decision the orchestra conductor will make during a school year. Even the most experienced conductors spend a great deal of time deciding on music for ensembles—knowing that finding just the "right" music for a group directly relates to the technical advancement of the students in that group.

How the Book Is Set Up

Teaching Music through Performance in Orchestra is organized in two parts. Part I includes chapters written by the six co-authors whose names appear on the cover of the book. Together, these individuals represent more than 150 years of successful teaching at all levels in the string and orchestra teaching and conducting fields. Each co-author has written on a subject that is crucial to building a superior orchestra program. Their "words of wisdom" provide valuable insight into teaching students about music in a performance setting.

Part II includes Teacher Resource Guides for teaching one hundred of the most significant works for string and full orchestra, including compositions for Grade 1 through Grade 6. Detailed information is given on each composition, including composer and composition background, historical perspective, technical considerations, stylistic considerations, musical elements, and form and structure, as well as suggested listening and other references and resources. The contributors of the Teacher Resource Guides are all professionals working in the orchestra field who were willing to share and contribute their talents and knowledge of these compositions to the orchestra profession.

Conclusion

It is hoped that this book will not only be used by practicing teachers and conductors, but also as a text at the college level for instrumental technique courses, string method courses, and string pedagogy courses at both the undergraduate and graduate levels.

The co-authors of this series sincerely hope that the publication of this book will help to upgrade the teaching skills of string and orchestra conductors already in the field, as well as greatly influence the quality and scope of the training of future teachers at the college and university levels.

CHAPTER 2

But What about the Sound? Toward Greater Musical Integrity in the Orchestra Program

James Kjelland

Consider the following concert program performed publicly by an orchestra in a time and place not long ago:

Beethoven:	*Leonore Overture No. 3*
Mendelssohn:	Symphony No. 4, Movement 1 ("Italian")
Bartok:	Concerto for Orchestra, Movements 3 and 4
Shostakovich:	"Finale" from Symphony No. 5

On first impression, this program would seem to be fairly well balanced, with a distribution of popular standard works covering the late classical through twentieth century periods. Certainly it is all great music—sure to please the listener and performer alike. It could be a program presented by a professional or university orchestra—the latter surely being challenged to handle the technique if not the endurance.

This program was performed by a high school youth orchestra of approximately sixty players whose average ability and experience level approximated that of a typical public high school ensemble, not including several adult coaches playing along. The conductor, clearly knowing the music well, displayed well-rehearsed gestures to a receptive audience primarily consisting of parents, local community members, and youth orchestra board members. When the last chord of the Shostakovich piece reverberated through the small auditorium, the audience applauded enthusiastically and cheered as they rose to their feet for the apparently routine standing ovation.

On the surface, this concert would be evaluated as a big success for all concerned. The students seemed excited to be playing original masterworks. The conductor was apparently having a good time sharing his interpretation of the music for the audience. The parents seemed pleased that their children were at least approximating the sound of those familiar melodies they knew and loved so well.

The one element that cannot be described easily in this scenario, however, is the most important ingredient of all—*the sound!* The reaction to and the observable behaviors of this performance were much better than the performance actually sounded. The brass were overwhelmed by the high tessitura of their parts, let alone the resulting forced-tone quality. The strings sounded more like a swarm of bees in certain rapid passages than a string section; bowings were haphazard, appearing to be some sort of group improvisation. And the woodwinds were playing notes so out of tune they might as well have been fingering different notes.

For the lay listener, perhaps simply attempting a performance of this difficult music might be enough: "These are kids, they're supposed to sound like kids." For the proud parents: "Isn't it (and everything else my child does) wonderful?" For the *bona fide* music educator, however, this performance is utterly without musical and educational integrity. Whatever other values remain are accidental and can be achieved better in other extra-musical ways.

What Is Over-Programming?

Over-programming refers to the practice of performing standard orchestral repertoire that is well beyond the technical capabilities of the players in the group. Over-programming is, of course, not limited to orchestras; however, the rich tradition of orchestra literature coupled with its widespread appeal and recognition makes the orchestra particularly prone to over-programming. The term is also applied to the performance of too much music in a program, thus over-extending the endurance of both the players and the audience.

Over-programming by difficulty level is a significant problem to address because many practitioners resist change—such as focusing more on quality than quantity of performance. Sounding better would mean scaling back the difficulty level of the music, and with that many practitioners feel would go some of the prestige of having such masterworks on the program. The above scenario can aptly be compared to the parable, "The Emperor's New Clothes," in which the imaginary substance of the clothing is analogous to the imaginary substance of the performance. In both situations, someone is fooled into thinking the substance is really there because of the social posturing and other extrinsic values that surround the event.

No suit of clothes is better than it looks, no performance better than it sounds, no wine better than it tastes. The point of music education is missed *entirely* when the quality of a performance takes a back seat to the prestige of the works being played, the desire of the conductor to add such repertoire to his or her résumé, or the misapplication of music appreciation.

To clarify, I am not talking about the characteristic flaws found in amateur players—the inevitable pitch, rhythm, or note inaccuracies relative to their developmental stages. I am also not just talking simply about bad teaching, which may or may not be the case in over-programming situations. I am talking about the kind of performance in which, in spite of ability evident within the ensemble, the performance is compromised because the players are locked in a desperate quasi-athletic struggle to get the notes and keep from completely falling apart before the finish line.

This kind of performance is too often tolerated in the name of music education, with no intrinsic value or virtue to be found. In reality, the great repertoire is being publicly sacrificed along with the image and reputation of music education. The *bona fide* music educator knows that the essence of musical experience and understanding generates from what is *done* with the notes, not from simply being able to play most of them in approximately the right order and at approximately the right time. By this definition, a middle school orchestra playing a relatively simple piece expressively has far more integrity than a high school group attempting to play original Brahms, Beethoven, or Tchaikovsky.

Adverse Effects of Over-Programming

- Students and parents come to believe that a performance is successful if the orchestra is able to get through the piece without breaking down—not unlike a marathon run where the finish line itself is the goal and the reward.

- Lay parents are seduced into thinking that their children are actually playing the works of the great masters—hence the cheering and standing ovation at the end of the concert.

- Students learn to turn up their noses at music that is easier or of lesser-known composers because they are now too good to trifle with anything less than the masterworks—independent of how it sounds, of course.

- Conductors come to rely on the difficulty of the music itself as an excuse for poor performance, hiding the fact that they may not know how to rehearse a group effectively regardless of the difficulty of the music.

- In their struggles to play notes that are too fast, too high, or too loud, students can develop poor playing habits that, in turn, can have serious long-term consequences for future success on the instrument. Such problems include excessive muscular tension in the arms and hands of string players; forced high notes with mouthpiece pressure or distorted embouchures in brass playing; loss of accuracy in pitch, tone, and embouchure control in woodwind playing.

- The lay public views the stature of the repertoire as more significant than how it is performed, thus creating a support system (and, therefore, demand) for more.

- Students develop inflated self-concepts of how they actually play, in turn making realistic assessment and evaluation difficult. This problem, of course, is widespread in all areas of education—an unfortunate by-product of the so-called self-esteem movement, where automatic rewards for effort become confused with, or substituted for, measures of students' true qualitative accomplishments.

What about Music Appreciation?

The issue of appreciation is often raised as a rationale for over-programming—that is, the supposition that the attempt to play it enhances the students' appreciation for those who do, in addition to providing exposure to even a rough approximation of the original. On the contrary, striving for musical excellence at a level appropriate to an individual's and ensemble's means is the more effective path toward music appreciation. To know what it means to shape a phrase beautifully, or to vary articulations to change the character, or to experience the effects of different tempos is to know and appreciate music far more deeply than to crash and slash through a Beethoven symphony.

Studying great music in guided listening experiences with historical and theoretical background outside the performance setting is extremely worthwhile. To attempt to play great music, however, brings about a distortion of what is perceived as quality in performance both for the performer as well as the listener. Diligent technical work coupled with good teaching is necessary. There are no shortcuts. To bypass the basics does everyone a disservice; it also deprives young musicians of the rich experience of the "real stuff" of music—its power of communication and expression.

The great standard orchestral literature is for adults to perform—that is, professionally trained musicians. We do not allow children access to certain adult experiences for a variety of reasons, some of which are akin to this situation—potential long-term damage to development, perceptions, and attitudes. Even if a young orchestra were able to get all the notes, the maturity, insight, and life experience required to understand and, therefore, convey its meaning is, in most cases, still years beyond them.

Used judiciously, great literature can be very effective in a learning environment to guide and motivate young musicians to strive to improve their technical and ensemble skills as well as their discrimination. Some

educators keep one or two pieces in the folders that are not publicly performed, but that are explored in rehearsal or used as a study guide for listening analysis. This experience offers a vision of where the young musicians need to be technically and can be a powerful motivator for achievement. Published collections of orchestral excerpts are currently available for just this purpose.

Choosing Appropriate Music for the Group

Not every piece selected for performance can possibly meet each individual's technical needs at precisely the right level. Obviously, you must make some compromises proportional to the range of ability within your ensemble, resulting in some (as few as possible) players being over-challenged. Effective programming, therefore, starts with having an accurate sense of what your students can do—that is, the threshold of their technical ability.

Once ability has been assessed, I recommend programming at (or one technical grade level *below*) the average of the group, with plenty of musical challenges. To program *above* the average level—for example, programming only to the best players in the group—is to use the music to teach technique, which is *an ultimately self-defeating practice*. Doing so is the opposite of what is needed for smooth development in both technique and musicianship. The expressive aspects of the music cannot and will not be realized if students are learning new technique simultaneously. The level of the music should, therefore, be technically accessible for the majority of the ensemble if a performance is to have musical integrity, confidence, and enjoyment.

Where do students develop technique if not through the music itself? Obviously, private lessons help, but in addition to and in lieu of such a resource, skills can be developed within the allotted rehearsal time, but separate from the context of rehearsing the music. Good publications are currently available for developing technique and musicianship in the orchestra that can help those who are not exposed to private study. Teacher-conductors must take responsibility for helping students who are not taking lessons while at the same time doing whatever possible to facilitate such opportunities. Currently developing the technique needed for your very next concert, or working on the same music over a protracted period of time can result in frustration and white-knuckle performances—not to mention the distortion of technical and musical development.

One effective guideline for selecting the grade level of performance music is simply this: Can the group get through the piece in the first or second reading without breaking down? In other words, does it come together fairly quickly after the sight-reading effects wear off? If skills are developed separately, rehearsals will, in fact, *be* rehearsals. The separation of technical development and music rehearsal is important not only for developing skills long-term—that is, beyond what is needed for the next concert—but also for

10

teaching students the difference between the two. Using music to teach technique blurs the distinction between the two in that, when the notes are learned, students think they have mastered the piece. After the concert, the music is filed away and the cycle repeats itself—never allowing students to gain mastery over the music or have the depth of satisfaction that comes with it.

Music educators often worry that all of the higher-level students will drop out if the music is not technically challenging to them. Such students should be guided by example to respond to musical challenges and subtlety of expression. They can also be given latitude and input in alternate fingerings, bowings, and interpretation. In addition, they could be released from some rehearsal time to work on chamber music or to teach lessons. Opportunities to compose and conduct can also be extremely rewarding and motivating. Furthermore, the youth orchestra experience ideally can supplement the necessity of the higher-level students to stay challenged at a level closer to their technique. To bring such experiences back to share with peers in the school group is the main rationale for positive relationships between school and youth orchestra.

Certainly the risks and the compromises are much fewer with under-programming than with over-programming. What are the relative consequences for performing music that is too easy? It can become stale and boring, especially if played the same way all the time without attention to its musical content. And without separate, more advanced technique work, progress will stagnate. Nevertheless, music that is technically accessible enables secure, confident, and expressive performance. It also allows for a greater variety and quantity of music to be performed. Again, I am speaking about music that is performed as opposed to that which is studied in other ways.

What Does a Grade Level Really Mean?

The technical and musical aspects of a piece are two very different dimensions that can vary a great deal independently. Musical difficulty refers to the relative complexity of ensemble-based aspects such as balance, phrasing, tempo changes, and number of independent parts separate from the rhythmic, bowing, and range demands. Because most string music is graded by technical more than musical difficulty and is usually oriented to left-hand skills such as range, key, and positions, a lower grade level piece can often be quite challenging for an ensemble.

Sustained bowing, such as in an adagio-style piece, for example, can be extremely challenging and may not be taken into consideration in the grade level determination. An arrangement of Bach's chorale, "Come Sweet Death," is marketed as a Grade 3 piece, when in actuality it could challenge a Grade 5 orchestra. For that matter, any advanced orchestra can be challenged musically by a sostenuto piece. Many instances of misgraded music

can be found, and as always, the proof is in how it works with *your* ensemble.

Another unfortunate situation with music grading, in addition to ignoring musical and right-hand challenges, is a kind of deflation of the grade levels themselves even on technical criteria. Many times a piece is labeled Grade 3 but should really be Grade 4 or even higher. Do some editors not understand the technical challenges of string music? Is there disagreement as to what a legitimate Grade 3 piece should be (for example, whether spiccato bowing is included)?

Many orchestra conductors may not know that the market for music per grade level roughly corresponds to a low-rise pyramid shape. That is, the greatest number of pieces at grade 1 represent the bottom of the pyramid, and as the grade level increases, the number of pieces become progressively fewer. Do publishers purposely mark the grade level down to reach a potentially larger market? I would hope not. Nevertheless, the instances of grade levels being underestimated are, in my experience, more frequent than vice versa.

A publisher's grade level is only a rough approximation at best, which contains a wide range of variability. A higher grade level does not correlate strongly with a higher quality of music, or with whether it meets the needs of each section of the orchestra at the same quality level.

What Can Be Done about Over-Programming?

Conductors who over-program flagrantly do not have the musical welfare of their students as their first priority. Intentional or not, technical development, perceptions, and attitudes are compromised. Pressure needs to be applied on conductors and organizations who support this practice consistently. Plenty of good music is available at all grade levels—high-quality original compositions and arrangements that, unfortunately, gather dust and go out of print quickly because of neglect in favor of the standards. One of the major contributions of this publication is to select and promote many excellent, original works that would otherwise go unnoticed. Such music may, indeed, be more appropriate for the balanced development of all sections of the orchestra compared to, say, the Mozart Divertimento, K. 136.

An important line of defense against over-programming is festival and competition adjudication. Too many times, those entrusted to uphold standards of performance quality enable over-programming to exist by not including, or by not emphasizing enough, the music selection factor in ratings and comments. Inflated ratings are awarded because of the attempt to perform hard music ("It's really a II rating, but I'll give them a I because they played hard music.") If adjudicators were to be truly honest in their evaluation, over-programming (and other forms of rating inflation) would virtually disappear. Unfortunately, adjudicators and other music organizations too often use difficulty level as the primary yardstick for measuring quality in a music program. If it sounds good, fine, but all too often sound takes a back seat to extrinsic values.

One of the acid tests of a conductor is what his or her orchestra can do with a technically easier piece. As mentioned, over-programming often is used to disguise a conductor's inability to effectively rehearse and improve the orchestra. If competitions and rated festivals were to be truly reflective of the ensemble's and conductor's ability, a lower grade level piece should be required in each group's performance to show by comparison their respective levels of true musicianship. Instead, music that is well within the grasp of the ensemble is sometimes considered a liability and, therefore, a reason to deduct points.

The bottom line in orchestra performance is quality of *sound* and the resulting musical and educational integrity that is embodied in it—regardless of the grade level of the music and the developmental level of the players. Let's promote deeper, more lasting musical values and experiences for our students by selecting literature that is within their means and by emphasizing the kinds of musical experiences that have brought us to the music teaching profession in the first place. When the sound is there, everyone wins; otherwise, what's the point?

This text is based in part on the author's article: "Over-Programming and The Emperor's New Clothes," originally published in *Orchestra News*, Scherl & Roth Co., Fall 1991.

CHAPTER 3

Selecting Music
for Your Orchestra

Robert Gillespie

A wealth of high-quality literature is available for school orchestras at all playing levels. Selecting music that is best for your orchestra is a process that involves advance concert planning and the ability to evaluate a piece of music in terms of the needs of your students, audience, and orchestra program. The process can be categorized into four steps.

Step 1: Predetermine the music needs of your concert season.

Start with the big picture: Plan your concert season well in advance. Predetermine the type of music needed for the year; focus on selecting a wide range of high-quality, expressive repertoire that meets the special needs of the concert year. The best time to plan the concert season is either before or during the beginning of the school year.

Consider the following questions when planning your concerts for the year:

- How many different concert programs will be performed?
- Which of the concerts will involve full orchestra, if any?
- How many weeks or rehearsals are available to prepare each concert?
- What is the special theme or purpose for each concert—pops, classical, patriotic, Broadway musicals, student recruitment, school assembly programs, National Standards focus, community support development?
- Will there be any contest or festival performances?
- What will be the acoustical properties of the concert sites?
- Who will primarily be in the audience—peers of the orchestra members, parents, people in the community who are not directly involved in the orchestra program, younger students, administrators?

Step 2: Determine the playing skills of your students.

After ascertaining the overall scope of the concerts that will be performed during the upcoming school year, you must next determine the playing skills of your students. Regular assessment throughout the school year is integral to choosing the best music for the orchestra. Start by administering skill checks and tests at the beginning of the year. This process will provide a base-line assessment that will either confirm that the difficulty level of the music you have already selected is appropriate or help you choose other selections.

Ongoing playing evaluation encourages students to continue to develop their skills to perform the music selected. Assessment at the end of the year helps you determine what music to program for the following year.

One factor to assess is the bowing skills of the students. What bow strokes can the majority of the students execute—détaché, staccato, hooked, spiccato, martelé, legato, tenuto? Left-hand skills to appraise may include finger patterns, cello extensions, shifting, and vibrato. Other factors to evaluate include how well students play in tune, which keys they can play in, and which rhythms and notes they are familiar with.

Be sure to understand your students' ability to understand and demonstrate expressive skills such as dynamics, phrasing, style articulations, and changes in tempo. Also assess the musical interests and maturation of the students. What types of music do they most like and dislike? Which styles of music do they prefer to play? What are their natural musical interests?

Step 3: Evaluate a piece of music.

Developing the ability to pedagogically evaluate a piece of music at sight is another one of the important steps in the process of selecting the best music for your orchestra. Quick, accurate assessment of a piece of music is critical to the process of music selection.

When first learning how to evaluate pieces, develop a list of sequential playing skills. Then use the list to help you quickly evaluate a piece. The list could include bowing skills, left-hand skills, and expressive skills, as described above.

Next begin to examine each piece. Determine what playing skills are necessary to perform the piece. For example, determine what bowing skills are required, such as détaché, staccato, string crossings, spiccato, slurring, and so on.

Evaluate what left-hand skills are required. What finger patterns occur for violin and viola? Are there any high third fingers for C-sharp and G-sharp or low second fingers for F-natural or C-natural for violin or viola? Are there any extensions for cello? Are there any accidentals? Do my students know how to play all the pitches and rhythms? To what degree are the parts rhythmically

 CHAPTER 3   Teaching Music through Performance in Orchestra

independent? Are there any shifts? If so, what positions are involved and do my students know them?

Is the bass part interesting rhythmically and melodically? Are there interesting musical lines for each instrument? Each instrument should get at least part of the melody occasionally. If not, students may consider their part, or maybe even their instrument, unimportant and may develop a negative attitude toward the piece. Attracting and maintaining interest in the music is key to a successful performance and educational experience for the students.

Also evaluate the musical expressiveness of the piece. Are the phrases clear and melodic? Is the tempo suggested appropriate? Does the style and tempo of the piece require vibrato to be musically expressive? Is the key of the piece familiar to students? Does the harmony appropriately support the melody? Do the suggested dynamics add to the musical character of the piece? Do the rhythms add to the musical interest of the work?

In *Reverie* by James Corigliano, for example, the phrases are clearly marked. The style marking of "Adagio" and the metronome tempo indicated fit the legato and expressive qualities of the piece. The viola part is important musically and rhythmically. The bowings support the musical line, and the dynamic markings are clearly indicated and add to the movement of the musical line.

in memory of Frank Console
REVERIE
for String Orchestra

James Corigliano

16

A Quiet Music by Douglas Wagner provides another example of a piece in which the viola part is integral to the musical line. In measures 5 through 10, the phrases are shared between first violin, second violin, and viola. The dynamic markings contribute significantly to the expressiveness of the piece. Also, the tempo marking is appropriate and the bowing contributes to the phrasing of the piece.

For Richard F. Dennis

A QUIET MUSIC

Douglas Wagner (ASCAP)

© Copyright 1999, Belwin-Mills Publishing Corp. (ASCAP)

How well are the score and parts edited? How much additional editing is needed to make the piece work for your students? Are the printed bowings appropriate for the skills of the students? Slurs that are too long for young players present problems. Are there any fingerings suggested, and if so do they make sense?

An excerpt from "Johnny's Planting Song," a movement from the *Johnny Appleseed Suite* by Robert Kerr, provides an example of a well-edited piece. The melody appears in the viola part, and the printed dynamic for that line is "forte," while the other parts are marked "mezzo-piano," helping students to understand that a melodic line must be heard over the harmony. All bowings are clearly marked, support the musical line, are accessible to young players,

and are easy to read. No other bowings are needed for students to perform the passage. The cello and bass lines are active and support the harmony at the same time. The case is the same for first and second violin.

excerpt from JOHNNY APPLESEED SUITE

How easily could you use this piece to teach the National Standards? Is it possible to research the life of the composer so you can correlate his or her life with related historical and artistic developments to teach the National Standards? If the piece is an arrangement, how close is it to the original? Is the original readily available? Is there a recording of the piece, other music by the composer, or other pieces of the same style? "Johnny's Planting Song" is an example of a piece that is well suited for teaching music in relation to history.

Publishers' grading systems can help you evaluate the performance requirements of a piece; however, unfortunately, not all publishers use the same system. In addition, not all pieces neatly fall within a stratified system.

Clearly determining the difference between a Grade 1 piece and a Grade 1.5 piece is frequently difficult. Publishers' grading systems help narrow the selection of pieces for you to examine, but nothing can substitute for the ability to quickly, efficiently, and accurately assess at sight the performance skills required by a piece of music.

Step 4: Match the music to your purposes.

The final step in the process of selecting the best music for your orchestra is to determine whether or not a particular piece matches the abilities of your students and your concert season. Consider the following questions:

- Do the technical and musical performance requirements match the playing skills of my students? Will my students be able to perform the piece well? Programming music that is too easy does not help students develop as musicians. Programming pieces that are too difficult demoralize students and do not contribute to their overall musical growth. (Refer to chapter 2 for more on over-programming.)

- Does the piece match the musical maturation of my students? Music that does not lend itself to the development of students' expressive experience is not worth their time or yours.

- Does the piece serve the special purposes or themes for the concerts during the year, or future years?

- Does the piece contribute to the goal of selecting repertoire that has a wide range of different musical styles, historical periods, and cultures?

- Does the piece reinforce the technical and musical development of my students? A complete school orchestra rehearsal includes a warm-up period that involves a creative review of previously learned skills, the introduction of new skills either by rote or through method book or written technical exercises, and reinforcement of new skills through orchestral music that includes those skills.

If you can answer these questions positively, the piece is probably a very good choice for your orchestra.

Conclusion

Much of the success of orchestra teaching in school depends on the music that students perform. The teacher's careful, intelligent, and informed analysis of music is integral.

Begin by determining the overall musical goals of your school year. Then

regularly assess the playing skills of your students and develop the ability to accurately evaluate the performance requirements of a piece of music at sight. If the piece fits your musical goals and the skills of your students, it will be good for the program.

CHAPTER 4

Teaching "Traditional" Contemporary Music in School Orchestra Programs: Let's Not Be Too Polite

Louis Bergonzi

As teachers we're given many responsibilities. Among them, we are important role models about American culture, conveying our values and viewpoints about music and the other arts. Students don't expect their orchestra teachers to put them in touch with every musical style that exists. But our attitudes toward popular music, folk music, and music from nonwestern cultures are contagious by the very position we hold as authorities in the students' world. Our decision about what musical materials we select to bring—and to leave out—of our orchestral curriculum speaks volumes about what we, as musicians and adults in their lives, consider important.

Students in an orchestra are also students of the orchestra as a social-cultural phenomenon; thus, the music from Western-European orchestral traditions should occupy a prominent place. After all, it is the music for which the orchestra as a musical ensemble exists. Certainly music from nonwestern cultures can be performed on stringed instruments, as is recommended in the National Standards in Music[1]. Nevertheless, music from other cultures may also be learned in other components of the school music program, whereas contemporary orchestra music is unique to the orchestral experience.

So what message do we convey about classical music? Is classical music by nature old and well preserved from another era, limited to well-established masterpieces, and predominantly from Europe? We need to communicate through our actions as musical arbiters to the young Americans in our charge that a tradition of classical music exists within their own country and that it is alive and well today.

School Music vs. Real Music

American composers write much of the music that is available commercially for school orchestras. Some of the best of this genre appears in this very volume. But music education philosophers and historians have written much about the inadequate relationship between the musical materials used in schools and those from the cultural-musical world outside of the educational system. According to Britton, "Music education...has always operated at a certain distance from the well-springs of American musical life, both popular and artistic.... The music educator has found himself in the position of trying to find understandable music that could be taken as 'classical.' The term 'polite' is perhaps as good as any other to characterize much of the music utilized in schools from the time of Lowell Mason to the present day."[2]

In his book *Contemporary Music Education*, Michael Mark derides the graded texts used in elementary classroom music programs and the method books used in instrumental music programs, as well as in music appreciation texts. According to Mark, "'educational music' derived in non-authentic fashion at a level of difficulty suitable for children...does not necessarily engage the students' interest."[3]

The leaders at the Yale Seminar of 1963 wrote eloquently about the need for better musical materials for school—materials that connect to musical practice outside of school. Initiatives of days past—such as the Young Composers Project (1959–62) and the Contemporary Music Project (1963–73)—and of present—such as "Meet the Composer"—attempt to connect American classical composers to the students in American schools.

Unlike our concert band colleagues, the orchestra and its music have prominent counterparts in the contemporary world of professional music. As such, the orchestra is in many ways the soccer team of music. Both have their origins in Europe, and a history of amateur practice that led to professional status prior to each being included in schools. Similar to soccer teams, orchestras also exist in the worlds of professional adults, amateur adults, and school children, with the latter practicing their art (sport) both in school and outside of school.

Because of this, not only do we need to include music by living American composers, but also the music of American composers whose work appears in the professional concert hall, or at least that most emulates it stylistically. How well do we meet this aspect of our professional responsibility? Clearly, each of us must judge that for himself or herself, but there is probably room for improvement.

Why We Might Avoid It

There is probably a variety of reasons why orchestra conductors avoid performing contemporary American music. Some teachers may believe that our primary job is to convey the orchestral masterworks; because we don't know which of today's pieces will develop that pedigree, we might be reluctant to devote precious time to contemporary music. Professional orchestra conductors and musicologists have dismissed this argument, however, as evidenced in their programming and writings.

On a more practical note, classical contemporary music often does not appear on the music lists of state/national professional organizations because—or perhaps as a result of this—scores and parts are difficult to obtain. With only a little extra effort, directors can secure scores and parts to many worthwhile contemporary works for orchestra. Often, scores and parts are less expensive for this repertoire.

Perhaps the most likely reason that contemporary American music is not often performed is that orchestra teachers/conductors aren't comfortable with this music. As may be the case with improvisation and jazz, we just don't know enough about it. This was determined to be the case in the 1960s with Contemporary Music Project.[4]

Before we can bring new music to our students, we need to orient ourselves. We need to learn what's new in contemporary music and then provide experiences that prepare our students for the journey.

Preparing Ourselves

Regardless of when composers write, they draw upon familiar musical practice, including aspects of musical sound such as harmony, instrumentation, rhythm, melody, and form. Our understanding of these concepts may need to be expanded to be more applicable to contemporary music. For example, rhythm may now be thought to include all representations and proportions of time, and instrumentation to include the aspect of how a sound is produced.

A thorough explanation of how each of these elements may be utilized in contemporary music is impossible here, but I offer these generalities:[5]

1. Harmony: Not necessarily based on thirds. Other intervals can be the basis of harmonic language (fourths/quartal harmony). Sometimes, composers think horizontally, not vertically.

2. Instrumentation: All voices are often viewed as equally important. Sounds assigned to second violin, bass, and viola have their own integrity and are not only at the service of other parts.

3. Rhythm: Rhythmic gestures are often more seminal in contemporary music than in earlier music.

4. Time Proportions: Composers consider themselves free of the tyranny of the bar line and control and convey the marking of real time in other ways.

5. Sound Production: Nontraditional sound production techniques (col legno, bowing behind the bridge, tapping the body of the instrument, etc.) are often the rule and not the exotic exception. Once we turn our thinking around on this, other qualities of the piece often fall into place.

6. Form: Sections may blur into one another, like a cinematic fade-in/fade-out rather than relate as do the chapters of a book. Also, a theme may be developed before it is stated.

Preparing Our Students

Although the sounds of contemporary music are not as foreign to students as we might think, they probably do have less experience performing this music than they do other styles. Students need an orientation so that they approach the experience with the seriousness of effort they afford more familiar music. Two analogies may assist you: making a new friend and speaking a new language.

Students of the age typically found in school orchestras are keyed into peer relationships and what it takes to develop them. Engaging students in a conversation about how one develops friendships will reveal that, although most of our friends look, dress, and act in ways similar to ourselves, we each have at least one or two friends who are unlike the majority of our others. We value our friendships with these persons in a special way—for the variety they bring to our lives. Learning a piece of contemporary music—because it is indeed so different from the other pieces we play in orchestra—can be as rewarding as knowing people who are unlike the majority of our friends. Moral of the story: Contemporary music may not be like the majority of music performed by a school orchestra, but if we take the time needed to understand it, we'll find it brings something special to our lives as musicians.

In today's world, students have the benefit of being exposed to a variety of languages other than English. In addition, our language is ripe with borrowed phrases and words. Even though we may not be familiar with a particular non-English language, applying what we know about our language to an unfamiliar language can provide us with key information about the speaker's intent. That is, we can often glean information about someone's message from a speaker's vocal quality—volume, range, modulation, and inflection—and body language, even if a person is speaking in a language of unfamiliar vocabulary, grammar, and syntax.

I have used the following classroom activity to make this point. The speaker can be the teacher or, with practice, an outgoing, comical student.

Teacher (to orchestra):
You're going to hear two messages being said to two people in the orchestra. The message will not be in a language with which any of you are familiar. It will be in a nonsense language. When we're done, I want you to tell me if the speaker felt the same way about each of the recipients and how you decided on your answer.

(Pause, during which speaker changes body posture and facial expression to indicate hatred of the student to whom he or she is about to "converse.")

Speaker to Student A (with low/loud voice, furrowed brow, facial grimace, body low to the ground and at an acute angle to student):
grrrr—kkppppppp–!!!—fffffff....

(Speaker should continue "speaking" in this manner using only consonants, no vowel sounds, to indicate and maintain an angry intent.)

Teacher:
Remember, you are to decide whether the speaker's intent is the same when he speaks to the next student and be able to tell me how you made your decision.

(Pause, during which speaker changes body posture and facial expression to indicate affection toward the second student.)

Speaker to Student B: (with modulating, midrange voice; a wide smile on face; an open stance, and arms that occasionally suggest an embrace of student):
ahhh.......oooooohhhhh....uuuuuuuuu.

(Speaker should continue in this manner using only vowel sounds to indicate and maintain an affectionate intent.)

Teacher:
Does the speaker feel the same way about each person he spoke to? (No. Likes one, dislikes the other.) How do you know this?

(Lead discussion summarizing contrasting vocal volume, voice modulation, use of consonants/vowels, facial expression, body posture.)

Moral of the story:
Even though you were completely unfamiliar with the vocabulary, syntax, and grammar of this language, you were able to discern the intent of the speaker by using what you know about personal communication and applying it. You could tell the intent of the speaker.

Throughout the history of orchestral music, there have been composers who have expanded the musical vocabulary of their time. Conversely, there have been musicians (performers, chamber ensembles, conductors, and orchestras) whose own familiarity with the music of their time has been pushed by these composers. And finally, these composers—for the most part—have asked audiences to move beyond the musical expectations of their time and to accept something new sounding.

We are going to learn a piece of classical music that has been written for orchestra (professional, if applicable) using a tonal, rhythmic, and expressive vocabulary that will be unfamiliar to you— and me. Together, we will work to determine the composer's intent and to present the piece to our audience.

To apply this idea to a musical example, improvise (you, a colleague, a local piano teacher, a student) a simple march and a nocturne on the piano using C and F-sharp majors at the same time. Keep the nocturne slow, soft, lyrical, temporally uneven (full of tenutos, *ritardandos*, etc.), while the march is clearly regularly rhythmic and loud. Ask the students if the two pieces were in the same style—or which was a march, the first or second example? And— most importantly—how did they decide that even though the pieces, unlike most of the music they've played, were in two keys at the same time? You can discuss these questions in a manner similar to the gibberish language stated earlier.

Rehearsal Guideposts

The above introductory classroom scenarios exemplify some important principles in approaching contemporary classical music: working from what is familiar to the students, identifying the composer's expressive intent and going after it, grabbing onto compositional handles, and—mostly important- ly—giving the composer and the piece a fighting chance. Let's examine each guidepost to see how they can be applied to one of the pieces in this volume.

When we hear a piece from a familiar style, perhaps by a composer whose music we know, we have the benefit of certain expectations about "how it goes." When we encounter new music, our need to know what we're doing compels us to try to establish reference points with known music or composers. It may be helpful to remind students that they actually do the same thing when they try a new type of cuisine for the first time: "Gee, it tastes like chicken." We might think: "Gee, this (measure, passage, movement, piece) sounds a little like x?"

We should feel comfortable using this survival instinct to identify a section or aspect of a piece that makes the most immediate sense to us. Without confining the piece too tightly into a straitjacket of conventionality, we should develop our ideas and opinions about the rest of the piece by using this handle.

A handle allows us to grab onto something to get us through the other sections of the piece that are not so immediately rewarding because of our unfamiliarity with the piece's convention. Handles offer students our most positive and committed connection to the work at the beginning of the preparation process. The technical requirements to play the handle should be well within the comfortable core of the ensemble's technique. To keep the focus on the expressive qualities of the piece, contemporary music should not be to stretch students' technique—although that may happen as well—but to expand their ears and sense of artistic commitment.

Critical to our progress in learning a new piece at this juncture is that we reserve judgment about the value of the piece until after we have given it a fair chance. Use words that describe, not evaluate. This attitude can be also conveyed to students by saying the same words with two meanings: Say "*Why is it this way?*" with a sense of serious curiosity and inquiry as opposed to "Why is it *this* way?" with a sense of skepticism and disbelief that it is the way it is.

Example of the Application of Rehearsal Guidelines

These guideposts can be applied to *A Little Bit of…Space…Time* by Samuel Adler, which can be found on page 116 of the Teacher Resource Guides.

1. **Grab on to the handles.** The major handle for the Adler piece is the contrast between nontraditional string sounds (and the physical space to produce them) and traditional sounds and how both are able to express something to the listener.

2. **Refer to the familiar** ("Tastes like chicken."), but don't force the piece to be something it's not. The tonal, scalar theme of the second movement is easy to remember. It could be taught by rote, having the students determine when to start the "round" building upon their familiarity with other rounds and canons. The intent of the final three measures is clear: "Here's the ending." We know this from the homorhythmic texture, loud dynamic, and solidly tonal nature, in this case D major. These qualities can be found in the final cadences of much that has been written for school orchestras.

3. **Give the composer and the piece a fighting chance.** The first movement makes more demands upon the player and listener. Use the elements found in the Teacher Resource Guide to attach students' interest to the most accessible features. Read how Adler himself did it during rehearsals for the first performance.

4. **Avoid labels that judge without cause.** The opening could be called "weird" or, equally damning, "interesting," both without any reference

to the sounds that lead toward that conclusion. But what about "expansive" *because of* the lack of pulse, or "captivating" *because of* the unfamiliarity of the sounds but the easily recognizable recurrence of the ideas.

5. **A piece has only one chance to make a first impression.** Take the most accessible and appealing section and get it to performance readiness as soon as possible—during the first encounter—so that musically expression can provide the reward needed to work your way through the rest of the piece. The intent of the ending of the Adler piece is probably the most accessible at first read-through. Work on getting the final three measures to performance level during the first rehearsal by insisting on strong bows just below the middle of the bow, strict rhythmic precision, adding a slight *crescendo* in the last measure toward the last eighth note—all contributing to an exciting finish.

Trust

Approaching contemporary music with our students requires trust at a variety of levels:

- We need to *trust* that the composer knew what he/she was doing when he/she wrote the piece; that the piece makes sense, even if we don't understand it at first.
- Students must *trust* us to help them through this new experience, even though it may be more of a stretch for us than for them.
- We must *trust* ourselves as musicians to have confidence in our interpretations about how a new piece "should go"; interpretations that we develop without benefit of the expectations we have for familiar music. However, this also liberates us to find our own "authentic" interpretation of a piece, as we are not boxed in by decades of traditions.

Why Contemporary Music?

In programming contemporary music, we demonstrate to ourselves and to our students:

- that we are lifelong learners. We show our professional willingness to approach current ideas and trends in our field. This may not be the same for other teachers, who must wait until developments in their discipline get processed by education publishers and included in new editions of an intentionally commercially viable textbook.
- that composers are people too, people who are alive in our world;

people we can even call on the telephone and speak to about their music.

- a pride in our own American music and our own time. We show that today's music is as musically interesting and expressive as older music was in its time.
- that classical music is not "museum music"; that there is a contemporary music in the Euro-American classical tradition; that there is contemporary music in America beyond that archived on movie soundtracks, radio, or television.

Contemporary music offers students more direct contact with music history in the making as they are engaged with a piece of music—in the case of a world premiere, for the very first time ever. This is particularly meaningful in our world of technology, where a piece is captured and preserved on ten different CDs and four videos, complete with historical commentary and analysis telling us all we need to know. With contemporary music, more of what we need to know is ours to find out, if we are ready and willing to do so.

Resources

Meet the Composer: http://www.meetthecomposer.org/

Morgan, Robert. *Twentieth Century Music*. New York: W. W. Norton & Company, 1991.

Sadie, Stanley, ed. *The New Grove Dictionary of Music and Musicians*. "Samuel Adler." New York: Grove's Dictionaries, 2000. Also available online at www.grovemusic.com

Watkins, Glenn. *Soundings: Music in the Twentieth Century*. New York: Schirmer, 1988.

---

1 Music Educators National Conference. *National Standards for Arts Education: What Every Young American Should Know and Be Able to Do in the Arts*. Reston, VA: Music Educators National Conference, 1994.
2 Britton, Allen P. Paul Henry Long, ed. "Musical Education: An American Specialty," in *One Hundred Years of Music in America*. (New York: Schirmer), 1961, 214–215.
3 Mark, Michael. *Contemporary Music Education*. 3d edition. (New York: Schirmer, 1996), 8–9.
4 Ibid., 29.
5 For appropriate background on contemporary music, I refer the reader to Glenn Watkins, *Soundings* (New York: Schirmer, 1992). I also want to thank John Graham, professor of viola and advocate-performer of contemporary viola, for his assistance with this section.

CHAPTER 5

The Impact of the National Standards on Music Performance

Dorothy Straub

Teaching Music through Performance in Orchestra directly addresses a significant change in music education at the end of the twentieth century in America. Orchestra performance is not an end in itself; it is one component of a comprehensive music education. Since the advent of the National Standards and developments that followed, a new definition of orchestra performance has emerged, along with a new definition of the role of the orchestra conductor.

The orchestra conductor, or more appropriately the orchestra teacher, is now viewed in a broader context, with the responsibility of providing a comprehensive music education for all children. The Arts Standards and two related projects, summarized here, are explained in detail at the end of this chapter.

- In 1994, *The National Standards for Arts Education: What Every Young American Should Know and Be Able to Do in the Arts* was published.
- In 1998, the American String Teachers Association published *Standards for the Preparation of School String and Orchestra Teachers*.
- In 2000, *Performing with Understanding* was published, written by participants in a seminar held at Northwestern University, "Performance in the Context of the National Standards for Music Education."

To ensure that music teachers understand that the National Standards are an expectation and responsibility for every music educator, regardless of grade level or area of specialization, the National Music Standards document states, "Each course in music, including performance courses, should provide instruction in creating, performing, listening to, and analyzing music, in addition to focusing on its subject matter."

When the National Standards are embraced, music, along with the other arts, is on a par with other academic subjects and, as such, calls for academic expectations on the part of the teacher as well as the students. The goal of the orchestra teacher is not solely the performance of the ensemble but also includes the development of the individual musical skills and knowledge of each student in the ensemble. The intent is to prepare well-educated musicians for active, lifelong musical participation.

The Orchestra Teacher as a Standards-Based Music Educator

THE CHALLENGE:

The orchestra teacher is indeed challenged by the expectations of the National Standards. It is assumed that the orchestra teacher is a well-rounded, well-educated musician. Theoretically, this should be the case. Colleges and universities are charged with the responsibility of preparing their graduates for successful careers in music education, but music education has changed. The National Standards are a new expectation, and many students entering college today have not had the opportunity to develop as well-rounded musicians, as defined in the National Standards. The breadth of the undergraduate program in music education is demanding and time consuming; the National Standards raise the bar.

CHANGE:

The National Standards call for change. Change is often not easy, particularly for teachers who, after years of teaching, have established patterns of instruction and are comfortable with existing expectations for students. To embrace the National Standards and the challenge of change, time is needed—time for reading and reflecting; time to discuss new curriculum and new pedagogy with colleagues, and to research new information; and time to prepare new lesson plans. Technology is a valuable tool in adapting to these changes, as a wealth of information is available on the Internet, and communication with colleagues near and far can be a useful process.

ASSESSMENT:

Music on a par with other academic disciplines assumes that assessment will be in place. Authentic assessment, or performance assessment, has made great strides in music since the advent of the National Standards. The Teacher Resource Guides included in this book have facilitated the process of assessment by specifying clearly the skills and knowledge students are expected to acquire.

RESOURCES AVAILABLE:

The primary purpose of *Teaching Music through Performance in Orchestra* is the Teacher Resource Guides. At your fingertips is information about selected pieces from orchestra and string orchestra literature to assist you in bringing a comprehensive musicianship approach to your rehearsals. Each piece selected includes information about the composer, the composition, a historical perspective, technical considerations, stylistic considerations, musical elements, form and structure, suggested listening, and additional references and resources.

The Teacher Resource Guides provide a format for approaching other musical selections. Analysis and research of new music should be less difficult once a pattern is established. Your students will come to expect a thoughtful and thorough presentation of each new piece of music.

THE RESULTS:

This is for you to determine. This is the interactive part of the chapter in this book. Will you find that your students are handling themselves as intelligent musicians, not just technicians on their instruments? Will they have a better understanding of the structure of the music, rhythmic patterns, melodic contour, harmonic progressions, and dynamic contrast? Will they be curious about composers and seek additional information? Will they be making comparisons between composers from the same musical period? Will they be able to sing the music they are playing? Will they be able to improvise on a melody in music they are playing? Will they be able to compose their own short piece using appropriate notational symbols? Will they be learning new music more quickly? Will they be more interested in listening to orchestral music—on a CD or at a live concert? Will they become more independent musicians, using their musical skills and knowledge to communicate expressively? Will they intensify their musical commitment? Will they aspire to continue playing their instruments when they leave your school orchestra?

Teaching Music through Performance in Orchestra implies that performance is not an end in itself, but rather a means through which we teach music. It has the potential to strengthen the orchestral experience for music teachers and their students.

The National Standards in Music

The National Standards in Music define what every student should know and be able to do in music. These standards call for a comprehensive music education for all children. They were developed through a national consensus process, and consistent with national standards in other disciplines, they are voluntary.

The *National Standards for Arts Education* were developed by the Consortium of National Arts Education Associations under the guidance of the national Committee for Standards in the Arts. The Standards were prepared under a grant from the U.S. Department of Education, the National

Endowment for the Arts, and the National Endowment for the Humanities.

The Content Standards specify what every student should know and be able to do. The nine Content Standards are:

1. Singing, alone and with others, a varied repertoire of music.
2. Performing on instruments, alone and with others, a varied repertoire of music.
3. Improvising melodies, variations, and accompaniments.
4. Composing and arranging music within specific guidelines.
5. Reading and notating music.
6. Listening to, analyzing, and describing music.
7. Evaluating music and music performance.
8. Understanding relationships between music, the other arts, and disciplines outside the arts.
9. Understanding music in relation to history and culture.

Achievement Standards specify the understandings and level of achievement expected by the completion of grades four, eight, and twelve. In the Music Standards document, an introduction summarizes the musical achievement of students in grades K–4, 5–8, and 9–12, as follows:

> *Music Standards, Kindergarten through Grade 4:*
> *Performing, creating, and responding to music are the fundamental music processes in which humans engage. Students, particularly in grades K–4, learn by doing. Singing, playing instruments, moving to music, and creating music enable them to acquire musical skills and knowledge that can be developed in no other way. Learning to read and notate music gives them a skill with which to explore music independently and with others. Listening to, analyzing, and evaluating music are important building blocks of musical learning. Further, to participate fully in a diverse, global society, students must understand their own historical and cultural heritage and those of others within their communities and beyond. Because music is a basic expression of human culture, every student should have access to a balanced, comprehensive, and sequential program of study in music.*

> *Music Standards, Grades 5 through 8:*
> *The period when students are in grades 5–8 is especially critical in their musical development. The music they perform or study often becomes an integral part of their personal musical repertoire. Composing and improvising provide students with unique insight into the form and structure of music and at the same time help them to develop their creativity. Broad experience with a variety of music is necessary if students are to make informed musical judgments. Similarly, this breadth of background*

enables them to begin to understand the connections and relationships between music and other disciplines. By understanding the cultural and historical forces that shape social attitudes and behaviors, students are better prepared to live and work in communities that are increasingly multicultural. The role that music will play in students' lives depends in large measure on the level of skills they achieve in creating, performing, and listening to music.

Music Standards, Grades 9 through 12:
The study of music contributes in important ways to the quality of every student's life. Every musical work is a product of its time and place, although some works transcend their original settings and continue to appeal to humans through their timeless and universal attraction. Through singing, playing instruments, and composing, students can express themselves creatively, while a knowledge of notation and performance traditions enables them to learn new music independently throughout their lives. Skills in analysis, evaluation, and synthesis are important because they enable students to recognize and pursue excellence in their musical experiences and to understand and enrich their environment. Because music is an integral part of human history, the ability to listen with understanding is essential if students are to gain a broad cultural and historical perspective. The adult life of every student is enriched by the skills, knowledge, and habits acquired in the study of music.

Standards for the Preparation of School String and Orchestra Teachers

Standards for the Preparation of School String and Orchestra Teachers defines the knowledge and skills needed for the successful orchestra teacher—as a musician, as an educator, and as a professional. These standards reflect the broad-based expectations of the National Standards specifically as they relate to the teaching of orchestra. The orchestra student is entitled to a comprehensive music education. The orchestra teacher, therefore, must be able to provide the experiences necessary for each student to develop the skills and knowledge defined as a comprehensive music education.

Performing with Understanding

Performing with Understanding represents the in-depth deliberation of recognized leaders in music and music education in response to the National Standards in music. Musical performance skills are significantly enhanced by appropriate musical knowledge as well as by the skills in creating music and

responding to music. Comprehensive musicianship, then, describes the musician who is capable of performing with understanding. Students who are developing as well-educated musicians, who are building their skills and their knowledge as well-rounded musicians, are capable of musical performance at an artistic level more meaningful to an audience and, importantly, more meaningful to each of the student performers.

References

American String Teachers Association. *Standards for the Preparation of School String and Orchestra Teachers*. Reston, VA: American String Teachers Association, 1998.

Music Educators National Conference. *National Standards for Arts Education: What Every Young American Should Know and Be Able to Do in the Arts*. Reston, VA: Music Educators National Conference, 1994.

Music Educators National Conference. *Performing with Understanding*. Reston, VA: Music Educators National Conference, 2000.

CHAPTER 6

Preparing Your Orchestra for Festival

Michael Allen

When discussing the type of preparation needed for a school orchestra to present a polished performance in a festival or contest setting, the question arises, "Shouldn't all performances be polished?" Each performance of a school orchestra has its own set of expectations and unique circumstances.

When participating in a state festival or contest, the ensemble is expected to present a performance that represents its collective best at a given moment. Music educators, however, become concerned when festivals and their concomitant ratings occupy an inappropriately dominant role in the overall goals of the school orchestra program. If the festival performance becomes the controlling objective of the year's efforts, other important learning opportunities may be overlooked.

Performances can and should serve a variety of functions in the musical development of students—the festival experience serving as one of many such opportunities. The challenge to the conductor is achieving a balance among the many performing opportunities for the school orchestra.

Achieving Balance

Several years ago I read an article by Donn Laurence Mills titled, "If I Only Had Less Rehearsal Time." The title alone made the article impossible to ignore, but the substance of Mills's argument was even more appealing. The basic premise of the article suggested that school orchestra conductors have too much rehearsal time. According to Mills, school orchestras tend to slow down their musical metabolism to match the time allowed to prepare for a performance. School orchestras have the luxury (or, in Mills's opinion, self-imposed burden) of preparing for concerts at a much slower rate than professional orchestras. If the conductor has four weeks to get ready for a

concert, then the conductor will take four weeks to get ready. If, on the other hand, the conductor has only four days to get ready, then the rehearsal schedule must be organized accordingly.

After reading Mills's article, I initiated a tradition at my school of passing out a new piece of music on Monday prior to a Thursday concert. Because we had only four days to get ready, the difficulty level had to be lower, but the experience was both popular and educational for the students. There was no time for drilling difficult passages and no time for multiple explanations. Although teachers might find many ways to bring variety and balance to a school orchestra program, I found that the experience of preparing a work for performance in a relatively short amount of time was a valuable experience for my students.

The Dress Rehearsal Phenomenon

Participating in a regional or state festival has many benefits, but the one that I value the most is how focused the students become during the last few weeks of rehearsal leading up to the performance. I recently attended the dress rehearsal of a high school orchestra and overheard the conductor tell the students, "If we concentrated in all of our rehearsals the way we concentrate at the dress rehearsal, imagine what we could accomplish."

Most musicians are keenly aware that an imminent performance brings about an intensity of thought and effort. This focus of attention is even more pronounced if the performance is to be adjudicated. Although I value judges' comments, performances by other groups, and related opportunities associated with festival participation, I believe the most important part is over by the time the students step on stage. Sustained focus over a significant amount of time contributes to the growth of any musical organization.

Music Selection: Over-Programming

Probably the single most important aspect of preparing an ensemble for festival is the thoughtful and careful selection of the music to be performed. Of all the dilemmas associated with the task of selecting music, the most prevalent problem is over-programming. While required lists and clumsy classification systems occasionally force orchestras to program literature beyond their collective ability level, most instances of over-programming can be ascribed to unsound decisions made by the conductor.

If the majority of students are able to play the notes *and* they are actively engaged in the issues of balance, blend, style, and phrasing, the conductor has not over-programmed. On the other hand, if the majority of students are absorbed in a frantic approximation of the notes with little or no regard as to *how* the notes should be played, the conductor has over-programmed. In an article that appeared in *Orchestra News*, James Kjelland stated, "The essence of musical experience generates from what is done with the notes, not in simply being able to play most of the notes at approximately the right time." If students are going to perform in an expressive manner, they must be able to efficiently handle the technical demands of the composition.

A Word about Arrangements

Orchestral arrangements are an important part of the literature available to school ensembles, but you should be cautious when programming arrangements for festivals. When choosing an original work to be performed, you should give a great deal of consideration to the quality of the work. No less care should be taken when selecting an arrangement.

By definition, an arrangement is a series of compromises; otherwise, an arrangement would not be necessary. If the compromises have harmed the quality and integrity of the music, the arrangement should be avoided.

You should be particularly careful when selecting a string arrangement of an original work for full orchestra. The abrupt changes in tone color can be most disruptive to the expectations of the audience, in this case the judges. When in doubt, choose original music; arrangements can be more safely programmed for other performances.

The Importance of Intonation

The standard MENC rating form for festivals includes the following seven categories: 1) tone, 2) intonation, 3) technique, 4) balance, 5) interpretation, 6) musical effect, and 7) other factors. Although the MENC rating form does not indicate that one category is any more important than the other, judges generally give more weight to the intonation category. I have often overheard judges discussing the hierarchies of importance, but in the final analysis, adjudicators do not forgive playing out of tune.

You can test this notion by observing trained musicians attending any recital or concert. Musicians will forgive a few instances of rushing if all other aspects of the performance are in order. Musicians will forgive a missed note or two if all other aspects of the performance are in order. But carefully observe the facial gestures of musicians listening to anyone playing dreadfully out of tune. It is a painful experience by any measure.

The Importance of Vertical Alignment

Any gathering of band directors will, in time, produce a discussion on the importance of vertical alignment in a musical performance. As important and obvious as vertical alignment is to a quality performance, I rarely hear this term used among string teachers. While string teachers often talk about playing together, they are rarely as sensitive as their wind counterparts in detecting small variations in ensemble precision.

Several years ago as a high school orchestra conductor in Texas, I asked the band director at my school if he would be willing to help me prepare for an upcoming concert. Colleague and friend Don Hanna agreed, and I soon realized that among his many talents was the uncanny ability to detect small imperfections in the rhythmical fabric of the music. His ears were unusually sensitive to the issue of vertical alignment, and as time went by, he helped me to become more perceptive in this area.

He also helped me to realize that vertical alignment plays a crucial role in intonation. A musical performance not properly aligned gives the illusion of being out of tune even if the notes are in tune.

Why Does Itzhak Perlman Seem So Relaxed?

A college music student returned to class one day after having attended a performance of the Beethoven Violin Concerto by Itzhak Perlman. The student was not only deeply moved by Perlman's artistry and talent but was also captivated by how relaxed Perlman appeared to be during the performance. The student's professor, who also attended the performance, pointed out that Perlman had probably played the Beethoven Violin Concerto in public on numerous occasions, and in each case, the outcome of the performance was never in doubt.

When performing a difficult work for the first time, particularly at a festival, both the students and the conductor may have serious doubts about the outcome of the performance. The natural anxiety of a first performance rarely allows the students or conductor to relax and enjoy the opportunity to share their hard work with others, in this case the judges. When possible, present the program to be performed at festival publicly at least once before going to festival. The wisdom of multiple performances *prior to* festival cannot be overstated.

A Word about Solos

Orchestra conductors often try to comfort their students by explaining that judges rarely consider solos when deciding the final rating. By employing this strategy, they attempt to control the pressure that a student internalizes regarding personal responsibility toward the group rating. To be sure, this is a kind and humane gesture, but I often think that conductors actually believe that judges dismiss the role of solo passages when determining the final rating.

I also think that many judges believe they do not take solo passages into account when rating an ensemble. Judges, for the most part, seem to agree that a shaky performance by the concertmaster in Bartók's *Romanian Folk Dances* should not affect the final scoring. But I have often listened to the same judges speak over lunch about the terrible intonation of the first oboe player in Bizet's *Carmen Suite* No. 1.

In short, I think judges, regardless of claims, are influenced both positively and negatively by solo passages in the literature. Prudent conductors will carefully consider the relative strengths of the individual members of the ensemble and choose music best suited to their abilities and talents.

Dividing the Violin Section

One of the most sensitive decisions a school orchestra conductor must make is how to divide the violin section. Needless to say, an entire chapter could be devoted to this delicate issue. In my experience, problems often result when conductors assign the more-accomplished players to the first violin section and place the younger, less-accomplished players in the second violin section. When this method is used, the judging panel often notices intonation problems and poor rhythmic stability in the second violin section, while the balance between the sections is often distorted.

Through the years, I experimented with many approaches to dividing the violin section before settling on a solution that produced excellent results (for me) and seemed educationally sound. I divide the students equally by ability between the first and second violin sections. I also rotate both sections between the first and second parts so that all students have a chance to play first violin and second violin parts in every concert. By using this approach, I have found that the musical results are superior and the number of complaints about playing in the second violin section drop noticeably.

Getting Help

At a recent festival I attended, a fine high school orchestra performed the last movement of Dvořák's *New World* Symphony. Afterward, I found the conductor and complimented her on an outstanding performance. The conductor explained that several other people should share the congratulations for their valuable contributions to the success of the concert. The conductor also explained that several string teachers from the middle schools in the area had offered their time to conduct sectional rehearsals. Not only had the conductor committed a substantial amount of time to prepare the wind players, but she had also requested the assistance of a local middle school conductor because he was a woodwind specialist. Several weeks before the festival, the conductor attended an inspiring clinic that the associate conductor of a nearby professional symphony had given, which included many valuable suggestions. In addition, the conductor scheduled a performance for the parents two weeks prior to the festival and sent a tape to his college conductor for suggestions.

This story illustrates how valuable obtaining outside help can be when preparing an orchestra for festival performance. Few conductors possess the ability to prepare an orchestra for festival performance alone, yet many try unnecessarily. The "extra set of ears" technique is frequently used by conductors of professional orchestras—surely it is a valuable technique for conductors of school groups. At the very least, record your orchestra prior to festival and allow the students to listen. This technique always gets their attention.

The Payoff

The dangers of festivals are well known to music educators. If the school year becomes focused on the results of a single event, the musical diet of both the teacher and the students becomes limited, and many wonderful opportunities can be missed. Orchestras should present at least one program each year that represents their best possible performance. Few areas of education are willing to present examples of their work for peer review.

Music educators have for years considered the festival experience to be an important opportunity to focus student efforts and to gain valuable feedback from respected leaders in the field. When viewed in a larger context, the festival experience can provide both confirmation of musical tasks well done and challenges to be considered for the future.

44

References

Mills, D. L. "If I Only Had Less Rehearsal Time," in *The Best of "The Soundpost"* (Port Clinton, OH: National School Orchestra Association, 1989), 1–7.

Kjelland, James. "Over-Programming and The Emperor's New Clothes," *Orchestra News*, Fall 1991, 5–7.

PART II

TEACHER RESOURCE GUIDES

Grade One

Teacher Resource Guide

Apollo Suite

Merle J. Isaac
(1898–1996)

Unit 1: Composer

Merle J. Isaac was one of the most prolific and well-received composers and arrangers of band, orchestra, and string music of his time. Born in 1898 in Pioneer, Iowa, he spent most of his life in the Chicago area. Isaac taught at Marshall High School in Chicago for fourteen years, where he directed an award-winning ninety-piece orchestra. He then served as an elementary school principal for twenty-one years.

Isaac began composing and arranging in 1934 and has several hundred works to his credit. His first published piece was an arrangement of Bohm's *Perpetual Motion*, which he arranged to meet the needs of his high school orchestra. He also wrote the *Merle Isaac String Class Method* to use at his high school.

Other well-known Isaac works in the Grade 1 and 2 string orchestra category include *Quinto-Quarto Suite*; *Early American Suite*; *Dancing Basses*; *Tango Trocadero*; *American Folk Song Suite Nos. 1, 2, and 3*; and *Lively and Rhythmic Suite Nos. 1 and 2*.

Unit 2: Composition

The publisher describes *Apollo Suite* as an "early, ensemble experience for String Orchestra." It has four movements: "Prelude" (Allegretto in 2/4), "Waltz" (Tempo di Valse in 1), "Scherzo" (Moderato in 2/4), and "Dance" (Allegro moderato in 2/4). *Apollo Suite* is approximately nine minutes in length and is best played by elementary-aged students with two to three years of playing experience.

That the title is related to the Apollo Space Mission seems unlikely from the names of the movements. More likely it is in honor of the Greek god Apollo, who was considered the most Greek of all gods and the god of light and music. Apollo was considered the master musician, a performer for Olympus on his golden lyre. Stravinsky wrote his ballet *Apollon musagète* also in honor of Apollo.

Unit 3: Historical Perspective

Apollo Suite was composed in 1972, when composers were just beginning to write original works for beginning string orchestras. Up to this point, many works were arrangements of well-known pieces collected in folios, such as *Early Classics* (Herfurth), *String Music of the Baroque Era* (Clarke), and the *Polychordia String Albums* (Brown). John Caponegro, Robert Frost, and Edmund Siennicki—all contemporaries of Merle Isaac—were just beginning to write original works for the young orchestra at about the same time *Apollo Suite* was published.

Unit 4: Technical Considerations

All students must be familiar with the G major key signature to play this piece. Violin students must be able to play a two-octave G major scale; viola, cello, and double bass students must be able to play a one-octave G major scale. Violin and viola students must be able to play C- and G-natural accurately on the upper two strings. Scales should be practiced in varying rhythm patterns at varying speeds using rhythmic patterns found in the work. The rhythm is very simple throughout the piece, but the students need to be able to count dotted-half notes and eighth notes accurately. The bowing, which is discussed under stylistic considerations, is the most technically challenging factor.

Unit 5: Stylistic Considerations

Movement 1, "Prelude," starts with pizzicato in all sections until it reaches the second theme, which is an Andante to be bowed in a legato style. Movement 2, "Waltz," calls for hooked bowing, pizzicato, legato, three-note slurs, and staccato in the accompanying parts. Movement 3, "Scherzo," requires pizzicato by all in the introduction, then the upper strings have repeated down-bows as they begin arco. When the theme runs through the third variation, the bowing changes to up-bow eighth notes followed by staccato and accented half notes.

The final movement, "Dance," requires a contrast in styles with the upper strings playing staccato. Cellos play legato with some staccato at the ends of phrases, and the double basses use pizzicato. A second theme is back to legato, but the violins use accented slurs to bring the melody alive. A third theme, titled "Czech Dance Song," uses heavily accented martelé, with the composer calling for separated tones. A middle section of the dance changes to legato.

Dynamics are marked throughout and add immensely to the piece. Tempo should remain steady, which is sometimes a challenge for students at this level.

Unit 6: Musical Elements

The entire suite stays in the key of G major. The melodic line appears mostly in the first violin part. Second violin and viola have simple harmonization of the melodic line. The piece, which is mostly homophonic, does use some counterpoint in the cello part, especially in repeated sections. Double bass parts are purely accompaniment.

Unit 7: Form and Structure

SECTION	MEASURES	EVENT AND SCORING
Movement 1: "Prelude"		
Form: ABA		
A	1–16	First violin has melodic line
A^1	17–32	Cello has countermelody; all other strings continue pizzicato
B	33–48	Chordal half notes
B^1	49–64	Cello has countermelody with double bass accompaniment
A		D.C. al Fine
Movement 2: "Waltz"		
Form: ABA		
Introduction	1–8	
A	9–24	Melodic line alternates between upper strings and cello against a staccato, waltz-style accompaniment
A^1	25–40	Melody and harmony becomes legato for all instruments
B	41–64	Uses a more contrapuntal texture
A/A^1		D.C. al Coda
Coda		G major descending arpeggios with chords
Movement 3: "Scherzo"		
Form: theme and variation		
Introduction	1–4	Cello ostinato; double bass contrary motion ostinato
Theme	4–24	First violin melody with cello ostinato continuing

SECTION	MEASURES	EVENT AND SCORING
Episode 1	24–39	Elongated melody in cello with chordal accompaniment in other voices
Transition	40–43	In upper strings
Episode 2	44–61	Rhythmic variation in upper strings
Codetta of chords	62–67	Four measures of ostinato; two measures

Movement 4: "Dance"
Form: compound ternary

A	5–12	First violin carries melodic line with simple harmonization of melodic line by second violin and viola
A^1	13–20	Cello has countermelody with contrasting rhythms and styles
B	21–28	Eight-measure melody that changes style in the upper strings
A	29–36	
Transition	37–40	
C	41–56	Czech folk song; first violin and cello in unison for first eight measures, then cello has countermelody
C^1	57–72	Varies stylistically from C
AA^1BA		*D.C. al Coda*
Coda		Four measures with chordal ending

Unit 8: Suggested Listening

Merle Isaac:
  Belvedere Suite
  Early American Suite
  Quinto-Quarto Suite
Igor Stravinsky, *Apollon musagète*

Unit 9: Additional References and Resources

Dillon, Jacquelyn A., and Casimer Kreichbaum. *How to Design and Teach a Successful School String and Orchestra Program*. San Diego: Neil A. Kjos Publishers, 1978.

Hamilton, Edith. *Mythology*. New York: Mentor Books, 1940.

Harley, Frances. "Merle, Magical Musician," *American String Teacher* 47 (Spring 1997): 25–32.

Contributed by:
Mary L. Wagner
Fairfax County Public Schools
Fairfax, Virginia

Teacher Resource Guide

Canyon Sunset

John Caponegro
(b. 1935)

STRING ORCHESTRA

Unit 1: Composer

Born June 20, 1935, John Caponegro attended the Manhattan School of Music, where he earned a Bachelor of Music in Composition and a Master of Music in Music Education. Recently retired, he taught elementary band and orchestra for more than thirty years in Long Island, New York. A prolific composer for young orchestras, Caponegro's works are technically educational while engaging to the young musician. Percussion parts are often added for interest. Some of Caponegro's other compositions include *March of the Bowmen* and *Rhumbolero*.

Unit 2: Composition

The composition was written in 1972 in a contemporary style. Performance time of the piece is approximately two minutes and thirty seconds for this Grade 1 composition. The form is A–B–A.

Unit 3: Historical Perspective

Over a thirty-year period, Caponegro has written more than one hundred works for young instrumental ensembles. *Canyon Sunset* was composed in 1972, when composers were just beginning to write original works for beginning string orchestras. Up to this point, many works were arrangements of well-known pieces collected in folios. Contemporaries of Caponegro who also wrote original works for young orchestras at that time included Robert Frost, Merle Isaac, and Edmund Siennicki.

Unit 4: Technical Considerations

The piece is in E minor. The note values of whole, half, dotted-half, quarter, dotted-quarter, and eighth note are utilized. The rhythmic pattern of dotted-quarter/eighth is used repeatedly. There is a *divisi* part in the first violins. Dynamic range extends from *pianissimo* to *forte* with *crescendos* and *decrescendos*.

Unit 5: Stylistic Considerations

A legato bow style is utilized throughout the composition. The rhythmic motive of dotted-quarter note followed by an eighth note needs to be carefully prepared so as not to emphasize the eighth note. It might be helpful to hook the rhythmic pattern at rehearsal letter C to avoid the accented up-bow.

Unit 6: Musical Elements

The optional percussion part utilizing temple blocks may symbolize donkeys descending into a canyon at sunset. The E minor tonality, along with the legato bow style, emphasizes the mood of a day's end. Presenting a slide show of canyon sunsets during the performance of the piece can be effective.

Unit 7: Form and Structure

SECTION	EVENT AND SCORING
Opening	Introduction (four measures)
Theme 1	Rehearsal A; flowing melody in first violin, with harmonic parts in second violin, viola, and bass; cello line provides the rhythmic energy
Theme 2	Rehearsal C
Theme 1	Rehearsal D

Unit 8: Suggested Listening

John Caponegro, *Canyon Sunset*
> Recorded by the Washington High School Orchestra at the 1976 Midwest International Band and Orchestra (Silver Crest Records, Huntington Station, New York)

Unit 9: Additional References and Resources

Proceedings of the 1976 Midwest International Band and Orchestra Clinic, Chicago, Illinois.

Music review of *Christmas Carols for Strings* by John Caponegro, *American String Teacher* 35 (Fall 1985): 87.

Contributed by:

Michele Winter
Orchestra Teacher
Lowell High School
San Francisco, California

Teacher Resource Guide

Cripple Creek

arranged by Edmund Siennicki
(b. 1930)

STRING ORCHESTRA

Unit 1: Arranger

Born in 1930, Edmund Siennicki received degrees from Kent State University
and the Teachers College at Columbia University. He worked his way through
college as a bassoonist and pianist, performing in country clubs, nightclubs,
shows, parks, churches, and on coast-to-coast radio and television. Special
performances included those with Ernie Kardos, associate concertmaster of
the Cleveland Symphony, and George Gobel, Henny Youngman, and Arlene
Francis.

Siennicki has had more than two hundred compositions and arrangements
published. These include works for band, orchestra, and bassoon. He won the
National School Orchestra Association Composition Contest two times, and
he has received numerous ASCAP awards. Twice he was appointed composer-
in-residence at the MacDowell Colony.

For more than thirty years, Siennicki was a junior high school instrumental teacher in the Cleveland Public Schools. Among his many students were
actor/comedian Drew Carey—a child that Siennicki describes as always full of
jokes—and George Voinovich, former mayor of Cleveland, governor of Ohio,
and now an Ohio senator. Siennicki received the Master Teacher Award from
the Martha Holden Jennings Foundation in 1964 and the Distinguished
Alumnus Award twice from Kent State University. Still active, Siennicki
continues to compose, arrange, and guest conduct.

Unit 2: Composition

Cripple Creek is a bluegrass fiddle tune that is performed frequently at fiddle contests throughout the United States. The exact origins of the tune are unknown, but it is titled after a stream located in the United States. The tune is an eight-measure melody that alternates with an eight-measure chorus. One set of words for the verses and chorus are as follows:

> I got a gal and she loves me,
> She's as sweet as sweet can be.
> She's got eyes of baby blue,
> Makes my gun shoot straight and true.
>> (Chorus)
>> Goin' down Cripple Creek, Goin' in a run,
>> Goin' down Cripple Creek to have some fun.
>> Goin' down Cripple Creek, Goin' in a whirl,
>> Goin' down Cripple Creek, to see my girl.
> I got a beau and he loves me,
> He's as sweet as sweet can be.
> He's got eyes of darkest brown,
> Makes my heart jump all around.
>> (Chorus)
> Goin' down to Cripple Creek fast as I can go,
> Goin' down to Cripple Creek, don't be slow.
> Raise my britches above my knees,
> Wade in Cripple Creek if I please.
>> (Chorus)

Siennicki arranged *Cripple Creek* for string orchestra. An optional third violin part doubles the viola part in treble clef. An optional piano part is also included. Performance time is approximately two minutes and thirty seconds. The bass line is cued in the cello part if basses are not available. Siennicki's arrangement of *Cripple Creek* is correlated with the *Strictly Strings Orchestra Series*, Book 1.

Unit 3: Historical Perspective

Cripple Creek is a bluegrass standard. Bluegrass style grew out of southern fiddle music in the 1930s. Fiddlers at the time began experimenting with adding blues pitches, continuous series of sixteenth notes, and complex double-stops to traditional fiddle music. By the mid 1950s, a distinct bluegrass fiddle style had developed. Bill Monroe, the Grand Ole Opry legend, is the recognized father of bluegrass music. The music took its name from his band, the

Bluegrass Boys. A typical bluegrass band is not electrified and consists of guitar, mandolin, five-string banjo, acoustic bass, fiddle, and vocals. The fiddle imitates the vocal line.

Unit 4: Technical Considerations

Cripple Creek is in D major. All parts are in first position except for an optional third-position D on the G string for double bass. Pitches for all instruments except the bass appear on the D and A strings, save an occasional open E string in the first violin part. Open string double-stops appear in first and second violin and viola. Simple détaché bowing is used throughout. Two-note slurs are incorporated. Bow markings are provided. Dynamics involve only *piano* and *forte*. Rhythmic note values include eighth, quarter, and half notes, and quarter rests.

Unit 5: Stylistic Considerations

The bowing style is legato détaché throughout. The cello and bass pizzicato against the violin/viola melodic statement adds crispness to the orchestral sound. The music should swing with a feeling of two large pulses per measure.

Unit 6: Musical Elements

"Allegro" is specified as the tempo. First violin, cello, and bass share the melody. An eight-measure countermelody section is to be played pizzicato. The melody can be easily heard when it is accompanied because of the simple scoring and pizzicato accompaniment. A typical bluegrass shuffle rhythm appears in the violin and viola line.

Unit 7: Form and Structure

SECTION	MEASURES	EVENT AND SCORING
Introduction	1–4	First two measures violin and viola; mm. 3–4 cello/bass pizzicato
Verse 1	5–12	First violin melody; second violin and viola harmony; cello/bass pizzicato roots of chords
Chorus	13–21	First violin chorus; second violin and viola harmony; cello/bass pizzicato chord progression
Verse 2	22–36	Cello/bass unison melody accompanied by violin and viola harmony in shuffle rhythm

Section	Measures	Event and Scoring
Chorus	37–45	Countermelody composed by Siennicki with melody in first violin; harmony in second violin and viola; bass line unison in cello and bass
Verse 3	46–54	Melody in shuffle rhythm in first violin; shuffle rhythm harmony in second violin and viola; chord progression in cello and bass
Verse 1	55–56	First two measures of melody; mm. 57–58 a V–I chord progression to the end of the piece

Unit 8: Suggested Listening

Bruce Chase, *Blue Grass Ball*
Andrew Dabczynski and Bob Phillips, *Fiddler's Philharmonic*
Merle Isaac, Fiddle Tune Nos. 1, 2, 3
Carold Nuñez, *Bluegrass Country*
Recordings of bluegrass bands
Dorothy Straub, *Simple Square Dance*

Unit 9: Additional References and Resources

Dabczynski, Andrew, and Robert Phillips. *Fiddler's Philharmonic*. Van Nuys, CA: Alfred Publishing, 1996.

Dabczynski, Andrew, and Robert Phillips. *Fiddler's Philharmonic Encore!* Van Nuys, CA: Alfred Publishing, 1999.

Willis, Barry. *America's Music-Bluegrass: A History of Bluegrass Music in the Words of Its Pioneers*. Kailua-Kona, HI: Pine Valley Music, 1998.

Contributed by:

Robert Gillespie
Professor of Music
The Ohio State University
Columbus, Ohio

Teacher Resource Guide

Dorchester Street Songs

Gregg A. Porter
(b. 1953)

STRING ORCHESTRA

Unit 1: Composer

Gregg Porter has taught orchestra and strings for more than twenty years at the elementary, secondary, college, and youth orchestra levels. His orchestras have appeared at the Illinois Music Educators Convention, Missouri Music Educators Convention, Midwest International Band and Orchestra Clinic, and the Music Educators National Convention. He has appeared throughout the country as a string and orchestra clinician, as well as guest conductor of many professional orchestras. Porter currently resides in Olympia Fields, Illinois, where he is a conductor, string teacher, and composer, with more than fifteen compositions in publication.

Unit 2: Composition

Dorchester Street Songs was the winner of the 1995 National School Orchestra Association Composition Contest. A Grade 1.5 composition for string orchestra, this piece was composed in dedication to all the wonderful string students Porter taught during his tenure as director of string activities at the University of Chicago Laboratory School. The title of this composition, as well as the names of the two movements, are street names bordering the string room at the Laboratory School in Hyde Park.

The second movement, "Kimbark Song," was composed as a special dedication to the fourth and fifth grade string orchestra at the Laboratory School. The memories of rehearsals will always be happy ones, and this movement should reflect that same spirit.

Unit 3: Historical Perspective

Porter's primary composition teacher, Karol Welcelean of Central Methodist College, encouraged Porter to proceed with writing even though his first love was always conducting. Porter currently has twelve selections published and looks forward to writing many more original and arranged compositions in the years to come. He feels that, too often, composers write music that doesn't address the needs for learning about dynamics, expression, and phrasing. But most of all, he tries to write something that the students will go out of the rehearsal room humming each day.

Unit 4: Technical Considerations

Both movements of *Dorchester Street Songs* are in the key of D major, a familiar and comfortable key signature for students of this level. Melodic structure is achieved through major thirds or arpeggios, with wide leaps being rare. All parts are playable in first position, although the cello part does include a C-sharp extension on the G string. The rhythms are usually the same for the upper and lower strings in the second movement.

Unit 5: Stylistic Considerations

Dorchester Street Songs is popular among both students and teachers, with hummable melodies. Both movements, whether beginning moderato or allegro, have slower Largo sections that will develop sensitivity to musicality and balance. There is a strong emphasis on dynamics in both movements.

Unit 6: Musical Elements

Major tonalities are prevalent, with the key of D major being used in both movements. The first movement, "Hyde Park Dance," is composed in a traditional A–B–A style with variations. The first violins introduce both the first and second melodies, with the viola, cello, and bass echoing the melody each time. The Largo section at measure 35 features the second violins and violas. Measure 35 should begin softly so that the *crescendo* in measure 37 can be most effective. Likewise, the following *decrescendo* should bring the music back to a *piano* dynamic. The energetic Allegro Moderato at measure 44 brings back both melodies, but this time they are played simultaneously. The movement comes to a close with a dramatic left-hand pizzicato played by the entire orchestra.

The second movement, "Kimbark Song," is a faster allegro, also in A–B–A form. A playful section begins at measure 25 for the first and second violins, and repeats at the end. In between is a Largo section at measure 44, that ends in a resolution cadence. The tempo, other than the short Largo section, should be lively, and every part should be played lightly, with a feeling of moving forward but without rushing.

Unit 7: Form and Structure

SECTION   MEASURES

Movement 1: "Hyde Park Dance"
A   1
A developed   10
A developed   18
A developed   26
B   35
A   44

Movement 2: "Kimbark Song"
A   1
A developed   25
B   41
A   49

Unit 8: Suggested Listening

Ludwig van Beethoven/arr. Gregg A. Porter, "Finale" from Symphony No. 9 (for string orchestra)

Reinhold Glière/arr. Gregg A. Porter, *Russian Sailor's Dance* (for string orchestra)

Gregg A. Porter, *Quatros Dance* (for string orchestra)

Gregg A. Porter, *Resolution Overture* (for full orchestra)

Arr. Gregg A. Porter, *Variations on a Christmas Lullaby* (for string orchestra)

Camille Saint-Saëns/arr. Gregg A. Porter, *Bacchanale from "Samson and Delilah"* (for string orchestra)

Gordon Young/arr. Gregg A. Porter, *Prelude in a Classic Style* (for string orchestra)

Unit 9: Additional References and Resources

Berman, Joel, Barbara G. Jackson, and Kenneth Sarch, eds. *Dictionary of Bowing and Pizzicato Terms*. 4th edition. Reston, VA: American String Teachers Association, 1998.

Lindeman, Carolynn A., and Robert Cutietta. *Strategies for Teaching Specialized Ensembles*. Reston, VA: Music Educators National Conference, 1999.

Lindeman, Carolynn A., Dorothy Straub, Louis Bergonzi, and Anne C. Witt. *Strategies for Teaching Strings and Orchestra*. Reston, VA: Music Educators National Conference, 1999.

Contributed by:

Gregg Porter
Conductor, string teacher, composer
Olympia Fields, Illinois

Teacher Resource Guide

Little Symphony

Carold Nuñez
(b. 1929)

STRING ORCHESTRA

Unit 1: Composer

Carold Nuñez, a native of Texas, received his Bachelor of Music in Composition and Master of Music in Education from North Texas State University. After twenty-nine years in the Texas Public Schools, he retired as director of the Denton High School Orchestra and coordinator of orchestras in the Denton Independent School District. In 1989, Nuñez was presented with the Texas Orchestra Director of the Year Award.

In addition to being in the Texas Music Educators Association and Texas Orchestra Directors Association, Nuñez has also been a member of the American String Teachers Association and Music Educators National Conference. Currently, he resides in Denton, Texas, where he is a professional composer and pianist, and continues his close association with music education as a clinician and adjudicator.

Other compositions by Carold Nuñez include the following string orchestra works: *Apache, Chapter One, Convergence, Introspection, Suite for Strings*, and *Festival*, a mass string orchestra piece. Nuñez is also author of *Uni-Tunes*, an elementary-level supplementary method designed to reinforce note recognition and reading skills.

Unit 2: Composition

Nuñez composed *Little Symphony* in 1995. The piece, approximately two minutes and thirty seconds long, has a strong emphasis on bowing technique from the classical period.

Unit 3: Historical Perspective

The piece gives young orchestras exposure to the classical period, which began in Italy in approximately 1750 and continued until approximately 1825. Music of the classical period emphasized balance of phrase and structure. Beethoven, Mozart, and Haydn were famous composers from the classical period.

Unit 4: Technical Considerations

The piece can be played in first position in the keys of G major and C major. Several bowing techniques are required to perform the piece. Eighth notes marked staccato are played using a light brush stroke, slightly off the string. Passages marked "legato" give the opportunity for smooth bow strokes. String crossings need to be mastered to perform this piece. Retrieving the bow to start an eighth note up-bow with the brush stroke is utilized in all instruments. Throughout the piece, the rhythmic pattern of an eighth rest followed by three eighth notes started up-bow recurs. Two measures have the rhythmic pattern dotted-quarter/eighth note. The rest of the piece is whole, half, quarter, and eighth notes.

Unit 5: Stylistic Considerations

The contrasting styles of legato and staccato are utilized throughout the piece. An understanding of the classical period bowing style is required. Players must utilize a wide range of dynamics, from *mezzo-piano* to *forte* with *crescendos* and *decrescendos*.

Unit 6: Musical Elements

The piece is marked "Moderato," with quarter note = 112. The time signature is 4/4 throughout. The rhythmic motive of an eighth rest followed by three eighth notes is challenging for the young player. Starting up-bow, using a brush stroke and retrieving the bow, or staying at the lower half of the bow can be rewarding for the student when mastered. First violins play a flowing melody over this rhythmic section.

Unit 7: Form and Structure

SECTION	EVENT AND SCORING
Theme 1	Flowing melody in first violin with rhythmic accompaniment in other parts
Theme 2	Rehearsal 17; string crossings section
Theme 3	Rehearsal 32; legato melody accompanied with a pizzicato bass line
Theme 4	Rehearsal 48; transition back to the first theme
Theme 1	Rehearsal 58; return of the first theme

Unit 8: Suggested Listening

Music composed during the classical period.

Unit 9: Additional References and Resources

Garverick, Jan Karen Daniel. *Selected Pedagogical Needs of the String Class as Addressed in the Compositions of Carold Nuñez.* Ph.D. Dissertation, Texas Tech University, 1998.

Contributed by:

Liz Murray
Parkway Southwest Middle School
Ballwin, Missouri

Teacher Resource Guide

Loch Lomond

arranged by Noah Klauss
(1901–1977)

STRING ORCHESTRA

Unit 1: Arranger

Noah Klauss, arranger of *Loch Lomond*, was born to German immigrant parents in Lebanon, Pennsylvania, in 1901. He grew up in Hershey, Pennsylvania, where he quit school to help support his family. Klauss later graduated and attended the Harrisburg Music Conservatory, where he studied violin. He established and conducted the Harrisburg Youth Orchestra. He was a violinist in the Harrisburg Symphony for thirty years and served as its assistant conductor.

Greatly admired by his students, Klauss composed and arranged much of the music his students played during his teaching career in the Elizabethtown Schools and Elizabethtown College. Some of his most notable works include Prelude for Orchestra, Fantasy for Orchestra, and his symphony titled *Evangeline*. Klauss died in 1977.

Unit 2: Composition

Loch Lomond, one of the most familiar Scottish folk songs, was originally arranged by Klauss to be played by his beginning string orchestra. Klauss often used folk songs as a basis for his arrangements and compositions because they expressed the heritage, daily life, and spirit of the people. *Loch Lomond* represents a sensitive sort of communication, characteristic of a great deal of folk music. Klauss has kept the accompaniment to this simple melody to a minimum. The piece is written for first, second, and third violin (viola treble clef), viola, cello, and double bass; it includes an optional piano part that doubles the strings. The arrangement is just under two minutes in length.

Unit 3: Historical Perspective

Loch Lomond is a song about lost love on the banks of Loch Lomond, the largest lake in Scotland, which lies in the Scottish Highlands about twenty miles northwest of the city of Glasgow. Folk songs such as *Loch Lomond* have been passed down orally through the generations, so slight changes in melody and words have occurred over the years.

> By yon bonnie banks and by yon bonnie braes,
> Where the sun shines bright on Loch Lomon',
> Where me and my true love were ever wont to gae
> On the bonnie bonnie banks o' Loch Lomon'.

> Oh! Ye'll tak' the high road and I'll tak' the low road,
> And I'll be in Scotland afore ye,
> But me and my true love will never meet again,
> On the bonnie bonnie banks o' Loch Lomon'.

Unit 4: Technical Considerations

Loch Lomond is written in the key of G major. The entire piece is playable in first position on all instruments of the string orchestra utilizing only the G, D, and A strings. Knowledge of the use of low second finger for violin and viola, and second finger for cello and double bass in first position on the A and D strings, is required. The rhythmic demands of this piece written in 4/4 are basic. Klauss uses only quarter, half, and whole notes, and quarter rests in this arrangement. All notes are to be played with separate bows: the only exceptions are one instance of a two-note slur found written for second violin, viola, and cello, as well as tied half and quarter notes.

Unit 5: Stylistic Considerations

Originally composed to be sung, the phrasing in *Loch Lomond* is made evident by the rests, thus allowing the young string player to sing. The style and articulations of the piece dictate a somewhat legato détaché bow stroke. The tempo is marked "Moderately with expression" and remains constant throughout. There are only a few dynamic markings with minimal contrast.

Unit 6: Musical Elements

The entire piece remains in the tonal center of G major. The first violins play the melody throughout, with the rest of the string orchestra playing a hymn-like accompaniment. Stepwise movement is prevalent throughout both the melody and harmony. The rhythmic pattern of half note/quarter note/quarter note occurs frequently in all voices simultaneously. The bowing, with some exceptions, should be identical throughout.

71

Unit 7: Form and Structure

The Klauss arrangement of *Loch Lomond* is a basic one-part form, with a short introduction and coda. The folk song itself is strophic, meaning that each new verse is sung to the same music.

Section	Event and Scoring
Introduction	Mm. 1–4
Theme A	Theme A begins in m. 4 with two pickup notes, preceded with a bow lift for the entire orchestra; the conductor's score has a first ending and a repeat sign written in at this point; however, the rest of the piece is written out in the orchestral parts
Theme A	Theme A is repeated, beginning with the pickup notes in m. 20
Coda	The last three measures are highlighted by a descending line in cello

Unit 8: Suggested Listening

Béla Bartók, *Romanian Folk Dances*
Gustav Holst, *Saint Paul Suite*
Felix Mendelssohn-Bartholdy, Symphony No. 3 ("Scotch")
Ralph Vaughan Williams:
    English Folk Song Suite
    Fantasia on a Theme by Thomas Tallis
    The Lark Ascending
Peter Warlock, *Capriol Suite*

Unit 9: Additional References and Resources

Eversole, James, and Jack Sacher. *The Art of Sound*. Englewood Cliffs, NJ: Prentice-Hall, Inc., 1971.

Klauss, Sylvia. Telephone conversation, June 7, 2000.

Lloyd, Norman. *The Golden Encyclopedia of Music*. New York: Golden Press, 1968.

MacColl, Ewan, ed. *Folk Songs and Ballads of Scotland*. New York: Oak Publications, 1965.

Ward, Arthur, ed. *The Singing Road*. New York: Carl Fisher, 1939.

The World Book Encyclopedia. Chicago: World Book, Inc., 2000. Volume 12, 409–410.

Contributed by:
Christa A. Speed
Grand Island Public Schools
Grand Island, Nebraska

Teacher Resource Guide

March of the Metro Gnome
Fred M. Hubbell
(b. 1924)

STRING ORCHESTRA

Unit 1: Composer

Born in 1924 in Rockford, Illinois, Fred M. Hubbell began studying clarinet in fifth grade under the instruction of his father, Roy Hubbell, who was a school band and orchestra director. Following high school, Hubbell attended the University of Illinois School of Music, where he studied composition with Alvin Etler and Burrill Phillips. After graduation, Hubbell taught for six years in the Mount Carroll, Illinois public schools and for twenty-four years in Park Ridge, Illinois, as both band and orchestra director and coordinator of instrumental music.

In 1988, Hubbell was honored with membership in the Illinois Chapter of Phi Beta Mu Bandmasters Hall of Fame; in 1998, he received the Star of Excellence Award from the Mendelssohn Club for his service and music contributions to Rockford, Illinois.

Hubbell has had more than seventy works for band, orchestra, solos, and ensembles published. *March of the Metro Gnome* was one of his first publications. Other published orchestral works by Hubbell include *Roundelay* for strings and *Busy Bows* for full orchestra.

Unit 2: Composition

March of the Metro Gnome is considered one of the classic pieces for beginning school orchestra. It was published in 1968 and remains a work that is still frequently performed by school orchestras across the country. *March of the Metro Gnome* is scored for strings and wood block. The bass part is optional. Performance time is approximately two minutes. Pizzicato lines are

incorporated. The wood block sounds four quarters per measure throughout except for the rest/quarter/quarter/rest in the last measure. The piece uses an eight-measure melody that is played three times by first violin, three times by second violin, three times by viola, and once by cello. Bass only accompanies, mainly by sounding open G and D strings.

Unit 3: Historical Perspective

Kendor Music, Inc. published *March of the Metro Gnome* as part of the *Playground String Orchestra Series*. The purpose of the series is to offer beginning string students in school orchestras an introduction to orchestra music. The music in the series introduces simple harmonization of melodies playable by typical first-year orchestra students. Rhythms involve only quarter notes and rests, half notes and rests, and whole notes.

Unit 4: Technical Considerations

March of the Metro Gnome is in G major. The octave of the G scale begins on the open G string for violin, viola, and cello in first position. Bowing is détaché. Rhythmic note values include quarter, half, dotted-half, and whole notes, and corresponding rests. Pitches occur only on the G and D strings. The melody, which occurs primarily on the G string, is great for reinforcing G string note reading. Logical bowings are provided, with some bow lifts during quarter rests. The piece could be performed without a wood block, if necessary. No piano accompaniment is provided.

Unit 5: Stylistic Considerations

The style is legato détaché throughout except for the accented quarter notes in the last measure. The pizzicato accompaniment played by cello and bass adds crispness to the overall effect of the work, particularly when grouped with wood block.

Unit 6: Musical Elements

Allegretto tempo with quarter note = 88–116 is specified. Dynamics from *piano* to *forte* are indicated. One *crescendo* appears over a four-measure *tutti crescendo* from *mezzo-forte* to *forte*. The wood block should be included in performance as it adds an effect that is musically interesting to both students and audience. The melody can be easily heard when it is accompanied because of the simple scoring. The passing of the melody from one instrument to another adds musical interest.

Unit 7: Form and Structure

SECTION	MEASURES	EVENT AND SCORING
Introduction	1–4	First two measures solo wood block; open string cello pizzicato with wood block mm. 3–4
A	Rehearsal A	First violin melody alone accompanied by cello playing open string pizzicato
A	Rehearsal B	First and second violin and viola melody in unison accompanied by cello and bass pizzicato
A	Rehearsal C	Cello melody accompanied by harmonization in violin and viola
A_1	Rehearsal D	First and second violin and viola melody stated in thirds; pizzicato accompaniment in cello and bass
A_2	Rehearsal E	Second violin and viola in unison melody with harmonization in cello
B	Rehearsal F	Eight-measure closing—violin and viola in harmonized melody for four measures followed by *tutti* chord progression in half notes; last measure involves pizzicato of a V–I chord progression

Unit 8: Suggested Listening
Ludwig van Beethoven/arr. Bruce Chase, *Ode to Joy*
John Caponegro:
    Canyon Sunset
    Fiddling A-Round
Arr. Carrie Lane Gruselle, *Crawdad Song*
Stephen Wieloszynski, *Round & Round & Round*

Unit 9: Additional References and Resources
Dillon, Jacquelyn, and Casimer Kriechbaum, Jr. *How to Design a Successful School String and Orchestra Program*. San Diego, CA: Neil A. Kjos Music, 1978.

Klotman, Robert. *Teaching Music*. 2d edition. New York: Schirmer Books, 1996.

Contributed by:
Robert Gillespie
Professor of Music
The Ohio State University
Columbus, Ohio

Teacher Resource Guide

Simple Square Dance

Dorothy A. Straub
(b. 1941)

STRING ORCHESTRA

Unit 1: Composer

Dorothy A. Straub is a graduate of Indiana University with a bachelor's and master's degree in music education, specializing in strings. She taught general music, strings, and orchestra in the Chatham Central Schools in Chatham, New York. At that time, she was a violist in the Hudson Valley Philharmonic and was instrumental in establishing the Columbia County Council on the Arts. She has also served as music coordinator of the Westport and Fairfield Public Schools in Connecticut.

Straub has served in various capacities for the Connecticut Music Educators Association, including president and chair of the Professional Affairs Commission. She is one of the original founders of the Fairfield County String Teachers Association. She has served as guest conductor for string festivals in Connecticut, New York, Massachusetts, and Nevada, and has presented numerous workshops on string education. Straub has served as president of MENC and member-at-large of the American String Teachers Association, and has been a consulting editor of the *American String Teacher* journal. She has served as chair of the MENC Committee for String and Orchestra Education and as president of the Eastern Division of MENC.

Unit 2: Composition

Simple Square Dance, published in 1990, serves as an excellent introduction to fiddle music. This Grade 1 composition is written for a beginning string orchestra. First violin generally has the melody. Second violin and viola have the same part; cello and bass generally are in unison. The piano duplicates the

four parts. This work is approximately one minute in length.

Unit 3: Historical Perspective

Simple Square Dance reflects America's rich musical cultural heritage. Folk music and old-time fiddling of the Appalachian Mountains for centuries have been passed down informally. Bluegrass music was started in the 1940s by Bill Monroe, a Kentucky musician. He incorporated blues, Irish tunes, and jazz into the Appalachian music. One characteristic of bluegrass is lowering the seventh scale degree. This piece is a good introduction to the Mixolydian mode.

Unit 4: Technical Considerations

The D major scale is required for all ensemble members. In addition, the cello section will need to play C-natural on the A string. The range of notes for all four stringed instruments mostly falls on the D and A strings. The first violins will need to play their open E string and F-sharp on the E string. Violas will need to know B-natural on the G string. Rhythms are basic, utilizing a combination of whole notes, half notes, eighth notes, and quarter notes. Two challenging, prominent rhythmic motives are four eighth notes/two quarter notes and two quarter notes/quarter rest/quarter note.

Unit 5: Stylistic Considerations

Uniform bow lengths and attacks are important, especially with the accented quarter notes. Bow control is needed for the whole note passage. Close attention to dynamic change is required. Sensitivity to balance is needed when cello has the melody at Rehearsal B. The rhythmic accompaniment in cello and bass needs to be metronomically precise. The tempo should remain constant throughout the work.

Unit 6: Musical Elements

The tonality of the work is D major with some modulation to G major indicated by accidentals in the cello part. The harmonic structure is predominately a I–IV–V–I progression. The entire composition is in common time.

Unit 7: Form and Structure

Overall form: introduction, A–B–A, ending

SECTION	MEASURES	EVENT AND SCORING
Introduction	1–4	Familiar open string double-stop fiddle kickoff
A	5–12	Eight-measure question/answer theme stated in first violin

SECTION	MEASURES	EVENT AND SCORING
B	13–20	Cello has the second theme using a half-step lowered seventh note (C-natural)
Transition	21–24	
A	25–32	All parts identical to mm. 5–12
Ending	33–34	Fiddle tag

Unit 8: Suggested Listening

Andrew Dabczynski and Bob Phillips, *Fiddler's Philharmonic* (accompaniment recording)

Clark Kessinger, *Oldtime Country Music*

Bill Monroe:
> *Bluegrass Ramble*
> *Kentucky Bluegrass*

Unit 9: Additional References and Resources

Dabczynski, Andrew, and Bob Phillips. *Fiddler's Philharmonic*. Van Nuys, CA: Alfred Publishing Company, 1996.

Quigley, Colin. *Music from the Heart*. Athens, GA: The University of Georgia Press, 1995.

Silverman, Jerry. *How to Play Old-Time Country Fiddle*. Hudson, NY: Saw Mill Music Corporation, 1983.

Silverman, Jerry. *Play Old-Time Country Fiddle*. Radnor, PA: Chilton Book Company, 1975.

Contributed by:

Selma Pyles
Hilliard City Schools
Hilliard, Ohio

Teacher Resource Guide

Three Tunes from Shakespeare's England

Go from My Window

Greensleeves

Nobodyes Gigge

arranged by Nicholas Hare
(b. 1940)

STRING ORCHESTRA

Unit 1: Arranger

Though often considered to be folk songs from anonymous sources and composers, further historical research indicates that the tunes that comprise this piece can be more specifically attributed. "Go from My Window" was a popular Elizabethan song, but its use as the basis for variations for an instrumental ensemble was probably initially done by William Cranford. Cranford lived in London during the first half of the seventeenth century, and the manuscript of these variations is found in Marsh's Library in Dublin. The beloved "Greensleeves" can be found in the *Jane Pickering Lute Book*, where it is fairly certainly written in Jane Pickering's (1615–1645) own handwriting. As is often the case, this written record is much later than the origins of the song: words were published as early as 1580, and Shakespeare includes it in *The Merry Wives of Windsor* in 1596. The dance tune, "Nobodyes Gigge," is found in the *Fitzwilliam Virginal Book*, attributed to Giles Farnaby's son Richard (b. c. 1594).

Arranger Nicholas Hare chose these pieces and set them to be musically and technically accessible for a string ensemble of young or developing play-ers. Hare has had an extensive career in music publishing and arranging (with Chester Music, London), and many of his works have been for early-level string groups.

Unit 2: Composition

This set of pieces is published in the *Playstrings: Music for String Orchestra Series*, appearing as the second composition in the easy level list. All of the pieces on this list have the following flexible instrumentation: violin 1, violin 2, violin 3 (viola 2), viola 1 (optional), viola 2 (optional, same as violin 3), cello 1, cello 2 (optional), and double bass (optional).

The arranger has used "Go from My Window" as the basis of a theme and four variations, in which each variation gives melodic interest to a different part. "Greensleeves" is primarily treated as an accompanied song, with the familiar melody moving among the violin, viola, and cello sections. A descant part for first violin provides contrapuntal interest. "Nobodyes Gigge," based on a dance form, is the liveliest and most contrapuntal of the pieces, using an arch structure to move from a single line accompanied by open fifths to simul-taneous and independent contrapuntal lines in all parts, back to a single, accompanied line. The return to a single line, now passed back and forth between first violin and cello, provides the opportunity to feature soloists.

Unit 3: Historical Perspective

As the title suggests, these tunes were probably popular in England during Shakespeare's lifetime, and certainly they typify music of the Renaissance. The great playwright died in 1616 at age fifty-two; the Renaissance period of music history is generally considered to include the years from about 1420 to 1600. Peter Warlock (pseudonym for Philip Hesseltine) is another compos-er/arranger who used Renaissance sources for string ensemble compositions (in his *Capriol Suite* and *Renaissance Dances*, for example), and much of the original music written for consorts of viols can be played by young and devel-oping string ensembles.

Viols are bowed string instruments with frets, played downward in the lap or between the legs—hence the name "viola da gamba" or simply "gamba." During the Renaissance and for some time to come (especially in France and England), the viol family was more popular than the violin family, in part because the construction and design of the instruments had developed some-what earlier. While viols may have existed as early as the eleventh century, the main documentary and pictorial evidence suggests that the violin family came into being some time in the 1520s. The first written reference to violins dates from 1523, and Ferrari painted a violin in *The Madonna of the Orange Trees* in 1529–30. Makers such as the Amati family—Andrea (1511–c. 1580), his sons Antonio (b. ca. 1540) and Girolamo (1561–1630), and Girolamo's son Nicolo (1596–1684)—and Gasparoda Salò (1540–1609) were contemporaries of Shakespeare, while Stradivari (1644–1737) and Guarneri del Gesù (1698–1744) lived and worked after Shakespeare's death.

Unit 4: Technical Considerations

This composition is intended for first- and second-year players. No shifting is required, except the possible use of half position for cello, and left-hand requirements are generally limited to the diatonic tetrachord (*Do, Re, Mi, Fa*). As noted, parts that exceed these requirements—high third finger in the viola 3 part, for example—can often be substituted with an alternate easier part. A particularly strong feature of these arrangements is the frequent exploitation of all four strings. Specific technical considerations are as follows:

"Go from My Window"
- Violin 1: low and high second fingers; all strings used
- Violin 2: high second finger only; all strings used
- Violin 3: all high second fingers; third finger required one time only
- Viola 1: often doubles violin 1; high third finger required; includes C string
- Viola 2: uses only open string; first and second finger; no third finger required
- Cello 1: 1–3–4 pattern only; all strings used
- Cello 2: *divisi* part; pizzicato required with adequate time to change
- Double bass: mostly open strings and first finger; only melodic interest is in last four measures.

"Greensleeves"
- Violin 1: low first finger (or high fourth) required; low second finger required
- Violin 2: requires low first or high fourth finger; double open strings
- Violin 3: *divisi*—top part requires open, 1, high 2; lower part is nearly all open strings
- Viola 1: high third; low first (or high fourth) fingers required
- Viola 2: *divisi*—top part mostly open and first finger; lower part mostly open
- Cello 1: requires second position or forward extension; fast arco-pizzicato change; the part calls for D-sharp and C-sharp on the G string; and "ossia" part suggests D-sharp, E, and F-sharp sul D
- Cello 2: *divisi*—top part uses mostly open and first finger; lower part uses 1 and 3, double open strings
- Double bass: uses all strings; mostly open and first finger; fast arco-pizzicato change

"Nobodyes Gigge"
- Violin 1: high third and low second fingers required; fourth finger recommended
- Violin 2: high second finger; fourth finger recommended; open double strings; left-hand pizzicato
- Violin 3: same as violin 2
- Viola 1: often doubles violin 1; high third, low first, and fourth fingers required; includes C string
- Viola 2: mostly open strings and first finger required; open double strings; left-hand pizzicato
- Cello 1: extension required (C-sharp on the G string); open double strings; left-hand pizzicato
- Cello 2: *divisi* part; open double strings; left-hand pizzicato
- Double bass: mostly open strings and first finger, with an occasional second finger; no melodic writing.

Unit 5: Stylistic Considerations

Hare's markings require the musical execution of several bowing styles that are at once challenging and appropriate for the first- or second-year student. These include slurs, détaché, lifted staccato, accents, dynamics, and musical silences (in "Go from My Window"); starting up-bow, sustaining *pp*, portato, and successive lifts (in "Greensleeves"); and a sustained dynamic arch (*pp–ff–pp*) across the length of "Nobodyes Gigge" followed by a climactic *tutti* arco chord at the end. For more information on the stylistic realization of Renaissance dances, Arbeau's *Orchesography* is a valuable resource.

Unit 6: Musical Elements

Characteristics of the Renaissance period include the use of modal tonalities (Dorian and Mixolydian are represented in *Three Tunes*, in addition to major and minor), homophonic (accompanied melody) and polyphonic (simultaneous countermelodies) textures, and frequent use of open fifths, drones, and a reiterated *cantus firmus*. Hare incorporates all of these devices, making the composition stylistically authentic, instructionally rich, and musically gratifying.

Unit 7: Form and Structure

Taken as a whole, the three pieces form a cohesive entity. "Go from My Window," marked "Alla Marcia" and ending on an A major chord, is followed by the Andante Espressivo of "Greensleeves" in E Dorian but concluding on an E major (Picardy) chord; the two are balanced by the "Nobodyes [Lively] Gigge," predominately in D major.

"Go from My Window" is structured as a theme and four variations, each eight measures in length. "Greensleeves" is strophic, with a violin descant defining the second statement of the song. "Nobodyes Gigge" is an arch form of increasing complexity and dynamic level (thirty-six measures), eight measures of *tutti ff*, and twenty measures *poco a poco diminuendo al Fine*.

Unit 8: Suggested Listening
Ralph Vaughan Williams:
>*Five Variants of "Dives and Lazarus"*
>*Variations on Greensleeves*

Peter Warlock:
>*Capriol Suite*
>*Renaissance Dances*

Unit 9: Additional References and Resources

Arbeau, Thoinot. *Orchesography*. New York: Dover Publications, Inc., 1967.

Bowed Instruments (video recording). Granada Television International; written and introduced by David Munrow, directed by Peter Plummer, produced by Peter Potter. (Early Music Instruments Series, Vol. 4) Princeton, NJ: Films for the Humanities, 1976.

Boyden, David D. *The History of Violin Playing from its Origins to 1761*. London: Oxford University Press, 1990.

Brown, Howard M. *Music in the Renaissance*. Englewood Cliffs, NJ: Prentice-Hall, 1976.

Brown, Howard M., and Stanley Sadie, eds. *Performance Practice: Music Before 1600*. New York and London: W. W. Norton & Company, 1989. (The Norton/Grove Handbooks in Music)

Cranford, William. *Consorts of Five Parts (Viol Consort Series No. 31)*. Albany, CA: PRB Productions, 1997.

An Index to Printed Sources of Folk Dance Tunes from the United States and British Isles. Berea, Ken.: North American Imprints, 1995.

Renaissance Works for Four Instruments. Editio Musica Budapest #12045 (score and parts).

Sadie, Stanley, ed. *The New Grove Dictionary of Music and Musicians*. New York: Grove's Dictionaries, 2000. Also available online at www.grovemusic.com

Contributed by:
Janet Jensen
Associate Professor of String Pedagogy
University of Wisconsin–Madison
Madison, Wisconsin

Grade Two

Teacher Resource Guide

Brandenburg Concerto No. 5, Movement 1

Johann Sebastian Bach
(1685–1750)

arranged by Merle Isaac

STRING ORCHESTRA

Unit 1: Composer
Johann Sebastian Bach was born on March 21, 1685, in Eisenach, Saxony (Germany), where his father, Johann Ambrosius, taught him to play the violin. So many Bachs in this area of Germany became musicians that everyone who was musical at all was thought to be a Bach. For more than 250 years, beginning in the baroque period, Bachs dominated the musical scene. When J. S. Bach was ten, his parents' deaths caused him to move in with his brother. His brother taught him to play the harpsichord and organ. In 1723, he was appointed cantor and musical director in Leipzig at the Saint Thomas School, where he remained until his death in 1750. While in Leipzig, Bach began the utilization of the tempered musical scale.

Unit 2: Composition
Brandenburg Concerto No. 5 is arranged for string orchestra in the original key of D major. The Allegro movement opens with a ritornello, which is an almost continuous flow of rapid notes. After the ritornello ends very definitely, the various string sections present short melodic ideas, with the upper and lower strings imitating each other playfully. The appearance of sections as soloists brings a lower dynamic level. After a while, the *tutti* returns loudly with a brief fragment of the ritornello, only to give way again to the separate string sections as soloists. This alternation between brief, loud ritornello

fragments by the *tutti* and longer, softer solo sections continues throughout the movement.

Unit 3: Historical Perspective

With his set of six Brandenburg Concertos, Bach brought immortality to a German aristocrat, the Margrave of Brandenburg. Bach met the Margrave in 1718, when he was music director for another patron. The Margrave loved music and asked Bach to send him some original compositions. About three years later, Bach sent him the Brandenburg Concertos. The individual composition dates for the Brandenburg Concertos cannot be precisely determined. The only thing that can be said with certainty about their chronology is that they were all composed by March 1721, the date on Bach's autograph copy. The instrumentation for Concerto No. 5 is flute, violin, viola, cello, and continuo.

Unit 4: Technical Considerations

Phrase dynamics play a very big part in this piece. Students need to be taught to *crescendo* as notes go higher and *decrescendo* as notes go lower. All eighth and quarter notes need to be played very detached. The bowing markings are excellent, as are the fingerings. The bass part moves between first and third position, and cellos have occasional extension C-sharps and G-sharps. Particular attention needs to be made to the accents, which always start in quarter notes, leading a particular string section with the melody. These accents must be played the same in the violins as in the bass section. Hooked bowings will also appear with dotted-quarter/eighth note figures, usually always down–down–up–up. Although the piece is written and conducted in 2/2, the *ritardando* in the last two measures is best conducted in 4/4.

Unit 5: Stylistic Considerations

The music of Bach may be perceived at many simultaneous levels of awareness. At one level, it is clearly baroque. At another, it sums up many earlier traditions. In addition, Bach's music served an important model for many composers who came after him. Finally, Bach's basic impulses seem to survive all manner of stylistic presentation. What makes Bach's music so special? There is no simple answer, but one possibility is that Bach's music has always invited descriptive adjectives such as mathematical, intellectual, and abstract. Viewed from this perspective, a Bach work may be considered as patterns of pure thought expressed in musical terms. Like a mathematical principle, the inner structure remains constant beyond the limits of style and time.

Unit 6: Musical Elements

Major tonalities are prevalent, with the key signature of D major. Even though the piece is written in 2/2, it can be rehearsed in 4/4 to work on the accents, separation, rhythm of the hooked bows, and building of *crescendos* and *decrescendos*. This movement is written in the standard A–B–A form.

Unit 7: Form and Structure

SECTION	MEASURES
A	1
B	16
A	69

Unit 8: Suggested Listening

Johann Sebastian Bach, Brandenburg Concerto Nos. 1–6

Unit 9: Additional References and Resources

Boyd, Malcolm. *The Brandenburg Concertos*. Cambridge: Cambridge University Press, 1993.

Leinsdorf, Erich. *The Composer's Advocate*. New Haven, CT: Yale University Press, 1991.

Contributed by:

Gregg Porter
Conductor, string teacher, composer
Olympia Fields, Illinois

Teacher Resource Guide

"Can Can" from Orpheus in the Underworld

Jacques Offenbach
(1819–1880)

arranged by Richard Meyer

FULL ORCHESTRA

Unit 1: Composer

Jacques Offenbach, a French composer of German descent, was born in Cologne on June 20, 1819. His father was a cantor in the Cologne synagogue.

Offenbach studied violin before taking up cello at age nine. He went to Paris at the age of fourteen. Because he spent most of his life in France, he is considered a French composer. Offenbach played in the orchestra of the Opéra-Comique and became conductor at the Comédie Française. In 1855, he opened his own theater, the Bouffes-Parisiens. Offenbach was a master of the operetta and was famous for his comic operettas; he wrote ninety-seven during his life. Audiences were delighted by these smart, witty, and satirical comic operas.

Offenbach's greatest successes were *Orpheus in the Underworld* (1858) and *La Belle Hélène* (1864). His work influenced the operettas of Gilbert and Sullivan. Offenbach died in Paris in 1880.

Unit 2: Composition

"Can Can" from *Orpheus in the Underworld* is a good example of Offenbach's music. It is characterized by an abundance of flowing, rollicking melodies, seasoned with humor suitable for the extravagant burlesques. The "Can Can" is performed in the last act of the operetta, which is a satirical treatment of Greek mythology. Richard Meyer arranged the "Can Can" for a young, full orchestra. This Grade 2 arrangement has one part each for flute, French horn, and trombone.

Unit 3: Historical Perspective

During the eighteenth century, operettas were short operas. *Opéra comique* used spoken dialogue instead of recitative, requiring fewer singers and players. The works were predominantly romantic in plot and melodious, graceful, and sentimental in music. In the nineteenth century, a special type of comic opera, *opéra bouffe*, was first performed in Paris. It emphasized the smart, witty, and satirical elements of the comic opera. *Orpheus in the Underworld* had a great influence in the development of comic opera in France. In England, Gilbert and Sullivan wrote operettas, and in the United States, Victor Herbert wrote several operettas.

Unit 4: Technical Considerations

The scale of G major and its related keys are required for the entire orchestra. The rhythmic demands are basic, with the use of half notes, quarter notes, and eighth notes. At measure 37, clarinets have a difficult rhythm: two eighth notes/eighth rest/eighth note. There is no tempo change, and special care must be given to ensure that the tempo is not rushed. Ranges for winds and strings are not difficult. Percussion consists of snare drum, bass drum, triangle, and crash cymbals.

Unit 5: Stylistic Considerations

The ensemble must be sensitive and demonstrate the constant dynamic changes and *crescendos*. An ensemble blend and balance are required throughout this work. The string section must produce an even spiccato bowing during the eighth note passages. Uniform bow lengths and attacks must match the wind section for the repeated, accented quarter notes.

Unit 6: Musical Elements

The tonal center of G major is used with some chromatic movement in the woodwinds, second violin, and viola. The entire work is in 2/4, and the eighth note is the smallest division of the beat. Rhythm in the accompanying parts moves vertically and imitates the rhythm of the theme.

Unit 7: Form and Structure

SECTION	MEASURES	EVENT AND SCORING
Introduction	1	Violin, woodwinds, and percussion
Theme 1	9	Violin, flute, and oboe
Theme 2	19	Woodwinds rhythmically blocked with trumpet
Transition	27	First violin, flute, and oboe
Theme 3	37	"Can Can" theme; first violin, flute, oboe, and trumpet
Closing theme	53	Flute and violin with countermelody in cello, bass, bassoon, trombone, and tuba

Unit 8: Suggested Listening

Gilbert and Sullivan, *The Mikado*
Ferdinand Hérold, *Zampa*
Jacques Offenbach:
  La Belle Hélène
  Orpheus in the Underworld
Ambroise Thomas, *Mignon*

Unit 9: Additional References and Resources

Faris, Alexander. *Jacques Offenbach*. Great Britain: Charles Scribner's Sons, 1981.

Grout, Donald Jay, and Claude V. Palisca. *A History of Western Music*. 6th edition. New York: W. W. Norton & Company, 2001.

Kracauer, S. *Orpheus in Paris*. New York: Alfred A. Knopf, 1938.

Sadie, Stanley. *The New Grove Book of Operas*. Great Britain: Macmillan Press Ltd., 1992.

Contributed by:

Selma Pyles
Hilliard City Schools
Hilliard, Ohio

Teacher Resource Guide

"Dance of the Tumblers" from Snow Maiden

Nikolai Rimsky-Korsakov
(1844–1908)

arranged by Sandra Dackow

STRING ORCHESTRA

Unit 1: Composer

Nikolai Rimsky-Korsakov was born in Tikhvin, Russia, in 1844 and died near Saint Petersburg in 1908. His education in music was informal, as he was planning on a career in the Navy. After a two-and-a-half-year tour of duty on a ship, he settled in Saint Petersburg, where he studied composition and shared ideas with the leading composers of the time. Later he was appointed to a position at the Saint Petersburg Conservatory, where he taught composition and orchestration.

Rimsky-Korsakov managed to combine his work as inspector of Navy bands and orchestras with his interest in composing and learning to play as many instruments as he could. He was especially admired for his understanding of what sort of writing would make each instrument sound particularly impressive. The composer loved setting well-known Russian folk tales to music, especially as operas, of which *Snow Maiden* is a good example. He is celebrated today for the sense of color, magic, and mystery he managed to include in so many of his pieces.

Unit 2: Composition

Snow Maiden is one of Rimsky-Korsakov's operas based on an old Russian folk tale. The "Dance of the Tumblers" is the best-known segment of the opera and the one most often performed at concerts. The work grows out of three basic diatonic ideas: the opening eighth/quarter note motive that becomes the main theme; the repeated eighth/sixteenth note ostinato at Rehearsal A; and a second theme, at Rehearsal G, which appears in the dominant. Rimsky-Korsakov generates large stretches of music using quite simple and straightforward ideas with seemingly endless possibilities.

Unit 3: Historical Perspective

Snow Maiden represents Russian opera fare typical of the late nineteenth century. Russia never enjoyed a true Renaissance with the rest of Europe; instead, it moved abruptly from older times to the nineteenth century. Though this was a time of reason and education, not everyone was willing to give up the legacy of legend and lore—hence, the magical, the fantastic, and the grandly historical were popular themes in literature and music. An evening at the opera in Rimsky-Korsakov's time could be compared to a trip to the latest special effects fantasy movie today. The music tried to transport the listener to a magical time and place.

During the eighteenth century, Russia looked to other cultures, particularly those of France and Germany, for example. During the nineteenth century, however, a sense of nationalism and pride in local history and fable became the norm. Rimsky-Korsakov belonged to a group of composers who sought to develop a nationalistic style of musical composition for Russia.

Unit 4: Technical Considerations

"Dance of the Tumblers" from *Snow Maiden*, as arranged for strings by Sandra Dackow, is an easy, Grade 2 arrangement, written for performance by second-year students. Written in the key of C major, it briefly visits the dominant before returning to the tonic. There is only one instance of chromatic writing, which is in the viola counterpoint (in quarter notes at Rehearsal H) to the theme in the dominant. All parts remain in first position in the basic C major/G major finger patterns. Rhythms are easy and repetitive.

The one rhythmic snag occurs toward the end of the arrangement when offbeats are required. This problem can be minimized if players with the theme lift the bow and come back to the frog after each dotted-quarter note so that the eighth note that follows is at the frog and off the string. If the piece is performed with all eighth notes and quarter notes off the string and at the frog, it can sound stylistically compelling, very impressive, and far more difficult than it actually is. It can be performed successfully at a variety of tempos but should never be rushed.

Unit 5: Stylistic Considerations

"Dance of the Tumblers," as the name would imply, is an athletic, exuberant work. A fast bow speed (*not* a fast tempo necessarily) is of greatest importance in realizing the best result. All eighth notes and quarter notes should be performed off the string and at the frog; the lifts between notes that result will give this piece the buoyancy that calls up the image of tumblers leaping and spinning through the air. When playing dotted-quarter notes followed by eighth notes, students should lift the bow after the down-bow dotted-quarter note and bring it back to the frog for the eighth note up-bow. This manner of playing is not only stylistically correct, but it will yield more sound and a more secure rhythm and sense of subdivision. Even the very youngest orchestras should strive to realize a powerful sound with energetic bow strokes.

Unit 6: Musical Elements

The design and elements of this short work are very simple and straightforward. The entire work is spun from three short and straightforward ideas, as mentioned earlier. Everything is diatonic except the one viola chromatic passage. Mixolydian mode is visited briefly to lend a breath of exoticism. Dominant pedal points, a signature nineteenth century Russian device, occur several times to great effect.

Unit 7: Form and Structure

This arrangement is essentially an A–B–A structure with coda. While the original full orchestra work develops material by running themes through several key areas and calls upon some exotic orchestration touches, this easy string arrangement abbreviates the argument while maintaining the same basic structure of A–B–A plus coda.

Unit 8: Suggested Listening

Alexander Borodin, "Polovetsian Dance" from *Prince Igor*
Modeste Mussorgsky, *Night on Bald Mountain*
Nikolai Rimsky-Korsakov:
> *Capriccio Espagnol*
> *Russian Easter Overture*
> *Scheherazade*
> Suite from *Le Coq d'or*
> Suite from *The Tsar Sultan*
Peter I. Tchaikovsky, "Cossack Dance" from *Mazeppa*

Unit 9: Additional References and Resources

Leonard, Richard Anthony. *A History of Russian Music*. New York: The MacMillan Company, 1956.

Rimsky-Korsakov, Nikolai. *My Musical Life*. New York: Alfred A. Knopf Inc., 1923.

Contributed by:

Sandra Dackow
Conductor, arranger, and music director
Ridgewood Symphony, New Jersey
Hershey Symphony, Pennsylvania

Teacher Resource Guide

Danny Boy

arranged by Harry Alshin
(1909–1995)

Unit 1: Arranger

Harry Alshin was born and raised in Brooklyn, New York. In the mid 1930s, he graduated from Juilliard with a bachelor's degree in violin performance. Shortly thereafter, he pursued a graduate degree in music education from Columbia University. For most of his life, he lived in New York, teaching in schools in Spring Valley, Hastings, and Scarsdale. He was also on the faculty at Hofstra University in Hempstead, New York.

Alshin was a dedicated teacher with an intense interest in helping young string students become the best musicians they could be. He was founder and conductor of the Westchester County Junior Strings and served as performer, coach, and conductor at the Aspen Festival Music Camp in Colorado each summer. Alshin arranged a large number of Grade 2, 3, and 4 pieces for string orchestra, including folk songs and works by Mozart, Mendelssohn, Vivaldi, Rossini, and other classical composers. In addition, he edited and annotated an intermediate to moderately advanced violin etude book based on famous excerpts, and he composed several original string compositions.

After Alshin retired from teaching in the mid-1970s, he moved to Florida, where he prepared his numerous string arrangements for publication. He died in 1995. Alshin made significant contributions to string music education and performance through teaching, conducting, arranging, and composing.

Unit 2: Composition

The tune "Danny Boy" is also known as "Londonderry Air," or simply "Derry Air." The tune as we know it can be traced back to 1855 where it first appeared in print in *The Petrie Collection of the Ancient Music of Ireland*, edited by George Petrie. The tune had no title.

Petrie indicated the tune had been collected by Miss J. Ross of Londonderry County, Ireland, who claimed to have notated it after hearing it from an itinerant piper. The tune became known as "Londonderry Air." Recent research (Shields, 1979, cited in M. Robinson) has linked the Ross tune, which is notated in duple meter, to an earlier version notated in triple meter found in *A Collection of the Ancient Music of Ireland* (1796) by Edward Bunting. Bunting's version in triple meter is closely related to the Ross melody, has Irish words, and is titled "Aisling an Ogfhir," or "The Young Man's Dream." The Irish words are not related in any way to the text of "Danny Boy." In actuality, the Ross tune has been paired with more than one hundred different song texts.

A version of "Danny Boy" was written in 1910 by an English lawyer and successful songwriter named Fred Weatherly (1848–1929). The original tune written by Weatherly was not highly received, but when his sister sent him the Ross version of "Londonderry Air," Weatherly realized it was perfectly suited for his "Danny Boy" text. Using the "Londonderry Air" tune, he published a successful, revised version of "Danny Boy" in 1913.

Most Americans believe that "Danny Boy" is a traditional Irish love song; however, the English text was written several years before it was paired with the Irish tune, negating cultural connection between text and tune. Another common interpretation is that the text describes a father's love for his son who has gone off to join the Irish Republican Army (IRA)—an unlikely theme given the English author. Neither Weatherly nor the song text specified the relationship of the singer to Danny, thereby creating a mystery concerning the intent of the song. No matter what interpretation is placed on the text, the popularity of the song "Danny Boy" and the tune "Londonderry Air" cannot be denied.

Alshin dedicated his arrangement to a close friend, Danny Schoenholz. Performance time is approximately three minutes.

Unit 3: Historical Perspective

With an increase in the number of youth orchestras and the number of string programs available in public schools in the 1970s and 1980s, string educators and composers were motivated to provide quality literature for young string students. In an effort to provide students with solid technique, a general understanding of musical style and history, and exposure to the wealth of classic literature for orchestra, educators and composers began to look at ways to make authentic literature accessible for young students.

Among those known in the past twenty years for their expertise in arranging folk songs and classical literature for young students, Harry Alshin, Sandra Dackow, Merle Isaac, and Vernon Leidig come to the fore. Each has contributed a wide variety and large number of arrangements that are playable for students and that are musically satisfying because the integrity of the works has been maintained. Like Alshin, Leidig also arranged the tune "Londonderry Air" in *Two Familiar Airs*.

Unit 4: Technical Considerations

Danny Boy is written in D major. All parts can be played in first position except for a short *divisi* section in the first violins, which requires third position in the upper octave. In first position, cellos are required to use forward extension, and upper strings must use a high third finger. Alternate fingerings are provided for more advanced players. Cellos and first violins share the melody. Tempo is slow, and lines in all parts are expressive and sustained.

The major challenge for young string players will be to maintain tone and to shape phrases musically. Bow speed and placement are critical. Inner voices are moving lines that contain arpeggiated figures with slurred string crossings. Rhythm is basic. Alshin provided alternate parts for less-experienced players or for use in a combined festival orchestra.

Unit 5: Stylistic Considerations

Alshin's arrangement and notation of *Danny Boy* clearly reflects the traditional Irish performance practice of playing slow airs expressively with intentional rubato, flexible rhythm, and melodic ornamentation. Inner lines have beautiful countermelodies that should support but never overpower the primary melody. Strategically placed *crescendos* and *decrescendos* lead to the shaping and tapering of phrases, encouraging young musicians to play with expression and a sense of direction.

Even bow speed and control are necessary to make smooth connections between notes and to create smooth string crossings in the inner voices. All lines should be played in a singing style. In measures 14, 26, and 30–32, use of tenuto bow style provides a natural rubato. Ornamentation in the primary melodic line provides interest in repeated verses and should be played with an easy, improvisatory style rather than in strict rhythm.

Unit 6: Musical Elements

The key of D major is maintained throughout the composition. Harmonic structure is basic and straightforward, with the exception of a deceptive cadence appearing immediately before the codetta. Inner lines are primarily countermelodies that include occasional accidentals appearing as passing tones. The string bass line is important for harmonic structure and depth, and should be played with solid and sustained tone.

Traditional Irish air melodies collected during the late eighteenth and nineteenth centuries encompass a wide range—an eleventh or twelfth. In the case of *Danny Boy*, Alshin maintained the integrity of the traditional melody, which encompasses the range of a fourteenth. Simple melodic ornamentation appears in the restatement of the opening phrase by the first violins in measures 18–22 and again in measure 30.

Meter is common time. Rhythmic elements in all parts are basic and often follow the rhythm of the melody. Optional parts consisting of mostly half and quarter notes add a fuller harmonic texture but at the same time detract from the integrity of the dotted-quarter/eighth note patterns prevalent in remaining parts.

Unit 7: Form and Structure

Alshin followed the original A–A–B–A form, which is the most common form for Irish songs of the time. Phrases are four measures each.

SECTION	MEASURES	EVENT AND SCORING
Introduction	1–2	Melodic interest in first violin
A	2–6	Melody in cello
A	6–10	Repetition of melody in first violin
B	10–14	Melody in first violin
A^1	14–18	Melody in first violin
A	18–22	Second verse; ornamentation of melody in first violin
A	22–26	Melody in primary form in cello
B	26–30	Melody in octaves in first violin; some variation at phrase ending
A^1	30–34	Melody in first violin
Codetta/A	34–35	Repetition of last two measures of the melody

Unit 8: Suggested Listening

"Danny Boy" performed by James Galway on *James Galway: The Celtic Minstrel* CD/BG268393
Percy Grainger, *Irish Tune from County Derry*
Irish Night at the Pops, Arthur Fiedler and Boston Pops, CD/60746-2-RG
The Irish Tenors, CD/MDT8552
"Londonderry Air," any instrumental recording

Unit 9: Additional References and Resources

Alshin, Mrs. Harry. Telephone interview, June 2000.

Fuld, James J. *Book of World Famous Music: Classical, Popular, and Folk.* New York: Crown Publishing, 1966.

Kendor Music Company. Telephone interview with Nadene Gardner, June 2000.

Rice, T., J. Porter, and C. Goertzen, eds. *The Garland Encyclopedia of World Music: Europe*. Vol. 8. New York: Garland Publishing Co., 2000.

Robinson, Michael. "'Danny Boy': The Mystery Solved," Folk Harp Journal, 95 (Spring 1997): 29–31.

Robinson, Michael. "'Danny Boy': The Mystery Solved!" http://www.standingstones.com

Sadie, Stanley, ed. *The New Grove Dictionary of Music and Musicians*. New York: Grove's Dictionaries, 2000. Also available online at www.grovemusic.com

Contributed by:

Kathlene Goodrich
The Hartt School
University of Hartford
Hartford, Connecticut

Teacher Resource Guide

"Entrance of the Queen of Sheba" from Solomon

George Frideric Handel
(1685–1759)

arranged by Harry Fisher

STRING ORCHESTRA

Unit 1: Composer/Arranger

George Frideric Handel was born and educated in Halle, in what is now Germany. Though he did not come from a musical family, his abilities soon became apparent, and he was permitted to study with the cathedral organist, Frederick Wilhelm Zachau. He entered the University of Halle to study law but left within a year to pursue a musical career. He studied in Italy from 1706–10 and met many of the finest composers active there, notably Corelli and Scarlatti.

Handel returned to Germany in 1710 as kappelmeister for the Elector of Hanover (later King George I of England). After an initial trip to London in 1711, he returned to settle there in 1712, becoming a British subject in 1727. He was recognized as one of the greatest composers of his day and, upon his death in 1759, was accorded the great honor of burial in Westminster Abbey.

Arranger Harry Fisher holds a bachelor's degree in music education from Gettysburg College and a Master of Music from Temple University in Philadelphia. He taught music in the public schools of New Jersey and Pennsylvania for thirty-four years. An active violist and organist, he is the founder of an early music ensemble called Musica Antiqua South Jersey.

Unit 2: Composition

That he would be remembered by future generations as a composer of oratorios would probably have surprised Handel, who regarded himself more as a composer of operas. In terms of musical style, however, there was very little difference between the two apart from the more extensive use of choruses in the oratorios. Handel was attracted to Biblical subjects for his oratorio texts, the most notable being *Messiah, Judas Maccabeus, Saul,* and *Solomon.*

The "Entrance of the Queen of Sheba" is, in effect, the prelude to the third act of *Solomon.* The Biblical story relates how the Queen of Sheba, hearing of Solomon's great wisdom, traveled to Jerusalem to meet him, entering with great pomp and ceremony to the city and the court. Handel illustrates this festive moment with a mini-concerto grosso movement using two oboes for the solo interludes (concertino) and the full string ensemble with continuo for the ripieno.

Unit 3: Historical Perspective

The concertino/ripieno practice of contrasting an ensemble of soloists with a larger ensemble is typical of many concerto grossos in the baroque style. Archangelo Corelli (1653–1713) is considered one of the first masters of the form, and his concertos of Opus 6 were widely diffused and imitated in Europe. The most common instrumentation for the concertino was two violins and cello, sometimes with their own continuo player (keyboard or a member of the lute family), while the ripieno contained parts for two violins, one viola, cello or bass, and another continuo player, usually a harpsichord or organ. The "Entrance of the Queen of Sheba" departs from the usual practice in that there is no bass part indicated to accompany the solo lines. The presence of oboe does, however, imply that bassoon would be used to reinforce the bass line of the cello or bass part, as in both the *Water Music* and *Fireworks Music* suites.

Unit 4: Technical Considerations

In this arrangement, the solo lines have been given to the violins, although oboes or even flutes could be substituted. Neither the solo nor the ripieno parts go above first position, but some players will find the use of upper positions easier for some of the figuration. The first violin part, and at times the second violin part, of the ripieno consists of repeated arpeggios, which must be executed accurately. Most of the other parts contain largely diatonic movement within the key centers of G, D, and A major, with brief episodes in related minors.

The rhythmic values of the original have been halved, so the eighth note is the smallest subdivision of the beat. In the original version, the oboes did not play the arpeggiated figuration in the ripieno sections but rather the slower rhythm at the beginning of the second violin part and the upper cello part.

An easier part for less-advanced violins and violas has been included for use in festival programs.

Unit 5: Stylistic Considerations

We are accustomed to thinking of the baroque style as the era of terraced dynamics, the ripieno ensemble being the *forte* section and the concertino the contrasting *piano* section. This does not imply that the concertino should play *piano*, but the sheer weight of numbers and the added viola part will give the ripieno a fuller sound. Much has been written about the baroque style of bowing, baroque bows themselves, and the characteristic sound of unwrapped gut strings on instruments set up in the baroque manner. For our purposes, we can be satisfied with achieving a clean, articulate, and basically détaché sound from the ensemble—the arpeggiated figures will sound that way anyway—and permit the solo lines to be a bit more legato for contrast. If an electronic keyboard with a pleasing harpsichord sound is available, its twang will add a charming sparkle to the piece.

Unit 6: Musical Elements

The texture of the piece is basically homophonic, with even the solo lines moving in parallel thirds or sixths. The harmonic movement is in straightforward progressions typical of baroque style. A descending scale line in the bass leading to a full dominant–tonic cadence is a recurring motive. The "busy" nature of the first violin arpeggios gives the piece its brightness and jollity, while the more flowing diatonic lines of the solo parts provide an appropriate contrast. This is not a movement packed with profound meaning but a joyous and exuberant celebration, in the same manner as the previously mentioned suites from *Water Music* and *Fireworks Music*.

Unit 7: Form and Structure

The piece is a large A–B–A form, the *da Capo* in measure 104 returning us to the beginning for the repeat of the A section. The B section (measures 33–104) begins with a concertino statement and continues as a dialog between the concertino and ripieno.

Unit 8: Suggested Listening

Archangelo Corelli, Concerti Grossi, Op. 6
George Frideric Handel:
    Fireworks Music Suite
    Solomon (oratorio)
    Water Music Suite

Unit 9: Additional References and Resources

Bukofzer, Manfred F. *Music in the Baroque Era*. New York: W. W. Norton & Company, 1947.

Dean, Winton. *The New Grove Handel*. New York: W. W. Norton & Company, 1982.

Donington, Robert. *String Playing in Baroque Music*. New York: Charles Scribner's Sons, 1977.

Dorian, Frederick. *The History of Music in Performance*. New York: W. W. Norton & Company, 1942.

Hogwood, Christopher. *Handel*. New York: Thames and Hudson, 1996.

Palisca, Claude V. H. Wiley Hitchcock, ed. *Music in the Baroque Era*. Englewood Cliffs, NJ: Prentice-Hall, Inc., 1968.

Contributed by:

Harry Fisher
Composer and arranger
Cherry Hill, New Jersey

Teacher Resource Guide

Fanfare and Frippery

Richard Stephan
(b. 1929)

STRING ORCHESTRA

Unit 1: Composer

Richard Albert Stephan was born in Buffalo, New York, in 1929. He earned degrees in music education from the State University of New York at Fredonia and the Eastman School of Music, with further study at the University of Buffalo and Brigham Young University. After a two-year tour of duty with the U.S. Army, where he served as an arranger-bandsman, Stephan began his teaching career in Buffalo, New York, followed by a position as coordinator of music in the Hamburg, New York public schools. In 1968, he became a member of the faculty of the Crane School of Music, State University of New York at Potsdam, until his retirement in 2000.

Throughout his career, Stephan has been active as a teacher, conductor, clinician, composer, and performing musician in both the symphonic and jazz areas. In 1984, he was honored with a Fulbright Senior Scholar Award to Australia. In 1986, his *Fanfare and Frippery* won the National School Orchestra Association Composition Contest. Other notable works by Stephan include *Fantasia on a Seventeenth Century Tune*, *Dance in D*, *Adirondack Sleighride*, *Australian Folk Suite*, *Vanguard Overture*, and *Fanfare and Frippery No. 2*.

Unit 2: Composition

Fanfare and Frippery was written specifically for submission to the National School Orchestra Association Composition Contest for middle school string orchestra in 1986. It won the competition and was subsequently published.

108

The term *fanfare* needs no explanation and should be performed in the expected majestic, festive manner. The term *frippery*, on the other hand, has elicited numerous queries. The term was borrowed from Lowell Shaw, a fine composer of many fripperies for French horn ensembles. The dictionary defines frippery as "a showy, unnecessary ornament." This definition somewhat alludes to the light and frivolous nature of the second movement.

Unit 3: Historical Perspective

Historically, music written for less-experienced players has mainly utilized traditional harmonic resources. *Fanfare and Frippery* is a very conservative attempt to use mildly dissonant harmonies in an accessible manner. The use of changing meters is also a device somewhat rare in music of this level. Both techniques were foreshadowed in an earlier arrangement of 1963, titled *When Johnny Comes Marching Home*.

The composer's experience as a bass player has undoubtedly influenced a desire to give every instrument an interesting part.

Unit 4: Technical Considerations

The set is written in the key of D major. A working knowledge of the D, G, and C major scales and G pentatonic scale is helpful. The first violin part has several measures in third position that are optional. The cello has a brief episode also in third position as well as some extensions on the C string.

Rhythms are mainly straightforward, block in nature, utilizing combinations of quarters, eighths, and sixteenths. Changing meters, however, add a challenge. Trills in the upper strings are also required.

Unit 5: Stylistic Considerations

A good, firm détaché bowing is appropriate for the body of the Fanfare, and a solid martelé stroke is needed for the accented portions. The middle section at Rehearsal E is best articulated with a short stroke at the tip or, if the players are up to it, spiccato at the balance point.

In the Frippery, the challenge, as always, is to keep the pizzicato from rushing—particularly the syncopated final measure of the eight-measure theme. The B section requires a legato stroke from all except the bass, gradually developing to a more aggressive stroke from Rehearsal I onward. A very broad, sonorous détaché is appropriate for the coda, perhaps belying the supposition that this was frivolous after all.

Unit 6: Musical Elements

The trills of the introduction set up a sparkling background for the restless fourths in the cello and bass leading to an ascending G pentatonic scale. The main theme at Rehearsal A is harmonized with simple triads in the upper three voices. A dissonance occurs when the bass voice is added to the triads at various points. Dissonances of major seconds in open chords are used to create tension. Simple triads in an unrelated key—that is, the F major triad used in the key of D—are added for color in the B section. Quartal harmonies also appear.

The melodies are generally diatonic and constructed of short rhythmic phrases. Changing meters and offbeat accents are the main challenges.

The Frippery is harmonized much more traditionally. The opening melody in the cello and bass turns out to be the bass line to the real main theme, which enters at Rehearsal G. A cycle of fourths borrowed from jazz vocabulary moves the orchestra through the B section. A bit of polyphony appears in the form of a two-part and then a three-part canon. The coda is a reharmonization of the melody in augmentation.

Unit 7: Form and Structure

SECTION	EVENT AND SCORING
Movement 1: "Fanfare"	
Introduction	7 measures
Theme 1	Rehearsal A; tonic
Theme 1	Rehearsal B; dominant
Theme 1	Rehearsal C; tonic; extended
Transition	5 measures before Rehearsal E
Theme 2	Rehearsal E; elements of introduction in bass
Transition	1 measure
Theme 3	Rehearsal F
Transition	2 measures
Theme 1	Rehearsal A; tonic
Theme 1	Rehearsal B; dominant
Theme 1	Rehearsal C; tonic
Coda	6 measures
Movement 2: "Frippery"	
Theme 1	First 8 measures
Theme 2	Rehearsal G; combined with Theme 1
Theme 3	Rehearsal H
Themes 1 and 2	Rehearsal I
Theme 2	Rehearsal J; two-part canon

110

SECTION	EVENT AND SCORING
Theme 2	Rehearsal K; three-part canon
Theme 3	Rehearsal H
Theme 2′	8 measures before Rehearsal L; augmentation
Coda	Final 7 measures

Unit 8: Suggested Listening

Samuel Adler, Concertino for Strings
Ernest Bloch, Concerto Grosso No. 2
Benjamin Britten, *A Simple Symphony*
Gioacchino Rossini, String Sonata in G
William Schuman, *Symphony for Strings*

Contributed by:

Richard Stephan
Crane School of Music
State University of New York at Potsdam
Potsdam, New York

Teacher Resource Guide

Kingsbridge March

William Dyson
(b. 1942)

STRING ORCHESTRA

Unit 1: Composer

William Dyson was born in Columbus, Georgia, in 1942 and lived in Alabama during his early years. In 1964, he received his B.S. in Music Education from Auburn University, and in 1967, he received his M.Ed. from the same institution. Dyson has taught band and strings in the public schools of Alabama, South Carolina, and Georgia. Since 1977, he has been employed by the Atlanta Public Schools as a strings specialist in high school, middle school, and elementary school. His current teaching assignment is at the elementary school level.

Active in the music teacher associations of Georgia, Dyson held numerous appointed or elected positions in the Georgia Music Educators Association. He is also active with the Georgia chapter of the American String Teachers Association and with the National School Orchestra Association, for which he serves as newsletter editor.

As a composer, Dyson currently has six compositions in print for string orchestra and eight compositions in print for handbells.

Unit 2: Composition

Kingsbridge March was composed in 1989 for that year's Atlanta Public Schools Area I Spring Arts Festival Elementary Honor Orchestra. When the music was composed, it was intended to be both a concert piece and a selection that could be performed as an end-of-the-year processional or recessional for graduation and promotional programs. *Kingsbridge March* is a stately and dignified processional or recessional march. The themes evolved into a piece similar in style to those of Elgar and Walton, with a decided English flavor. Its title is derived from this association with England. *Kingsbridge March* is a versatile piece. It can be used as a selection for concert, graduation, promotional exercises, awards programs, contests, or festivals.

Unit 3: Historical Perspective

At the time of the composition of this piece, there were no middle schools in the Atlanta public school system. Students attended elementary school from grades K–7 and high school from grades 8–12. Most of the students who first performed *Kingsbridge March* were in grades 6 and 7. Consequently, the piece was written with this age group in mind. *Kingsbridge March* is, thus, best suited for middle school or junior high school level students, although it can be (and has been) used for high school graduations as well.

Unit 4: Technical Considerations

Kingsbridge March can be performed by students who have had as few as two years' instruction in elementary school. All of the music can be played in first position on all instruments. Of all the shoulder instruments, only the first violin is required to use the fourth finger, and this occurs only at measures 22 and 23.

Students must be familiar with the use of low second finger (shoulder instruments) and second finger (floor instruments). The music starts in the key of G major and changes to C major before returning to G major once again. These keys were chosen deliberately to teach the chromatic use of the second finger on all instruments.

The tempo of *Kingsbridge March* is quarter note = 92. This tempo stays constant throughout the composition to encourage a stately processional/recessional. The meter, 4/4, is also constant. Rhythmically, the only new concept for the less-advanced student is the use of eighth note triplets. Only in the first violin part do the notes within the triplet change. In the other parts, the pitches are the same within the triplet figure.

Unit 5: Stylistic Considerations

The first section of this piece is played in a détaché style. At the change of key at measure 25, there are two kinds of contrasts: the bowing style becomes more legato as compared with measures 1–24, and the floor instruments are playing pizzicato against the legato upper voices.

Instances of hooked bows are found throughout the piece. These must be used to perform the piece effectively. At the change of key at measure 25, shoulder instruments only are required to slur throughout this section.

This piece can be very effective if all dynamics are scrupulously followed. Not observing dynamics will result in a static performance.

Unit 6: Musical Elements

At one time or another, all shoulder instruments play the melody in *Kingsbridge March*. At measure 9, the second violins have the melody with all other instruments on harmony parts. The students playing second violin must project the part at this place and use a large amount of the bow to be heard.

Starting at measure 26, the style is more legato, and all shoulder instruments are in unison until measure 35. Again, a large amount of the bow should be used, with particular emphasis on intonation. In this section, the floor instruments should take great care to keep a steady tempo without rushing.

Throughout *Kingsbridge March* the harmonies are traditional. There are no atonal elements, and no harmonic surprises will be found.

Unit 7: Form and Structure

Form: A (aba)–B–A (aba) plus coda

SECTION	MEASURES	EVENT AND SCORING
Theme 1	1–8	First violin has the melody
Theme 2	9–16	Second violin has the melody
Theme 3	17–24	First violin has the melody
Theme 3	25–42	Shoulder instruments have a unison melody through m. 34, then first violin has the melody with the other instruments playing harmony parts; this continues through m. 42, where there is a *da capo* to m. 1
Coda		The jump to the coda is at m. 22; a four-measure coda concludes the piece

Unit 8: Suggested Listening

Sir Edward Elgar, *Pomp and Circumstance*
   (five marches for orchestra, Op. 39)
Gustav Holst, "Jupiter" from *The Planets*
Ralph Vaughan Williams, *English Folk Song Suite*
Sir William Walton, *Crown Imperial*

Unit 9: Additional References and Resources

Ewen, David. *The World of Twentieth-Century Music*. Englewood Cliffs, NJ: Prentice-Hall, Inc., 1969.

Grout, Donald Jay, and Claude V. Palisca. *A History of Western Music*. 6th edition. New York: W. W. Norton & Company, Inc., 2001.

Randel, Don, ed. *The New Harvard Dictionary of Music*. Cambridge, MA: Harvard University Press, 1986.

Contributed by:
William Dyson
Atlanta Public Schools
Atlanta, Georgia

Teacher Resource Guide

A Little Bit of...Space...Time
Samuel Adler
(b. 1928)

STRING ORCHESTRA

Unit 1: Composer

Samuel Adler was born in Mannheim, Germany, in 1928, and came to the United States in 1939. During his tenure in the U.S. Army, he founded and conducted the 7th Army Symphony Orchestra. Because of this ensemble's great psychological and musical contribution to the European cultural scene, he was awarded the Army's Medal of Honor. Adler's catalog includes over four hundred published works in all media, including five operas, six symphonies, eight string quartets, eight concerti (organ, piano, violin, cello, flute, guitar, saxophone quartet, woodwind quintet), many shorter orchestral works, works for wind ensemble and band, chamber music, and a great deal of choral music. His works have been performed by major symphonic, choral, and chamber organizations all over the world. He has published three books, *Choral Conducting—An Anthology*, *Sight-Singing*, and *The Study of Orchestration*, as well as numerous articles in major magazines and reference books in the U.S. and abroad. Adler was Professor of Composition at the Eastman School from 1966 until his retirement in 1994. He currently lives near Toledo, Ohio, and still composes and conducts concerts around the world. He is also on the faculty of the Juilliard School in New York City.

Unit 2: Composition

A Little Bit of...Space...Time was commissioned by the Rockville (NY) Center School District and published in 1978. The work lasts approximately three minutes and is in two movements: "...Space" and "...Time." It is number 14 in the Contemporary String Orchestra Editions of Ludwig Music Publishing

Company. It would be tempting to view the format of the title, with its ellipses, as an attempt to indicate graphically a sense of void or expansiveness related to the concepts contained in the title; however, according to Adler, the ellipses were inserted by the publisher after the piece was written.

Unit 3: Historical Perspective

Like many American composers, Adler has long been committed to new works for young orchestra as a composer, teacher, and conductor. He conducted the premiere of the piece and reports that not all of the string teachers in the Rockville Center School District were pleased with the composition. They were concerned that it did not teach "proper tone production" and that the students would not like it. In fact, Adler reports that two members of the elementary orchestra came up to him before rehearsal and said that their private teachers thought he knew nothing about writing for strings.

The piece debuted ten years after the release of the film *2001: A Space Odyssey.* Although not part of Adler's thinking in writing the piece, a connection with the movie did prove relevant to the premiere. Adler reports that there was little support from either the teachers or the students for the first movement and that he had to volunteer to rehearse and conduct the entire work at the concert.

At the first rehearsal, Adler tapped into the students' familiarity with the Kubrick film by asking them if they wanted to perform "some 'space' music." He then taught the students how to bow behind the bridge on their instrument and conducted, composed, and improvised a sound-scape based on the resulting sounds, which was similar to the opening of the piece. Initiated into the tonal landscape of the movement by this experience and oriented by the connection Adler made to the students' lives outside of school, he was able to rehearse the piece for the concert.

At the concert, the audience and the students enjoyed the first movement so much that Adler was asked to repeat it three times before he insisted on going on to the final movement.

Unit 4: Technical Considerations

As part of the commission, Adler was requested not to write using fourth finger for the upper string players. With one exception, this is indeed the case.

The entire piece can be played in first position. The violin parts require experience in the 1–23–(4) and 12–3–(4) patterns, to which violists must also add familiarity with 1–2–3(4). There is one misprint in measure 24 of "...Time" in the inside second violin part: the pitch should be F-sharp, not F-natural. There is one backward extension (E-flat on the D string) in the cello part. The bass part has two slow, sustained pitches in half position; the rest of the part is in first position. Most of the piece is played arco with and without mutes. There is some *divisi* writing in each movement, which could be done by stand or by a subgroup of a section.

"...SPACE":

Nontraditional sound production is evident only in the first movement, as musical sounds are produced by playing on open string in back of the bridge, trilling with fingers on the body of the instrument, using mutes, and knocking on the body of the instrument. Written in 4/4 with simple "book 1" rhythmic material, the rhythmic content includes entrances off the beat and quarter note syncopation over two measures, none of which is difficult at the tempo marking: "Very slowly, quarter note = 44." In fact, it provides a good evaluation of students' counting skills outside of the folk song-like style found in most "Book 1" string class method books.

"...TIME":

The second movement does not employ nontraditional sound production technique. The cello and double bass begin the movement by plucking an extended open-string ostinato. At the tempo marking of "Quite fast, quarter note = 116," the double bass players employ the jazz pizzicato technique of anchoring the thumb on the fingerboard and using two fingers to pluck—1 followed by 2, or 2 by 1—almost in a twisting motion. This will be more successful than trying to pluck the open E string as rapidly as is required using a single finger. Tonally the movement is in D major and G major, with each of the upper string parts playing a five-measure scalar theme that is imitated within each *divisi* section and among sections.

Unit 5: Stylistic Considerations

"You never know what's going to come from me stylistically," says Adler. This is true, as the two movements are stylistically very different. The first is a sound-scape suggesting sound or music from outer space. This programmatic notion is confirmed by Adler (see Unit 3: Historical Perspective). The second is a multi-voiced, imitative march over an ostinato, which also creates a sound wall once it gets going, but with a thick texture and, therefore, in contrast to the thin, non-atmospheric texture of space. There is perhaps an implied relationship between the two movements that some students, particularly budding composers, will find fascinating. Adler creates a sense of "space" in the first movement by removing "time." The 4/4 meter and the bar lines are visual markers only for the convenience of rehearsing, not to create the suggestion of metric pulse. Whereas in "...Time," the tempo is fast and the music march-like—or in "time."

"...SPACE":

There is a contrast between nontraditional and traditional sounds as they relate to physical space, not outer space. To produce nontraditional sounds,

118

one can consider the physical space used to produce them, specifically knocking on the hollow boxes of string instruments (their "inner space"), bowing in the space in back of the bridge, and utilizing the horizontal and vertical planes of the bow and fingerboard. Traditional string sounds with lots of "space" between pitches create sounds we typically associate with "space music."

The opening should begin inaudibly up-bow, as should lower strings in measures 18–19. During sustained whole notes, students should change their bows *ad libitum*. Nevertheless, the difficulty here is to ensure that students are rhythmically precise so the pitch clusters change simultaneously within and among sections. Students tend to see whole notes and think they can sort of "ooze" from pitch to pitch. Students also need to be sure rests are counted at their full value, as in the important beat of silence found at the beginning of measure 4.

"…TIME":
The opening four-measure introduction needs to be filled with energy and precision. Violins should begin on the string just below the middle of the bow for the *ff*. The theme is stated by each part with détaché half-bows. Dynamics between sections need to be taken into consideration. Unlike in a fugue, it is acceptable that each part is not heard as it enters. The interest here should be the thickening of the texture and then the textural changes at measures 16 and 20, and especially at the first and second endings. These measures are vital because they are the only places where the orchestral texture is homorhythmic—that is, everyone plays at the same time.

Unit 6: Musical Elements
"…SPACE":
Stacks of open fifths contrast with nontraditional sounds. The movement is not so much in the form of statement–departure–restatement as it is one of evolving textures.

"…TIME":
D-major tonality is reserved for the scalar themes, while the purpose of the ostinato is rhythmic rather than tonal. Other information on musical elements is found in Unit 7: Form and Structure.

Unit 7: Form and Structure

SECTION	MEASURES	EVENT AND SCORING
Movement 1: "…Space"		
	1	Opens with contrast between upper strings' bowed sounds (vertical plane) and lower strings' fingerboard taps (horizontal plane); two motives

SECTION	MEASURES	EVENT AND SCORING
		composed of similar materials: a three-measure unit followed by one twice as long, hinged together by a silent downbeat in m. 4; dissolves into….
	10	Sustained traditional string tones that are (a) tone clusters in middle voices (close in space) and (b) at wide (open space) intervals in double bass and first violin
	17	Lower strings release on downbeat and violins move together from m. 16 so the open fifths will be in sharp contrast to the wider orchestral sound of m. 16; this begins a contrasting section using traditional means of sound production; timeless upper string parts, free bowing
	23	Return of the opening material, but the upper and lower strings have switched roles; clean release by upper strings is required in m. 25
	28	Fingerboard taps have disappeared; finally a unison mode of sound production with everyone bowing behind the bridge during the critical *diminuendo*, mm. 26–39; ends with a brand new sound—a knock (done more easily if left hand is used) that appears only here
Movement 2: "…Time" (in five sections)		
Introduction	1	Rhythmic ostinato in lower strings; energy-filled, upper-string fanfare figure
Section 1	5	Scale-based, six-note theme imitated by another voice after two beats; after the first six beats, pitches appear in the same order within each part, but rhythmic values are different; Theme 2 in first violin appears in m. 8

SECTION	MEASURES	EVENT AND SCORING
Section 2	16	Ostinato stops; only treble voices continue; theme actually begins midway through m. 15 in outside first violin; viola functions as bass voice and needs to be heard; free bowing is encouraged
Section 3	21	Upper strings play double "time" eighth notes with slurred articulation; countermelody from m. 8 appears in lower strings and in imitation; leads to first homorhythmic measure in m. 24, which is an important moment; repeat sign leads back to m. 5
Coda	25	Importance of m. 24 is clearer as it is now the beginning of the coda; in the middle of the two-measure coda is the movement's only unison silence followed by D octaves, which must be clear to listeners; lower string parts can be changed to arco to add weight to the movement's conclusion

Unit 8: Suggested Listening

Samuel Adler:
    Concertino No. 1 for String Orchestra
    Suite of Five American Folk Songs
Ligeti, *Atmosphères*
Orff, *Carmina Burana*
Varése, *Intégrales*

Unit 9: Additional References and Resources

Morgan, Robert. *Twentieth Century Music*. New York: W. W. Norton & Company, 1991.

Sadie, Stanley, ed. *The New Grove Dictionary of Music and Musicians*. "Samuel Adler." New York: Grove's Dictionaries, 2000. Also available online at www.grovemusic.com

Watkins, Glenn. Soundings: *Music in the Twentieth Century*. New York: Schirmer, 1988.

Contributed by:

Louis Bergonzi
Associate Professor of Music Education (Strings)
Eastman School of Music
University of Rochester
Rochester, New York

Teacher Resource Guide

Little Fugue

George Frideric Handel
(1685–1759)

arranged by Edmund Siennicki

STRING ORCHESTRA

Unit 1: Composer/Arranger

George Frideric Handel was born in 1685 in Halle, Saxony. He wrote operas, chamber music, choral music, orchestral music, keyboard music, and vocal music.

Arranger Edmund J. Siennicki was born in 1920 in Cleveland, Ohio. He started composing and improvising music on the piano at the age of thirteen. He holds a Bachelor of Music from Kent State University and a Master of Arts from Teacher's College at Columbia University. In the 1960s, Siennicki established an electronic music lab called Musique Concrète where his students composed *avante garde* music. He has taught junior high instrumental music in Cleveland, Ohio.

While a student at Kent State University, Siennicki wrote the Kent State fight song that is sung today. He also composed and arranged music for the instrumentation of his public school classes. In 1959, Robert Rimer encouraged him to write for orchestras. His first composition, *Park Avenue Hoedown*, was written for the National School Orchestra Association Composition Contest. Siennicki recently was honored with the Kent State Distinguished Alumnus Award for his career achievement in music education.

Unit 2: Composition

Siennicki remembers discovering this Handel work and arranging the selection to introduce his students to the fugue form and to help build their tone.

This C major fugue is approximately two minutes in length.

Unit 3: Historical Perspective

The original fugue was composed during the baroque period. The arrangement was written in 1970. The fugue form was developed during the seventeenth century and brought to its highest perfection by J. S. Bach. A fugue's dominating characteristic is two or more independent musical lines combined. The most important element in a fugue is the subject heard by one voice at the beginning. The subject is replied to by an answer, which is the subject repeated in another voice, often combined with a countermelody.

Unit 4: Technical Considerations

The composition is in the key of C major, and the tempo is marked "Allegro." The quarter note is the smallest note value. The string bass part has some third position parts; all other parts can be played in first position. The first violin part requires use of a low first finger; the first and second violins utilize a high third finger. The cello and bass parts are doubled. Although classified as a Grade 2 selection based on the notes, this selection is a Grade 3 piece musically. This selection has many sustained parts that will require intonation precision. Vibrato would greatly enhance these sustained passages.

Unit 5: Stylistic Considerations

Each entrance needs to be emphasized. A very fast, energetic staccato bow stroke will make the selection more characteristic of the baroque string sound. There should be a slight space between the notes. The pulse of the music is very important. Students should be taught to slightly accent the first beat of the measure, and the end of every measure should move into the next measure.

Unit 6: Musical Elements

The short first violin melody stated at the beginning is imitated by the other string sections in close succession. The melody or short motifs reappear throughout the entire piece in all voices. The quarter notes need to be metronomically precise and with a slight separation.

Unit 7: Form and Structure

Little Fugue is a form of imitative counterpoint. The fugue starts with first violin followed by second violin a fourth lower; the viola entrance is an octave below first violin. The cello and string bass parts are doubled. The selection builds from *piano* to the *fortissimo* ending.

Unit 8: Suggested Listening
J. S. Bach:
  Fugue in G Minor
  Well-Tempered Clavier
G. F. Handel:
  Concerto Grosso in B-flat Major, Op. 6, No. 7
  Entrance of the Queen of Sheba

Unit 9: Additional References and Resources
Dillon, Jacquelyn A., and Casimer B. Kriechbaum Jr. *How to Design and
  Teach a Successful School and Orchestra Program.* San Diego: Neil A. Kjos
  Publishing, 1978.

Contributed by:
Judy Evans
Pine Ridge Middle School
Naples, Florida

Teacher Resource Guide

Petite Tango

Casimer B. Kriechbaum, Jr.
(1923–1991)

STRING ORCHESTRA

Unit 1: Composer

C. B. "Casey" Kriechbaum, Jr. earned his Bachelor of Music from Baldwin Wallace College in Ohio and his Master of Arts from Western Reserve University in Ohio. He was director of the Music Department of the North Olmsted School System in the Cleveland area. Under his direction, the North Olmsted High School Band and Orchestra performed at the Midwest Band and Orchestra Clinic in 1970. Kriechbaum was a Scherl and Roth clinician and wrote numerous articles for music education magazines. After his retirement from the North Olmsted school system, he taught at Ashland University in Ohio. Co-author of the book *How to Design a Successful School String and Orchestra Program*, he was an active member of Phi Delta Kappa, American School Band Directors Association, Music Educators National Conference, and National School Orchestra Association.

Unit 2: Composition

Petite Tango was written for young string players who have at least one year of playing experience or have completed a first-year method book. The work is two minutes in length. *La Boca Grande* is another Spanish-style selection by Kriechbaum.

Unit 3: Historical Perspective

Kriechbaum wrote *Petite Tango* for second-year string players. *Petite Tango* was published in 1975 when original Grade 2 string orchestra music was limited.

Unit 4: Technical Considerations

The composition is in the key of C major. All parts are playable in first position. Violin and viola parts contain low second fingers. The tempo is marked "Moderato" with quarter note = 116. The first violin, cello, and string bass sections have dotted-quarter/eighth note tango rhythms. This selection is perfect for the introduction of the brush stroke. Student parts contain alternating pizzicato and arco parts. The cello and bass parts contain slurred staccato bowing. This selection allows for work on bow control while performing *crescendos*, *decrescendos*, *forte*, *piano*, and uneven rhythm patterns.

Unit 5: Stylistic Considerations

Petite Tango has a fun, Spanish flavor. It provides the opportunity for the inclusion of diversity in the orchestra class. Optional piano, claves, and bongo parts are included. The piano part is not necessary, but the claves and bongo parts should be played. The contrasting styles of pizzicato, legato, and brush stroke are used throughout the composition.

Unit 6: Musical Elements

The three contrasting melodic lines are in C major. The harmony uses I and V chords. The tango rhythm part should remain constant throughout.

Unit 7: Form and Structure

The rondo form is A–B–A–C–A with four-measure phrases. The A and B theme phrases always end with a *decrescendo*.

Section	Event and Scoring
Introduction	Four measures pizzicato
A	First and second violin have the melody in thirds (eight measures)
B	Violin and viola; a bow four-measure *decrescendo* phrase (repeated)
A	(repeat)
C	Viola and cello have the melody in octaves
A	Repeat A for four measures and with a hint of B

Unit 8: Suggested Listening

Georges Bizet, *Carmen*
Ernesto Lecuona, *Andalucia Suite*

Unit 9: Additional References and Resources

Dillon, Jacquelyn A., Casimer B. Kriechbaum Jr. *How to Design and Teach a Successful School and Orchestra Program*. San Diego: Neil A. Kjos Publishing, 1978.

Kriechbaum, C. B., Jr. *La Boca Grande* for string orchestra. San Diego: Neil A. Kjos Publishing, 1978.

Contributed by:
Judy Evans
Pine Ridge Middle School
Naples, Florida

Teacher Resource Guide

La Réjouissance
George Frideric Handel
(1685–1759)

arranged by Richard Meyer

STRING ORCHESTRA

Unit 1: Composer/Arranger

George Frideric Handel lived between 1685 and 1759. He was born in Halle, Saxony, and lived in Germany, Italy, and England, where he became a naturalized British subject in 1726. Most of Handel's music was written in either opera or oratorio form. His two best-known pieces are *The Water Music Suite* and *Music for the Royal Fireworks*, composed in 1749.

Arranger Richard Meyer is the conductor for the Pasadena Youth Symphony Orchestra and an arranger of band, orchestra, and string orchestra music. He received a Bachelor of Arts from California State University in Los Angeles and taught instrumental music for more than sixteen years. He has received prestigious composition awards from the National School Orchestra Association and the Texas Orchestra Directors Association.

Unit 2: Composition

La Réjouissance (The Rejoicing) is a typical example of late baroque instrumental music. It is the fourth of six pieces from the *Music for the Royal Fireworks* suite. The suite was composed to celebrate the signing of the Peace of Aix-la-Chapelle (War of the Austrian Succession) in 1748. England's King George planned a grand fireworks celebration and asked Handel to compose martial music for the event. Thus, the original work had to be scored for winds and percussion, much to Handel's disgust.

129

Before the big celebration, Londoners were invited to Vauxhall Gardens to hear the debut of *Music for the Royal Fireworks*. An estimated 12,000 people were in attendance. Only the Overture was played at the fireworks celebration, and it was claimed to be a big success. The rest of the evening was not; rain ruined most of the fireworks, and the scaffolding specifically built for the big celebration caught fire. Immediately following this performance, Handel scored the work to include strings. This arrangement for string orchestra is marked "Allegro" and is two minutes and thirty seconds in length.

Unit 3: Historical Perspective

Music for the Royal Fireworks was written toward the very end of the baroque period. Handel's contemporaries were Johann Sebastian Bach, Antonio Vivaldi, Henry Purcell, and Georg Telemann. Orchestral suites had become popular in Germany in the late 1600s until about 1740. They comprised dance movements with a French overture; the grouping eventually became known as a *suite*. Called *ouverture suites*, Bach wrote four; Telemann and other German composers wrote them as well.

Unit 4: Technical Considerations

La Réjouissance is in the key of D major. It correlates with *Strictly Strings* Book 1, page 29, so it only uses a one-octave scale. The violas and cellos do not have to play any C-sharps or F-sharps on the lower strings. The rhythmic demands require some independence and use of eighth, quarter, half, dotted-half, and whole notes. The rhythmic independence required is a bit too challenging for students in the first year of study but is recommended for second- and third-year students. Even then, parts will need to be clapped out and bowed on open strings before adding the printed pitches. Students should practice the scale with staccato and hooked bowings.

Unit 5: Stylistic Considerations

La Réjouissance introduces the baroque style to young students through the use of staccato, slurred staccato, and hooked bowings. The bow stays on the strings at all times. In the B section of the piece, the dynamics are particularly noticeable with the first motive *piano* and the sequence that follows eight measures later, *forte*. The tempo should remain steady throughout the selection.

Unit 6: Musical Elements

The melody occurs only in the first violin part, though the second violin and viola get a measure of melody periodically. The cello part is contrapuntal, making this selection polyphonic. While the second violin, viola, and bass parts seem to be homophonic, the cello part is written in counterpoint. The form of this piece is binary with three themes in the selection. This arranger has opted for the binary form, while some recordings repeat the A section.

Unit 7: Form and Structure
Binary form: A–B

Section	Measures	Event and Scoring
A	1–17	Melody stated in first violin with simple harmonization in second violin, viola, and bass parts; cellos start with descending arpeggios and at m. 9 continue with an independent part; Handel uses sequences and motives within the melody line
B1	17–24	Melody consists of a sequence and a motive with violin and viola playing in unison rhythmically; cello echoes with a slightly louder motive
B2	25–36	Melody consists of descending sequences in first violin with chordal accompaniment from second violin and viola; the cello line is completely independent beginning in m. 27
B1	37–44	Section repeats exactly
B2	44–56	Section repeats with final cadence

Unit 8: Suggested Listening
J. S. Bach:
    Ouverture (Suite) No. 1, BWV 1066
    Ouverture No. 2, BWV 1067
    Ouverture No. 3, BWV 1068
    Ouverture No. 4, BWV 1069
George F. Handel, *Water Music Suite*
Henry Purcell, Suite from *The Fairy Queen*

Unit 9: Additional References and Resources
Donington, Robert. *String Playing in Baroque Music.* New York: Charles Scribner's Sons, 1977.

Grout, Donald Jay, and Claude V. Palisca. *A History of Western Music.* 6th edition. New York: W. W. Norton & Company, Inc., 2001.

Hogwood, Christopher. *Handel.* London: Thames & Hudson, 1996.

Lang, Paul Henry. *George Frideric Handel*. London: Dover Publications, 1996.

Machlis, Joseph. *Music: Adventures in Listening*. New York: Grosset and Dunlap, 1968.

Sadie, Stanley. *Handel: Works for Orchestra*. CD recording. Polygram Classics, 1984.

Contributed by:
Mary L. Wagner
Fairfax County Public Schools
Fairfax, Virginia

Teacher Resource Guide

Rondeau (Theme from "Masterpiece Theater")
Jean-Joseph Mouret
(1682–1738)

arranged by Vernon Leidig

STRING ORCHESTRA

Unit 1: Composer

Jean-Joseph Mouret was born on April 11, 1682, in Avignon and died on December 22, 1738, in Charenton. His father was an amateur violinist. The younger Mouret trained in the choir school of Nôtre Dame du Dom in Avignon, where Rameau was temporary organist. From 1714–18, Mouret conducted the orchestra for Paris Opera, and in 1718, he received a royal privilege to publish his own music. His music was very popular until 1734, when he lost his post at the Concert Spirituel after it was taken over for financial reasons by the Académie Royale de Musique. Mouret relied financially on the kindness of former patrons, but in 1737, he showed the first signs of insanity and was sent to the Fathers of Charity at Charenton, where he died.

This version of Mouret's *Rondeau*, published by Alfred Publishing, was arranged by Vernon Leidig.

Unit 2: Composition

This piece is well known because of its long-standing association as the theme from "Masterpiece Theater" on public television. A good deal of Mouret's output is music for the stage, including opera and ballet. *Rondeau*, taken from the first movement of the Suite de Symphonies No. 1, was written in 1729. Later

133

editions include those by R. Viollier (Paris, 1937) and M. Sanvoisin (Paris, 1970).

Unit 3: Historical Perspective

According to the entry in the *New Grove Dictionary of Music and Musicians*, the stage music of Mouret was of the same pioneering spirit as Lully and Rameau. His music for small ensembles moved more to the concept of an orchestra by his use of a set instrumentation. French music in the baroque was almost always composed for specific occasions, either for staged works (ballet and opera) or for ceremonial occasions, and was noted for formality and elegance.

Unit 4: Technical Considerations

The students need to be able to make the physical and aural adjustment between D major and D minor. Upper strings (violin and viola) need to be able to execute a detached slur in eighth notes, which occurs throughout the piece, generally following a separated eighth note passage. Third position will be useful for first violin. In the D minor passage, both upper and lower strings need to be able to play slurred eighth notes with a light stroke. This arrangement avoids viola, cello, and bass acting as mere punctuation by varying the rhythms they need to play: dotted half notes followed by quarter notes, dotted-quarter and eighth notes, and traditional quarter note bass lines.

In the D minor passage, first violins need to be able to adjust to the F-natural on the E string. This adjustment is particularly important as cello and bass play a passage centered on F-natural in measure 30. Violists should be able to play the G-sharp in measure 32 with an extended third finger, but advanced students could play the minor section mostly in third position. Cellists will find second position useful, particularly in order to avoid the open A string. Most bass players will alternate between first and half position.

Unit 5: Stylistic Considerations

In the original, the pageantry of the fanfare is created through the use of timpani and trumpet, so the strings need to maintain a crispness of bowing and emulate the brilliance of a brass instrument. The bow will generally remain in the lower half except for the half notes and dotted-half notes. Cello and bass have several passages with half notes and will need to avoid the extreme upper half because they generally need to get back to the lower half for a quarter or eighth note sequence. All sections should make every effort to avoid open A strings.

Bass and cello need to imitate the resonance and articulation of the timpani. In the D minor section, both upper and lower strings may experiment with making the second eighth note of the eighth note slurs lighter than the first. Leidig creates dynamic contrast in measures 32–40 by having all instruments alternate between *forte* and *piano*. The *piano* passages occur on the second beats of measures 33 and 38, which will require all sections to plan bow placement.

Unit 6: Musical Elements

This piece provides an opportunity for students to refine their ability to play as an ensemble while still moving in an essentially homophonic rhythm. In the rondeau theme, listening to the cello and bass sections will help the upper strings place their moving passages within the framework. In the first contrasting theme, while first violins play the melody, all of the other string sections need to keep the quarter note/quarter rest pattern quite steady.

In Theme B, or the D minor section, the upper and lower strings have a short choral-response passage, followed by a steady quarter note passage in which the chief interest is achieved by dynamic contrast. Students need to practice the up-bow detached eighth notes both as individuals and in sections to achieve a lilting style. Another bowing issue is the ability to sustain the dotted-quarter note without accenting the eighth note that follows. Second violin and viola often have the middle voice of the triad and need to adjust within the two outer voices.

Unit 7: Form and Structure

SECTION	MEASURES	EVENT AND SCORING
Opening fanfare	1–2	Identical rhythm in all sections
Rondeau theme	3–9	Theme played twice; first phrase ends on the subdominant, second ends on the tonic
Theme A	13–20	In contrasting style to the rondeau theme
Rondeau theme	21–28	
Theme B	29	In D minor
Extension of Theme B	36	
Da capo		Return of the rondeau theme

Unit 8: Suggested Listening

At the Court of the Sun King. Philips: CD 454 423-2
Cuivres en Fête. College de Cuivres de Suisse Romande. Cascavelle: 1015
Mad about Baroque. PGD/Deutsche Grammophon: 39147
The Mighty Tubadours. Crystal Records: CD420

Unit 9: Additional References and Resources

Anthony, James R. *French Baroque Music: From Beaujoyeulx to Rameau.* 2d edition. Portland: Amadeus Press, 1997.

Kennedy, Michael. *The Concise Oxford Dictionary of Music.* 3d edition. Oxford, England: Oxford University Press, 1980.

Sadie, Stanley, ed. *The New Grove Dictionary of Music and Musicians*, New York: Grove's Dictionaries, 2000. Also available online at www.grovemusic.com

Web sites:
    http://hector.ucdavis.edu/Handy/composr/mouret.htm
    http://www.philclas.polygram.nl/class/454/454423.htm

Contributed by:
Gail V. Barnes
University of South Carolina
Columbia, South Carolina

Teacher Resource Guide

"See, the Conquering Hero Comes" from Judas Maccabaeus

George Frideric Handel
(1685–1759)

arranged by Edward Jurey and Frank Erickson

FULL ORCHESTRA

Unit 1: Composer

George Frideric Handel, one of the baroque era's most celebrated composers, was born Georg Friedrich Händel in Halle, now in Germany, on February 23, 1685. His father, a barber-surgeon, took a second wife, Dorthea Taust, at age sixty-one; George was the second son of that marriage.

The young Handel was a precocious child who had great interest in music. On a trip with his father to Saxe-Weissenfels, his musical talent was noticed by the Duke Johann Adolf. At Adolf's insistence, George was sent to Halle to study organ with Friedrich Wilhelm Zachau. Zachau gave him lessons on harpsichord and organ, and in the fundamentals of composition. The young Handel proved to be an excellent student and progressed so quickly that he was able to substitute for Zachau as an organist for services whenever necessary. He also composed trio sonatas and motets for Sunday church services.

Following the death of his father, Handel entered the University of Halle in 1702 and was named probationary organist for the church there. Equally skilled as a violinist, he took a position in 1703 in Hamburg as a "violin di ripieno" for the Hamburg Opera. During his tenure there, his first opera, *Almira*, was premiered in 1705. He departed Germany in 1706 for a long journey through Italy, where he visited Florence, Rome, Naples, and Venice. During this four-year trip, he wrote and premiered a variety of compositions, including operas, chamber music, and oratorios. He returned to Germany in 1710 and was named Kapellmeister to the Elector of Hanover. Throughout the next several years, Handel made several trips to England, where he had a variety of works premiered. They all proved to be so successful that they won him royal favor and an annuity of two hundred pounds sterling. Then in 1714, his protector, the Elector of Hanover, became King George I of England. The king bestowed many favors on Handel and augmented his annuity to four hundred pounds sterling. In 1727, Handel became a British subject and anglicized his name to George Frideric Handel, dropping the umlaut.

During the next several years, Handel embarked on a career of writing mostly operas that met with only marginal success. Frustrated that his operatic works were not achieving the success he intended, he turned his energies toward writing oratorios. In historical perspective, this was a great turn of fate because he achieved greatness in this genre. The last twenty or so years of his life were spent composing oratorios and other types of incidental music in service to the king. Around 1750, Handel had to limit his activities due to failing eyesight. His last public appearance was in London on April 6, 1759, where he saw a performance of *Messiah*. He died eight days later on April 14, 1759. Upon his death, Handel left an enormous collection of published works that include opera, oratorio, instrumental chamber music, cantatas, and numerous sacred works.

Unit 2: Composition

The oratorio *Judas Maccabaeus* was one of Handel's later compositions, written in the summer of 1746. Along with *Messiah* and *Alexander's Feast*, it was one of his most popular works both in his lifetime and in the two centuries after his death. During Handel's lifetime, the work was performed fifty-four times; Handel himself conducted thirty-three of these performances. Based on a libretto by Thomas Morell, the oratorio had universal appeal because it told the story of an old Jewish leader whose nation was struggling to fight off a Roman invasion.

The movement where "See, the Conquering Hero Comes" first appears is in the latter part of the third act. It is initially sung by a three-part boys choir and then joined by the entire chorus, including the full orchestra, organ, and timpani. The effect is dramatic as Handel adds to the orchestration. The section then concludes with an orchestral march that presents some of the same themes and includes a prominent snare drum part.

This arrangement is scored well for the young orchestra because most of the parts are doubled or cued so that the integrity of the piece will remain even with weak or missing players. This arrangement also represents an old-fashioned method of orchestration that includes alto and tenor saxophone parts.

Unit 3: Historical Perspective

Handel, like Bach, is one of history's most formidable composers. Unlike Bach, Handel was not satisfied to remain in the tradition of his ancestors. He chose instead to leave the confines of what he considered a politically backward Germany and move to the more progressive atmosphere of England. In this atmosphere, Handel was able to expand the oratorio genre to a grand, almost operatic form set in English. His oratorios had all of the musical grandeur of an opera yet lacked nothing without staging. His central focus was always the choruses, which afforded great contrapuntal and dramatic development to the English hymn tradition. Then he juxtaposed the soloists against these tremendous dramatic moments and, thus, created a form rich with drama, excitement, and subtlety. The size of his choruses, many much larger than an entire opera company, involved great numbers of people who, along with the soloists and the orchestra, were not just listening to the music, but were experiencing the music.

Unit 4: Technical Considerations

The piece was written originally in G major, but that key is difficult for young wind players, so the arrangers transposed it down to F major. This is polyphonic music, so there is an emphasis on the horizontal line. The parts are all quite playable for the second- or third-year student. All the wind parts are in registers that students can comfortably negotiate. The upper string players can execute this piece without shifting, but they will have to play low first and low second finger to play in F major. For some second- or third-year players, this may be a new key that requires preparation. The cellists will have backward and forward extensions, and the double bass part will require shifting into second position. Chromatic alterations are in almost every part but are mostly confined to concert C-sharp.

The rhythms are usually confined to quarter, half, and whole notes, with a few dotted-quarter notes slurred to eighth notes. One potential problem for the young orchestral musician is the four eighth-note slur and the four quarter-note slur. This piece emphasizes the long, sustained line; young wind players may have breath support problems, while young string players may *decrescendo* on down-bows and *crescendo* on up-bows. String players will employ the basic bow strokes of détaché and legato. Slurs across two strings may also be somewhat of an issue. These skills will have to be developed prior to working on this piece.

Unit 5: Stylistic Considerations

Although this piece is written in 4/4 time with the score indicating quarter note = 120, the piece really should be thought of in *alla breve* to bring out the line by grouping larger beats. In most cases, the groupings of the notes are in larger groups of two within the measure. Baroque music needs to have a

feeling of forward motion; young orchestras may tend to think about individual beats and lose the line. Conducting it in two might be a better way to keep the orchestra moving and retain the sense of line and motion.

Unit 6: Musical Elements

Young orchestra literature is usually more densely scored than more advanced repertoire because young performers do not have full command of their technique. The hazard of this type of orchestration is that the piece can become too thick and heavy sounding. The original begins with a smaller segment of the orchestra before adding more parts, while this arrangement begins with the entire orchestra at *mf* dynamic level. It is critical that the orchestra keeps to this dynamic or the dramatic effect of the last section will be lost. Because this music is song repertoire and is strophic, the musical treatment of each of the verses comes in the orchestration. It is important that the young performers pay strict attention to the musical elements of dynamics, phrasing, and note length, or the musical and dramatic effect will not be heard.

Unit 7: Form and Structure

The song in its original form is strophic and has a verse and a short refrain. The structure is revealed through the orchestration. Each subsequent entrance of the verse has a different setting and requires attention to the dynamics and phrasing.

Unit 8: Suggested Listening

George Frideric Handel:
> *Judas Maccabaeus*
> *Messiah*
> *Music for the Royal Fireworks*
> *Water Music*

Unit 9: Additional References and Resources

Borroff, Edith. *The Music of the Baroque.* Dubuque, IA: W. C. Brown Co., 1970.

Burrows, Donald, Ed. *The Cambridge Companion to Handel.* New York: Cambridge University Press, 1997.

Donington, Robert. *A Performer's Guide to Baroque Music.* New York: C. Scribner's Sons, 1974.

Sadie, Stanley, ed. *The New Grove Dictionary of Music and Musicians.* New York: Grove's Dictionaries, 2000. Also available online at www.grovemusic.com

Slonimsky, Nicolas, ed. emeritus. *Baker's Biographical Dictionary of Musicians*. New York: Schirmer Books, 2001.

Contributed by:
Kathleen A. Horvath
University of Illinois
Urbana, Illinois

Teacher Resource Guide

Simple Gifts

arranged by Marsha Chusmir Shapiro
(b. 1950)

FULL ORCHESTRA

Unit 1: Arranger

Marsha Chusmir Shapiro was born in Rhode Island in 1950 and grew up in South Florida, where she played French horn and double bass, and sang in school and community bands, orchestras, and choruses. Shapiro earned her bachelor's and master's degrees in music education from Florida State University. As a student at Florida State, she served as a music copyist to band arranger Charles Carter, with whom she later studied. Shapiro enjoyed performing Carter's band arrangements because French horn had interesting countermelodies to play instead of the usual afterbeats. From this initial realization, Shapiro went on to develop a horizontal compositional style for educational music, dedicated to giving each instrumentalist interesting, singable parts with which to develop his or her technique.

Shapiro has taught at all levels in the Volusia County, Florida schools since 1972. She was the winner of the 1985 National School Orchestra Association Composition Competition. Shapiro has had numerous compositions published for school orchestras, as well as the elementary-level musical, *The Scientific Dream*.

Unit 2: Composition

As with many of Shapiro's earlier works, *Simple Gifts* was arranged for her own middle school students in the mid-1980s. Although she had published string orchestra arrangements, *Simple Gifts* was Shapiro's first published full orchestra piece. She was attracted to the famous Shaker melody, which she originally heard in Aaron Copland's *Appalachian Spring*, because of its intrinsic beauty and also because of the possibility of combining the two sections of the melody as one contrapuntal form. The melody stuck in her mind. Not until after scoring the melody from memory, however, did she go back and further research its origin.

Like *Simple Gifts*, many of Shapiro's compositions and arrangements for school orchestra employ elements of counterpoint and are based upon the folk music of various ethnic groups. These include *African Accents*, *Eiré*, *Folk Songs of Israel*, *Folk Songs of the British Isles*, *Folk Songs of the Mountains*, *Folk Songs of the Orient*, *Folk Songs of the West*, and *Three Songs for Chanukah*.

Unit 3: Historical Perspective

The tune "Simple Gifts" was composed in 1848 by a 51-year-old Shaker elder named Joseph Brackett. It was one of more than twelve thousand songs that came out of the Shaker community during the mid-nineteenth century. "Simple Gifts" was originally a dancing song, and some of the words were instructions for dancing, as well as for living.

> 'Tis the gift to be simple, 'tis the gift to be free,
> 'Tis the gift to come down where we ought to be,
> And when we find ourselves in the place just right,
> 'Twill be in the valley of love and delight.
>> When true simplicity is gained
>> To bow and to bend we shan't be ashamed
>> To turn, turn will be our delight,
>> 'Til by turning, turning we come round right.

But it wasn't until 1944, when Aaron Copland immortalized the tune in his ballet score *Appalachian Spring*, that "Simple Gifts" became popularized. After that, the Shaker melody could be found in composer Sydney Carter's hymn "Lord of the Dance," which was later adapted by Irish dancer Michael Flatley in a rock concert and recorded by folk singer Judy Collins. Musical versions of "Simple Gifts" were performed at presidential inaugurations and funerals. Music Educators National Conference named it one of four songs every American should be able to sing.

In addition to Shapiro's arrangement, Aaron Copland's *Variations on a Shaker Melody* (Grade 6, full orchestra) and Clark Tyler's *Simple Gifts* (Grade 1, band) are also published for student musicians.

Unit 4: Technical Considerations

Simple Gifts moves through the keys of C, F, B-flat, and G, with varying tempos and sudden changes of dynamics and instrumental texture. Frequent use of polyphony, orchestration by choirs of instrument families, solos (flute, oboe, clarinet, and trumpet), and open scoring require independence and assurance from student musicians. Most wind parts remain within comfortable range, with F concert as the highest tone. An optional *divisi* places advanced first violins in third position from measure 47 to the end. This part is explicitly edited. At the same point, the string bass moves through half, second, and third position, again with fingerings well marked.

Rhythmic requirements are uncomplicated. The arrangement is scored for two flutes (generally unison), oboe, two B-flat clarinets, E-flat alto saxophone, bassoon, one French horn, two B-flat trumpets, two trombones (generally unison), tuba, timpani in F–C (B-flat), bells, suspended cymbal, snare drum, bass drum, first and second violins, viola, cello, and string bass. Optional parts are provided for tenor saxophone and third violin/viola treble clef.

Unit 5: Stylistic Considerations

Simple Gifts is marked by contrast of timbre, tempo, and dynamics. It begins with a slowly unfolding chorale. The legato style continues as the tempo increases with each variation. The gentle, playful woodwind counterpoint at measure 29 is interrupted by a boisterous brass fanfare that is suddenly disrupted with a slow, calming oboe solo. In final contrast is the full, broad ending, combining both themes *forte* as the piece slows to its final chord.

Unit 6: Musical Elements

The two melodic lines of *Simple Gifts* are each eight measures in length. The first melody is rhythmically simple, conjunct, and consists of an ascending and descending line before and after the half cadence. The second melody is also conjunct but begins with a descending line of longer rhythmic value, recognized by a half note/dotted-quarter note/eighth note pattern. Although *Simple Gifts* repeats the same theme, the harmonic structure varies considerably through the use of counterpoint in the polyphonic sections and substitute chords (a few chromatics) in homophonic sections. The open fifths in the accompaniment at measure 29 create a bagpipe effect. The use of instrumental choirs is employed as a major technique of variation, rendering changes in timbre most important.

Unit 7: Form and Structure

SECTION	MEASURES	EVENT AND SCORING
Theme 1	1–8	C major; slow woodwind/string chorale; introduced in clarinet and violin, with thickening texture
Theme 1	9–16	Slightly faster; in F major; trumpet duet; sustained chordal accompaniment in woodwinds and strings

SECTION	MEASURES	EVENT AND SCORING
Theme 2	17–24	Full orchestra in unison, fanning out harmonically; sudden drop in dynamics and texture with lower voices on melody, ending with lighter texture
Transition	25–28	Clarinet and oboe perform contrapuntal motif as tempo accelerates in transition to B-flat major
Theme 1	29–38	Clarinet, saxophone, bassoon, and strings in open fifths all imitate a bagpipe; snare drum maintains a steady pulse, above which flute and clarinet soloists lightly dance in counterpoint
Theme 2	39–44	Sudden change in dynamics with replacement by brass choir; in four-part polyphony; pausing with fermata at m. 44
	45–46	Clarinet soloist slowly and quietly completes the end of the phrase
Themes 1 and 2	47–54	Themes combined in G major; upper voices contrasting with lower voices, broadening to a *ritardando* with the final statement of the first motif in the lower voices

Unit 8: Suggested Listening

Sydney Carter, *Lord of the Dance*
Aaron Copland, *Variations on a Shaker Melody*
Marsha Chusmir Shapiro:
    African Accents
    Asia Minor
    Folk Songs of Israel
    Folk Songs of the Orient
    Minor Variations
    Three Songs for Chanukah
    Variations on a Ground

Unit 9: Additional References and Resources

Crumm, David. "One Hundred Fifty Years of 'Simple Gifts'." November 11, 1998. http://www.freep.com/fun/music/qshaker11.htm

Shapiro, Marsha Chusmir. "Student Conducting in the Junior High." *The Instrumentalist* 24 (November 1974): 30.

Shapiro, Marsha Chusmir. "Teaching Strings: A Special Opportunity for Wind and Percussion Majors." *American String Teacher* 24 (Summer 1974): 6–10.

Shapiro, Marsha Chusmir. "Teaching Young Bassists, Part I." *The Instrumentalist* 27 (April 1983): 97–99.

Shapiro, Marsha Chusmir. "Teaching Young Bassists, Part II." *The Instrumentalist* 36 (May 1983): 44–46.

Smith, Jeffery. "Not So Simple Gifts: Copland's Use of Folk in Appalachian Spring." http://www.newyorkphilharmonic.org/copland/article_2.htm Completely Copland Festival.

Contributed by:

Marsha Chusmir Shapiro
Ormond Beach Middle School
Ormond Beach, Florida

Teacher Resource Guide

Sinfonia from Trio in A Minor

Georg Philipp Telemann
(1681–1767)

arranged by Robert Bennett Brown

STRING ORCHESTRA

Unit 1: Composer/Arranger

Georg Philipp Telemann was born in Magdeburg in 1681 and died in Hamburg in 1767. Telemann worked in Leipzig, Eisenach, Frankfurt, and Hamburg, where he wrote forty operas, twelve complete cycles of cantatas and motets, forty-four passions, a large number of oratorios, other church compositions, and hundreds of chamber and orchestra works. In 1704, Telemann founded the Collegium Musicum of the University, an extracurricular musical society that performed contemporary music, of which Bach later became director. Telemann worked as a church music director and in his time was recognized as among the most versatile and prolific composers.

The arranger, Robert Bennett Brown, has worked as District Supervisor of Music for the Levittown Public Schools in New York. He taught in Bronxville, New York, where as chairman of music he brought about an extremely high level of school orchestral achievement. He was educated at the New York University and Teachers' College at Columbia University.

Unit 2: Composition

Despite the dramatic and grandiose developments in music of the last two centuries, the luster and appeal of baroque music is still popular. Brown's 1965 arrangement of the Sinfonia paraphrase from Trio in A Minor retains the character and style of baroque orchestral string music. Simple rhythms and bow styles make this work accessible and allow a rich, full sound for a young string orchestra. This work, approximately three minutes in length, opens with a Largo section and is followed by a driving and energetic Allegro.

Unit 3: Historical Perspective

Music of the baroque period, 1600–1750, is rather clearly defined, much more than other periods. Generally, the baroque period is an era of ecstasy and exuberance of dynamic tensions and of sweeping gestures.

Unit 4: Technical Considerations

Most of the composition is in A minor. There are no extreme demands rhythmically because the rhythms include only eighth, quarter, half, and whole notes. The introduction is in 3/2, a meter that may need to be explained to young performers. For violins, use of low first finger is a must, and cellos must be familiar with extensions. Bass players must be comfortable on the E string, and both the cello and bass sections must play leaps of an octave. Bowing of sustained notes and détaché are used throughout.

Unit 5: Stylistic Considerations

This composition uses strict baroque style with détaché bowing on quarter notes throughout the Allegro passage. There is also use of traditional baroque terraced dynamics. However, phrasing of repeated eighth notes may include a *crescendo* from measures 5–30 and 44–end at the conductor's discretion. The long notes found in the introduction and middle section require a sustained and sonorous bowing technique. The upper melody is played with a precise bowing style while the commanding pulse is found in the cello and bass parts.

Unit 6: Musical Elements

The primary texture is homophonic with the melodic structure mostly achieved by diatonic means. The most common chords are I, IV, and V. First violins play an ostinato pattern at measure 31, which is transferred to the cellos at measure 39. The cellos play the main motive, a three-note A–C–A pattern, throughout the entire Allegro. Driving rhythms and varied dynamics build intensity throughout the piece.

Unit 7: Form and Structure

SECTION	MEASURES
Introduction	1
A	5
B	31
C	45
A^1	64

148

Unit 8: Suggested Listening

Arcangelo Corelli, Concerti Grossi
Georg Philipp Telemann:
    Trumpet Concerto
    Viola Concerto
Antonio Vivaldi, Concerti Grossi

Unit 9: Additional References and Resources

Sadie, Stanley, ed. *The New Grove Dictionary of Music and Musicians*. New
    York: Grove's Dictionaries, 2000. Also available online at
    www.grovemusic.com

Slonimsky, Nicolas, ed. emeritus. *Baker's Biographical Dictionary of Musicians*.
    New York: Schirmer Books, 2001.

Contributed by:

Sheila Morris
Las Vegas, Nevada

Teacher Resource Guide

Variations on a Ground

Marsha Chusmir Shapiro
(b. 1950)

STRING ORCHESTRA

Unit 1: Composer

Marsha Chusmir Shapiro was born in Rhode Island in 1950 and grew up in South Florida, where she played French horn and double bass, and sang in school and community bands, orchestras, and choruses. Shapiro earned bachelor's and master's degrees in music education from Florida State University. As a student at Florida State, she served as a music copyist to band arranger Charles Carter, with whom she later studied. Shapiro enjoyed performing Carter's band arrangements because the French horns had interesting countermelodies to play instead of the usual afterbeats. From this initial realization, Shapiro went on to develop a horizontal compositional style for educational music, dedicated to giving each instrumentalist interesting, singable parts with which to develop his or her technique.

Shapiro has taught at all levels in the Volusia County, Florida schools since 1972. She was the winner of the 1985 National School Orchestra Association Composition Competition. She has had numerous compositions published for school orchestras, as well as the elementary-level musical, *The Scientific Dream*.

Unit 2: Composition

Variations on a Ground is one of many orchestral compositions and arrangements that Shapiro has prepared for young musicians. These pieces are designed to give each student musician the opportunity to play singable, melodic lines. Shapiro noted that when viola and string bass players were given this type of challenging music with which to develop their skills, they broke the stereotype of being less accomplished technically than their peers who played violin and cello. This particular composition was written during the period of time when the composer was on maternity leave from teaching and was able to devote more time to writing.

A *ground* is a short melody that is performed over and over again, normally by a bass instrument or voice. Above the theme, a string of continuous variations unfold. In the case of *Variations on a Ground*, however, the ground melody moves from one instrument to another, similar to a passacaglia, but in double rather than triple meter. Other music by Shapiro that employs the use of variations includes *Minor Variations* and *Simple Gifts*.

Unit 3: Historical Perspective

Variations on a Ground was composed in 1987. It is a modern piece that draws on baroque form (passacaglia, but in duple meter) and also employs the style of contrapuntal variation often used in the sixteenth and seventeenth centuries. The orchestrations are derived from a series of settings developed and taught by the late contemporary band composer, Charles Carter.

Unit 4: Technical Considerations

The composition remains throughout in 4/4 meter in the key of D major. As the viola part frequently lies in the lower range of the instrument, the music is well edited with reminders to use a low first finger to play C-sharp on the C string and a high third finger to play C-sharp on the G string. Cello extensions are also duly noted. All instruments remain in first position except for string bass, which plays in third position on the G string. Again, fingerings are marked. As a double bass player, the composer has made deliberate efforts in all her music to encourage young bass players to move up into higher positions rather than drop the octave.

Bow directions are indicated, and the bow lifts halfway through the ground and at the end of the phrase should be observed. Students will be required to use détaché, staccato, and two-note slurs. There is also a pizzicato section.

Rhythmically, the composition is not demanding. A solo section for viola and cello may also be performed *soli*. Because viola and string bass students, who are less often called upon to play the melody, are here challenged to do so, they are usually paired with another instrument for security. There is a third violin (viola treble clef) part available, but it is usually one octave too high.

Unit 5: Stylistic Considerations

The composition imitates a classical style, generally employing a precise, carefully controlled, and lightly separated bow style (détaché). There are contrasting stylistic sections at measure 17, where the upper strings slur in a more expressive manner, and at the pizzicato section that begins with the pickup notes to measure 49. The dynamics remain moderate and controlled

(*mf*, *mp*) throughout the composition. While the ground motif will always need to be recognized, contrapuntal lines are equally important and should be dynamically balanced. The consistent tempo is marked "Moderato" (quarter note = 116).

Unit 6: Musical Elements

The ground motif is an eight-measure melody consisting of a four-measure antecedent and a four-measure consequent (subject and answer). This melody repeats intact seven times, though played by different instruments. Motif fragments may be found, in quasi-fugal style, in the upper strings in the closing segment. The conjunct melody is always in D major, within the range of a sixth. Many of the variations are polyphonic, but even so, the underlying harmonic progression is always I–IV–V^7–I. Even with the counterpoint, phrases are divided into a four-measure antecedent and a four-measure consequent. The meter is consistent and balanced with simple, repetitive rhythmic patterns.

Unit 7: Form and Structure

As previously noted, *Variations on a Ground* consists of a recurring theme, presented as a passacaglia-like ground, but in duple meter, with a series of mostly contrapuntal variations in other voices.

MEASURES	EVENT AND SCORING
1–8	Theme introduced in the lower strings
9–16	Theme in the upper strings with countermelody in cello and bass
17–24	Cello and bass theme with three-part chordal accompaniment based on quarter/half/quarter rhythm in upper strings
25–32	Theme in first violin with second violin a third below; viola, cello, and bass have rhythmically independent, scalar accompaniment
33–40	Viola and cello play the ground; violin plays a counter melody using quarter and eighth note rhythms
41–48	Solo viola with cello an octave and a third below
49–56	Pizzicato melody in upper strings with an arpeggiated accompaniment in the lower strings
57–65	Theme in cello and bass, with other voices using imitative fragments of the theme in a mini-fugal form

Unit 8: Suggested Listening

Marsha Chusmir Shapiro:
African Accents
Asia Minor
Folk Songs of Israel
Folk Songs of the Orient
Minor Variations
Simple Gifts
Three Songs for Chanukah

Unit 9: Additional References and Resources

Shapiro, Marsha Chusmir. "Student Conducting in the Junior High." *The Instrumentalist* 24 (November 1974): 30.

Shapiro, Marsha Chusmir. "Teaching Strings: A Special Opportunity for Wind and Percussion Majors." *American String Teacher* 24 (Summer 1974): 6–10.

Shapiro, Marsha Chusmir. "Teaching Young Bassists, Part I." *The Instrumentalist* 27 (April 1983): 97–99.

Shapiro, Marsha Chusmir. "Teaching Young Bassists, Part II." *The Instrumentalist* 36 (May 1983): 44–46.

Contributed by:

Marsha Chusmir Shapiro
Ormond Beach Middle School
Ormond Beach, Florida

Teacher Resource Guide

Westminster Prelude and Fugue

David Shaffer
(b. 1953)

STRING ORCHESTRA

Unit 1: Composer

David Shaffer holds a Bachelor of Music Education from The Ohio State University and a Master of Music from Miami University in Oxford, Ohio. Following eight years of public school teaching, Shaffer started Music on the Move, Inc., an organization providing music teacher staffing services for private and parochial schools in Ohio. In 1985, Shaffer was appointed assistant director and principal arranger for the Miami University Marching Band. An active composer, Shaffer has more than two hundred compositions and arrangements published by C. L. Barnhouse Company, Heritage Music Press, and Lake State Publications. His compositions are performed at clinics and music festivals around the world and have been placed on contest repertoire lists in the United States, Canada, Europe, and Asia.

Unit 2: Composition

Westminster Prelude and Fugue was published in 1987 by Lake State Publications as part of the *Wizard Easy String Series*. It is scored for first violin, second violin, third violin (viola treble clef), viola, cello, double bass, and optional piano. Although the title suggests two distinct movements, the harmonic design makes it imperative that the work be performed as a whole. Performance time is approximately three minutes and thirty seconds. The contrasts between the energetic tolling of bells in the Allegro, the lyrical melody of the Andante, and the cheerful subject of the Fugue make this piece interesting and appealing to middle school string players and their audiences.

Unit 3: Historical Perspective

The first movement is titled "Westminster Chimes." The work opens with a four-note motive adapted from the English chime tune "Cambridge Quarters." The complete chime tune, which requires only four different bells, is a set of five short motives. The rhythm of each motive is three quarter notes followed by a dotted-quarter, and the melodies are as follows:

1. *mi re do sol*
2. *do mi re sol*
3. *do re mi do*
4. *mi do re sol*
5. *sol re mi do*

The motives of the chime tune indicate each quarter hour as follows:

- Quarter past the hour: motive 1
- Half past the hour: motives 2 and 3
- Three-quarters past the hour: motives 4, 5, and 1
- On the hour: motives 2, 3, 4, and 5.

This leaves the chime mechanism ready to repeat the first motive after having tolled the hour on a single bell. The mechanism for playing quarters on church bells or clock chimes is similar in principle to the barrel inside a music box. The Cambridge Quarters mechanism was first erected in Saint Mary's Church, Cambridge, in 1793–94. In 1859–60, it was copied at the Houses of Parliament in Westminster, and the chime tune became popularly known as "Westminster Quarters" or "Westminster Chimes."

The "Prelude and Fugue" referred to in the title has its roots in the baroque. A *prelude* is a piece of music designed to be played as an introduction to another composition. A *fugue* is a multi-voice composition based on a theme, or subject, which is stated at the beginning by one voice alone and then imitated by the other voice or voices in close succession. The subject will reappear throughout the piece in one voice or another. Johann Sebastian Bach's famous two-volume work, *The Well-Tempered Clavier*, contains twenty-four preludes and fugues, one for each major and minor key.

Unit 4: Technical Considerations

This piece is well suited to the technical abilities of the Grade 2 string player. Finger patterns from G major and C major are predominate. B-flats, E-flats, and D-flats appear briefly in the Fugue. Double bass shifts to the D above middle C, but all other instruments remain in first position throughout. Cello does not need to use forward extensions, but viola must reach F-sharp on the C string (high third finger).

Unit 5: Stylistic Considerations

The notes that imitate the striking of bells are marked with accents. Use speed rather than weight at the beginning of each bow stroke to produce a bell-like accent.

At the opening of the Andante, the accompanying voices have dotted-half notes followed by quarter notes. Avoid unwanted accents on these quarter notes by managing bow speed and altering the contact point, saving bow on the long notes and bowing a little farther from the bridge on the short notes.

The long notes in the opening Allegro and the Andante offer an opportunity to practice extended bow strokes and vibrato.

Unit 6: Musical Elements

Westminster Prelude and Fugue is in G major throughout. The only departure from diatonic harmony occurs in a brief episode in the fugue. (See Unit 7.) The melodic material is simple and memorable, and Shaffer gives the melody to each section at one time or another. Common time is the meter throughout, and simple rhythmic elements (whole, half, dotted-half, quarter, and eighth notes) are used to great effect. Ties are the most challenging rhythmic element in the piece, but even they are used with such natural grace that they should pose no problem to middle school musicians. Players will enjoy bringing out the various timbres implicit in each section of the work: the opening Allegro requires the strings to sound like bells, the Andante calls for a rich string orchestra sound, and the Fugue highlights the timbre of each string section.

A suggested ear-training activity is:

- The class sings "Westminster Quarters" from solfège notation.
- First violin plays the opening measure of *Westminster Prelude and Fugue*.
- The class sings that motive in solfège and notates it in solfège (*sol, do, re, sol*).
- Students discuss the differences in rhythm and melody, determining which of the motives in "Cambridge Quarters" is most similar to the motive used by Shaffer.

A suggested composition activity is:

- Students form groups of five to compose a new chime tune.
- Each group chooses a pentatonic scale for their chime tune.
- The group members decide which notes of the scale to use. (Be sure to include the tonic.)
- Each group chooses a meter and a rhythm pattern for their chime tune.
- Each member of the group composes a four-note motive for the chime tune.
- Group members sing or play their motives for each other.

156

- The group decides upon the most effective order in which to present the motives.
- The group sings or plays the chime tune as a tune, then again as "quarters."
- All groups perform for each other.

Unit 7: Form and Structure

The work opens with an Allegro section in which the entire string orchestra imitates the sound of bells tolling. In the Andante section that follows at measure 15, first violin introduces a lyrical theme repeated by viola and cello sections in unison. Returning to the original Allegro tempo at measure 35, first violin states the four-measure Fugue subject in the tonic key of G major.

Next, second violin and viola in unison state the subject in the subdominant key of C major. After cello and double bass state the subject in the tonic, there is a six-measure episode that, through a series of secondary dominant chords, ventures into closely related flat keys. The Fugue closes with a statement of the subject in the tonic by cello and double bass.

Contrary to expectation, the piece does not end here. A *Da Capo al fine* brings back the tolling bells of the opening Allegro and the lyrical theme of the Andante to round out the composition in a satisfying ternary form.

Unit 8: Suggested Listening

Johann Sebastian Bach, *The Well-Tempered Clavier*, Books 1 and 2, Jeno Jando, piano, NAXOS 8.553795-6 and 8.550970-1
Johann Sebastian Bach/arr. Robert Frost, *Church Bells of England*, Saydisc CD-SDL 378
A. Corelli/arr. Theldon Myers, *Prelude and Dance*
J. K. F. Fischer/arr. Theldon Myers, *Prelude and Fugue*
Henry Purcell/arr. Lester DeValve, *The Bell Anthem*
Gerald Sebesky, *Prelude and Fugue for Young Strings*
David Shaffer, *Impravada*
D. Shostakovich/arr. Harry Alshin, *Prelude and Polka*

Unit 9: Additional References and Resources

Randel, Don, ed. *The New Harvard Dictionary of Music*. Cambridge, MA: Harvard University Press, 1986.

Sadie, Stanley, ed. *The New Grove Dictionary of Music and Musicians*. New York: Grove's Dictionaries, 2000. Also available online at www.grovemusic.com

David Shaffer's web page:
http://www.fna.muohio.edu/musweb/faculty/shaffed1.html

Contributed by:

Michele Winter
Orchestra Teacher
Lowell High School
San Francisco, California

Teacher Resource Guide

When Johnny Comes Marching Home

Richard Stephan
(b. 1929)

STRING ORCHESTRA

Unit 1: Composer

Richard Albert Stephan was born in Buffalo, New York, in 1929. He earned degrees in music education from the State University of New York at Fredonia and the Eastman School of Music, with further study at the University of Buffalo and Brigham Young University. After a two-year tour of duty with the U.S. Army, where he served as an arranger-bandsman, Stephan began his teaching career in Buffalo, New York, followed by a position as coordinator of music in the Hamburg, New York public schools. In 1968, he became a member of the faculty of the Crane School of Music, State University of New York at Potsdam, until his retirement in 2000.

Throughout his career, Stephan has been active as a teacher, conductor, clinician, composer, and performing musician in both the symphonic and jazz areas. In 1984, he was honored with a Fulbright Senior Scholar Award to Australia. In 1986, his *Fanfare and Frippery* won the National School Orchestra Association Composition Contest. Other notable works by Stephan include *Fantasia on a Seventeenth Century Tune*, Dance in D, *Adirondack Sleighride*, *Australian Folk Suite*, *Vanguard Overture*, and *Fanfare and Frippery No. 2*.

Unit 2: Composition

Stephan's first published piece, *When Johnny Comes Marching Home*, was written specifically for a student string quartet at the Junior High School in Hamburg, New York, where he taught. It was adapted for string orchestra in 1963. The original impetus was to introduce the students to a more

159

contemporary harmonic style than the basic junior high school repertoire offered. The challenge was to create a work that was modern and yet within the technical capabilities of the students. The composer chose a familiar melody as the basis upon which he introduced new or unfamiliar rhythmic and harmonic techniques.

Unit 3: Historical Perspective

The original tune and words have a particular connection to our Civil War of the 1860s and have been sung throughout the ensuing generations. Traditional or folk music has had an important influence upon the music of most countries. Its influence upon American composers is seen especially in the works of Aaron Copland and Roy Harris. Copland, William Schuman, and Ralph Vaughan Williams were major influences upon Stephan's writing during the 1950s and 1960s.

Unit 4: Technical Considerations

The scale of E natural minor is used throughout, with a few F-naturals and C-sharps thrown in for harmonic variety. The entire piece is in first position except for the E above middle C in the cello part. The technical challenge, however, is mainly rhythmic, with the use of various quarter, eighth, and dotted-eighth note combinations within 6/8 time. The sections in 3/4 and 2/4 are less demanding rhythmically.

Unit 5: Stylistic Considerations

A firm martelé bowing, preferably in the lower half, should be used to articulate the accents and maintain the *fortissimo* dynamic of the introduction. The lower strings continue the march-like accompaniment while the upper strings present the melody in a carefully controlled, on-the-string bowing, all at a reduced dynamic level. The conductor may wish to change the bowing at letter A to fit the capabilities of students. The middle section requires smooth détaché and slurred bowing with gradually increased dynamics, reaching a climax seven measures before Rehearsal I. The concluding section calls for a return to martelé bowing, much of it in the lower half of the bow.

Unit 6: Musical Elements

The introduction and ending utilize quartal harmony. The body of the work is harmonized in traditional major and minor triads with an occasional open fifth sound. However, seven measures before Rehearsal I and five measures after Rehearsal J, students encounter major and minor seventh chords.

The modal melody and developed fragments are generally treated homophonically except for the brief canonic imitation at Rehearsal C. The countermelody at Rehearsal E must be equal in strength of tone to the original melody when it reappears at Rehearsal F.

As the meter changes from 2/4 to 6/8 and back again, a steady unifying two pulse must be maintained.

Unit 7: Form and Structure

This is basically a theme and three variations. Superimposed on the variations is a three-part form: fast, slow, fast.

SECTION	EVENT AND SCORING
Introduction	First six measures
A	Rehearsal A
A^1	Rehearsal C; canonic treatment of A
Transition	Six measures before Rehearsal E
A^2	Rehearsal E; A in augmentation
Transition	Rehearsal I
A^3	Rehearsal I plus seven measures; A developed
Codetta	Last six measures; related to the introduction

Unit 8: Suggested Listening

Benjamin Britten, *Simple Symphony*
Aaron Copland, "Hoedown" from *Rodeo*
Edvard Grieg, *Holberg Suite*, Op. 40
Paul Hindemith, *Acht Stücke*, Op. 44, No. 3
Gustav Holst, *Saint Paul's Suite*

Unit 9: Additional References and Resources

Glass, Paul. *Singing Soldiers* (The spirit of the sixties); a history of the Civil War in song. Arrangements for piano and guitar. New York: Grosset & Dunlap, 1968.

Silber, Irwin. *Songs of the Civil War.* Piano and guitar arrangements by Jerry Silverman. New York: Columbia University Press, 1960.

Songs of the Civil War [sound recording]. NW 202. New York: New World Records, 1976.

Wellman, Manly Wade. *The rebel songster; songs the Confederates sang.* With commentary and illus. by Manly Wade Wellman. Music scores by Frances Wellman. Charlotte, NC: Heritage House, 1959.

Contributed by:

Richard Stephan
Crane School of Music
State University of New York at Potsdam
Potsdam, New York

Grade Three

Teacher Resource Guide

Allegro in D

Antonio Vivaldi
(1678–1741)

arranged by Steven Frackenpohl

STRING ORCHESTRA

Unit 1: Composer/Arranger

Antonio Vivaldi was born on March 4, 1678, in Venice and died on July 28, 1741, in Vienna. He was the eldest of six children. His father was Giovanni Battista, who was originally a baker before becoming a professional violinist. His father was hired at St. Mark's Basilica in Venice in 1685 under the surname "Rossi," which could be an indication that he had the famous red hair of his son, who was commonly known as "the red-haired priest."

Vivaldi was hired in 1703 as the *maestro di'violino* at Pio Ospedale della Pietà, one of four institutions in Venice where orphaned and abandoned girls were sent. Also in 1703, he began his priestly duties. He was excused from saying Mass a year later because of his chronic asthma. Vivaldi's contract with the Pietà was not renewed in 1709, most likely due to budgetary restraints, but it might have been the result of Vivaldi building an elite core of violinists who could carry on his teaching, which made him dispensable. In 1711, however, he was back at Pietà and in 1716 was promoted to *maestro de' concerto*; he continued some sort of association with the institution until his death.

An indication of Vivaldi's fame beyond Venice was the publication of *L'Estro Armonico* in 1711 by a publisher from Amsterdam. Several Italian composers switched publishers at the same time because of the superiority of the engraving process and a demand for Italian music in Northern Europe. It is known that Bach was familiar with the work of Vivaldi because he transcribed as many as ten of Vivaldi's works to the keyboard. Most of the history

of his work is contained in letters documenting the financial transactions. One of his biographers, Michael Talbot, states that Vivaldi's preoccupation with money was excessive, but ironically, he died in poverty.

Steven Frackenpohl, the arranger of Allegro in D, has been a public school string and orchestra teacher for many years. He was also a teacher in the West Genessee School District in Camillus, New York.

Unit 2: Composition

Of the 470 concertos that Vivaldi composed, only thirty-four are for like instruments, and of those, only a few are for brass. The Pio Ospedale della Pietà would not hire instructors for these instruments, both because of the expense and because they were not considered appropriate for young ladies. This was probably due to the association of brass instruments with the world of the courts and of hunting. Allegro in D is based on the Concerto for Two Trumpets in C. The trumpet concerto has three movements, but the second is mostly a brief transition to the third. In both the original work and this transcription, the chief compositional devices are imitative counterpoint for the two soloists (or solo sections) and the ritornello (orchestral refrain) for the *tutti* passages.

Unit 3: Historical Perspective

Vivaldi is generally thought to have refined the concerto to its current form of three movements. He had a reputation for avoiding fugal writing, but that is disproved in this piece with the several examples of imitation and counter-point. He is also thought to be the first composer to give the slow movement of a concerto equal importance with the two allegro movements, but that is not the case in the Concerto for Two Trumpets. The driving rhythm and fresh-ness of Vivaldi keeps his hundreds of concertos popular today. Vivaldi's contemporaries were Avison, J. S. and C. P. E. Bach, Goldoni, Locatelli, Marcello, and Tartini.

Unit 4: Technical Considerations

The Concerto has been transposed from the original C to D major. There is a brief transition to the dominant key of A major (around measure 35) before returning to end in D major. Necessary left-hand skills include second and third position for violins. The viola part could be played entirely in first position, but several passages would be easier and have a more facile quality with knowledge of half and second position. Cellists play in half, first, and low and high third position. Bassists utilize first, second, and third positions. Students not only need to know the positions, but they also must possess the ability to shift quickly and accurately between them.

Unit 5: Stylistic Considerations

The recorded versions of this concerto are played in a variety of speeds, with quarter note = 80 to 118 beats per minute. Frackenpohl advises that the tempo should not be too fast. To achieve the sparkling Venetian style, students need a fair command of the bow. Sixteenth notes should be played in a brush stroke at the balance point of the bow, and eighth notes need to be detached. There are several instances where students need to detach between an eighth and two sixteenth notes. Students need to be able to replace the bow from a quarter note to crisp eighth note/eighth rest patterns. The students at the Pietà school were known for their disciplined playing, and students today may appreciate the challenge of creating the brilliance and precision documented from those days.

Unit 6: Musical Elements

In the ritornello theme, all sections must allow the D major triad to have the full value of the quarter note before beginning the next figure. Players need to be vigilant with the varying lengths of rests between rhythmic motives. Eighth note upbeats need to be played precisely on the second half of the beat. In passages that begin after quarter note rests, players need to carefully anticipate the first beat of that passage. One example of this is at Rehearsal A, where first violins may be anxious about the shift to third position and make an early entrance. Instead, they need to allow viola, cello, and bass time to complete their figure. In measures 12–13, students may tend to rush on the descending scale line. If they isolate the scale passage and experiment with rhythmic variation, they should begin to internalize the harmonic outline; this should help steady the ensemble. Another passage that offers potential for rushing is at measures 14–16. Violin needs to maintain stability with the broken thirds, while viola and cello propel the passage with the repeated sixteenth note patterns. At Rehearsal B, first and second violin must exercise this mutual rhythmic respect in each of the solo passages. At Rehearsal D, care must be taken to keep the G-sharp leading tone high enough throughout the A major section. Interest is maintained by observance of the edited dynamic markings. At Rehearsal H, first and second violin must clearly articulate the sixteenths or they will sound like a sustained note. At the end of the piece, lower strings control the *ritardando*.

Unit 7: Form and Structure

The ritornello is an introduction by the orchestra that returns periodically through the piece. Material in the solo passage can be from the ritornello or can be entirely new.

MEASURES	EVENT AND SCORING
1–18	Opening ritornello

MEASURES	EVENT AND SCORING
18–27	Theme A; first and second violin in imitation
27–31	Four measures of ritornello
31–38	Theme B; transition to A major
38–55	Ritornello; A major
55–65	A´ third solo passage; incorporating elements of the first
65–81	Final ritornello

Unit 8: Suggested Listening

Classic Wynton, Sony Classical: SK 60804

Musiche Veneziane/Concerti, Accademia Instrumentalis Claudio Monterverdi. Claves: CD 50-602

Vivaldi, Concerto for Two Mandolins and Fourteen Concertos—The Academy of Ancient Music. L'Oiseau-Lyre 455 703-2

Unit 9: Additional References and Resources

Davie, Cedric Thorpe. *Musical Structure and Design.* New York: Dover Publications, Inc., 1966.

Grout, Donald Jay, and Claude V. Palisca. *A History of Western Music.* 6th edition. New York: W. W. Norton & Company, 2001.

Sadie, Stanley, ed. *The New Grove Dictionary of Music and Musicians.* New York: Grove's Dictionaries, 2000. Also available online at www.grovemusic.com

Slonimsky, Nicolas, ed. by Richard Kassell. *Webster's New World Dictionary of Music.* New York: Schirmer Books, 1998.

Talbot, Michael. *Vivaldi.* London, England: J. M. Dent & Sons, Ltd., 1978.

Web sites:
http://genetics.washington.edu/~nlkosuk/ECP/past_seasons/5.24.98/vivaldi.html
http://www.hyperion-records.co.uk/notes/67073.html

Contributed by:

Gail V. Barnes
Assistant Professor, Music Education
University of South Carolina
Columbia, South Carolina

Teacher Resource Guide

A "Bark" Gigue
Ralph Hultgren
(b. 1953)

STRING ORCHESTRA

Unit 1: Composer

Ralph Hultgren has been composing and arranging since 1989. An Australian, he is a well-known composer of all levels and types of orchestral and band music, including scores for radio, television, theater, and cabaret. His contemporary, traditional classical, and folk music works in recent years have been for young musicians. His commitment to enable young Australians to play music by Australian composers is well known. Hultgren has been nominated for Penguin and Sammy Awards for his television sound tracks and has been awarded the Most Outstanding Composition Award at the 1985 and 1987 Australian National Band and Orchestra Clinic.

Unit 2: Composition

A "Bark" Gigue is a single-movement piece based on the Australian folk song, "The Old Bark Hut." In a jolly, swaggering, 6/8 meter, marked "Allegro" (dotted-quarter note = 116–132), the piece lasts approximately one minute and fifty seconds.

Unit 3: Historical Perspective

The piece was written in 1994 and reflects Hultgren's interest in providing repertoire by Australian composers to young musicians of that country. The folk song, from the early 1900s, portrays the trials and tribulations of a once well-to-do person who is now "stumped up" and living in a bark hut. The verses detail the person's battles with weather, furnishings, food, and fleas. The lyrics are colorful, but not objectionable, and hold a strong appeal to middle

school students. The lyrics for "The Old Bark Hut" can be found at: <http://www.uq.edu.au/~mlwham/banjo/old_bush_songs/the_old_bark_hut.html>

Unit 4: Technical Considerations

ENTIRE ORCHESTRA:

Right hand: The notes of the shortest subdivision are six eighth notes, with most of the piece being quarter note followed by eighth note in 6/8. There are some pizzicato with quick transitions to arco in accompanying voices, but the folk song material is played arco using a light, détaché stroke. Some of the accompaniments and parts of the development section require use of a heavy, strong, détaché stroke in the lower half of the bow.

Left hand: The piece is predominantly in G major, with a three-measure excursion into E-flat major. A nine-note chromatic scale in three quarter note down-bows over a measure is one of the signature gestures of this work that will come off beautifully. All parts require limited, simple shifts.

FIRST VIOLIN:

First position is primarily used. At the recapitulation, *divisi* octave writing requires use of third position to play the tune. A simple third position passage is also part of the coda.

SECOND VIOLIN AND VIOLA:

Mostly G major finger patterns are used. Chromatic alterations are within C major and B-flat major patterns. A measure-long scalar passage into third position exists for second violin. These two parts start the fugato section in unison and play a countermelody/ostinato at the recap, which students will enjoy.

CELLO:

There are a few passages in third and fourth positions that lie well for the most part. There are also some rapid, rollicking string crossings.

DOUBLE BASS:

Writing is in first and half positions, with shifting on the G string to extend the range. The bass part doubles the cello part in most instances, so it is rewarding to play.

Unit 5: Stylistic Considerations

The use of the folk song by Hultgren is very much in the style of his British predecessors, Holst and Vaughan Williams. Attention should be given to the phrasing of the accompaniment writing. Dynamics and style range from a light, bouncy initial presentation of the tune at the beginning to a joyous, carefree *ff*. Excitement is maintained throughout by the variety of the settings of the tune relative to a very consistent tempo and extremely accurate rhythm.

Throughout the movement, the folk song's chorus is often taken only by second violin; thus, a European seating format with first violin to the conductor's left and second violin to the conductor's right will highlight this feature of the writing. Placing cellos to the inside of the conductor's left and basses in a row along the back of the ensemble will augment the lower string sound so that the rollicking eighth note passages will drive the piece.

The conductor should always keep in mind that the pervasive style is of an Australian folk song, so having the orchestra sing the folk song with its inherent exuberance will convey the Australian spirit of the original in a way that the traditional rehearsal process can only approximate. An audience sing-along at the concert will enhance everyone's experience with the work.

Unit 6: Musical Elements

The folk tune is used as the outer sections of this three-part movement. Here, the harmony is diatonic, with chromatic passing tones for stylistic definition. Countermelodies and ostinatos are used in the accompaniment to maintain interest. The development section employs shifting tonal centers, chromaticism, imitation (fugato), stretto, and syncopation (three against two).

Unit 7: Form and Structure

SECTION	MEASURES	EVENT AND SCORING
Introduction	1–4	Four-measure passage that establishes style and tempo over an underlying dominant pedal
Verse	5–20	Melody played arco in first violin; pizzicato accompaniment in the style of British folk song instrumental suite
Chorus	21–36	Chorus (period construction, eight-measure phrase) stated in second violin with countermelody in first violin
Transition	37–41	Introductory material used as transition; surprise cadence to B-flat is a false modulation
Development	42–71	Theme for the development is fashioned melodically from the sequential nature of the Chorus and its descending anacrusis; imitative entrances by first violin and cello/bass are interestingly not symmetrical; sudden tonal shift to E-flat major, followed by the rhythmic development (three over two) of the fugal theme

SECTION	MEASURES	EVENT AND SCORING
Transition	72–75	Introductory material used as transition to Return
Return (verse)	76–91	Melody in first violin in *divisi* octaves; rollicking, fiddle-like countermelody in second violin and viola; bass/cello provide solid, stately bass line (beginning in m. 84)
Return (chorus)	92–109	Chorus in second violin; additional countermelody added in viola; melodic interruption in mm. 105–106 brings back the three over two gesture from the development (m. 60)
Coda	110–121	Introduction material extended by statement of opening phrase of verse is used as a rousing closing

Unit 8: Suggested Listening

Gustav Holst, *First Suite in E-flat*
Ralph Vaughan Williams, *English Folk Song Suite* (for orchestra or band)

Unit 9: Additional References and Resources

Lyrics to other Australian folk songs can be found at:
    <http://www.uq.edu.au/~mlwham/banjo/old_bush_songs>

Contributed by:

Louis Bergonzi
Associate Professor of Music Education (Strings)
Eastman School of Music
University of Rochester
Rochester, New York

Teacher Resource Guide

Brandenburg Concerto No. 3 in G Major

Johann Sebastian Bach
(1685–1750)

arranged by Merle Isaac

STRING ORCHESTRA

Unit 1: Composer

Johann Sebastian Bach was born in 1685 into a musical family in Eisenach, Germany. He became an outstanding organist, violinist, violist, teacher, and prolific composer who is recognized as the greatest genius of baroque music. Bach's output as a whole is unparalleled in its encyclopedic character and embraces practically every musical form of his time.

Bach composed works in both sacred and secular idioms; the creative development of his music roughly corresponds to the positions of employment he held during his life. During his appointments affiliated with the church, Bach composed cantatas, oratorios, and an immense variety of works for the organ. While employed as a court musician, he devoted himself to secular instrumental music. He composed his great cycles of keyboard music, notably the *Well-Tempered Clavier*, the Inventions and Suites, during this time. His chamber music works include sonatas for various instruments and continuo, concertos for solo and instrumental groups, and orchestral suites.

Bach's two wives bore him twenty children. Of those who survived early childhood, four sons became recognized performers and composers. The date of Bach's death in 1750 generally marks the close of the baroque period in music history.

Unit 2: Composition

The Brandenburg Concerto No. 3 in G Major (1721) is one of six concertos by J. S. Bach dedicated to the Margrave of Brandenburg. It is believed the concertos were not written expressly for the Margrave but were presented to him as a sample of Bach's earlier work. Unlike the standard baroque *concerti grossi*, the six Brandenburg Concertos use a variety of solo combinations from the heterogeneous mixing of brass, woodwind, string, and keyboard instruments. The great variety of instrumental combinations continues the coloristic tradition of Venice, but the emphasis on wind instruments is of typically German heritage.

Bach took as his model the modern baroque concerto style of Vivaldi, but in his hands it became a thoroughly personal composition. Because of the marvelously balanced concerto themes, solid counterpoint, and rhythmic exuberance, these concertos represent courtly entertainment at its height.

The original Brandenburg Concerto No. 3 presents a homogenous string sound composed for three each violins, violas, and cellos with continuo; it is a true ensemble concerto. The arrangement by Isaac uses the traditional string orchestra setting of two violins, viola, cello, string bass, and piano. This abridged concerto, approximately seven minutes and thirty seconds in length, has two movements: "Moderato" and "Allegro." The second movement is more technically demanding for each instrument than the first.

Unit 3: Historical Perspective

Bach and his contemporaries were subject to the European patronage system in both court and church. Their compositions reflect the demands and desires of their employers. The Brandenburg Concertos, written for a court orchestra, are an excellent example of this dependency of composers on their sponsors. Bach's life came in the waning years of the baroque period, and his music was considered outdated by most of his contemporaries. Unrecognized at the time, Bach opened up new dimensions in virtually every area of creative work he touched—in format, density, musical quality, and technical demands. Fully in touch with new developments, such as the instrumental concertos of Vivaldi, the *concerti grossi* of Telemann and Corelli, and the oratorios of Handel, Bach combined the best that the German, French, and Italian styles had to offer, resulting in a higher musical level.

Unit 4: Technical Considerations

Most of the composition is built around the keys of G, D, and C major, although more extensive modulation in Movement 2 also encompasses the keys of E and B minor. Violin and viola use third-finger extensions on the lower strings, and cello also employs extensions. Position work for first violin, cello, and string bass extends through third position.

Rhythmic demands are basic, although steadiness of the pulse should be maintained through string crossings and descending passages. Movement 1 is a Grade 3 selection; Movement 2 is considerably more difficult with the extensive use of half and second positions, a faster tempo, and more difficult modulation sequences. It should be rated a Grade 4.

Unit 5: Stylistic Considerations

The use of baroque-style bowing is crucial to the exuberant rhythmic nature of this composition. The bow should be used in the mid- to upper half in the violin and viola parts and in the mid- to lower half in the cello and string bass parts. Longer note values should be slightly detached, though not stiff and stopped. Shorter note values are connected smoothly. The cello and string bass sections should be careful not to overplay the bass line because the line is doubled.

Isaac has added dynamic markings to aid young players in recognizing the natural flow of the music. It is wise to remember that the Brandenburg Concerto No. 3 is a chamber music composition. Large ensembles need to be especially sensitive to style and balance in order to enhance and clarify the contrapuntal style of this period.

Unit 6: Musical Elements

During the baroque period, fast movements seemed to have been most popular—as they are with young players today. The two movements in this concerto display lively rhythmic vitality and rich polyphonic texture.

The first movement is based on a tiny three-note rhythmic motif that is quickly expanded into a long, arching opening phrase in G major. This phrase is comprised of five motives that are then used in a variety of combinations and extensions of the thematic material.

The second movement is a gigue, a stylized dance in binary form with great swirling melodic lines that are swept along on a steady stream of sixteenth notes. Both movements exhibit contrapuntal texture with imitative and sequential figures typical of baroque composition. The harmonic structure is rich in modulations and is an exceptional model for teaching movement from key to key.

Unit 7: Form and Structure

SECTION   MEASURES

Movement 1: "Moderato"
This movement opens with a long, arching phrase of sixteen measures that can be divided into the following three measure motives:

A	1–3
B	4–6

SECTION	MEASURES
C	7–9
D	10–12
E	13–16

These basic motives are employed interchangeably as material for the six following phrases. At times they are used against each other, the three-note rhythmic motif (two eighths and one quarter note), and other countermelod-ic material. Major harmonic cadences determine the phrases. The last five measures of this movement employ a technique borrowed from Vivaldi in which all instruments join in unison to draw special attention to the upcoming cadence and signal the end of a major section. In the original work, this technique is used numerous times, not only at the end of the movement.

Phrase 1	1
Phrase 2	17
Phrase 3	31
Phrase 4	46
Phrase 5	62
Phrase 6	80
Phrase 7	92
Coda	106

Movement 2: "Allegro"
This movement is a gigue in extended, rounded binary form.

Part 1 (repeated)

A	1	Tonic
	8	Dominant
	15	Supertonic
Closing material	24	Dominant

Part 2 (repeated)

A´	25	Dominant
	27	Submediant
	42	Mediant
	73	Subdominant
A	81	Tonic
Closing material	96	Tonic

Unit 8: Suggested Listening
J. S. Bach:
   The Brandenburg Concertos
   Four Orchestral Suites
Arcangelo Corelli, Twelve Concerti Grossi

George Frideric Handel, *Messiah*
Antonio Vivaldi, *The Four Seasons*

Unit 9: Additional References and Resources

Berman, Joel, Barbara G. Jackson, and Kenneth Sarch, eds. *Dictionary of Bowing and Pizzicato Terms*. American String Teacher Association with National School Orchestra Association Publications Library, 1987.

Bukofzer, Manfred E. *Music in the Baroque Era*. New York: W. W. Norton & Co., 1946.

Downes, Edward. *Guide to Symphonic Music*. New York: Walker and Co., 1976.

Geiringer, Karl. *Johann Sebastian Bach*. New York: Oxford University Press, 1966.

Keenan, Kent W. *Counterpoint*. Englewood Cliffs, NJ: Prentice-Hall, Inc., 1972.

Palisca, Claude V. *Baroque Music*. Englewood Cliffs, NJ: Prentice-Hall, Inc., 1968.

Randel, Don, ed. *The New Harvard Dictionary of Music*. Cambridge, MA: Harvard University Press, 1986.

Sadie, Stanley, ed. *The New Grove Dictionary of Music and Musicians*. New York: Grove's Dictionaries, 2000. Also available online at www.grovemusic.com

Contributed by:

Kathleen DeBerry-Brungard
Orchestra Clinician/Adjudicator (retired)
Plano Senior High School
Plano, Texas

Teacher Resource Guide

Contredanse

Antonio Salieri
(1750–1825)

arranged by Edvard Fendler

STRING ORCHESTRA

Unit 1: Composer/Arranger

Antonio Salieri, fifth son of merchant Antonio Salieri, was born in Legnago, Italy. He was first taught the violin and harpsichord by his older brother but received formal training on the violin, in singing, and reading and playing from the score in Vienna. While in Vienna he met Gluck, who was to become his patron and lifelong friend.

Salieri is most well known for his operas, achieving his greatest triumphs in Paris. He served the Viennese court for more than fifty years as a composer, teacher, and notable member of the musical establishment. He had dealings with many artists and scholars of the late eighteenth and nineteenth centuries, and was the teacher of a large number of musicians born between 1770 and 1810, including such notables as Beethoven, Schubert, and Liszt.

Arranger Edvard Fendler was born in Leipzig, Germany, in 1902. He graduated in conducting from the Stern Conservatory in Berlin. In 1927, he began conducting various groups in Europe, including the orchestra of the Paris Conservatoire. He was conductor of the Mobile, Alabama Symphony Orchestra beginning in 1952 and later the Beaumont Symphony (Texas), where he remained until his retirement in 1971. He was a naturalized American citizen and during his career appeared as a guest conductor with major orchestras throughout the world, among them the New York Philharmonic Orchestra. Beginning in the late 1930s, in addition to his podium responsibilities, Fendler served as an editor for numerous editions of classical repertoire.

Unit 2: Composition

The organization of this composition is typical of many found in the classical period. The symmetry of form is precise and clear. The music is homophonic and tonal, with the phrases and cadences well defined. Two contrasting, four-measure phrases are combined into a double phrase. Rhythm elements are simple and constant with clearly punctuated rhythm cadences. The harmony is simple, utilizing primary chords, their inversions, and various seventh chords. The harmonic rhythm moves slowly and is subordinate to the melody. The structure is closely aligned with the rondo form. It is a Grade 3 composition. Approximate performance time is two minutes and thirty seconds.

Unit 3: Historical Perspective

The contredanse was a popular eighteenth century instrumental form that can be found in the works of Mozart and Beethoven. The origin of this composition is not known; however, its stylistic and melodic elements are consistent with other compositions of the classical period. The contredanse, however, was used in French opera, and with Salieri's operatic success in Paris, it is possible that this composition may have operatic connections. This arrangement, published in 1964, came at a time when a renewed interest was developing in school orchestras.

Unit 4: Technical Considerations

The melodic elements fall naturally in the keys of D major and B minor. The first violin part requires third position; all other parts can be easily played in first position. The double bass does not go higher than D above the staff. Rhythmic elements are basic: quarter, eighth, sixteenth, dotted-quarter/eighth notes, and eighth notes/eighth rests. A few simple double-stops in fifths, sixths, and octaves using open strings are found in the inner voices.

Unit 5: Stylistic Considerations

No style indications are given; however, a staccato style on the repeated eighth note patterns will add energy to this composition. Eighth notes followed by eighth rests are played with a series of up-bows and are best played with a crisp bow stroke beginning on the string. Dynamics are sudden, dramatic, and occur at the beginning of new phrases. Pizzicato is used occasionally in the accompaniment.

Unit 6: Musical Elements

The A theme is mostly diatonic, a four-measure phrase in unison paired with a four-measure phrase in harmony. Harmonic movement in the A theme is restricted to I and V chords. The B theme at Letter A contrasts the A theme melodically and rhythmically. Harmonic movement is expanded to include I, IV, and V chords. The C theme at Letter C has two contrasting themes, one

in B minor and one in D major. The harmonic structure is again limited to the I and V chords. Letter E includes the repetition of the C theme in B minor but is extended to include limited use of chromatics, primarily in the first violin.

Unit 7: Form and Structure
Modified rondo: ABACDCA coda

SECTION	EVENT AND SCORING
Beginning, Theme 1	Repeated; double phrase (antecedent and consequent) built upon two four-measure phrases
A, Theme 2	Repeated; double phrase
B, Theme 1	Repeated; exact repetition of melodic, rhythmic, harmonic, and dynamic treatment
C, Theme 3	Repeated; double phrase in B minor
D, Theme 4	Repeated; double phrase in D major
E, Theme 3	Developed; double phrase in B minor developed
F, Theme 1	Repeated; double phrase extended to coda
G, Coda	Development of harmonic and rhythmic elements of Theme 1 using scales, double-stops

Unit 8: Suggested Listening
Ludwig van Beethoven, Twelve Contredanses
Franz Benda/arr. Fendler, "Sinfonia" from *Barber of Seville*
L. Clerambault/arr. Fendler, Symphonia Quarta
Jean-Baptiste Lully/arr. Fendler, Chaconne
Wolfgang Amadeus Mozart, Contredanses K. 267, K. 609, K. 462

Unit 9: Additional References and Resources
Hitchcock, H. Wiley, and Stanley Sadie. *The New Grove Dictionary of American Music*. New York: Macmillan, 1986.

Randel, Don M., ed. *The New Harvard Dictionary of Music*. Cambridge, MA: Harvard University Press, 1986.

Sadie, Stanley, ed. *The New Grove Dictionary of Music and Musicians*. New York: Grove's Dictionaries, 2000. Also available online at www.grovemusic.com

Wold, M., G. Martin, J. Miller, and E. Cykler. *An Outline History of Western Music*. 7th edition. Dubuque, IA: Wm. C. Brown, 1990.

Contributed by:
Robert S. Frost
Composer/Arranger, Author, Conductor
Smithfield, Utah

Teacher Resource Guide

Danza

Vaclav Nelhybel
(1919–1996)

STRING ORCHESTRA

Unit 1: Composer

Vaclav Nelhybel was born in Czechoslovakia. He studied composition and conducting at the Prague Conservatory of Music and musicology at the universities of Prague and Fribourg, Switzerland. He held various conducting posts, including the Czech Philharmonic (1945–46), Swiss Radio (1946–50), and Radio Free Europe (1950–57). He emigrated to the United States and became a citizen in 1962, where he was active as a composer, conductor, and lecturer.

Nelhybel published over four hundred pieces, including works for orchestra, band, chorus, small ensembles, and operas. He is especially known for his symphonic band works, and his music ranges from middle school to professional difficulty level. A 1962 National MENC student ensemble performance inspired Nelhybel to begin composing for school ensembles.[1] His music is known for its driving rhythms, modal melodies, varied used of dissonance and texture, and broad dynamic range. Notable works by Nelhybel for symphonic band include *Suite from Bohemia*, *Trittico*, and *Festivo*.

Unit 2: Composition

Danza, written for young string players, was commissioned by and dedicated to Professor Vernon H. Stinebaugh, founder of the Manchester College String Festivals, Manchester, Indiana. It was first performed for the 25th Anniversary Concert in April 1971. The piece, approximately seven minutes in length, has three contrasting sections: Adagio, Allegro, and Vivo. Nelhybel's affinity for Renaissance and baroque period music is evident in the use of modal melodies, parallel intervals in conjunct motion, and fugal techniques, including imitative entries, stretto, and augmentation. *Danza* is published by E. C. Kirby, Ltd., and distributed by Hal Leonard.

Unit 3: Historical Perspective

Nelhybel, along with his contemporaries Persichetti, Schuller, and Copland, has been recognized for his contributions to a growing list of original and well-constructed works for band.[2] Nelhybel's music, similar to his countryman Janacek's, uses modal and autonomous melodies that do not follow functional harmonic techniques.

Unit 4: Technical Considerations

The composition is written in A-natural minor/Hypodorian mode with chromatic alterations (F-sharp and B-minor) in the Allegro. The piece provides minimal left-hand difficulties because all parts can be played in first position. All double-stops are to be played non-*divisi*. In measures 83, 85, and 87, cello has the option of playing open A string or the E a fifth above. There is an optional viola/third violin part written in treble clef. A mute is required for all instruments. Much of the technical challenge comes from the rhythmic and melodic independence of the parts, syncopation and tied notes, and such tone production and bowing issues as producing a wide dynamic range from *pp* to *ff*, sustained sound in the Adagio, accents in the Allegro, and quick bow lifts in the Vivo.

Unit 5: Stylistic Considerations

This work, strongly Slavic in character, progresses from the initial nostalgic Adagio through a rhythmic Allegro into a frenzied finale.[3] Choosing the appropriate tempos for the three sections is critical for a successful performance. Tempo marks are given in the score. The Adagio requires students to play legato style with sustained strokes. The Allegro and Vivo should be played in a gypsy style with faster rhythms performed near the frog, on the string, or—for more advanced students—brushed spiccato.

Unit 6: Musical Elements

Danza is a monothematic composition based on a five-note theme. Independent melodic lines; imitation; melodic movement in parallel thirds, fourths, and fifths; selective use of dissonance; and frequent texture and dynamic changes provide melodic interest. Short rhythmic fragments that often contain repeated eighth notes generate rhythmic momentum. Unison rhythms in measures 37, 71–77, 91–96, 109–110, 125, and 150–156 provide contrast and serve as points of rhythmic arrival. *Danza* offers many opportunities to develop ensemble skills by drawing student attention to rhythmic and timbral changes, coordinated bowings, and tuning intervals, particularly in the unison rhythm passages.

Unit 7: Form and Structure

The three-part form of the composition is typical of many Slavic folk dances. Because plagal and authentic modes are linked through a shared final note D, several sections are written in D minor/Dorian mode.

ADAGIO:

This segment is divided into two sections at mm. 1–27 and 28–43, with mm. 40–43 functioning as a coda. Both sections begin and end on unison A. The sections have coordinated dynamic and texture changes where instrumentation increases in mm. 21 and 37 to support the dynamic climax. The five-note theme, A–D–C–B–A, is first stated by viola and cello in mm. 1–5.

ALLEGRO:

This segment begins in D minor/Dorian and ends in A minor/Hypodorian. It is divided into three sections with boundaries that are marked by rhythmic and, in the case of the third section, melodic unison. The Allegro contains three major elements: (1) the five-note theme, (2) an extension of the five-note theme that begins with an accented syncopation, and (3) two quarter note slurs. All three elements are present in the last statement of the theme in m. 140.

SECTION	MEASURES	EVENT AND SCORING
Section 1	45	Following a four-measure introduction, the five-note theme punctuated by a half rest after the second note is played first by second violin at m. 49 and then by first and second violin in canon by fifths at m. 62; succeeding passage at m. 72 consists of unison rhythms
Section 2	78	This section consists of two similar parts in mm. 78–111 and 112–126 that *crescendo* from *p* to *f*; theme presented in a one-measure canon by first violin and cello, and then in m. 112 by viola, cello, and double bass; five-note theme is presented in repeated eighth notes at m. 78 and in a more legato style in m. 79; third element is first introduced in m. 94; unison passage from the first section extended in mm. 95–111 and 123–126; ends with a harmonically unstable passage leading to A minor

SECTION	MEASURES	EVENT AND SCORING
Section 3	127	This section is divided into three parts at mm. 127–139, 140–149, and 150–156, where rhythmic momentum builds in a stretto-like fashion from a one-measure canon in violin in fifths to a two-beat canon in all four instruments (m. 140); second part, written in D minor/Dorian mode, resolves in the third part to *ff* unison A

VIVO:

This segment, the shortest in duration and length, is composed in binary form.

SECTION	MEASURES	EVENT AND SCORING
Introduction	157	Five-note theme presented in eighth note double-stops; canonic entrances are in fifths
A	160	Introduction material serves as a background for the five-note theme in first violin
B	168	Unison rhythm in parallel fifths in violin and viola; theme includes a three-beat tie over the bar line and quick bow lifts
A^1	175	Theme is presented three times in a two-beat canon, from highest to lowest range instruments; violins state the theme in E minor while the other instruments are in A minor
B^1	183	Theme is presented twice in a one-measure canon in fifths at *ff* by two groups of instruments (violin and viola, cello and contrabass)
Extension	189	Three-note stepwise ascending line of the B theme is augmented
Coda	199	*Subito pp* whole notes progress from a Neapolitan sixth B-flat to its root E-flat, which also functions as a Neapolitan in D that leads to an accented *sfz* unison on the final D

Unit 8: Suggested Listening
Vaclav Nelhybel:
> *Festivo*
> *Suite from Bohemia*

Unit 9: Additional References and Resources
Knapp, Joel Davis. "Vaclav Nelhybel: His Life, Influences on His
    Compositional Style, and a Review of His Published Choral
    Compositions." Ph.D. diss., University of Missouri-Kansas City, 1991.

Sadie, Stanley, ed. *The New Grove Dictionary of Music and Musicians.* New
    York: Grove's Dictionaries, 2000. Also available online at
    www.grovemusic.com

University of Scranton, University Bands and Choirs:
    http://academic.uofs.edu/department/bandsing/nelhybelbio.html

Contributed by:
Margaret Haefner Berg
University of Colorado
Boulder, Colorado

---

1 Alliance Publications Composer List: http://www.op.org/api/complst2.htm
2 Michaelides, Peter. "Vaclav Nelhybel: Composer for Concert Band." *Music Educators
    Journal*, Vol. 54/8 (April 1968), 51.
3 Nelhybel, Vaclav. *Score Notes*. London: E. C. Kirby, Ltd., 1971.

Teacher Resource Guide

Fantasia on an Original Theme
Joseph Phillips
(b. 1962)

STRING ORCHESTRA

Unit 1: Composer

Joseph Phillips was born in Beacon, New York. He holds degrees from the Crane School of Music of the State University of New York at Potsdam and the University of North Texas. He is currently Supervisor of Music Education for the Carmel Central School District in Patterson, New York. Prior to his present position, he served as Director of Fine Arts, Magnet, and Gifted/Talented Programs for the Galveston (Texas) Independent School District. He has also served as a band and orchestra director in New Hampshire, Texas, and New York. Recipient of the 1998 Texas Orchestra Directors' Association Composition Contest Prize, Phillips's compositions have appeared on several bestseller and editors' choice lists. In addition to his published compositions (such as *Dorian Dance* and *Westminster Strings*), he has also written for *The Instrumentalist* magazine. Phillips lives in southeastern New York State with his wife and three children.

Unit 2: Composition

The original title of this work was Fantasia on an Original Folk Song, but it was changed by the publishers because the words "original" and "folk song" are contradictory. The melodies in the work, as the original title suggests, were written to be imitative of folk songs, with no specific nationality in mind. The sparse use of certain pitches, most notably *fa* in the opening and closing sections of the work, gives it a slightly modal flavor.

186

Unit 3: Historical Perspective

This is one of Phillips's first compositions for string orchestra. It received its premiere performance with the composer conducting his middle school orchestra in Fort Worth, Texas.

Unit 4: Technical Considerations

The keys of C major and A minor are used in the work. The opening viola solo, while not technically difficult, will require a performer with good tone. Bowings and articulations used in the piece include détaché, slurs, slurred staccato, pizzicato, and tremolo. The middle section should be fast enough to provide contrast to the outer slower sections. Some performance problems conductors may encounter include rushing in the cello and bass pizzicato lines in measure 35 as well as clean execution of the dotted-eighth/sixteenth rhythms. When the first violin part is divided in octaves, it is recommended to assign only a few players to the top part for the sake of balance and to improve intonation. The top line of the *divisi* first violin part at measure 17 and measure 52 may be left out if a group does not have players who can play with good intonation in second position. The harp part, while easy, contributes to the variety of timbre in the work.

Unit 5: Stylistic Considerations

The work requires expressive playing throughout. Smooth bow changes will add to the lyrical nature of the piece. Good dynamic contrast will also improve the effectiveness of the piece.

Unit 6: Musical Elements

In both the opening and closing sections of the piece, the harmonic framework is provided by counterpoint melodies in the accompanying parts. In the middle section, the theme is introduced in viola and cello accompanied by tremolo chords. It is then passed to first violin, with chordal accompaniment provided by second violin and viola, along with a walking pizzicato bass line in the cello and bass parts. The third time the theme is stated, violin plays the theme in canon with viola and cello.

Unit 7: Form and Structure

The piece is in ternary (ABA) form.

SECTION	MEASURES	EVENT AND SCORING
A		
a	1	Solo viola
a	9	Violin 1
b	17	Violin 1

SECTION	MEASURES	EVENT AND SCORING
B		
Transition	25	
c	27	Viola, cello
c	35	Violin 1
c	43	Violin 1 and 2; viola and cello in canon
A		
a	52	Violin 1; in octaves
b	60	Violin 1; in octaves
Coda	67	

Unit 8: Suggested Listening

Gustav Holst, *Saint Paul's Suite*, Movement 4
Joseph Phillips:
    Dorian Dance
    Westminster Strings
Ralph Vaughan Williams:
    Fantasia on Greensleeves
    Fantasia on a Theme by Thomas Tallis

Contributed by:

Joseph Phillips
Supervisor of Music Education
Carmel Central School District
Patterson, New York

Teacher Resource Guide

Farandole from L'Arlésienne Suite No. 2

Georges Bizet
(1838–1875)

arranged by Merle Isaac

STRING ORCHESTRA

Unit 1: Composer

Georges Alexandre César Léopold Bizet was born in Paris on October 25, 1838, and died on June 3, 1875. Bizet was the only child of professional musicians. He was granted early admission to the Paris Conservatory at the age of nine. He developed into a brilliant pianist, winning a first prize for piano in 1852, for organ in 1855, and in 1857 the Paris Conservatory's most prestigious prize, the Prix de Rome. This prize enabled Bizet to focus his attention on composing in Rome for three years. While there, he became a hardworking composer, turning out a number of songs, piano pieces, and works for orchestra, but at the same time never neglecting his main ambition, to write a successful opera. Upon his return to Paris, Bizet continued to compose. His most lasting impact on the musical world came with the premiere in 1875 of his opera, *Carmen*, just three months before his death. Other notable works by Bizet include the Symphony in C, *Pêcheurs de Perles*, *Petite Suite*, *Jeux D'Enfants*, and *L'Arlésienne Suite*.

Unit 2: Composition

Bizet wrote the incidental music for *L'Arlésienne* ("The Girl from Arles"), a play by Alphonse Daudet. None of the pieces for *L'Arlésienne* are in extended form, and many of the short mélodrames (the French term for "background music to the dialogue") are fewer than twenty measures long. Except for a few short choruses, all of the music is instrumental. Farandole was originally composed as one of twenty-seven numbers to accompany the dialogue. Bizet, a Parisian, was greatly influenced by the area of Provençe in southern France, in particular the old city of Arles. As a result, he used Provençal tunes such as Farandole, known also as "Danse dei chivau-frus" and March of the Three Kings ("Marcho dei rei") along with melodies Bizet composed himself for *L'Arlésienne*.

Merle Isaac (1898–1996) arranged the Farandole from *L'Arlésienne* Suite No. 2 for string orchestra in 1978. Isaac, who was well known as an educator and for his arrangements of great orchestral works, provided a piece with all of the style of the original. The approximate playing time is just over three minutes.

Unit 3: Historical Perspective

Bizet was commissioned to write the music for *L'Arlésienne* using only twenty-seven musicians because of limited funds. The mélodrame form had such low reputation at the time that Bizet's music went largely unnoticed. It was not until he selected four movements, reorchestrated them for full orchestra, and performed them as the *L'Arlésienne* Suite No. 1 that his music met with success. The first suite consists of the Overture, Menuetto, Adagietto, and Carillon. Bizet's close friend, Ernest Guiraud, selected and reorchestrated the pieces for the *L'Arlésienne* Suite No. 2 following the composer's death in 1875. This suite includes the Pastorale, Intermezzo, Menuetto, and Farandole. Guiraud's version of the Farandole is a free arrangement of Bizet's material from Nos. 22–24, including the March of the Three Kings and Farandole.

Unit 4: Technical Considerations

The Isaac arrangement of Farandole is in the keys of G minor, G major, and E minor. The suggested Tempo di marcia is quarter note = 120 in the opening section in 4/4 time. The Allegro section changes to 2/4 time, with quarter note = 144. The rhythmic demands are basic for the most part; however, there are a few sixteenth note patterns, grace notes, and a prevalent combination of eighth note/sixteenth rest/sixteenth note. Farandole requires a minimal amount of position work. Optional notes have been written in measures 182–187 for first violin to avoid the need for third position, but measures 37–52 are ideal for third position, although not required. Cellists must have an understanding of extensions and must shift second position for a brief time. The double bassists will utilize half, first, and second positions, as well as a few harmonics played an octave above the open string.

Unit 5: Stylistic Considerations

Farandole was written during the romantic period. The music of this period sees many contrasts in dynamics, rhythm, and style, and the Farandole is no exception. Dance was typically included in the French opera, and Bizet also included the Farandole, a dance, in his incidental music for *L'Arlésienne*. The dance-like melody begins at the Allegro and must be played lightly. This is in contrast to the opening theme, which should be played using accented and separated bow strokes to convey the marcato style of the march. The use of a variety of bowing styles—détaché, spiccato, legato, and martelé—are necessary in order to express the contrasting themes in this piece. The rhythmic accompaniment in the low strings and percussion must remain precise.

Unit 6: Musical Elements

The rhythmic main theme of the opening begins in G minor, with the same theme then played canonically. The Allegro introduces two new themes in the key of G major. The opening theme returns in E minor and is heard first in unison before being harmonized. Contrapuntal devices of the three themes in G major and a richer harmonic accompaniment conclude the piece, enriched with additional use of percussion.

Unit 7: Form and Structure

SECTION	MEASURES	EVENT AND SCORING
A	1–9	March of the Three Kings stated in G minor
A	9–17	Played in canonic imitation
B	17–36	Farandole stated in G major, also known as the Provençal *Danse dei chivau-frus*; percussion added to the simple chordal accompaniment played on each downbeat
C	37–52	Introduced by first violin and viola, lightly accompanied by pizzicato chords in cello, with second violin playing quarter notes preceded by grace notes
A	53–69	Returns to first violin, harmonized by a simple eighth note pattern played lightly by the rest of the orchestra
C	69–84	Presented *p* by second violin
B	85–101	Thicker-textured, straight eighth note pattern accompaniment played in unison by violin

SECTION	MEASURES	EVENT AND SCORING
A returns	101–132	E minor; played in unison by the entire orchestra until m. 125, when it is harmonized but remains rhythmically the same
A and B	133–149	G major; A and B in counterpoint
A and C	149–164	Played in counterpoint
A and B	165–180	Return simultaneously with a denser eighth note accompaniment in low strings and percussion
B varied	180–end	The coda is a variation of Theme B; the energy and intensity of the closing measures increase by the repeated eighth note being changed to sixteenth notes and additional percussion; block chords conclude Isaac's arrangement

Unit 8: Suggested Listening
Georges Bizet:
   Carmen
   L'Arlésienne Suite Nos. 1 and 2
   Petite Suite
   Symphony in C
Charles Gounod, *Funeral March of the Marionette*
Edvard Grieg, *Peer Gynt Suite*, Op. 46, No. 1
Felix Mendelssohn-Bartholdy, *A Midsummer's Night Dream*
Modest Moussorgsky, *Pictures at an Exhibition*
Camille Saint-Saëns, *Carnival of the Animals*

Unit 9: Additional References and Resources

Bizet, Georges. *L'Arlésienne* Suite Nos. 1 and 2. Fritz Hoffman, ed. New York: Dover Pub., Inc., 1977.

Curtiss, Nina. *Bizet and His World*. New York: Knopf, 1958.

Dean, Winton. *George Bizet, His Life and Work*. London: J. M. Dent and Sons Ltd., 1965.

Harley, Francis. "Merle, Magical Musician," *American String Teacher*, Spring 1997, Vol. 47, No. 2, 25–32.

Jackson, Barbara, Joel Berman, and Kenneth Sarch. *The A.S.T.A. Dictionary of Bowing Terms for String Instruments*. 3d edition. Bloomington, IN: Tichenor Publishing Group. American String Teachers Association, 1987.

Sadie, Stanley, ed. *The New Grove Dictionary of Music and Musicians*. New York: Grove's Dictionaries, 2000. Also available online at www.grovemusic.com

Slonimsky, Nicolas, ed emeritus. *Baker's Biographical Dictionary of Musicians*. New York: Schirmer Books, 2001.

Contributed by:

Christa Speed
String Specialist
Grand Island Public Schools
Grand Island, Nebraska

Teacher Resource Guide

Folk Tune and Fiddle Dance

Percy Fletcher
(1879–1932)

STRING ORCHESTRA

Unit 1: Composer

Englishman Percy Eastman Fletcher was born December 12, 1879, in Derby and died in Windsor on September 10, 1932. He moved to London at the age of twenty and conducted at various theaters, including the Prince of Wales', Savoy, Drury Lane, and His Majesty's. His style of composition was light and melodious, as evidenced by the titles of several of his orchestral works, such as *Woodland Pictures*, *Sylvan Scenes*, *Parisian Sketches*, *Rustic Revels*, *Three Frivolities*, and the *Vanity Fair* Overture. He also wrote a short sacred cantata entitled *Passion of Christ*. Fletcher composed for and adjudicated brass bands in England.

Unit 2: Composition

Folk Tune and Fiddle Dance, composed in 1914 for string orchestra, keeps Fletcher's memory alive in music history. Fletcher had an active conducting career in London for over thirty years, and some of his works are still played by wind ensembles. The paucity of listings in his discography and in encyclopedias should not negate the value of *Folk Tune and Fiddle Dance* in the string orchestra repertoire.

Unit 3: Historical Perspective

Folk Tune and Fiddle Dance is perhaps the earliest example of educational music in the repertoire that is still performed with regularity, although it was not written with students in mind. String students of 1914 played material from the few existing method books as well as some arrangements of the standard orchestral repertoire. Holst's *St. Paul's Suite* (1913) and *Brook Green Suite* (1933), Hubert Parry's *English Suite* (1914–15), and Peter Warlock's *Capriol Suite* (1926) fit into the same historical era and fill an important niche in the British string orchestra repertoire that is now played by young people.

Unit 4: Technical Considerations

First violin, cello, and bass are required to shift. The keys of A major and E major, and accidentals within the prevalent E minor, will necessitate forward extension for the cellos and high third finger in the upper strings. Certain other accidentals will also pose fingering problems. Numerous tempo, key, and stylistic changes in "Folk Tune" make this a tricky movement. In "Fiddle Dance," the major problem is the rapid sixteenth notes prevalent in violin and viola. Cello and bass must maintain a steady tempo under the running sixteenth notes.

Unit 5: Stylistic Considerations

"Folk Tune" is replete with broad, lyrical sections that require musical sensitivity, moreso than for "Fiddle Dance" because of the inherent contrast in the nature of the two movements. Numerous dynamic shadings and tempo changes are indicated in "Folk Tune." "Fiddle Dance," by a British composer, has obvious connections to American fiddle music, which performers will easily grasp.

Unit 6: Musical Elements

The harmonic structure of the chords in both movements is simple; altered chords are usually secondary dominants. The most unusual chord is the Neapolitan at six measures after number 7 in the first movement, and that chord occurs only once. The melodies are folk-like, are predominantly stepwise and diatonic, and sometimes occur canonically. The prevalent compound meter of 6/8 in "Folk Tune" is usually a harder concept for younger players to master than simple meter.

Unit 7: Form and Structure

SECTION	EVENT AND SCORING
Movement 1: "Folk Tune"	
A	Beginning; 6/8; flowing melody in E natural minor in violin and cello; answered by second violin
Variation 1	Number 4; "a little quicker"; drone E provided by viola and cello; thinner texture
B	Number 6; 3/4; A minor; "In Minuet time"; four-measure introduction; binary dance form

SECTION	EVENT AND SCORING
A Variation 2	Number 8; 6/8; A major; "Quickly and lively" with the feeling of a jig
C	Number 10; 2/2; D major; "In a rough and jovial manner"; ostinato in cello and bass; theme presented by second violin and viola, joined later by first violin
A Variation 3	Number 14; 6/8; E minor; canonic treatment of A theme
Coda	Number 17; E major; nine-measure coda; "smoothly and tenderly"; another variation on A

Movement 2: "Fiddle Dance"

Introduction	Beginning; 2/4; eight measures of open strings in first and second violin; in the manner of a hoedown
A	Number 1; vague key center of G major/E minor
A^2	Number 2; E minor; continuation of A section
A	Number 5; exact repeat of numbers 1–2
B	Number 7; A minor; viola and cello present the melody, which is then taken over by second violin with a lyrical countermelody in first violin
A	Number 12; accompaniment different from that of number 1
Coda	Number 13; begins as a bridge to A at number 14; ends in G major

Unit 8: Suggested Listening

Percy Fletcher:
> *An Epic Symphony* (band)
> *Labour and Love for Brass Band* (tone poem)

Gustav Holst:
> *Brook Green Suite* (string orchestra)
> *St. Paul's Suite* (string orchestra)

C. Hubert H. Parry, *English Suite* (string orchestra)

Peter Warlock (pseudonym for Philip Heseltine), *Capriol Suite*

Unit 9: Additional References and Resources

Mayer, F. R., ed. *The String Orchestra Super List.* Reston, VA: Music Educators National Conference, 1993.

Slonimsky, Nicolas, ed. emeritus. *Baker's Biographical Dictionary of Musicians.* New York: Schirmer Books, 2001.

Contributed by:

David Littrell
Professor of Music
Kansas State University
Manhattan, Kansas

Teacher Resource Guide

Four Royal Dances
Eric Ewazen
(b. 1954)

STRING ORCHESTRA

Unit 1: Composer

Eric Ewazen was born in Cleveland, Ohio, in 1954. He received a B.M. degree from the Eastman School of Music, as well as M.M. and D.M.A. degrees from the Juilliard School of Music, where he has been a member of the faculty since 1980. His music has been performed in major concert halls throughout the United States, Europe, and Asia, as well as at the Aspen, Caramoor, Tanglewood, Estherwood, Warwick, and Tidewater Music Festivals, and at the Music Academy of the West. A recipient of numerous composition awards and prizes, Ewazen's works have been commissioned, performed, and recorded by many chamber ensembles and orchestras in the U.S. and overseas. His compositions have been championed by such organizations as the Detroit Chamber Winds; the American Brass Quintet; St. Luke's Chamber Ensemble; the Chicago Chamber Musicians; the Charleston Symphony; the West Virginia Symphony; the New World Symphony; the U.S. Military Band at West Point; the U.S. Army Band and Marine Bands of Washington, D.C.; the Air Force Band in Langley, Virginia; the Bellevue Philharmonic; the Western Piedmont Symphony; the Fairfield Chamber Orchestra; Cantabile Chorale; and the School for Strings, among others.

Unit 2: Composition

Ewazen composed *Four Royal Dances* specifically with young string players in mind, yet its performance is satisfying for advanced ensembles as well. The publisher says it is "suggested for intermediate level string orchestra students with three to four years of instruction" and is listed as "Grade 3: Challenging."

198

The title reflects the four distinct moods established by the individual movements of the work: The Lord, The Lady, The Jester, and The Knight. Written following an extended stay in Great Britain, the individual movements are evocative of their respective monikers and present a particularly accessible opportunity for student musicians to focus on expression and musicality. The piece is consistent with Ewazen's style of composition, which has been called neoromantic, yet it is distinctly contemporary in a most refreshing way. The entire work lasts approximately seven minutes. It is scored for first and second violin, viola, cello, and bass, with optional piano part.

Unit 3: Historical Perspective

Four Royal Dances was composed in 1991 at the invitation of the publisher, Boosey & Hawkes, as one of the initial pieces in a new educational series for string orchestra. While the composer is best known for significantly enriching the brass literature in recent years, this piece demonstrates his equal fondness for and comfort with strings. Ewazen, himself, is an accomplished cellist. As in his chamber works, chamber orchestra, and full orchestral compositions, *Four Royal Dances* is full of Ewazen's signature rhythms, chord progressions, and melodic gestures. Unlike many other composers of his generation, Ewazen's compositions are grandly melodic and are consistently well received by audiences.

Unit 4: Technical Considerations

Four Royal Dances requires musicians to be comfortable with modal scale and arpeggio patterns, particularly Dorian and Mixolydian, as well as related major and minor figures. Violin and viola remain in first position throughout the four movements; cellists need extend only to an E and E-flat above first position once in each of the second and fourth movements, respectively; bassists must be prepared to occasionally play C and D above the staff. Some unexpected chromaticism arises in all parts during the second movement. Rhythmic figures are generally basic in the first three movements, with simple, yet effective, syncopations throughout. The final movement is more rhythmically challenging, with mixed meter (6/8, 9/8, 3/4) and hemiola. All sections of the orchestra receive opportunities to play the melody. Tempos of the four movements are not extreme: quarter note = 116, 80, and 132, and dotted-quarter note = 84, respectively.

Unit 5: Stylistic Considerations

As mentioned, expressivity lies at the core of *Four Royal Dances*. Contrasts in dynamics and articulation abound but can be easily anticipated and executed by players. The first movement, "The Lord," requires baroque-like eighth note articulation, with an emphasis on syncopations. The second movement, "The Lady," requires great sensitivity within a *p* context. The third movement,

"The Jester," must be jovial and lively, with contrasting legato eighths and short quarters. The last movement, "The Knight," requires rhythmic precision, ability to use bouncing bow strokes, and accuracy within a triplet feel. Strong attack strokes are also required, as is the ability to play sudden dynamic changes.

Unit 6: Musical Elements

As noted, the melodic elements of each movement are primarily modal in nature. D Dorian permeates the first movement, E Aeolian the second, C Mixolydian the third, and G Aeolian the fourth. The conductor should familiarize the students with these modal scales.

The two-part theme of the first movement is played by high and then low strings, and in each setting is complemented by contrasting rich, modal chords and syncopated rhythms.

A pulsating drone introduces the haunting melody of the second movement. It contains canonic elements with richly scored chordal accompaniment; some unexpected chromaticism is included. The movement closes with a fade to silence.

The third movement, like the first, is based on a two-part theme with short motifs that receive a brief development before a recapitulation of the entire theme; rhythmic augmentation of the theme is effectively the movement's coda.

The complexity of the fourth movement contrasts with the first three. After a rhythmic introduction in 6/8, the main theme is presented in first violin and is closed by an interesting phrase extension by way of a 9/8 measure. A brief, syncopated transition takes the primary theme to the lower strings, the transition reappears, and a second, related theme in 9/8 is introduced. A canonic setting of the first theme—with strong chordal accompaniment—gallops toward the extended hemiola of the coda. The conductor should prepare students with rhythmic studies that explore alternating two- and three-beat subdivision of 6/8.

Unit 7: Form and Structure

MEASURES	EVENT AND SCORING

Movement 1: "The Lord"

1–8	Primary theme A1; D Dorian; presented in first violin; chordal accompaniment in rest of strings
9–16	Secondary theme A2; closely related to the primary theme, but in major mode; presented in thirds in first and second violin; related rhythmic accompaniment in viola and cello

Measures	Event and Scoring
17–24	Modified A1; presented in second violin and viola; chordal accompaniment in rest of strings
25–32	A1; presented in cello and bass; chordal accompaniment in rest of strings; ending with transition
33–40	New thematic material B; toggles between minor and major; presented in thirds in first and second violin; motifs drawn from Primary theme; rhythmic and syncopated accompaniment in viola and cello
41–42	Transition
43–48	A1; restatement by first violin, this time in parallel sixths with second violin; accompaniment in other sections is the rhythmic equivalent of that found in mm. 33–40
49–52	Codetta; a rhythmic augmentation of the final two measures of A1

Movement 2: "The Lady"

1–2	Introduction; sustained E in octaves provides an introduction; presented in seconds, viola and cello; presence of an underlying pulse, here in bass, that continues through the first thirteen measures
3–9	Primary Theme A; seven-measure theme; essentially in E Aeolian; presented first in violin, with seconds entering with parallel harmony in m. 6; rhythmic chords in viola and cello
10–14	Primary theme; presented with a tonal center of B, here in second violin and viola; first violin and bass maintain a sustained B in octaves; cello maintains the underlying rhythmic pulse
15–38	Primary theme developed; development of motifs; traded among all sections and played within constantly shifting key centers
39–48	Primary theme material; continued development by extending and rhythmically augmenting the primary theme phrase; conclusion in E Aeolian, with *sfz/subito p* climax in m. 48
49–53	Coda; underlying sustained E and bass pulse recall introduction; stretto entrances of opening phrase in first violin, second violin, and viola; ends with a Picardy third/sustained E major chord with fade

MEASURES	EVENT AND SCORING

Movement 3: "The Jester"

1–14	The movement is based on one thematic unit; following a rhythmic one-measure introduction, the theme, in C Mixolydian, is presented in two-measure phrase sections, alternating between statements by first and second violin, then by viola/cello; steady quarter note rhythm initially presented as introduction material continues as the dominant accompaniment figure; statement of the theme is concluded with a three-measure phrase extension that overlaps with a restatement of the theme by cello
14–35	Development of thematic motifs traded among all sections and played within shifting key centers
36–45	Recapitulation of theme and tonal center; bass joins viola and cello in the statement of mm. 38–41
43–45	Final three measures of the primary theme are rhythmically augmented to establish a codetta

Movement 4: "The Knight"

1–2	A brief *crescendo* of a chordal 6/8 pattern establishes the rhythm, character, and tonal center of the movement
3–9	Primary theme; Theme A in G Aeolian is presented in first violin, with steady quarter/eighth accompanying rhythmic figure in all other sections; closes with one 9/8 measure that serves as an unexpected phrase extension
10–11	A repeat of the introductory measures, here serving as a transition
12–19	A restatement of the A theme, this time by cello, with the same quarter/eighth accompanying pattern in bass; supporting dotted-quarter chords in violin and viola; 9/8 measure is not heard this time; theme ends in 6/8
20–26	A secondary theme; "B" in E-flat and C tonal centers is based on alternating rhythmic subdivisions within 6/8 (hemiola 6/8 subdivision in three alternating with subdivision in two)
27–28	Repeat of transition material from introduction
29–36	A third theme; C in G Aeolian; in 9/8; an antecedent four measures played in unison and thirds by first and second violin; consequent two-measure statement in cello and bass, and closing with another segment in thirds by first and second violin with broadly rhythmic chordal accompaniment

MEASURES	EVENT AND SCORING
37–42	Stretto entrances of A theme material in first and second violin, with underlying lower strings chords in shifting tonal centers
43–44	Final transition using the introduction motif mm. 45–50; recapitulation of A theme, up one octave, in first violin with the same quarter/eighth accompanying pattern in the other strings
51–54	Phrase extension/codetta in 3/4; established by hemiola and *ritardando*; a rhythmically augmented ending to the movement; the piece closes with G major chord, with a fermata, and a Picardy third

Unit 8: Suggested Listening

Eric Ewazen:

Among Friends, featuring Steve Witser, trombone, Albany Records, TROY

Chamber Music of Eric Ewazen, featuring the St. Luke's Chamber Ensemble and the American Brass Quintet, Well-Tempered Productions, WTP 5172

David Taylor, featuring David Taylor, bass trombone, New World Records, 80494-2.

Discoveries, featuring the Borealis Wind Quintet, Helicon Records, HE 1030.

From the Hudson Valley, featuring Margaret Swinchoski, flute, Albany Records, TROY 371.

Music for the Soloists of the American Brass Quintet, Well-Tempered Productions, WTP 5189.

New American Brass, featuring the American Brass Quintet, Summit Records, DCD 133.

New York Legends, featuring Joseph Alessi, trombone, Cala Records, CACD 0508.

New York Legends, featuring Philip Smith, trumpet, Cala Records, CACD 0516.

Noises, Sounds and Strange Airs, featuring Eugene Becker, viola, Clique Track, CT 0576.

Paving the Way, featuring Summit Brass, Summit Records, DCD 171.

Street Songs, featuring Center City Brass, d'Note records, DND 1030.

Unit 9: Additional References and Resources

Web site: "Southern Music Company" — http://www.southernmusic.com/
Contains listings and access to published works.

Web site: "Spindrift Music Company" —
http://www.spindrift.com/ctbio2.html
Contains biographical information and descriptions of published works.

Web site: "The Juilliard School" — http://www.juilliard.edu/faculty/efac.htm
Contains biographical information.

Web site: "The Music of Eric Ewazen" —
http://www.ericewazen.com/newsite/index.html
Contains biography, reviews, access to recordings and music, music that
can be downloaded, calendar of performances, and other relevant items.

Contributed by:

Andrew H. Dabczynski
Professor of Music Education
Brigham Young University
Provo, Utah

Teacher Resource Guide

The Ghost of John

arranged by Susan C. Brown
(b. 1949)

STRING ORCHESTRA

Unit 1: Arranger

Susan Cahill Brown was born in New York City in 1949. She received a Bachelor of Music degree from Ithaca College and a Master of Fine Arts from Sarah Lawrence College, where she was a student of Dorothy DeLay. She recorded music of Lou Harrison, Germaine Tailleferre, and Roy Hargrove as concertmaster and soloist. She is on the faculties of Cabrillo College and University of California at Santa Cruz. Notable works include *Two Octave Scales and Bowings for Violin and Viola*, and string orchestra pieces for children entitled *Tiptoe* and *Dona Nobis Pacem*. Future works include *Orchestral Excerpts and Studies for Strings* and *Shabbat Shalom* for Chamber Orchestra.

Unit 2: Composition

Brown wrote *The Ghost of John* after hearing her youngest daughter, Jeannette, sing this folk song around Halloween:

> Have you seen the Ghost of John?
> Long white bones with the skin all gone.
> Ooo Ooh Oo Oo Ooh
> Wouldn't it be chilly with no skin on!

The piece is in round form for strings, piano, and percussion. There is a short introduction of the "ghost" followed by the round, continuing with a jazz ballad and a coda that utilizes tapping on the instruments that mimic the sound of a skeleton.

Unit 3: Historical Perspective

The Ghost of John was written in Mainz, Germany, in 1991, while Brown was on sabbatical leave from teaching. Her intent was to create a song for her daughter in the spirit of Halloween. The text of the folk song gave way to updated sounds used in contemporary music for strings. A little American jazz walking bass line interrupts the traditional round in the middle of the piece.

Unit 4: Technical Considerations

The piece uses the A minor scale extensively with some chromatic movement for the upper strings in the middle of the piece. Most of the piece stays within a two-octave range except for the violin solo part, which shifts into fifth position. The rhythmic considerations are straightforward and utilize quarter, half, and eighth notes. The string techniques that create the ghost-like effects are reasonably challenging. They consist of pizzicato *glissandi*, bass slap pizzicato, tremolo behind the bridge, and arco *glissandi* as high as possible. One other technique is tapping on the instrument lightly with the fingertips.

Unit 5: Stylistic Considerations

The traditional round is presented in a serious manner with the surrounding parts yielding to a more humorous and diabolical mood. The bowing styles encompass legato, martelé, and détaché. Brown also incorporates late twentieth century techniques for strings such as behind the bridge tremolo and light tapping on the top of the instrument. While the quarter/eighth note pulse is steady and noticeable throughout, the piece goes through several longer and shorter tempo changes, including a slower jazz ballad. The eighth notes should be played straight in this jazz section (i.e., without swinging them). *The Ghost of John* melody is played with a singing détaché sound that is often accompanied by accented rhythms played martelé and spiccato. The printed agogic accents should be emphasized. Most of the dynamics fall into a medium range, but there are sudden forceful notes and a *diminuendo al niente* at the end.

Unit 6: Musical Elements

The harmony is in triadic form based in A minor. Elements of the blues scale are also incorporated with a flat five notated as a diminished fifth E-flat or augmented fourth D-sharp. As the new voice enters the round, a polyphonic melodic structure is created. In measure 45, fragments of the round form a ground bass line. A new theme is introduced to accompany the round in measure 53.

Unit 7: Form and Structure

SECTION	MEASURES	EVENT AND SCORING
Introduction	1–8	Lower strings and piano
Theme 1	9	The round begins in violin 1 followed two measures later by violin 2 and viola, and two measures after that in m. 13 by cello and string bass
Theme 2	37	Theme appears in solo violin; walking bass line in lower strings
Themes 1 and 2	53	Played together with Theme 2 in violin 1 and Theme 1 in lower strings
Coda	61	Introduction material in lower strings; rhythmic pulse changes timbre to a drumming sound played with left-hand fingers lightly tapping on the instruments

Unit 8: Suggested Listening

Béla Bartók, Ten Pieces from *For Children*
Percy Grainger, *Mock Morris*
Germaine Tailleferre, *Pastorale*
John Williams/arr. James Curnow, *Dance of the Witches*

Unit 9: Additional References and Resources

Alfred Publishing Co., Inc., P.O. Box 10003 Roscoe Blvd., Suite 200, Van Nuys, CA 91406

ASCAP (American Society of Composers, Authors and Publishers), ASCAP Building, One Lincoln Center Plaza, New York, NY 10023

Contributed by:

Susan Brown
Director of Strings & Ensembles, Cabrillo College
Director of Chamber Music, University of California at Santa Cruz
Santa Cruz, California

Teacher Resource Guide

Good Daughter Overture (La Buona Figliuola)

Niccolò Piccini
(1728–1800)

arranged by A. Louis Scarmolin

FULL ORCHESTRA

Unit 1: Composer

Niccolò Piccini was born in Bari, Italy, on January 16, 1728. As a child, he was exposed to music at a very early age because his father was a violinist at Bari's Basilica di San Nicola. He demonstrated musical promise at an early age, and with the help of the archbishop of Bari, Muzio Gaeta, he was able to enroll in the Naples Conservatorio di S. Onofrio, where he studied with Leo and Durante. Upon graduation, he commenced his career as a composer of opera. His first opera, *Le Donne dispettose*, a comedy, was premiered in Naples in 1754. Over the course of his lifetime, Piccini wrote prolifically for the stage, composing more than one hundred operas. He began his career in Italy and, with the performance of more than fifty operas, achieved a great deal of success.

Nevertheless, in 1776, he left Italy for Paris because the French court offered him a lucrative position. Piccini, a married man with seven children, decided to avail himself to this offer. This career move precipitated a rivalry for public opinion between him and Gluck. Despite their public competition, Piccini did have some success, and in 1784, he was appointed teacher of voice at the École Royale de Chant et de Déclamation Lyrique in Paris. Because of the French Revolution of 1789, Piccini lost his post and his pension and returned to Naples in 1791. After the Revolution, he returned to Paris in 1798, where he obtained partial restoration of his pension and was appointed as the sixth inspector at the Conservatory. By this time, however, he was too ill to carry out his duties. He died in Passy, France, on May 17, 1800, at the age of seventy-two.

Unit 2: Composition

La Cecchina, also known as *La Buona Figliuola* (the *Good Daughter*), has long been considered the most popular *opera buffa* of the mid-eighteenth century. Its premiere performance in Rome on February 6, 1760, created such a stir that it was an immediate success. Based on Samuel Richardson's famous and first controversial novel of 1740, *Pamela,* or "Virtue Rewarded," was translated into Italian and adapted for the stage by Carlo Goldoni. This production was so successful that it was performed at every major Italian opera house. It became so widely known internationally that it was performed for the next twenty years in German, French, and English translations in such major cities as Paris, London, Hamburg, Dresden, Graz, and Esterház.

This arrangement is remarkably similar to the original. There is an opening trumpet fanfare and Andante Sostenuto section, where themes are presented in D minor and in 3/4 time. The Allegro section that follows in D major is close to the original score.

Unit 3: Historical Perspective

The eighteenth century saw opera continue as a sophisticated art form. The opera overture was designed to set the stage for the whole production by displaying musical elegance and technical mastery. Piccini's compositional style was perfectly matched to the comic opera setting because he was capable of making rapid dramatic shifts with his orchestration and melodic lines. He changed emotional content rapidly from the serious to the comic by linking a musical motif with each character. Each motif had a specific meter, tempo, and dramatic expression. When he brought these various sections together, the dramatic changes in musical character amplified the text.

Unit 4: Technical Considerations

This piece begins in D minor and then changes mode to D major after the first major section. The arranger effectively uses doubling and cueing so that even a small ensemble will be able to perform this selection if other instruments perform the cues. The arranger writes the transposing wind parts without a key signature and uses accidentals instead. This makes it easier for young wind players to keep track of the multiple sharps. Inexperienced wind players will find the parts playable in the most widely used registers but will need to become familiar with the keys associated with four and five sharps. In addition, there are some beautiful, lyrical lines shared by the winds and strings, so intonation may be somewhat of an issue for the young orchestra.

The second violin and viola parts are all playable in first position, but much of it lies well in third position if students need experience with this. The first violins require rudimentary knowledge of third position, and the cellos need to shift into second position for one passage. The double basses need to use both the half and first positions, but this piece can also be performed in alternate positions if the players need to build this skill. In general, the bow strokes employed will be détaché, spiccato, and hooked. Second violins and violas will need to rehearse the articulation so they do not overpower the melody.

All parts are rich with chromatic alterations, which will be most difficult for the string players. The upper strings will use the first four Bornoff finger patterns (low 1, high 3, and both low and high 2). This may be an area that must be prepared before students will feel confident with the parts.

Unit 5: Stylistic Considerations

As with most of the operatic compositions of this period, the Overture presents the primary melodic information for the entire opera; therefore, the piece has many transitions of tempo, dynamics, and style, and is consistent with the classical style. The opening eight measures present a trumpet fanfare introduction to get the audience's attention; it is in 3/4 and in minor. After the fanfare, the remaining introductory section consists of alternating sixteen-measure phrases with lyrical melodies in moderate or slow tempo, and then a transition into D major for the Allegro. This introduction was clearly written by the arranger to set off the more flamboyant Allegro section that follows. The editor did a wonderful job with the string parts marking articulations, bowing, fingerings, and phrasing, so it is very clear what the composer intended.

This piece represents the high classical style and should be regarded with all of the usual considerations of performance practice from the era. Balance, clarity, dynamics, intonation, and articulation should be primary concerns of the overall ensemble. The winds will have to work for melodic clarity in A major and E major, particularly in the *piano* sections when lack of breath support may cause intonation problems. The strings will have to concentrate on chromatic alterations, bow stroke clarity, and string crossings, particularly with slurs across two strings. Off-the-string spiccato will greatly add to the clarity. Overall, the rhythms are very even with only a few dotted-eighth/sixteenth patterns. With the exception of a few sections of syncopation, this piece does not present any major challenges.

Unit 6: Musical Elements

Clarity and structure characterize music of the classical era. This music is homophonic in nature, so there is a definite melody, some countermelodies, and a bass line. The texture is transparent and depends on precise articulations. Classical pieces for the intermediate full orchestra are often overplayed because young players frequently elongate note lengths and play the louder dynamics too forcefully. A classical era *f* is not as loud as a romantic era *f*. The melody always needs to emerge from the texture even when there are running notes underneath creating movement. The character of this piece is jovial and light; excessive dynamic range or note length will take away the impact of the piece. It should be performed with light, delicate, and short articulations with careful attention to dynamics.

Unit 7: Form and Structure

MEASURES	EVENT AND SCORING

Section 1:

| 1 | D minor; 3/4; trumpet fanfare with string accompaniment |
| 7 | Transition; *ritardando* |

Section 2: "Andante sostenuto"

9	A; thinly scored with woodwinds, horn, and strings; *p*
17	Number 1; A
25	Number 2; B; eight-measure section repeated with first and second endings
37	Number 3; A; *a tempo*
45	Number 5; B; *mf* with the addition of trombone; second ending is transition to next section at number 6
53	Number 5; second ending of B; transition with full orchestration of winds, brass, percussion, and strings, with a *ritardando* to the final cadence in A major

Section 3: "Allegro"

59	Number 6; D major; 4/4; f; Theme 1 of the Exposition of an abbreviated sonata allegro form
68	Theme 2; D major
73–74	Two-measure transition back to Theme 1
75	Restatement of Theme 1
83	Number 9; Theme 3; D major
92	Number 10; transition to A major and A minor in the Development
105	Number 12; Development
133	Number 13; Recapitulation

Unit 8: Suggested Listening

Wolfgang Amadeus Mozart, *The Marriage of Figaro*
Niccolò Piccini, *La Cecchina*

Unit 9: Additional References and Resources

Howard, Patricia. Gluck: *An Eighteenth-century Portrait in Letters and Documents*. Oxford: Clarendon Press, 1995.

Hunter, Mary Kathleen. *The Culture of Opera Buffa in Mozart's Vienna: a Poetics of Entertainment*. Princeton Studies in Opera. Princeton: Princeton University Press, 1999.

Lawson, Colin James. *The Historical Performance of Music: An Introduction*. Cambridge Handbooks to the Historical Performance of Music. Cambridge: Cambridge University Press, 1999.

Rosen, Charles. *The Classical Style: Haydn, Mozart, Beethoven*. New York: W. W. Norton & Company, 1972.

Sadie, Stanley, ed. *The New Grove Dictionary of Music and Musicians*. "Piccini," Dennis Libbey. New York: Grove's Dictionaries, 2000. Also available online at www.grovemusic.com

Contributed by:

Kathleen Horvath
Assistant Professor of Music Education
University of Illinois
Urbana, Illinois

Teacher Resource Guide

"Grand March" from Aida
Giuseppe Verdi
(1813–1901)

arranged by Merle Isaac

FULL ORCHESTRA

Unit 1: Composer

Giuseppe Verdi was born October 9, 1813, in the Duchy of Parma and died in
Milan on January 27, 1901. He studied in nearby Busseto until he left for further study in Milan at the age of eighteen. Incredibly, he failed the entrance
exams in keyboard proficiency and composition, so he studied counterpoint,
canon, and fugue diligently. He won the post of *maestro di musica* in Busseto
in 1834 and wrote his first opera, *Oberto, Conte di San Bonifacio*, which
achieved success at La Scala in 1839. His *Nabucco* of 1842 is his first opera to
remain in the repertoire. Verdi's aria, "La donna è mobile" from *Rigoletto*,
became one of the most popular operatic tunes of the day. *Il Trovatore* and *La
Traviata*, both dating from 1853, were successful worldwide. After he wrote his
great *Requiem* of 1873, Verdi composed *Otello* and *Falstaff*. Historic evaluation
of his music changed several times after his death, due in part to the opposite
stylistic preferences of the Wagner camp.

Unit 2: Composition

Verdi wrote the beloved opera, *Aida*, as a commission by the opera house in
Cairo, Egypt, where *Rigoletto* had appeared a year earlier. *Aida* premiered on
Christmas Eve in 1871. The production was hailed as a world event; the composition became one of the most famous in opera history. The Grand March
is a spectacle number; elephants in the procession have been employed in
some staging of the opera.

Unit 3: Historical Perspective

Aida represents a high point in Verdi's career. The opera has never gone out of favor, and the Grand March, with a duration of over four minutes, still holds great appeal for its grandeur, as evidenced by its performance at numerous graduation ceremonies. The mid-nineteenth century in Italy saw an emerging body of operas—chiefly those by Rossini, Bellini, Donizetti, and the young Verdi—that were becoming a mainstay of many opera houses' repertoire through repetition of performances over a span of years. Rossini's death in 1868 was significant in the history of Italian opera, even though his last opera, *Guillaume Tell*, was composed in 1829. His death coincided with the rising tide of Italian nationalism and the popularity of Wagner and his Germanic style, the musical antithesis of the Italian style and tradition as evidenced in Verdi's music. Isaac arranged the Grand March in 1962 for full orchestra.

Unit 4: Technical Considerations

The primary keys of G major, D major, and G minor should pose few problems. Precision in performing the abundance of dotted-rhythms, with triplet patterns interspersed, will require attention to rhythmic detail. This is a showpiece for trumpets because of the fanfares and the main theme being presented by first trumpet at number 4. Cellists and trombonists will enjoy the running eighth note line at number 13.

Unit 5: Stylistic Considerations

The Grand March requires precision for the dotted-rhythms on the part of almost everybody for the numerous fanfares interspersed throughout as well as for the main themes themselves. The strings must play hooked bows with crispness on the dotted-rhythms, and the winds and brass need to play with precise tonguing. There is only one truly legato theme, at number 13, which calls for a broad sweep of sound.

Unit 6: Musical Elements

The harmonic language is uncomplicated, with numerous diminished seventh chords that are so prevalent in the romantic style. Keys are all closely related except for one excursion to the mediant at number 8—not at all unusual for this period. Melodies are diatonic, with accidentals appearing in modulatory sections.

Unit 7: Form and Structure

Section	Event and Scoring
Fanfare	mm. 1–2; G major
A	Number 1; G major
B	Number 2; D major

SECTION	EVENT AND SCORING
A	Number 3; G major
C	Number 4; G major
C	Number 8; B-flat major
A	Number 11; G major
B	Number 12; D major
D	Number 13; G major; brief excursion to G minor
Codetta	Number 15; G major based on C theme

Unit 8: Suggested Listening

Giuseppe Verdi:
>Aida
>Overture to *I Vespri Siciliani*
>Overture to *La Forza del destino*
>Overture to *Nabucco*
>*Requiem*

Unit 9: Additional References and Resources

Aida. Libretto in English and Italian. Boston: Oliver Ditson. Verdi's opera Aïda, containing the Italian text, with an English translation, and the music of all the principal airs. New York: Kalmus, n.d.

Martin, George. *Verdi: His Music, Life and Times*. New York: Da Capo Press, 1963, rev. 1983.

Mayer, F. R., ed. *The String Orchestra Super List*. Reston, VA: Music Educators National Conference, 1993.

Osborne, Charles. *Verdi: A Life in the Theatre*. London: Weidenfeld and Nicholson, 1987.

Price, Leontyne. *Aïda as told by Leontyne Price*. (illustrated by Leo and Diane Dillon.) San Diego: Harcourt Brace Jovanovich, 1990. (Juvenile Literature)

Slonimsky, Nicolas, ed. emeritus. *Baker's Biographical Dictionary of Musicians*. New York: Schirmer Books, 2001.

Contributed by:

David Littrell
Professor of Music
Kansas State University
Manhattan, Kansas

Teacher Resource Guide

Jazz Suite for Strings and Rhythm

Leighton Tiffault
(b. 1917)

STRING ORCHESTRA (PLUS RHYTHM SECTION)

Unit 1: Composer

Leighton Tiffault was born in Winsted, Connecticut, on October 19, 1917. He earned a master's degree in composition and education from Syracuse University in New York. Tiffault retired from Fayetteville-Manlius High School, where he taught creative writing, humanities, history of music, and class piano. He was also a visiting teacher at Ithaca College, Potsdam University, and Syracuse University, where he taught vocal, arranging, and keyboard harmony.

Unit 2: Composition

Jazz Suite is one of the two suites that Tiffault composed for strings, rhythm section, flute, and vibes. The rhythm section includes guitar, piano, bass, and drums. The piece is written for young string players and has three contrasting movements: Blues, Ballad, and Waltz.

Unit 3: Historical Perspective

Jazz Suite was published in 1980 when composers and arrangers were offering new repertoire that was different from traditional school orchestra music. This work was originally written for a double string quartet of students at Fayetteville-Manlius High School. Tiffault rescored the piece for string orchestra and later wrote a second suite. It is hoped that a third suite will be published soon. Tiffault believes that "string players are just as hip as anyone."

Unit 4: Technical Considerations

Jazz Suite is based on C major, D major, and G major for the respective movements. Rich harmonic progressions and chromatic accidentals will require careful attention for accurate tuning. All the string parts can be played in first position. More advanced players can be challenged by using upper positions. Bow distribution and syncopated rhythms are techniques required in the performance of this work.

Unit 5: Stylistic Considerations

A mature, experienced rhythm section is vital to the successful performance of *Jazz Suite*. String players will become familiar with "swinging" the eighth notes in the Blues movement. "Ballad," the second movement, is played as written with a light triplet feel in the rhythm section. Sustained bow control is necessary, especially in first violin. The Waltz movement features a driving, syncopated rhythm to be played at the frog, with a contrasting legato section.

Unit 6: Musical Elements

The Blues movement features melody in first violin and accompanying chords in rich jazz harmonies for the rest of the string section. Ends of phrases are punctuated with syncopation and *glissando* by the entire string section. First violin carries the melody in the Ballad movement, with the moving chromatic lines in second violin and viola, along with sustained whole and half notes in the string section. The Waltz movement again gives the melody to first violin. The syncopated rhythm, which is the signature of this movement, is stated in block chords by the entire string section. Harmonies throughout this work are based on rich chord progressions. The most complex occur in the Ballad movement. The following example comes from three measures before the end of the Ballad movement:

A-flat 13–G13–G-flat13–E-flat7 (11) + E/D

Improvisation is a possibility for rhythm section players but not necessary, as all parts are written out.

Unit 7: Form and Structure

MEASURES	EVENT AND SCORING
Movement 1: "Blues"	
1	Introduction based on A-flat9 and G9
5	Phrase in C with blues progression
17	Phrase develops introduction based on D-flat9 and C9 chords
25	C blues progression
36	Coda based on introduction; in C, with last progression of Em7–E-flatm7–Dm7–D-flatmaj7–Cmaj7

217

MEASURES   EVENT AND SCORING

Movement 2: "Ballad"
1   Theme 1 in C
12   Theme 2 in F
20   Theme 1 in C
28   Theme 2 in F; melody in flute and vibes
36   Theme 1 in D

Movement 3: "Waltz"
1   Theme 1 in G; syncopated figure
9   Theme 1 in G; repeated
17   Theme 2 in C; contrasting legato style
33   Theme 1 in G
41   Theme 1 in G; repeated
49   Theme 2 in C; melody in flute; syncopated figure from
                  Theme 1 as accompaniment in strings
33   Theme 1 in G; *Dal Segno*
66   Coda in G

Unit 8: Suggested Listening
Stéphane Grappelli:
    For Django
    Jazz 'Round Midnight
    Violin Summit
Stéphane Grappelli, Oscar Peterson, *Skol*
Stéphane Grappelli, Yo-Yo Ma, *Anything Goes*
Turtle Island String Quartet, *Metropolis*
Turtle Island String Quartet featuring The Billy Taylor Trio, *On the Town*
Jean-Luc Ponty:
    Individual Choice
    Open Mind

Unit 9: Additional References and Resources
Davis, Adam. "Jazz for String Players." *The Instrumentalist*, November 1999.

Feather, Leonard. "Da Capo." *The Encyclopedia Yearbook of Jazz*, 1992.

"Going Native: The Turtle Island String Quartet." *The Strad*, December 1996.

"Grappelli, Stéphane." *Compton's Encyclopedia Online 3.0.* 1998.

"Jazz." *Compton's Encyclopedia Online 3.0.*, 1998.

Lieberman, Julie Lyon. *Improvising Violin*. Woodstock, New York: Homespun Tapes, Ltd., 1988.

"Remembering the Genius of Stéphane Grappelli." *The Strad*, March 1998.

Taylor, Hollis. "French Jazz." *Strings*. September/October 1995.

"The Singing Cellist: Eugene Friesen." *The Strad*, December 1996.

"Violon sans frontières: Jean-Luc Ponty." *The Strad*, May 1996.

Contributed by:

Ida Steadman
Orchestra Conductor
Morehead Middle School/ Coronado High School
El Paso, Texas

Teacher Resource Guide

Lullaby

William Hofeldt
(b. 1952)

STRING ORCHESTRA

Unit 1: Composer

William Hofeldt was born in Chicago in 1952. He earned a degree in music education and accounting from the University of Illinois in 1974 and began teaching strings in Middleton, Wisconsin. He studied composition at the graduate level at the University of Wisconsin in Milwaukee. His *Centennial Overture* for full orchestra and *Nocturne* for string orchestra won the 1987 and 1988 National School Orchestra Association Composition Contests, respectively. Hofeldt then retired from teaching and currently works in accounting.

Unit 2: Composition

Lullaby was composed in 1984, inspired by Hofeldt's infant son. The theme is lyrical and supported by rich, rolling harmonies that are interesting for all players—not a coincidence for violist Hofeldt. The work has modern harmonic language but a simple beauty similar to Brahms's famous lullaby, also in triple meter.

Unit 3: Historical Perspective

Lullaby was composed at a time when original works for student orchestras were encouraged and supported by publishing companies and the orchestra teaching profession. This piece was written for the specific abilities of middle school or intermediate string players; it is successful in that goal. Hofeldt holds a place at the forefront of several other outstanding composers who wrote for school orchestras during this time.

Unit 4: Technical Considerations

This piece is in the key of D major with temporary moments in F major. The cello part is notable for its slurred, arpeggiated notes. The first violin part is lyrical, with third and fifth position sections in obbligato to the melody. Second violin and viola not only have interesting supporting harmonies but also present the melody. The simplest part is the bass, with sustained tones and a short passage that goes beyond first position. Rhythms never go beyond eighth notes in complexity.

Unit 5: Stylistic Considerations

This piece is reflective of the romantic musical period exemplified by rich harmonies, more involvement of all parts, warm melodies needing vibrato, and relaxation of tempo at section endings. Performers must play legato in a singing style. Dynamic contrasts are by section, with gradual softening and slowing at the end of the louder sections. Each statement of the theme begins in the original tempo.

Unit 6: Musical Elements

The main theme is in D major. One aspect of the harmony is the progression I–IV–ii–V–I. The harmonic support is the same in each statement of the main theme. The second theme begins in D major but is characterized by sudden shifts to E minor and F major with a mournful cadential sequence of G minor, D minor, arriving at A major for the return to the original theme. In the coda, the notable harmony is a B-flat chord preceding the final D major, giving a final feeling of hush.

Unit 7: Form and Structure

Section	Measures	Event and Scoring
Opening	1–2	Cello D major arpeggio
Theme 1	3–18	Melody in first violin; repeated in mm. 19–34 with melody in second violin and obbligato in first violin
Theme 2	35–50	Melody in first violin beginning in D major and temporarily straying into E minor and F major
Theme 1	51–66	Melody up an octave in first violin and more involved accompanying parts
Theme 2	67–82	Melody in second violin divided into octaves; the loudest section of the work, with first violin making interrupted entrances that are very unsettling

Section	Measures	Event and Scoring
Theme 1	83–97	Final statement of the theme in cello and viola in a reassuring manner
Coda	98–103	Final peaceful conclusion

Unit 8 Suggested Listening
Samuel Barber, *Adagio for Strings*
Aaron Copland, Corral and Nocturne from *Rodeo*
Larry Daehn, *As Summer Was Just Beginning*

Unit 9 Additional References and Resources
Mayer, F. R., ed. *The String Orchestra Super List*. Reston, VA: Music
   Educators National Conference, 1993.

McCord, David. *One at a Time*. Boston: Little, Brown, 1974.

Silverstein, Shel. *Where the Sidewalk Ends*, New York: Harper Collins, 1974.

Contributed by:
Joanne Erwin
Associate Professor and Director of Music Education
Oberlin College
Oberlin, Ohio

Teacher Resource Guide

M to the Third Power

Carold Nuñez
(b. 1929)

STRING ORCHESTRA

Unit 1: Composer

Carold Nuñez was born in Port Arthur, Texas, in 1929. He earned his Bachelor of Music in Composition and Master of Music Education from North Texas State University, now known as the University of North Texas. He taught for twenty-nine years in the Texas public schools, where his orchestras and bands consistently received first division ratings. He retired from public school teaching in 1985. In addition to composing numerous works for high school orchestra, he served in leadership positions at the region and state level. He now resides in Denton, Texas, where he remains active as a clinician, adjudicator, composer, and professional pianist.

Unit 2: Composition

M to the Third Power is a teaching piece for string orchestra. The term "Third Power" refers to the Minor Meter Mix. It is a single-movement work in a perpetual motion style with a performance time of approximately three minutes. It is a Grade 2 composition except for the limited first violin position work.

Unit 3: Historical Perspective

During the 1980s, interest in new repertoire for school orchestras, especially at the elementary and middle school levels, played a dominant role in the curriculum. Orchestra conductors sought new arrangements of the classics, as well as original works. Few original works, however, used twentieth century techniques, especially meter changes. M to the Third Power, published in 1985, was refreshing with its simple harmony and accessible melody. It was not

technically difficult and provided an opportunity for students to become acquainted with this twentieth century compositional technique.

Unit 4: Technical Considerations

The D melodic minor scale is fundamental to the composition. The rhythmic elements include an understanding of simple and compound meter, and that the eighth note remains constant when there is a change of meter. All parts can be played in first position with the exception of two measures in third position for first violin and a few measures in third position for double bass. Cellists will need to know backward and forward extensions.

Unit 5: Stylistic Considerations

Basic bowing styles are legato and marcato with only a few measures that contain slurs and accents. The repetitive nature of the melody, rhythmic figures, and doubled sixteenth notes creates a perpetual motion type of composition.

Unit 6: Musical Elements

Melodic themes are simple, restricted in range, and predominately diatonic with occasional use of thirds. Phrase lengths are unusual, however, usually six or twelve measures, and comprise melodic material in two-, three-, or four-measure groupings. Phrases begin in simple meter, change to compound meter, then return to simple meter. The texture is homophonic, with the basic chord structure frequently implied with only two or three voices. Although rhythmically repetitive, interest is achieved through changes in voicing.

Unit 7: Form and Structure

Free form is used with no return to the original theme. Melodic variations are limited to phrase endings.

Section	Measures	Event and Scoring
Theme 1a	1–12	Unison melody in violin and viola
Theme 1b	12–26	
Theme 2	27–36	Melody in harmony between violin and viola
Theme 2	37–43	
Theme 1c	43–60	Unison melody; subtle changes in scoring
Transition	60–63	
Theme 3	64–72	Unison melody in viola and cello
Theme 3a	73–81	
Theme 4	82–89	Unison melody in viola and cello; similar to Theme 3
Theme 4a	90–97	

SECTION	MEASURES	EVENT AND SCORING
Transition	98–101	Material similar to mm. 60–63
Theme 3	102–110	Melody in first violin; change in accompaniment
Theme 3b	111–119	
Theme 4	120–129	Melody in sixths between violin and viola
Theme 4b	130–135	
Theme 3	136–143	Unison melody in violin; change in accompaniment
Theme 3c	144–149	Unison melody in octaves in violin, viola, and cello
Coda	150–157	Unison material using thematic rhythmic patterns

Unit 8: Suggested Listening

Carold Nuñez:
> *Chapter One*
> *Convergence*
> *Suite for Strings*

Unit 9: Additional References and Resources

Dallin, L. *Techniques of Twentieth Century Composition*, 2d edition. Dubuque, IA: Wm. C. Brown, 1964.

Randel, Don M., ed. *The New Harvard Dictionary of Music*. Cambridge, MA: Harvard University Press, 1986.

Wold, Milo, Gary Martin, James Miller, and Edmund Cykler. *An Outline History of Western Music*, 7th edition. Dubuque, IA: Wm. C. Brown, 1990.

Contributed by:

Robert S. Frost
Composer/Arranger, Author, Conductor
Smithfield, Utah

Teacher Resource Guide

"March to the Scaffold" from Symphonie fantastique

Hector Berlioz
(1803–1869)

arranged by Anthony Carter

FULL ORCHESTRA

Unit 1: Composer

Hector Berlioz was born in La Côte-St. André, France, on December 11, 1803. The son of a doctor, Berlioz was introduced to a wide range of studies, including music, during his childhood. In 1821, his father enrolled him in medical school in Paris, but Berlioz soon abandoned his medical career for the study of music at the Conservatoire under Jean-François le Seuer. A composer, performer, and great orchestrator, Berlioz's musical contributions are measured not only in technical terms, but more importantly for their emotional content. With *Symphonie fantastique*, Berlioz crafted a large-scale composition based on his emotions rather than classical technique and structure. Other great works by Berlioz include *Harold in Italy*, *Romeo and Juliet*, and *The Damnation of Faust*.

Unit 2: Composition

The *Symphonie fantastique*, composed in 1829–30, was written to gain the attention of Shakespearean actress Harriett Smithson. She did not know Hector Berlioz at the time he composed this symphony as a result of his obsession with her; however, they did eventually marry. The work depicts an artist's dreams of his beloved during an opium overdose. The fourth movement, "March to the Scaffold," describes the artist's march to his execution after murdering his beloved, heard in two contrasting march themes. Nevertheless, when he reaches his executioner, he thinks of his beloved once more. The *idée fixe*, or fixed idea, represents his beloved and is played by clarinet (three measures before X) as the artist imagines his love before he is beheaded. The large chord following this thought represents the beheading, with the following pizzicatos in the strings representing the sounds of the falling head.

Unit 3: Historical Perspective

The *Symphonie fantastique* was composed during the early years of the romantic era. Following the classical symphonic structure, Berlioz's emotional interpretation of the symphony paved the way for future tone poems and programmatic music from Liszt, Smetana, and even Tchaikovsky. After attending the premiere of the work on December 5, 1829, Franz Liszt was so moved by the piece that he invited Berlioz to dinner, and they eventually became good friends. Composed during the Revolution of 1830, Berlioz wrote of the *Symphonie fantastique*, "I dashed off the final pages of my orchestral score to the sound of stray bullets coming over the roofs and pattering on the walls outside my window."

Unit 4: Technical Considerations

The A minor natural and melodic scales, as well as F major, C major, and A major are required of the entire orchestra. In the strings, bass must be able to shift up to high G, violin 1 into third position, and cello into fourth position. The clarinet solo of the *idée fixe* reaches high E on a B-flat clarinet. Sections to give specific attention are as follows: (1) Strings at T must achieve clear and crisp articulation; starting with an up-bow and playing in the lower half of the bow may help achieve the desired sound. (2) The sextuplets may need some slow practice for upper woodwinds from P–Q. (3) It is hard to obtain a unified sound from violins from M–O; rehearse each violin section separately before combining the violins and then all the strings.

Unit 5: Stylistic Considerations

The entire movement, although written in common time, should be felt and conducted in two with a metronome marking of half note = 120–132. This pulse will bring out the broad and heavy sound needed for both march themes. In contrast to the broad sounds of the marches, all eighth note and dotted-eighth/sixteenth note passages should be staccato. The dynamics range from *ppp* to *fff* with many sudden contrasts. There are also many varied rhythms throughout the piece, often overlapping each other; all should be played with distinct accuracy, especially the triplets and sextuplets.

Unit 6: Musical Elements

The piece begins in A minor, including the first march statement in the strings at B, which then modulates to F major at D before returning to the tonic. The principal march theme at H is in C major, the parallel major key, and is in this key every time it returns. One of the more interesting sections in the piece at P–Q uses the original march motive in the lower winds and brass while accompanied by sextuplets in the upper woodwinds and an ascending scale in the strings. This section modulates from tonic to dominant, each time restating the march motive until it reaches the original march theme one last time. The melodic structure of the piece is based around the two march themes. Much of the accompaniment is homophonic in structure, in support of these strong march themes. A characteristic of Berlioz is his predilection for complexity of rhythms and the layering of contrasting rhythms. A prime example can be found between M and O, where he combines the theme in the winds with an almost rhythmic chaos in the strings.

Unit 7: Form and Structure

SECTION	EVENT AND SCORING
Opening	Introduction: timpani, cello, and bass set up the tonality while brass, clarinet, and bassoon call in the distance
Theme 1	B–C: slow march stated in the strings; C–D: same string statement with solo oboe
Theme 1A	D to three measures after F; F major; slow march in woodwinds and upper strings with countermelody in the low strings
Theme 1	Three measures after F to H: slow march in pizzicato strings with bassoon solo accompaniment outlining the tonal center in straight eighth notes
Theme 2	H–K: main march theme stated in C major by winds and brass; strings have light accompaniment
Transition	K–M: small transition section followed by brief return to Theme 1
Theme 2	Repeated, M–O: march stated in winds and brass again but with complex string accompaniment this time
Transition	O–P: states original transition theme, then states the Theme 1 motive three times in the brass accompanied by ascending sextuplets and scales in the winds and strings
Theme 1	Repeated, Q to fermata before X: final statement of the opening march from Q–S followed by a large section in the tonal center of the theme

SECTION	EVENT AND SCORING
Coda	Fermata to the end: begins with the *idée fixe* in the clarinet followed by a series of chords in A major for a grandiose finish

Unit 8: Suggested Listening

Ludwig Van Beethoven, Symphony No. 6 ("Pastoral")
Hector Berlioz :
    Damnation of Faust
    Harold in Italy
    Symphonie fantastique
Franz Liszt, *Les Préludes*
Felix Mendelssohn, Symphony No. 4 ("Italian")
Bedřich Smetana, *Má Vlast*

Unit 9: Additional References and Resources

Berlioz, Hector, *New Letters of Berlioz*, Trans. by Jacques Barzun, New York: Columbia University Press, 1954.

Berlioz, Hector. *The Memoirs of Hector Berlioz, Member of the French Institute*. Trans. and ed. David Cairns. London: Granada, 1981.

Grout, Donald Jay, and Claude V. Palisca. *A History of Western Music*. 6th edition. New York: W. W. Norton & Company, 2001.

Sadie, Stanley, ed. *The New Grove Dictionary of Music and Musicians*. "Hector Berlioz." New York: Grove's Dictionaries, 2000. Also available online at www.grovemusic.com

Contributed by:

Rachel Dirks
Director of Orchestras
USD #373
Newton, Kansas

Teacher Resource Guide

Modus à 4

Shirl Jae Atwell
(b. 1949)

STRING ORCHESTRA

Unit 1: Composer

Shirl Jae Atwell was born in Kansas City, Missouri, in 1949. She earned a Bachelor of Music Education degree from Kansas State Teachers College and a Master of Music degree in Theory and Composition from the University of Louisville, where she studied composition with Nelson Keyes. She has also completed post-graduate work in composition at the University of South Carolina.

In 1984, Atwell received the Clifford Shaw Memorial Award for Kentucky Composers. In 1993, her scores were placed in the permanent collection of the Bibliothèque Internationale de Musique Contemporaine in Paris at the invitation of the Contemporary Music International Information Service. *Modus à 4* won the National School Orchestra Association composition contest in 1996.

Atwell is a string teacher in the Jefferson County Public Schools in Louisville, Kentucky.

Unit 2: Composition

Modus à 4 combines four different melodies in both a homophonic and contrapuntal setting. All four melodies combine in a rich, homophonic texture as the piece nears its completion.

Unit 3: Historical Perspective

Many pieces have entered the school orchestra repertoire because of contests that encouraged composers to write for student ensembles. *Modus à 4* was the

230

winning entry in the 1996 National School Orchestra Association contest, a competition that has been responsible for many pieces still in the school orchestra repertoire today.

Unit 4: Technical Considerations

Though listed at a Grade 3 level, there are few technical problems. Rhythms are simple, no syncopations exist, and the bowings are uncomplicated. The double bass part requires some shifting unless the bassist plays the optional notes an octave lower. The cello and first violin parts each require only one shift to fourth and third position, respectively. A quick change from pizzicato to arco at measure 54 occurs in the violin parts.

Unit 5: Stylistic Considerations

The lyricism of the melody and many of the accompaniments require a legato style of bowing. Care must be given to bring out the contrapuntal melodies and not let them be overpowered by the accompanying voices.

Unit 6: Musical Elements

The piece is written almost entirely in A natural minor. The "white-note" harmony and melody are almost completely diatonic; only two accidentals occur in the entire piece.

Unit 7: Form and Structure

THEME	MEASURES	EVENT AND SCORING
1	1	Theme in violin and viola
2	9	Theme in violin in counterpoint to Theme 1 in viola and cello
3	17	Theme in cello and bass
4	36	Theme in first violin; repeated in viola at m. 45
	54	Interlude
4	61	Fragment of Theme 4 as bridge
1–4	65	Contrapuntal treatment of all four themes: 1 in first violin, 2 in second violin, 4 in viola, 3 in cello; Themes 3 and 4 are fragmentary

Unit 8: Suggested Listening

Béla Bartók, 44 Violin Duos
Gustav Holst, *Brook Green Suite*
Ralph Vaughan Williams, "Fantasia on Greensleeves" from *Sir John in Love*

Unit 9: Additional References and Resources

Mayer, F. R., ed. *The String Orchestra Super List*. Reston, VA: Music
  Educators National Conference, 1993.

Contributed by:

David Littrell
Professor of Music
Kansas State University
Manhattan, Kansas

Teacher Resource Guide

"Russian Sailors' Dance" from the Red Poppy
Reinhold Glière
(1875–1956)

arranged by Merle Isaac

STRING ORCHESTRA AND FULL ORCHESTRA

Unit 1: Composer

Reinhold Moritsevich Glière was born in Kiev in 1875. At the Moscow Conservatory he studied violin with Hřímalý and theory and composition with Arensky and Ippolitov-Ivanov. From 1920 to 1941, he was Professor of Composition at the Moscow Conservatory and an important teacher who influenced leading Russian composers such as Sergei Prokofiev. He was also chairman of the organizing committee of the USSR Composers Union. Working in the Russian romantic tradition, Glière composed mostly in the large forms of opera, ballet, symphony, and symphonic poems. His intense interest in the folk music of Azerbaijan is demonstrated in his opera *Shah-Senem* of 1925. His ballet music is marked by brilliant color and pictorialism. *The Red Poppy* and *The Bronze Horseman* are still among the most popular ballets in Russia.

Unit 2: Composition

"Russian Sailors' Dance" is a fiery movement from Glière's popular ballet of 1927, *The Red Poppy*. It is distinctly Russian in its rhythmic impetuosity and nationalistic sound. The presentation is awkward and heavy to suggest Russian sailors attempting to negotiate intricate dance steps. As the orchestral power increases steadily and swiftly to a mad climax of excitement and exhilaration, the sailors manage to complete the dance with a desperate lunge aided by an enthusiastic rush in the orchestra. Its form is that of theme and variation, and Glière exhibits his talent for orchestration as virtually every instrument is featured. Composed in the romantic programmatic style, this selection is approximately three minutes in length and is a great concert finale.

Unit 3: Historical Perspective

The life of Reinhold Glière spanned a period containing three major world events: the Russian Revolution and World Wars I and II. With the formal proclamation of the Union of Soviet Socialist Republics in 1922, a new Russian state inherited the vast Czarist Empire that enveloped the whole of central Asia, including large numbers of peoples of differing nationalities, languages, and religions. Their composers eagerly embraced the rich folklore of the various peoples of this new union. In addition to Glière, who is deemed the greatest Ukrainian composer, Aram Khatchaturian applied the principles of the nineteenth century romantic nationalistic school to Armenian folk idioms in his ballet music for *Spartacus* and *Gayane*.

Unit 4: Technical Considerations

The Aeolian, Mixolydian, and Phrygian modes based on G are employed throughout this composition. Tonal centers are within easy reach of all instrument groups, especially winds and brass. Merle Isaac transposed the clarinet and trumpet parts to their natural keys of B-flat, and the French horns to F. The score is cross-cued for small groups or those lacking particular instruments. Solo indications in the score are used to highlight melodic material and are not to be taken literally as one on a part. First violins must play sixteenth note scalar passages covering two octaves at ninety-six beats per minute. Clarinet 2, bassoon, trombone 1, viola, cello, and double bass must play running eighth note passages, with quarter note = approximately 150. A one-octave chromatic scale is also required. Special attention should be given to the absolute placement of the bow on the string near the frog during offbeat rhythmic passages. The bow should be placed on the string on the primary beat and pulled away on the offbeat.

Unit 5: Stylistic Considerations

The accentuation of non-primary beats with a marcato style is used to depict the rough, unrefined personalities of Russian sailors. Legato and leggiero styles add to the derisive merriment of certain variations. Detached tonguing in the woodwinds must match pizzicato articulation in the string section. The upper strings must execute offbeats precisely at the frog; a metronome would be a good teaching aid. Dynamics encompass a wide range of intensity from *pianissimo* legato sections to *sfz-crescendo* explosions. Articulations are well marked in the score and must be accurately observed to elicit the Russian atmosphere of this programmatic composition based in nineteenth century romantic style.

Unit 6: Musical Elements

The introduction is based on G Phrygian followed by the main theme stated in G Aeolian mode. The variations use these modes as well as Mixolydian. Modes figure prominently in Central Asian folk music and impart a Russian flavor. The melodic structure is achieved mostly through diatonic means. Variations on the theme are not achieved through melodic alteration but rather through imaginative orchestration and changes of tempo. Countermelodic material does occur in the bass lines of Variations 5, 6, and 10. Obbligato embellishment is performed by first violin in Variation 3. Minor chromatic movement occurs in the introduction and coda. The composition ends triumphantly with a final G major chord.

Unit 7: Form and Structure

SECTION	MEASURES	EVENT AND SCORING
Opening	1–25	Introduction
Theme	26	Rehearsal 3
Variations 1–11	38	Each variation is twelve measures in length beginning at Rehearsal 4
Coda	160	Rehearsal 15 to end

Unit 8: Suggested Listening

Alexander Borodin, *On the Steppes of Central Asia*
Reinhold Glière:
   The Bronze Horseman
   Overture on Slav Themes
   Taras Bulba
Mikhail Ippolitov-Ivanov, *Caucasian Sketches*
Aram Khatchaturian, *Gayane* Ballet
Nikolai Rimsky-Korsakov, *Russian Easter Overture*
Peter Tchaikovsky, *Marche Slav*

Unit 9: Additional References and Resources

Hindley, Geoffrey, editor. *The Larousse Encyclopedia of Music*. New York: Barnes and Noble Books, 1994.

Longyear, Rey M. *Nineteenth-Century Romanticism in Music*. Englewood Cliffs, NJ: Prentice-Hall, 1973.

Piston, Walter. *Harmony*. New York: W. W. Norton & Company, 1962.

Sadie, Stanley, ed. *The New Grove Dictionary of Music and Musicians*. New
    York: Grove's Dictionaries, 2000. Also available online at
    www.grovemusic.com

Contributed by:

Kathleen DeBerry-Brungard
Orchestra Clinician/Adjudicator (retired)
Plano Senior High School
Plano, Texas

Teacher Resource Guide

Serenade for Strings

Robert Washburn
(b. 1928)

STRING ORCHESTRA

Unit 1: Composer

Robert Washburn was born in Bouckville, New York, in 1928. He received a
Ph.D. in Composition at the Eastman School of Music, where he worked with
Bernard Rogers, Alan Hovhaness, and Howard Hanson. He later studied with
Darius Milhaud at the Aspen Music School and with Nadia Boulanger in Paris.
After four years of service with the USAF as a member of the Air Force Band
of the West and the Air Force Sinfonietta, he earned his Bachelor's and Master's
degrees at the Crane School of Music of the State University of New York at
Potsdam. He joined the faculty there in 1954 and now serves as Dean Emeritus
and Senior Fellow in Music. As a composer, conductor, author, and teacher, he
has been active in the United States, Canada, Mexico, Europe, and the Middle
East. Washburn is the composer of more than 150 published works, which have
been performed by major professional symphonic, choral, and chamber groups
as well as many school and university organizations. He has received numerous
commissions and awards, including those from ASCAP, the Ford Foundation
administrated by the MENC, the Danforth Foundation, the Juilliard Repertory
Project, the Rockefeller Foundation, the U.S. Endowment for the Arts and
Humanities, and the Fulbright Commission.

Unit 2: Composition

The Juilliard School Repertory Project commissioned Washburn's Serenade
for Strings. This endeavor had as its objective the creation of works for school
and amateur performing groups that would be accessible to players of moderate technical skills without compromising contemporary stylistic resources.

He is the composer of many works for strings and utilizes his knowledge of the idiom as a string player to advantage. The use of tonalities that are congenial to string playing is notable, as is open string usage, which gives strong resonance to the pitches involved and frequent intonation checks.

Unit 3: Historical Perspective

The work is in four short movements making use primarily of classical forms. Compositions by Ralph Vaughan Williams, Gustav Holst, Benjamin Britten, David Diamond, and Paul Hindemith have served as models. The development of strong string programs in many American schools has been an incentive for Washburn to contribute to the rich literature for this medium. The need for works for strings has been emphasized by educators in recent years to provide the opportunity for string players to hear clearly what they are playing without the heavy doubling of the winds, which is heard in most compositions and arrangements for full orchestra at the school and amateur level.

Unit 4: Technical Considerations

The principal tonalities employed are C major, D major, G major, and E minor. The composer has given melodic statements to all of the instrumental parts that call for considerable independence from the players. Although performance by full string orchestra is preferable, the contrabass part is optional with some adjustment of *divisi* and double-stops in cello in the absence of bass. Rhythmic considerations are very basic and include syncopation, dotted-note values, conventional meters, and some use of ostinato. Range demands involve only the use of first position, except in the case of first violin, using third position at times.

Unit 5: Stylistic Considerations

Performance of the Serenade requires consideration of articulation, bowing relationship to articulation, expression, and phrasing. A warm, singing tone is appropriate for the legato portions of the work, while a more aggressive marcato style is appropriate for the rhythmically incisive sections. In staccato passages, the notes should be slightly separated, with repeated eighth note accompaniment passages metronomically precise. Careful balance between the parts should be maintained as the melodic passages are exchanged in the various sections of the string orchestra.

Unit 6: Musical Elements

Rhythmically the work employs conventional meters. The principal tonalities are major and minor, although modal scales and harmonies are sometimes employed. There are occasional uses of bitonal chords in accompaniment patterns. There is also some use of quartal harmonies and extended tertian chords. The dynamic range extends from *pp* to *ff*. Texturally there is considerable use of canonic imitation.

Unit 7: Form and Structure

The four movements of the Serenade for Strings are in neoclassic forms, principally ABA or ABACA rondo. The first movement, marked "Allegro con moto," employs a song-like theme initially heard played by first violin and restated at letter A in cello with melodic alterations. The middle section at letter B is to be played somewhat slower, with second violin, viola, and cello separating the notes slightly. At letter C the first theme returns, this time heard canonically in first violin, cello, and bass. The movement comes to a close with a delicate *diminuendo e poco ritardando*.

The second movement is in a simple ABA form with a bitonal flavor in the A sections. The middle section is imitative two-part counterpoint between the lower and upper strings. In the return of the A section, the bitonal scheme resumes but resolves agreeably on a final D major chord.

The third movement again employs the three-part rondo form in a reflective mood marked "Adagietto." The prevailing tonality is D minor, although the contrasting middle section moves to E minor and is a three-voice fugato. At letter K, after a brief *poco rit.*, the principal section returns to cadence finally on a D major chord. The concluding movement, marked "Allegro vivo," is in a more extended rondo form, ABACABA, with inverted variants of the theme presented.

Unit 8: Suggested Listening

Benjamin Britten, *Simple Symphony*
Paul Hindemith, educational pieces
Gustav Holst, *St. Paul's Suite*
Robert Washburn:
    Queen Noor Suite
    Sinfonietta for String Orchestra

Unit 9: Additional References and Resources

ASCAP Biographical Dictionary. New York: R. R. Bowker Company, 1980.

Hitchcock, H. Wiley, and Stanley Sadie. *The New Grove Dictionary of American Music*. London: Macmillan, 1986.

Sigma Alpha Iota. Composers Bureau Online:
    http://www.sai-national.org/phil/composers/compaz.html

Slonimsky, Nicolas. ed. emeritus. *Baker's Biographical Dictionary of Musicians*. New York: Schirmer Books, 2001.

Contributed by:

Robert Washburn
Dean Emeritus and Senior Fellow in Music
Crane School of Music
State University of New York at Potsdam
Potsdam, New York

Teacher Resource Guide

St. Lawrence Overture

Robert Washburn
(b. 1928)

FULL ORCHESTRA

Unit 1: Composer

Robert Washburn was born in Bouckville, New York, in 1928. He received a Ph.D. in Composition at the Eastman School of Music, where he worked with Bernard Rogers, Alan Hovhaness, and Howard Hanson. He later studied with Darius Milhaud at the Aspen Music School and with Nadia Boulanger in Paris. After four years of service with the USAF as a member of the Air Force Band of the West and the Air Force Sinfonietta, he earned his Bachelor's and Master's degrees at the Crane School of Music of the State University of New York at Potsdam. He joined the faculty there in 1954 and now serves as Dean Emeritus and Senior Fellow in Music. As a composer, conductor, author, and teacher, he has been active in the United States, Canada, Mexico, Europe, and the Middle East.

Washburn is the composer of more than 150 published works, which have been performed by major professional symphonic, choral, and chamber groups as well as many school and university organizations. He has received numerous commissions and awards, including those from ASCAP, the Ford Foundation administrated by the MENC Danforth Foundation, the Juilliard Repertory Project, the Rockefeller Foundation, the U.S. Endowment for the Arts and Humanities, and the Fulbright Commission.

Unit 2: Composition

St. Lawrence Overture was written during Washburn's year-long Ford Foundation/MENC Young Composers' Grant in 1960, which he spent in Elkhart, Indiana, writing for school and community groups. The work is thought to be descriptive of a boat excursion on the St. Lawrence River, with the varied passing scenery being suggested in mood rather than actual description. At times the feeling is pastoral, while at other times the listener's creative imagination infers a suggestion of the busy passage through Montreal. The themes are all original with the composer, although some of the thematic material is folk-like.

Unit 3: Historical Perspective

The Ford Foundation/MENC grants mentioned earlier were awarded to twelve emerging composers to place them in direct contact with the school and community groups for which they were composing. The intent was to give them the experience of working with the actual performers of their compositions and, thus, develop a more realistic approach to their art. It was also hoped that the program would produce a body of contemporary literature for moderately advanced players without artistic compromise, which was felt to be lacking at the time. This became a reality as the various works of the composers were published and widely heard.

Washburn has continued to produce works of this level for full orchestra, string orchestra, band, chamber, and choral groups along with others intended for more advanced professional-level ensembles.

Unit 4: Technical Considerations

Washburn's principal considerations were to make the work accessible to less-advanced players without sacrificing aspects of a contemporary sound in melody, harmony, and rhythm. This meant staying within the practical ranges of the instruments: first violin uses first and third positions; second violin, viola, cello, and bass stay in first position; woodwinds and brass remain in their safe ranges; instruments that might be less strong or missing are doubled and cued; syncopation, rhythmic displacement, rapid articulation, and other devices are employed that are challenging but not beyond the ability of younger players. Washburn used easier major keys and scales, such as G, C, and F, but with various chromatic notes used for more colorful harmonies and in modal passages.

Unit 5: Stylistic Considerations

In this work, the stylistic considerations for the players are conventional: standard bowing techniques for the strings include legato singing style, staccato for rhythmic incisiveness, and marcato for emphasis. Players use pizzicato and spiccato. Woodwinds and brass have prominent parts, many of them solo passages. Short percussion solos give additional color. Dynamic considerations are traditional, ranging from p to ff.

Unit 6: Musical Elements

Regarding the elements of rhythm, harmony, and melody, the focus is on contemporary materials that are quite accessible to players and audiences. Rhythmically, the meters are straightforward 2/4 and 4/4 with considerable syncopation and other offbeat accent patterns. Harmonically, there are borrowed triads from other keys, triads that shift out of the principal key frequently while accompanying tonal melodies. In addition to Washburn's use of bitonality, there are also extended tertian chords (such as sevenths, ninths, and elevenths), use of superimposed triads, quartal chords, a brief whole-tone harmonization of a major scale melody, and modal harmonizations. These devices give a feeling of a twentieth century sound without excessive dissonance. Melodically, the themes are folk-like and, in some cases, modal.

Unit 7: Form and Structure

SECTION	MEASURES	EVENT AND SCORING
A	1–6	Introduction; the rhythmic figure—two sixteenths/eighth—recurs throughout the piece as a unifying element; followed by a unison scale and a quartal "pyramid" leading to a reversal of the opening rhythmic figure in the percussion
B		First theme in G Mixolydian mode is stated by oboe over a quarter note string accompaniment of parallel sixths in Dorian, an example of polymodality; nine measures after letter B, the theme is repeated by violin in C major; followed by a brief contrasting theme in the woodwinds; principal theme returns nine measures after letter B in violin harmonized by parallel triads borrowed from other keys in the lower strings and brass
C		Four measures before letter C, the first two measures of the principal theme are heard as an ostinato, joined at letter C by viola and cello playing a secondary theme, which is actually the inversion of the principal theme in augmentation; at letter D, the main theme returns in augmentation with a

SECTION	MEASURES	EVENT AND SCORING
		countermelody in oboe and clarinet; opening measures of the main theme are heard repeated, played by oboe harmonized with parallel thirds from the whole-tone scale; at letter F, the theme is heard played by the trumpet with contrapuntal F major scales that begin beneath the melody, pass through it, rise above it, and then descend through it to the lower instruments
D		A simplified version of the middle part of the first theme section is heard in the key of F major while the bass instruments alternately play B-natural and F-sharp; this suggests a tonic-dominant progress in B major, suggesting a polytonal relationship that is a diminished fifth from the tonal center of F
E		The "Marziale moderato" marking begins the middle section of the piece with a new theme in F Mixolydian accompanied by parallel triads that are borrowed from other keys; after a contrasting middle section with trumpet solo, the Mixolydian theme returns canonically
F		The "head" of the theme becomes a foreshadowing of the return of the A section of the piece at Tempo I, which is accompanied by mixed tertial and quartal chords; at letter J, the short contrasting theme is heard in rhythmic displacement—the same pitches as formerly but with a different and highly syncopated rhythmic pattern; at letter K, the structure is similar to that referred to above in section C, but the ostinato is heard in cello below the melody, which is played by violin and flute; this continues until nine measures

SECTION	MEASURES	EVENT AND SCORING
		after letter L when two successive canonic versions of the theme are heard, the second being double canon by augmentation
G		In the final section of the piece, the two main themes are heard contrapuntally; in the last four measures, the opening theme is heard being played simultaneously in its original form and in augmentation; the rhythmic pattern heard at the work's beginning is then heard in the percussion, bringing the work to a close

Unit 8: Suggested Listening

Aaron Copland, *Appalachian Spring*
Gustav Holst, First Suite for Band in E-flat
Darius Milhaud, *Suite Française*
Robert Washburn, Symphony for Band

Unit 9: Additional References and Resources

ASCAP Biographical Dictionary. New York: R. R. Bowker, 1980.

Sadie, Stanley, ed. *The New Grove Dictionary of Music and Musicians*. New York: Grove's Dictionaries, 2000. Also available online at www.grovemusic.com

Sigma Alpha Iota. Composers Bureau Online: http://www.sai-national.org/phil/composers/compaz.html

Slonimsky, Nicolas. *Baker's Biographical Dictionary of Musicians*. New York: Schirmer Books, 1991.

Contributed by:

Robert Washburn
Dean Emeritus and Senior Fellow in Music
State University of New York at Potsdam
Potsdam, New York

Teacher Resource Guide

Stringtown Stroll

Doris Gazda
(b. 1934)

STRING ORCHESTRA

Unit 1: Composer

Doris Gazda graduated from the Eastman School of Music and Penn State University with concentrations in violin and music education. She played professionally in Rochester, New York, and Washington, DC, and taught instrumental music in the Montgomery County, Maryland public schools. She founded and conducted two youth orchestras that have grown and flourished over the years. She served as national president of the National School Orchestra Association and as a board member for ASTA with NSOA. Gazda has written numerous published works for string and full orchestra and is co-author of *Spotlight on String, Levels 1 and 2*, string method books for beginning and intermediate players. She also composed *High Tech for Strings*, a recently published technique book for string ensemble or individual instruction.

Unit 2: Composition

Gazda composed *Stringtown Stroll* for the students in her string classes. Two of her schools were connected by Stringtown Road, a windy country lane that she traversed when traveling from her morning to her afternoon schools. Occasionally, it became a wonderful spot for taking a stroll under the giant trees that lined the road. It seemed natural to give the title *Stringtown Stroll* to the easygoing melody. Written in the style of a swing band tune, this work gives young string musicians the opportunity to experience the feel and sound of jazz without an overabundance of complexity. It contains a touch of improvisational style and could be performed in such a way that actual improvisation would occur. Because string students rarely experience playing jazz, *Stringtown Stroll* gives them a unique opportunity to explore this important musical genre.

Unit 3: Historical Perspective

Jazz originated in New Orleans towards the end of the nineteenth century within the African-American population. Combining the styles of African music with Christian hymns gave rise to singing spirituals with their strong rhythmic emphasis and repetitive phrases. The work songs and spirituals of the African-Americans that developed into the "blues" were generally sad songs containing a characteristic lowering of the third and seventh tones of the scale. These tones were called "blue notes." The scale usually had other alterations and omissions that vary from piece to piece. The style depended on playing by ear and improvising on the melodies rather than playing from a written score. When small orchestral groups started playing the songs and spirituals, they used the name "jazz" to describe the music.

Among the first published blues pieces were "Memphis Blues" and "St. Louis Blues" written by cornettist and band leader W. C. Handy. Blues, with its new name, "jazz," traveled quickly to Memphis, Chicago, and New York. By 1935, some of the jazz orchestras had grown to number fifteen players and were called swing bands. "Swing" was the word used to describe the rhythmic characteristics of the dance music that these groups played. The swing bands were made up of saxophones, trumpets, trombones, keyboard, rhythm, string bass and, occasionally, a few violins. Some of the famous musicians of the swing era of jazz were Count Basie, Lionel Hampton, Benny Goodman, and Glenn Miller.

Unit 4: Technical Considerations

Stringtown Stroll is written in the syncopated style of jazz and is meant to be played with a strong swing beat. Understanding and performing the rhythmic figures that depend upon a syncopated style present the primary technical problems. Syncopation, which can be defined simply as either the removal of an accent where you expect it or placing an accent where you least expect it, requires learning the bowing skills needed to play accents on weak beats and keep the bow poised and ready following a rest. Cello and bass need to keep a steady beat while playing the "walking bass" line. In addition, the pairs of eighth notes need to swing into the feel of a triple rhythm with the first eighth note of the pair receiving 2/3 of the beat. The eighth note pairs in swing style can be learned by practicing on scales with hooked bowing. To play the final chord of the piece correctly, the entire orchestra needs to learn how to play *tremolo sul ponticello* at the tip of the bow.

Unit 5: Stylistic Considerations

Meant to be played at a relaxed tempo, the composition should convey the easygoing style of a big swing band. In the middle section, the melody in violin provides the feel of improvisation above a steady bass beat. It would be in keeping with the style for one or two members of the orchestra to improvise on the melody line between measures 19 and 27. It would also be entirely appropriate to add a rhythm section and brass or woodwind instruments to the entire piece. This opportunity to improvise will encourage students to experiment and experience the freedom that is appropriate to jazz.

Unit 6: Musical Elements

The melody is a simple, song-like tune accompanied by a repetitive rhythmic figure. After being played by the violin section, the melody repeats in the tenor voice played by the viola section. The violin section then plays an eight-measure section that sounds like improvisation. Care should be taken throughout to maintain the "swing" feel in the eighth note passages. Except for the central eight-measure section, the bass line sustains a steady rhythmic and harmonic pattern that is called a "walking bass" line. When working on intonation while moving from one seventh chord to another, practicing the progressions with slow, sustained chords will be most helpful.

Unit 7: Form and Structure

SECTION	EVENT AND SCORING
Opening	Introduction of two measures
Theme 1	Eight-measure melody in the treble instruments accompanied by the "walking bass" line
Theme 1	Repeated; melody played by viola and cello with syncopated chords in the treble lines
Theme 2	Eight-measure, improvisation-style melody with seventh chord progression in the accompaniment
Theme 1	Repeated
Theme 2	Repeated
Theme 1	Repeated
Tag ending	Final chord is a ninth chord played *tremolo sul ponticello*

Unit 8: Suggested Listening

Reissues of big band recordings from the Swing Era (Benny Goodman, Glen Miller, Lionel Hampton, and Count Basie)

Unit 9: Additional References and Resources

Davis, Adam. "Jazz for String Players." *The Instrumentalist,* November 1999.

"Going Native: The Turtle Island String Quartet." *The Strad*, December 1996.

Lieberman, Julie Lyon. *Improvising Violin*. Woodstock, NY: Homespun Tapes, Ltd., 1988.

Contributed by:
Doris Gazda
Composer, Retired Teacher/Professor
Tempe, Arizona

Teacher Resource Guide

Symphony No. 1 in C Minor, Movement 4

Johannes Brahms
(1833–1897)

arranged by Vernon Leidig

FULL ORCHESTRA

Unit 1: Composer/Arranger

Johannes Brahms was the son of a double bass player. He was born in Hamburg, Germany, on May 7, 1833. He received his first music lessons from his father and later studied piano with Otto Cossel and Eduard Marxsen. Because of his family's poverty, Brahms had to earn a living playing piano in disreputable taverns as a young man. He also taught piano during this time, and began to compose songs, piano pieces, and his first piano trio. In 1853, he toured Germany with Hungarian violinist Eduard Reményi. This tour and his association with Reményi left him with a lifelong love for gypsy and Hungarian folk music. Through Reményi, Brahms met and was influenced by Robert and Clara Schumann. From 1857 to 1860, Brahms was part-time music master to the Prince of Lippe-Detmold; from 1860 to 1863, he led a chorus in Hamburg; and from 1863 to 1864, he directed the concerts of the *Singakademie* in Vienna. After 1863, his ever-increasing popularity as a composer went hand in hand with increasingly significant appointments and honors. His *Variations on a Theme by Haydn, German Requiem, Hungarian Dances*, and his First Symphony put him in the front rank of orchestral composers of his generation.

Most of his mature years were spent in Vienna or in nearby mountain resorts. He contracted a cold while attending Clara Schumann's funeral in

250

1896 that aggravated the cancer of the liver from which he had suffered for several years. After he attended his last concert on March 7, 1897—a performance of his Fourth Symphony—he fell more gravely ill and died on April 3, 1897, in Vienna.

The arranger of this work, Vernon Leidig, is Professor Emeritus of Music at California State University–Los Angeles, where he has received the Outstanding Professor Award for teaching, scholarship, research, and professional advancement. His previous experience includes teaching instrumental music in the secondary schools in Los Angeles, where his teaching principles earned him a Certificate of Merit from the United States Department of State. Well known throughout the United States as a clinician, adjudicator, and conductor, Leidig has published many music education materials, including college texts and magazine articles, as well as numerous arrangements for school and community orchestras and bands.

Unit 2: Composition

Fourteen years elapsed from the time Brahms started making his sketches for his First Symphony until its completion. Brahms was quite intimidated by the genius of Beethoven. "You will never know how the likes of us feel when we hear the tramp of a giant like Beethoven behind us," he wrote in 1862. The symphony was finished in 1876 when Brahms was forty-three, at a time when his creative personality was fully matured. This symphony is now one of the world's most popular symphonies because of its glorious lyrical passages and magnificent broad lines. As in the original finale, the arrangement begins with the famous Alpine horn call, followed by the primary themes of the movement. This arrangement omits the difficult technical passages of the original while still keeping the integrity of the movement intact.

Unit 3: Historical Perspective

The first sketches of Symphony No. 1 were started in 1862 during the American Civil War, and the symphony was completed in 1876, the year Bell invented the telephone. When Brahms began writing this symphony, he gave his first public performance as a pianist in Vienna on November 16, 1862. During this time, Brahms met Richard Wagner and was influenced by the latter's *Die Meistersinger*. While writing his First Symphony, Brahms was active in the concert hall and in composing other works. The Karlsruhe Orchestra conducted by Dessoff performed the symphony for the first time on November 4, 1876. Brahms himself conducted the symphony on November 15, 1876, in Munich with the Munich Orchestra. This symphony has been compared to Beethoven's Ninth Symphony because of the similarity of themes in the finales of both works. Most musicologists agree that Brahms's First Symphony is more closely aligned in spirit and technique with Beethoven's Fifth

Symphony. Hans von Bülow called it the "Tenth Symphony" to indicate that Brahms was the symphonic heir to Beethoven. Von Bülow also coined the phrase "the three B's" to associate Brahms with Beethoven and Bach.

Unit 4: Technical Considerations

Leidig's arrangement begins with the upper strings muted at measure 4, with all the mutes removed at letter B (measure 34). The violins leave first position for the first time at measure 66. First violins are required to shift throughout the piece, but this is certainly not beyond the limits of the average high school violinist and well within the limits of a Grade 3 selection. Second violins must leave first position at measure 71 and again at measure 90; however, at measure 90, the notes are doubled an octave lower. The violas never leave first position. The cellos have shifts in two places; otherwise, their high notes can be played with extensions. Double bass shifts are always doubled at the octave.

Rhythmically, there is nothing more difficult than eighth notes. At the coda, the meter shifts from 4/4 to *alla breve* and the eighth notes become sixteenth notes; however, this is definitely not beyond the limits of a Grade 3 orchestra. There are no rhythms in this piece that students in a Grade 3 orchestra have not previously seen, and there is little that will pose any problem. The wind/percussion writing is well within the limits of Grade 3 and will pose little difficulty to the average high school woodwind, brass, or percussion player.

The tonality of this movement is firmly in C major. The primary challenge of this piece will be for the conductor to lead the students in a precise performance. There are ample opportunities for the students to not play together—especially during the pizzicato section at letter C (measure 51) against the legato playing of the winds. Another section that will present similar problems will be at the *alla breve* section of the coda. The precision here must be exact to achieve the marcato effect the arranger desires.

Unit 5: Stylistic Considerations

This composition falls squarely in the romantic period and, as such, should be interpreted as a lush and dramatic piece. The strings will need to use a well-defined bow arm to perform the legato passages smoothly and effectively. The dynamics in this piece range from *pp* to *ff*, and there is ample opportunity for the brass to show its robust nature. This piece can be made effective by emphasizing the dynamics to bring about the contrasts that the arranger intended. In the *alla breve* section of the coda, there will be a tendency for the brass to overblow and become raucous. In the last few measures, the dynamics are *f* to *ff* with sustained chords for an extended period of time. Much care should be taken here to avoid poor tone quality and poor balance in the brass section of the orchestra.

Unit 6: Musical Elements

Because this is an arrangement of such a famous composition, the harmonies, melodies, rhythms, and timbres in this piece are straightforward, with no surprises. The usefulness of this arrangement, and others like it, is to provide an opportunity for the student musician to gain an understanding of the major themes and kinds of rhythms in the work before moving on to the original composition. This arrangement presents these themes and rhythms very effectively while omitting the very technical aspects of the original, which would cause the work to be unplayable by less-mature student musicians.

Unit 7: Form and Structure

SECTION	EVENT AND SCORING
Introduction	"Più Andante"; chorale-like introduction that features the winds, especially French horn, in C major; ends on a G^7 chord at m. 33
Theme 1	"Allegro Non Troppo"; the most famous theme of this movement; begins in the strings in the lower register at m. 34, with a light woodwind/French horn accompaniment; theme shift at m. 49 to the winds, with the strings accompanying pizzicato
Theme 2	Theme begins at D (m. 64), marked "animato"; also in C major, stated by the full orchestra; this theme, marked "fortissimo," is very dramatic, in contrast to the first theme; uses motives from Theme 1
Theme 3	Starting at m. 78, there is a shift in the mood of the piece to a more subdued, less dramatic feel; however, the tempo remains "animato"; dynamics change to softer tones; strings state this theme; at letter F (m. 92), the tempo becomes slower and the piece becomes more introspective as the arranger makes a transition back to Theme 1; again, strings state this transition with the woodwinds/French horn in accompaniment until the Dal Segno at m. 103
Coda	The jump to the coda comes at m. 75, after the restatement of Theme 2; the coda starts with staccato quarter notes in all instruments, ending the G major tonality from Theme 2 and leading to C major at the *alla breve* in m. 107
Theme 4	Introduced at m. 107 in the strings—a staccato theme marked "Più Allegro" (marcato); woodwinds answer in m. 112, and dialogue between the woodwinds and the strings ensues until m. 119 when the winds take over the

SECTION   EVENT AND SCORING

theme for four measures; at letter G (m. 123), the tempo suddenly changes to "Broad"—slower with no *ritard*. To anticipate the tempo change; from this point until the end, the orchestra is playing a chorale reminiscent of the introduction but not using the same thematic material; restatement of Theme 4 in the strings at letter H (m. 149) until m. 155, where there is a typical romantic symphonic ending played by the entire orchestra

Unit 8: Suggested Listening

Ludwig van Beethoven, Symphony No. 5 in C Minor

Johannes Brahms:

     Symphony No. 1 in C Minor

     Symphony No. 2 in D Major

     Variations on a Theme by Haydn

Richard Wagner, Overture to *Die Meistersinger*

Unit 9: Additional References and Resources

Ewen, David. *The Complete Book of Classical Music.* Englewood Cliffs, NJ: Prentice-Hall, Inc., 1965.

Grout, Donald Jay, and Claude V. Palisca. *A History of Western Music.* 6th edition. New York: W. W. Norton & Company, 2001.

Hadow, Sir W. H. *Studies in Modern Music.* Port Washington, NY: Kennikat Press, 1970.

Musgrave, Michael. *The Music of Brahms.* Boston: Routledge & Paul Kegan, 1985.

Randel, Don, ed. *The New Harvard Dictionary of Music.* Cambridge, MA: Harvard University Press, 1986.

Contributed by:

William Dyson
Elementary Strings Specialist
Atlanta Public Schools
Atlanta, Georgia

Teacher Resource Guide

Ten Pieces for Children
Béla Bartók
(1881–1945)

arranged by Leo Weiner

STRING ORCHESTRA

Unit 1: Composer

Béla Bartók is recognized as a composer, ethnomusicologist, and pianist. He was born in Nagyszentmiklós, Hungary (now Sinnicolau Mare, Romania) on March 25, 1881. His father was director of an agricultural school and was also an amateur musician who played the cello and piano. His mother, a pianist, gave Bartók his first piano lesson at age five. Bartók's father died when he was young, and his mother was forced to support the family by giving piano lessons.

In 1894, the family moved to Pozsony (Bratislava), where Bartók studied piano and theory. He entered the Budapest Academy of Music in 1899 to study piano and composition. He did not complete his studies in Budapest until 1903 because of illness. Early influences on his compositions came from Liszt, Wagner, Debussy, and Richard Strauss. He was also influenced by the growing sense of Hungarian nationalism. He began to wear national dress and opposed the use of German by his family for everyday language.

In 1905, Bartók made contact with Zoltán Kodály who had recently published his first study of folk music. They began a lifelong collaboration to record and popularize the folk music of Hungary. In 1907, Bartók was appointed as a professor of piano at the Budapest Academy of Music, which allowed him to settle in Hungary and continue his research. He also began to collect Slovak and Romanian songs. Also in 1907, he discovered the pentatonic origins of Hungarian peasant song as well as the old modal scales. His research

inspired his first folk song arrangements, which include the piano pieces for children (1908–09) and the Ten Easy Pieces (1908). The first of his compositions that synthesized the folk song and art music was the First String Quartet in 1908. By 1918, Bartók had collected 2,721 Hungarian, 3,500 Romanian, and 3,000 Slovak folk songs.

Often ill both as a child and an adult, Bartók's physical condition left him unfit to serve in World War I, and he continued to compose. After the war, Bartók was unable to travel where he wanted for his research because of the political situation in Hungary. In 1920, he was accused of a lack of patriotism. This caused Bartók to consider emigration, but he found himself unable to do so.

By that time, Bartók's music was recognized internationally; he spent the next few years touring as a performer and an accompanist. His success in Europe also improved his standing in Hungary. Bartók continued to compose and also publish collections of folk songs, some in collaboration with Kodály. He also published a number of articles on the influence of folk songs. In 1934, he was dismissed from his teaching position at the Budapest Academy of Music, and the Hungarian Academy of Sciences commissioned him to publish a Hungarian folk song collection.

In the early 1930s, Bartók took a stand against fascism and was attacked in the Hungarian and Romanian newspapers. In 1940, the Bartóks left for the United States. Columbia University awarded him an honorary Ph.D. in 1940, and for the next two years he continued folk song research for the university. After 1942, Bartók's health began to fail from leukemia; he died in New York City in 1945.

Unit 2: Composition

During 1908 and 1909, Bartók wrote a four-volume series of eighty-five pieces for children. These pieces were influenced by Hungarian and Slovakian folk songs. The series, titled *Gyermekeknek, sz. 42*, was revised in 1945 using only seventy-nine pieces. *Ten Pieces for Children*, arranged for young orchestras by Leo Weiner, is from this series.

Unit 3: Historical Perspective

Music in the nineteenth century was characterized by a growing sense of nationalism. Often the music reflected melodic ideas and rhythms rather than folk songs themselves. In the early part of the twentieth century, Kodály and Bartók were concerned that the original folk songs might be lost as people began to move and communications improved. They collaborated in an extensive research project to record the folk music of Hungary, and Bartók enlarged his study to include Slovak and Romanian songs. Using the newest technology available to him, Bartók began traveling throughout the countryside making recordings using an Edison phonograph. His research inspired his first folk song arrangements.

Unit 4: Technical Considerations

Rhythm studies with a variety of bowing patterns and bowing styles will help prepare the students for this composition. Exercises in simple double-stops and pizzicato chord playing will be helpful for chord playing. The work is scored for violin I, II, and III (ossia viola), cello, and bass (*ad lib.*). The viola part is identical to the third violin part with the exception of being notated in the alto clef. First violin and cello parts encompass the first four positions and provide young players with excellent opportunities for short-term position work. The second violin part is playable in first position with the exception of two notes. Third violin and viola parts are playable in first position for violin and requires only a fourth finger extension for viola. The bass part requires first through fourth positions. Bowing is marked, but no fingerings are provided.

Unit 5: Stylistic Considerations

Preparatory listening to Hungarian, Romanian, and Slovakian folk music will help students to understand and interpret the music. The bowing as marked is essential to the stylistic interpretation, as are the designated fluctuations in tempos and dynamics.

Unit 6: Musical Elements

No key signatures are provided in any of the pieces, and accidentals are numerous. The pieces range in tempo from Andante to Vivace. Tonality is major, minor, and modal. The pieces are all in simple meter, the first nine in 2/4 and the tenth in 4/4. Accents, as well as note values, create a syncopated effect in many of the pieces. Each piece requires a wide range of dynamic contrast.

Unit 7: Form and Structure

The pieces feature regular phrase patterns in ABABA or ABBABBA form. Number 6 is a canon.

Number 1	Andante grazioso; sixteen measures in length; tonal center of C
Number 2	Vivace; five-note melody patterns in ABCABC form with C being *ritardando*; tonal center of C
Number 3	Moderato sostenuto; tonal center of A; two-measure patterns repeated
Number 4	Allegro robusto; tonal center of A; four-measure patterns repeated
Number 5	Allegretto; tonal center of G; four- and six-measure phrases alternated
Number 6	Vivace risoluto; tonal center of E; canon in six-measure phrases

Number 7	Poco Allegro; tonal center of G; six-measure phrase patterns
Number 8	Allegro giocoso; tonal center of D; seven-measure phrases alternate with five-measure patterns of *poco ritardando/a tempo*
Number 9	Andante sostenuto; tonal center of F; three-measure patterns; ABBAABBA
Number 10	Risoluto; tonal center of G; unifying rhythmic patterns with syncopation

Unit 8: Suggested Listening

Béla Bartók:
> *Mikrokosmos*
> *Music for Strings, Percussion, and Celesta*
> *Ten Easy Pieces for Piano*

Zoltán Kodály, *Háry János Suite*

Unit 9: Additional References and Resources

Grout, Donald J., and Claude V. Palisca. *A History of Western Music*. 6th edition. New York: W. W. Norton & Company, 2001.

Randall, Don Michael, ed. *The Harvard Biographical Dictionary of Music*. Cambridge: HarvardUniversity Press, 1996.

Sadie, Stanley, ed. *The New Harvard Dictionary of Music*. Cambridge: Harvard University Press, 1986.

Slonimsky, Nicholas, ed. *Baker's Biographical Dictionary of Music and Musicians*. 8th edition. New York: Macmillan, Inc., 1992.

Stevens, Halsey. *The Life and Music of Béla Bartók*. New York: Oxford University Press, 1953.

Contributed by:

Mary Lou Jones
Shawnee Mission South High School
Shawnee Mission, Kansas

Teacher Resource Guide

Vier Kleine Stücke

Karel Husa
(b. 1921)

STRING ORCHESTRA

Unit 1: Composer

Karel Husa is a Pulitzer Prize winner and was a professor at Cornell University until his retirement in 1992. He was born in Prague in 1921, and he has been an American citizen since 1959. Husa studied at the Prague Conservatory and the Academy of Music. He continued his studies in Paris and received diplomas from the Paris National Conservatory. His teachers include Arthur Honegger, Nadia Boulanger, Jaraslave Ridky, and conductor Andre Cluytens.

Husa's String Quartet No. 3 received the 1969 Pulitzer Prize. His *Music for Prague 1968* is known both in orchestral and band versions. It has had over eight thousand performances worldwide. Husa's musical language is contemporary, with driving rhythms and rich, modern harmonies. Bitonality and the use of modes are often a part of his tonal vocabulary.

Unit 2: Composition

Vier Kleine Stücke (Four Small Pieces) was composed in 1955 for string orchestra. The movements have metronome markings and timings, and are entitled "Variazioni," "Notturno," "Furiant," and "Coda." The longest and most complicated is "Variazioni," which is seven minutes and thirty seconds long. Titles of the variations are Thema, à la Marcia, à la Gavotta, à la Elegia, à la Siciliana, à la Danza, and Finale. The Notturno, marked "Adagio" is two minutes and forty-five seconds long. The Furiant (Czech danza), marked "Allegretto," lasts two minutes and thirty seconds, and leads attacca to the Coda, marked "Maestoso," which lasts only one minute and forty-five seconds.

Unit 3: Historical Perspective

This work shows the influence of early twentieth century masters Stravinsky and Bartók. It also has the ethnic folk characteristics of other Czech composers—Smetana and Dvořák—from the nineteenth century. The driving rhythms and modal scale forms used here hark back to even more primitive times. The overall effect of the piece, however, is modern and contemporary. Some sections even feel like modern jazz or rock.

Unit 4: Technical Considerations

Violin parts do not go beyond first position; viola does use some treble clef, but it stays mostly in first position. The cello and bass parts will require shifting. Unless you have five-string basses or extensions, basses will have to transpose some low notes up an octave. All parts are active; all instruments get an opportunity for melody and harmony. The challenges in this music will be rhythm, style, tone, and emotion. Dynamic contrasts, mood, and tempo changes will challenge the conductor and ensemble. Key centers include mixed modal scales in E and a closing movement in C minor. The muted siciliana of the first movement pits first violin in C Lydian mode against the rest of the strings in the F-sharp Lydian mode. There is no bowing or editing in this music. It uses the string technique of *sul ponticello*, and mutes are required.

Unit 5: Stylistic Considerations

In the first movement, there are six different stylistic variations. The opening theme is a canon in legato style; other variations are march, gavotte, elegy, siciliana, and a dance. The second movement, "Notturno" (evening song), is muted, legato, and dark. The third movement, "Furiant," is a Bohemian folk dance in which two-beat and three-beat patterns alternate. It is followed by a trio and *da capo*. The final Coda is marked "Maestoso and largamente." It is deliberate, heavy, and esoteric.

Unit 6: Musical Elements

Husa's opening theme of the variation movement is in E minor mixed mode. The Dorian and Phrygian modes are possible because both F-natural and F-sharp are present. The cadence at the end of the theme adds to the mixed mode feeling: on beat one it is an A major triad but moves on beat three to a suspension or half cadence. The following march is clearly in C major. The melody is related to the first theme in that intervals have been inverted and rhythms are twice as fast. The next variation, a gavotte, is in G major. The elegy has open harmonies and is very chromatic. It ends with dissonant pizzicatos. Bitonality is used in the siciliana. The first violin tune is in C with an F-sharp as part of the scale, resulting in the Lydian mode. The seven sharps of the other string parts are also in Lydian, the tonic being F-sharp. The harmony and scale forms of this section will be a challenge for most ensembles.

Variation 5 is a dance starting in a key center of C with a middle section of G Lydian and closing with a C major chord. A canon closes out the finale section, with the first theme now transposed a fifth higher. The first movement closes with an E Dorian sound. The second movement, "Notturno," is chromatic and dissonant, ending with a perfect fourth. "Furiant," the third movement, begins and ends in C major; the middle section is a trio in G major. The final movement, "Coda," is clearly in C minor with a final chord of C major.

Unit 7: Form and Structure

SECTION   EVENT AND SCORING

Variation 1:
Thema   Eleven measures long with two phrases, grouped by five
                   measures plus six measures; five measures in canon; thema
                   also a canon
Marcia   Two phrases, each eleven measures
Gavotta   Two phrases, each eight measures
Elegia   Chorale-like; odd groupings separated by fermata
Siciliana   Triple meter; song-like tunes in contrasting tonalities
Danza   Three sections; unison rhythms; secco melody; return
Finale   Theme in canon

Variation 2: "Notturno"
AABC

Variation 3: "Furiant"
ABA   Allegretto–trio–de capo

Variation 4: "Coda"
Coda   Two six-measure phrases with repeat

Unit 8: Suggested Listening
Béla Bartók:
Divertimento for Strings
Romanian Folk Dances
Karel Husa, *Music for Prague 1968*
Bedřich Smetana, *My Country* (Má Vlast)

Unit 9: Additional References and Resources
Miles, Richard. *Teaching Music through Performance in Band.* Chicago: GIA
    Publications, Inc., 1997.

Slonimsky, Nicolas, ed. emeritus. *Baker's Biographical Dictionary of Musicians.*
    New York: Schirmer Books, 2001.

Contributed by:

Jonathan D. Lane
Orchestra Director
Shawnee Mission East High School
Indian Hills Middle School
Shawnee Mission, Kansas

Grade Four

Teacher Resource Guide

Adieu

Todd Coleman
(b. 1970)

STRING ORCHESTRA

Unit 1: Composer

Todd Coleman was born in Mesa, Arizona, in 1970. His interest in music began at an early age. In addition to popular music of the day, his father often played recordings of the music of Bach and Beethoven as well as electronic music. Coleman's first composition was a ten-minute work for strings, oboe, harp, piano, and timpani. His high school orchestra premiered the work in 1988. The following year Coleman composed a new work for string orchestra. This work, entitled *Adieu*, won the MENC's National Student Composition Contest in 1989.

Coleman's formal music training began in 1992 at Brigham Young University. There he received several honors for composition, including the Mayhew Composition Award for his song, *The Silver Swan*, the Dean's Excellence Award, and the Creative Work Award for his first orchestral work, *In the Beginning*.

Following the completion of his undergraduate studies, Coleman taught high school orchestra in Arizona for a year. He then attended the Eastman School of Music in Rochester, New York, earning his Masters degree in 1999. He is currently completing his Doctorate in Composition at the Eastman School, anticipating graduation in 2002. Recent awards include winning the Chicago Symphony Orchestra's 1999 First Hearing Competition, receiving the Eastman School's Howard Hanson Orchestral Prize, and being a finalist in the Alexander Zemlinsky International Composition Competition. He received a Barlow Commission to write a double bass concerto, *SivaSakthi*, which was premiered in October 2000, and he was the Grand Prize winner of the ScorchMusic.com Composing and Arranging competition.

Unit 2: Composition

Adieu was written at the encouragement of Coleman's high school orchestra director. As a senior in high school, Coleman had composed only one work previously. In order to submit the work to the MENC's biannual composition contest, he had only three weeks to write the new work before the entry deadline. After a week and a half of struggling to come up with ideas for the work, a simple melodic line came to him. The rest of the work was completed in a matter of days, the remainder of the piece being an outgrowth of this initial theme. Just a few months later, Coleman was to leave to serve as a missionary for his church, teaching Laotian, Thai, and Vietnamese refugees living in Minnesota. In anticipation of his farewell to family and friends, he chose to title the new work *Adieu*. It was premiered in Washington, DC, in 1990. This was Coleman's first published work; it has been widely performed throughout the United States and abroad.

Unit 3: Historical Perspective

Due in part to the composer's young age and lack of exposure to the major trends in twentieth century music at the time he wrote this work, *Adieu* is allied much more closely with the works of the eighteenth and nineteenth centuries. Its simple diatonic language and beautiful melodic lines reflect the composer's love for the music of the common practice period. As can be seen with most composers in the early stages of their development, this work reveals the influence of composers from previous generations. In this case, the influence of American composer Samuel Barber is clearly evident in the texture, form, and style of the work. Indeed, to this day Coleman cites Barber's Adagio for Strings as one of the motivating forces in his early growth as a composer. Coleman's more recent compositions have utilized many of the innovations of twentieth century compositional techniques, but he continues to maintain an affinity for music that is expressive and builds upon the traditions of the past.

Unit 4: Technical Considerations

Adieu was originally written in the key of E major to make use of the low E in double bass. However, the number of sharps in the key signature made it more difficult for younger performers to play with accurate intonation. The work was transposed down to D major for publication to facilitate performance by less-experienced musicians. As a result, the bass players need to tune down their E string to play the low D's in the piece; this also creates difficulties. However, the key of D has certain advantages as well. Because of the sympathetic vibrations of the open strings, D major has a greater resonance. Most of the music lies comfortably in the lower positions of each of the instruments. As the music grows to a climax in the middle section of the work, the cellists must play in thumb position. To increase security of intonation in the upper registers, and especially in the transition to thumb position, the cellists should practice three-octave scales, focusing on the highest octave, both ascending and descending. Immediately following the peak of the composition, at measure 33, double bass plays the main theme in unison with the cellos. Many young bass players are inexperienced at sustained legato playing in this register. Practicing slow, slurred scales spanning from open G up to the octave harmonic and gradually increasing in speed through repetition can develop greater facility.

Unit 5: Stylistic Considerations

Throughout most of this composition, there are always two distinct components to the musical texture: a cantabile melodic line and a sustained homophonic accompaniment. The melodic line should be played with expressive vibrato and full bows, in the style of late romantic works such as the Adagietto from Mahler's Symphony No. 5. It is essential that the melody be sustained through the entire phrase, not dying out on the longer notes in the middle of each phrase. The accompanying parts must take care to balance with each other in a unified, well-blended sound without covering up the melody. When playing an accompaniment part, less vibrato should be used than when playing the primary melodic line. Open strings should be avoided as much as possible in all parts because the timbre does not blend well with the overall texture.

Unit 6: Musical Elements

Adieu is written in D major throughout. It is a completely diatonic work, containing no accidentals from outside the key signature. There are two primary themes, the second being similar to the first but consisting only of eighth notes. The first theme features two common musical devices: sequence and suspensions. Timbre is another important musical element in this work. The use of mutes and careful doublings between muted and unmuted instruments creates a variety of sound combinations. The combination of different instruments, such as viola and cello playing the same melodic line in unison, also creates timbrel variety from one statement of the theme to the next. The rhythms are simple and straightforward throughout. Primary attention should be given to expressive projection of the main themes and the differences in timbre, dynamics, instrumentation, and register from statement to statement.

Unit 7: Form and Structure

Section	Measures
Theme A	1
Theme B	8
A	10

SECTION	MEASURES
B	14
Development	17
A	33
B	36
Closing	41
Coda	49

To enhance the overall shape of the piece, special consideration should be given to the use of the bow. The opening and closing sections of the work, where the music is the most delicate, calls for playing *sul tasto*. As the music grows in intensity and climbs in register at the middle of the work, players should bow a little closer to the bridge. The coda, beginning at measure 49, should be especially slow and soft. The last note should die away slowly to the point where the cut-off is imperceptible, thus bringing the work to an expressive close, as if the music never really ends.

Unit 8: Suggested Listening
Samuel Barber, Adagio for Strings
Gustav Mahler, Adagietto from Symphony No. 5

Unit 9: Additional References and Resources
There are a number of Internet web sites containing more information on Todd Coleman and his music. As URL's change frequently, the surest approach is to conduct an Internet search for "Todd Coleman, composer" using one of the popular search engines. More information may also be available by contacting the Eastman School of Music at www.toddcoleman.net

Contributed by:
Todd Coleman
DMA Graduate Student, Composition for Non-majors Instructor
Eastman School of Music
Rochester, New York

Teacher Resource Guide

Air for Strings

Norman Dello Joio
(b. 1913)

STRING ORCHESTRA

Unit 1: Composer

Norman Dello Joio was born into a musical family in 1913 in New York City. His father, grandfather, and great-grandfather were all church organists. He received his early composition training from his father and his godfather, Pietro Yon. He later attended the Juilliard School and Yale University, where he studied composition with Paul Hindemith. Dello Joio held teaching positions at Sara Lawrence College (NY) and the Mannes College of Music in New York City. He was also the Dean of the School of Arts at Boston University from 1972 to 1979.

Dello Joio received several awards for his compositions. Among these were the New York Music Critic's Circle Award in 1962 for the opera *The Triumph of St. Joan*, the Pulitzer Prize for music in 1957 for *Meditations on Ecclesiastes* for string orchestra, and an Emmy Award in 1965 for the orchestra work *Scenes from "The Louvre."* He was also associated with the Contemporary Music Project for Creativity in Music Education, which placed young composers in high schools throughout the United States to write music that was suitable for school ensembles.

Unit 2: Composition

Air for Strings, written in 1967, is a four-minute work for string orchestra that is suitable for performance by an advanced high school string ensemble. It is marked by a lyrical, singing melodic line that resembles an Italian *bel canto* operatic aria. While the harmonic language is primarily tonal, Dello Joio's liberal use of chromatics tends to blur the tonal center in places. A syncopated

rhythmic accompaniment heightens the tension between the melodic line and the other voices, particularly in the last section of the work. It is cast in a classic rondo form with a brief introduction and short coda.

Unit 3: Historical Perspective

Dello Joio's early musical influences were nineteenth century Italian opera, Catholic church music, and popular and jazz music of New York City in the 1920s and 1930s. Perhaps the most important influence on his compositional style was the brief training he had with Paul Hindemith, who espoused the principles of tonality, diatonicism, and music that was accessible to a vast general audience. Dello Joio's music is characterized by a directness of expression, strong melodic appeal, rhythmic vitality, restrained harmonic language, and clearly defined classic formal structures.

Unit 4: Technical Considerations

Most of the composition is built around the keys of E-flat and C major. However, the chromatic alterations in the C major sections may present an intonation challenge; they will need to be practiced slowly in sectional rehearsals. The syncopated rhythmic accompaniment figure in the last C major section will need to be isolated and practiced without the melodic line. Most of the parts remain in first position, except for first violin and cello, which shift to third position.

Unit 5: Stylistic Considerations

The cantabile sections of this composition should be performed in a legato style that brings out the lyrical character of the melodic line. Careful attention should be paid to phrasing and dynamic shadings. The chordal section presents a stark contrast to the cantabile sections and should be performed in a marcato style with heavy, accented bow strokes. The concluding coda section should be performed in such a manner that the final bowed chord fades away, followed by a light, almost inaudible pizzicato chord.

Unit 6: Musical Elements

The cantabile sections are set in E-flat major with few chromatic alterations. In contrast to this, chromatics are used freely in the C major sections so that an illusion of frequent modulation is created. Lyrical countermelodies in the second violin and viola parts are set against the cantabile melody in the first violin part. A tempo marking of quarter note = 88 is given. The entire work is set in triple meter and is not rhythmically complex except for the syncopated rhythmic figure in the chordal section.

Unit 7: Form and Structure
Classic rondo form: ABACA

SECTION	MEASURES	EVENT AND SCORING
Introduction	1–4	E-flat major
A section	5–15	E-flat major; introduction of the lyrical melody in first violin
B section	15–26	C major modulates back to E-flat major at m. 25; new chromatic melodic line used in imitative fashion in different voices
A section	26–34	E-flat major; lyrical melody in first violin accompanied by countermelodies and an undulating eighth note figure
C section	34–55	C major; loud; accented chords followed by the introduction of a syncopated rhythmic accompaniment at m. 42
A section	55–65	C major; return of lyrical melody in first violin with syncopated accompaniment in viola
Coda	65–74	C minor to C major at m. 71; *diminuendo* chord mm. 71–73; C major pizzicato in m. 74

Unit 8: Suggested Listening
Norman Dello Joio:
    Air for Strings
    Air Power Symphonic Suite
    Choreography
    Epigraph
    Meditations on Ecclesiastes
    New York Profiles
    Serenade
    Triumph of St. Joan
    Variations, Chaconne, and Finale

Unit 9: Additional References and Resources
Bumgardner, Thomas A. *Norman Dello Joio*. Boston: Twayne Publishers, 1986.

Chase, Gilbert. *America's Music from the Pilgrims to the Present*. Revised 2d edition. New York: McGraw-Hill, 1966.

Downes, Edward. "The Music of Norman Dello Joio," *Musical Quarterly*, 48 (April 1962), 149–72.

Hitchcock, H. Wiley. *Music in the United States: A Historical Introduction.* Englewood Cliffs, NJ: Prentice-Hall, 1969.

Hitchcock, H. Wiley, ed. *The New Grove Dictionary of American Music*, Vol. 1. London: MacMillan Press Ltd., 1986.

Salzman, Eric. *Twentieth Century Music: An Introduction.* Englewood Cliffs, NJ: Prentice-Hall, 1969.

Contributed by:

Dr. Camille M. Smith
Associate Professor of Music
University of Florida–Gainesville
Gainesville, Florida

Teacher Resource Guide

Andante Festivo

Jean Sibelius
(1865–1957)

STRING ORCHESTRA

Unit 1: Composer

Jean Sibelius, known especially for his large symphonic works and Finnish nationalistic pieces, was born in Hämeenlinna, Finland, in 1865. He composed his first piece at the age of ten, though he did not formally study violin till the age of fourteen. During his school years in Helsinki in 1885–89, he studied composition with Hegelius, then later with Becker in Berlin. His early output consisted mostly of chamber music, the medium with which he was most familiar. Nevertheless, he demonstrated his skill as a symphonist with the premiere of the *Kullervo* symphony in 1892. The piece was based on the Finnish epic *Kalevala* and established Sibelius as the musical leader of Finnish nationalism. This was a reputation with which Sibelius wrestled all his life. He composed several more tone poems based on nationalistic, mythical, and natural themes, many of them containing Scandinavian musical characteristics. The well-known *Finlandia* (1900) is one of those. At the same time, he composed seven symphonies that were primarily more absolutist and cosmopolitan in nature. Sibelius retired in the mid-1920s, composing almost nothing except for the Eighth Symphony, which he reportedly destroyed, until his death in 1957. He lived the rest of his life as a Finnish national treasure and symbol of the country's independence gained in 1917 from Russia, and was celebrated nationally on his major birthdays. His music was enormously popular in the United States and the United Kingdom throughout most of his life.

Unit 2: Composition

Andante Festivo was originally a string quartet, composed on commission for a factory in 1922,[1] revised in the 1930s for string orchestra with timpani. It has a solemn, hymnlike, processional character, moving homophonically with rich romantic string sonority throughout. There are no rhythmic, tonal, or textural complications, and it is conservative in style, in many ways reminiscent of *Finlandia* (1900). Sibelius used the thematic material of this piece for "The Village Church," the first of *Five Characteristic Impressions*, Op. 103, for piano. He wrote one other piece for string orchestra and percussion, *Rakastava* (1911), recomposed from an earlier choral work, though it is quite different in style. Andante Festivo is approximately four minutes and thirty seconds in length.

Unit 3: Historical Perspective

Sibelius composed Andante Festivo near the end of his creative life, at a time when he was writing a great number of small pieces to support himself and his family, but before the Sixth and Seventh Symphonies and the monumental tone poem *Tapiola*. In these latter works, Sibelius reached the pinnacle of his unique symphonic style, which had no real corollaries in the works of other composers of the time because of his unique blend of nationalistic, programmatic, and abstract elements. Andante Festivo does, however, hark back to an earlier style; it bears more resemblance to works like Grieg's *Heart Wounds* and *Last Spring* than to the aforementioned works. Ironically, it is the only piece by Sibelius that was recorded with the composer conducting, performed for a live radio broadcast (by hookup) at the New York World's Fair. It is still used for solemn state occasions in Finland and, like *Finlandia*, is important mostly for its patriotic significance.

Unit 4: Technical Considerations

This piece requires broad, sustained *son filé* bow strokes in all the string parts to give it full string sonority. It is solidly in G major with no real modulations and few chromatic alterations. Harmonically and rhythmically it is simple, and the shifting requirements are minimal: fourth position in first violin and second position in cello. The shaping of phrases to give the piece direction may be its most challenging aspect; since it is so chordal in texture, the ensemble must be precise. The three timpani rolls entering in the last four measures are on A, D, and G.

Unit 5: Stylistic Considerations

The piece has a rich, hymnlike texture and should be played in a very sustained, legato style, somewhat like that of Barber's Adagio for Strings, also originally written for quartet though tonally much different. It also contains a dynamic range from *pp* to *ff*, and because the harmony, texture, and rhythm are somewhat static, this contrast should be exaggerated in keeping with the romantic tradition.

Unit 6: Musical Considerations

Utilizing a technique characteristic of several of his works, Sibelius seems to have derived much of the melodic material for this piece from the opening five-note arch (do–re–mi–re–do) motive in G major. It figures prominently in the A and B sections and, in inversion, is the basis for the tonal motion in the C section as well. In the coda, its upper and lower neighbors are utilized as well, so it becomes do–re–mi–fa–mi–re–do–ti–do. In the C section, cello and bass play a syncopated G pedal point for six measures, while in the next six measures they change pitches on each beat. This helps to generate the most harmonic variety in the piece, cadencing in A major in measure 46 before settling back into G major. Rhythmically, the dotted-quarter/eighth note figure is used throughout as a unifying element. An unusual formal feature occurs in the A theme, which cadences on the IV chord in the middle of the fourth measure, resolving to ii in measure 7. This bit of imbalance provides extra interest in what is otherwise a very straightforward structure.

Unit 7: Form and Structure

The overall form might be described as two-part, the second a reordering of the first:

Section		Measures	Event and Scoring
I	A	1	Theme consisting of one period; two nearly identical phrases (a–a), the second extended by one measure to arrive at the dominant
	B	16	Theme derived from A; two identical six-measure phrases (b–b)
	C	28	Through-composed derivative material throughout with G pedal for first seven measures
II	D	40	a; modified to cadence on the secondary dominant, plus b
	C	52	Modified in last measure to lead back to b
	B	64	
Coda		69	Material derived from A and B; timpani on last four measures

Unit 8: Suggested Listening

Samuel Barber, Adagio for Strings
Edvard Grieg:
    Heart Wounds
    Last Spring
Jean Sibelius:
    Finlandia
    Rakastava ("The Lover")
    Symphony No. 2
    The Village Church, Op. 103, No. 1 (piano)

Unit 9: Additional References and Resources

Abraham, Gerald, ed. *Sibelius: A Symposium*. London: Drummond, 1947.

Burnett-James, David. *Sibelius*. London: Omnibus Press, 1989.

Goss, Glenda D., ed. *The Sibelius Companion*. Westport, CT: Greenwood Press, 1996.

Layton, Robert. *Sibelius*. New York: Schirmer Books, 1997.

Rickards, Guy. *Jean Sibelius*. London: Phaidon Press, 1997.

Sadie, Stanley, ed.. *The New Grove Dictionary of Music and Musicians*. S.v. "Jean Sibelius" by Robert Layton. New York: Grove's Dictionaries, 2000. Also available online at www.grovemusic.com

Slonimsky, Nicolas, ed. emeritus. *Baker's Biographical Dictionary of Musicians*. New York: Schirmer Books, 2001.

Tawaststjerna, Erk. *Sibelius Volume III: 1914–57*. Translated and edited by Robert Layton. London: Faber and Faber, 1997.

Wood, Ralph W. "Sibelius's Use of Percussion." *Music and Letters*, 23 (1942).

Contributed by:

Judy Palac
Associate Professor of Music Education
Michigan State University
East Lansing, Michigan

---

1 Robert Layton, *Sibelius* (New York: Schirmer Books, 1993), p. 123.

Teacher Resource Guide

Peer Gynt Suite No. 1, Op. 46, Movement 2 ("Ase's Death")

Edvard Grieg
(1843–1907)

STRING ORCHESTRA

Unit 1: Composer

Edward Hagerup Grieg was born in 1843 and died in 1907 in Bergen, Norway. Grieg wrote many pieces that spoke of his homeland and gave his music a nationalistic voice. He studied music at the Conservatory at Leipzig, Germany, as a pianist and composer. He founded the Norwegian Academy of Music. Grieg's German publisher, C. F. Peters, popularized much of his music. Notable works include violin sonatas, *Holberg Suite*, A Minor Piano Concerto, *Norwegian Dances*, *Peer Gynt Suite* Nos. 1 and 2, two string quartets, and 150 famous songs, including "The Wounded Heart."

Unit 2: Composition

"Åse's Death" is the second movement of Grieg's Suite No. 1, Op. 46; "Morning" is the first movement. The story of *Peer Gynt* comes from Henrik Ibsen's Norwegian drama written in 1876. Åse is Peer Gynt's mother who dies while Peer is speaking to her. This lamentation is a very powerful musical piece of approximately four minutes and thirty seconds for muted strings. It is marked "Andante doloroso" and quarter note = 50.

Unit 3: Historical Perspective

Grieg wrote *Peer Gynt* as incidental music to Norwegian author Henrik Ibsen's drama of the same name. The music premiered in Oslo, Norway, and was soon performed throughout Europe, becoming Grieg's most famous piece. The order of the four movements in Suite No. 1 were chosen by Grieg for his often-

performed piece. The background music of the second movement, "Åse's Death," presents itself as a lush lament from the later romantic period. Polish composer Frédéric Chopin was the most influential composer on young Edvard Grieg. He also established ties with English composer Arthur Sullivan and Norwegian composer Rikard Nordraak. After Nordraak's death, Grieg dedicated himself to his own musical heritage of Norway through his folk songs, dances, and pieces.

Unit 4: Technical Considerations

The opening uses B minor in its various forms within a two-octave range. The technical difficulties lie in the *divisi a 3* for cello with the upper voices in fifth position in a melodic minor scale pattern. First violin *divisi* appears in octaves in third and fourth positions. This movement is lush in a connected legato and expressive détaché style. Making a pure and beautiful sound quality within scalar and chromatic movement in *ff* to *pp* dynamic ranges becomes the difficult challenge.

Unit 5: Stylistic Considerations

The Andante doloroso, played with mutes, sets the tone for this melancholy movement. The short, forty-five measures are restrained dynamically until the *fortissimo* climax, which is followed by a soft, reflective second half. The long legato and sustained détaché bowings shift into a *fortissimo* climax in which every note is accented. The timbre of the piece is created with muted strings for the duration of the movement. A romantic, lush sound with a vibrato responsive to dynamic intensities will bring a stylistic purity to this movement.

Unit 6: Musical Elements

This movement is in B minor until letter A, where the chords progress from D major to B major before returning to B minor. Grieg orchestrated the homophonic four-measure phrases as *divisi* for a richer texture at the *ff* section. The chromatic movement of the melody in section A is played against an augmented rhythm in the bass line.

Unit 7: Form and Structure

SECTION	EVENT AND SCORING
Theme 1	Theme 1 appears in violin 1 with rhythmic and harmonic similarities in other voices; the "Åse's Death" theme is repeated in violin 1 one octave higher with intertwining melody in the cello *divisi a 3*
Theme 2	Letter A, a chromatic phrase in a quarter and half note pattern; Theme 2 repeats an octave lower at m. 33 with the full strings; at m. 42, the rhythm is augmented until the end

278

Unit 8: Suggested Listening
Frédéric Chopin, Piano Concertos Nos. 1 and 2
Antonín Dvořák:
  String Quartet in F Major, Op. 96 ("American")
  Symphony No. 9 in E Minor ("From the New World")
Edvard Grieg:
  Holberg Suite
  Norwegian Dances
  Piano Concerto
Sir Arthur Sullivan, *The Mikado*

Unit 9: Additional References and Resources

Benestad, Finn. *Edvard Grieg*. Lincoln: University of Nebraska Press, 1988.

Cross, Milton, and David Ewen. *New Encyclopedia of the Great Composers and Their Music*. New York: Doubleday and Company, Inc., 1969.

Horton, John. *Grieg*. London: Dent, 1974.

Schjelderup-Ebbe, Dag. *A Study of Grieg's Harmony*. Oslo: J. G. Tanum, 1953.

Contributed by:
Susan Brown
Director of Strings & Ensembles, Cabrillo College
Director of Chamber Music, University of Southern California
  at Santa Cruz
Santa Cruz, California

Teacher Resource Guide

"Basse Danse" and "Mattachins" from Capriol Suite

Peter Warlock
(1894–1930)

STRING ORCHESTRA

Unit 1: Composer

Philip Heseltine, writer, composer, music editor, and critic, was born in London in 1894. For most literary works he signed his given name, but for musical compositions and works about music he used the pen name Peter Warlock. He had little formal music training but had a strong interest in sixteenth and seventeenth century English music and poetry. Primary influences in Warlock's compositional style were friends and mentors: Delius with a chromatic style; van Dieren with a contrapuntal technique; and Bartók with his use of discordant sound. Warlock composed over one hundred songs, edited three hundred early English and French songs and a collection of early English and Italian dances, and wrote books on Delius, Thomas Whythorne, and Gesualdo. His works for orchestra include *Capriol Suite* and *Serenade for Strings*. In 1923 Warlock received the Carnegie Award for *The Curlew*, a song cycle for tenor, flute, English horn, and string quartet. He served as editor for the controversial music opinion journal, *The Sackbut*. He suffered from severe depression and committed suicide by gas poisoning in his London flat in December 1930. Warlock made a significant contribution to scholarly research and the resurgence of interest in early English music. Most of his compositions and much of his editing are a result of his scholarship.

Unit 2: Composition

Capriol Suite was written in 1927 for string orchestra and arranged for full orchestra in 1929. The suite contains six short, contrasting dance movements whose monodic melodies were originally notated in Thoinot Arbeau's sixteenth century dance manual, *Orchesographie*. Arbeau, a pen name for Jehan Tabourot, wrote the dance manual in the form of a dialogue between a teacher, Arbeau, and a formal pupil, Capriol—hence the name *Capriol Suite*. Warlock followed Arbeau's melodies faithfully, adding simple yet original harmonic and rhythmic elements that include counterpoint, chromaticism, discord, hemiola, and accents. "Basse Danse," the first movement, was a dance originally for the upper class, but by the time Arbeau notated it in 1589 it had lost its popularity. Dance steps were stately and feet were kept close to the floor, as reflected by the title, "Basse." Performance time is approximately one minute and thirty seconds. "Mattachins," the last movement in the suite, is a fast-paced sword dance based on one of Arbeau's variations of the tune of the buffoons. Performance time is one minute. Movements from *Capriol Suite* have been arranged for a number of ensembles, including recorder choir, guitar ensemble, and concert band.

Unit 3: Historical Perspective

Vocal and instrumental music written during the first half of the twentieth century reveals a strong interest in revival of melodies from medieval, renaissance, and folk sources. For some composers like Cyril Scott (1879–1970) and Peter Warlock, maintaining the integrity of the melodies was important while the harmonic and rhythmic accompaniments reflected newer techniques of composition: impressionistic, chromatic, discordant. On the other hand, Respighi (1879–1936) harmonized extant renaissance dance melodies in traditional sixteenth century style when he composed his three suites for orchestra, *Ancient Airs and Dances*. His orchestration, however, reflects twentieth century techniques. Other composers, including Vaughan Williams (1872–1958), Elgar (1857–1934), and Delius (1862–1934), used folk-like melodies or early dance-like tunes as the basis for composition but rarely quoted actual sources. In each instance the settings, orchestrations, and voicings are highly individualized among composers, transforming and transcending the vernacular.

Unit 4: Technical Considerations

The tonality of "Basse Danse" is centered around D minor with short excursions into relative and parallel majors. First violin has a *divisi* passage with upper notes in third and fifth positions. The same passage also requires a light spiccato bowing. String bass will need to shift to third and fourth positions on the G string. Remaining instrumental parts require only first position but afford the opportunity for shifting as well. All players must stay alert rhythmically, as Warlock tends to shift rests and accents around; just when players think they have the pattern, Warlock changes it. The tempo is "Allegro moderato."

"Mattachins" is in F major for the first half of the movement. At the second repetition of theme one, first violin is divided in octaves, with the upper octave in third and fifth positions. Remaining parts, except string bass, have double-stops alternating with *divisi* parts. Notes are not difficult, but the page tends to look crowded, so sight-reading can be a challenge. The second half of the movement is original Warlock—a series of clashing double-stops alternating with *divisi* parts. Intonation and aural understanding will be the challenge. First violin will use third position, and string bass will use second position. First position will work for remaining parts with the use of low first fingers or extended third or fourth fingers for accidentals. Tempo is "Allegro con brio." Once again, Warlock creates interest with changing rhythmic patterns.

Unit 5: Stylistic Considerations

Dances require a vertical approach to the music. Accents are important to the style and momentum of the dance. A slight separation between notes is appropriate. The music should be played as if the performers were moving. "Basse Danse" is a stately dance in triple meter. A hooked style bowing (down, up–up) in measures containing three quarter notes will provide separation and a natural accent on downbeats without allowing the tempo to rush. Written accents should not be heavy but should rather lean into the note. All three themes use the same articulation until letter C where the mood becomes pesante and the tempo becomes a bit broader because of the suggested series of down-bows in the violins. The last two measures require a heavy marcato style bowing.

"Mattachins" is a fiery and quick sword dance in duple meter. From the beginning to letter B, the use of hooked bowing in all parts for the quarter/two eighth note patterns (down, up–up) will again provide the clarity and natural accents desired to maintain the tempo and the jovial spirit of the dance. Hooked eighth notes should be light and off the string. Letter B to the end is reflective of Bartók's influence on Warlock. The harmonic structure requires solid tone via firm left-hand connection and bow speed. Dotted-rhythms should be bowed separately, and cluster chords should be played with more force and separate marcato bows. Accents should have a sting to them, as does a sword when it nicks a worthy opponent.

Unit 6: Musical Elements

"Basse Danse" is primarily built around D minor with most themes taking a short excursion to the relative or parallel major key. The third theme moves to a minor and its parallel major. Texture is basically two voices. The melody is highly rhythmic and generally moves in stepwise motion. First violin, followed by immediate restatement in second violin, introduces each of the three themes. Contrast in restatement of themes is found in unexpected and delightful harmonic shifts and variations in rhythmic accompaniments. First and second violin should strive to match tone and style on statement of themes, thereby allowing the listener's attention to focus fully on the surprises in the accompaniment.

"Mattachins" begins in F major with both themes presented by first violin. Themes are stepwise and encompass less than an octave. Texture is homophonic. As themes are restated at letter A, accompaniment figures divide, resulting in a fuller sonority. Harmonic structure also changes creating a rich contrast to the simple figures in the initial statement of themes. At letter B, a series of highly rhythmic and discordant double-stops provide an aural image of the sword dance. The coda includes a two-measure discordant quarter note triplet that ends on an F major chord. Dynamics range from *p* to *fff* and include many accents.

Unit 7: Form and Structure

SECTION	MEASURES	EVENT AND SCORING

"Basse Danse"
Warlock chose three of the four original themes notated in Arbeau's basse danse. He added a short coda that was not present in Arbeau's notation.

Section	Measures	Event and Scoring
Theme 1	1–8	Stated in first violin; mm. 9–16 identical restatement in second violin
Theme 2	17–24	Between first and second violin; mm. 25–32 identical restatement
Theme 3	33–40	Between first and second violin; mm. 41–48 restatement in second violin
Theme 1	49–56	Restatement in octaves in first violin
Theme 2	57–64	Restatement in octaves in first violin
Codetta	65–68	

"Mattachins"		
Introduction	1–4	Cello; open fifths
Theme 1	5–12	Stated in first violin
Theme 2	13–20	Stated in first violin; mm. 21–28 identical restatement in first violin
Theme 1	29–36	Restatement in octaves in first violin
Theme 2	37–44	Restatement in octaves in first violin
Closing/Coda	45–76	Discordant harmony and double-stops

Unit 8: Suggested Listening

Frederick Delius, *Two Aquarelles*
Ottorino Respighi, *Ancient Airs and Dances*
Ralph Vaughan Williams, *Five Variants of "Dives and Lazarus"*
Peter Warlock:
    Capriol Suite
    Serenade for Strings

Unit 9: Additional References and Resources

Arbeau, Thoinot. *Orchesography*. Trans. Mary Stewart Evans. New York: Dover Publications, 1967.

Sadie, Stanley, ed. *The New Grove Dictionary of Music and Musicians*. New York: Grove's Dictionaries, 2000. Also available online at www.grovemusic.com

Slonimsky, Nicolas, ed. emeritus. *Baker's Biographical Dictionary of Musicians*. New York: Schirmer Books, 2001.

Web site:
    http://www.peterwarlock.org

Contributed by:

Kathlene Goodrich
Assistant Professor of Music Education, String Specialist
The Hartt School
University of Hartford
Hartford, Connecticut

Teacher Resource Guide

"Berceuse and Finale" from The Firebird Suite

Igor Stravinsky
(1882–1971)

arranged by Merle Isaac

FULL ORCHESTRA

Unit 1: Composer

Igor Fedorovich Stravinsky was born in Oranienbaum (Lomonosov) near Saint Petersburg on June 17, 1882, and died in New York City on April 6, 1971. Stravinsky's father was a superstar singer at the St. Petersburg opera in Russia. Through his father, he heard all the great Russian operas of his time, and he even met most of the great Russian singers and composers. For example, he not only heard the Saint Petersburg premiere of Tchaikovsky's fairy tale ballet, *The Nutcracker*, but he was introduced to Tchaikovsky himself. Sadly, Stravinsky's father died when Igor was a young man. Happily, Igor was virtually adopted by his father's friend Rimsky-Korsakov, the composer of the orchestral fairy tale, *Scheherazade*. Stravinsky studied composition and learned how to earn a living as a composer from Rimsky-Korsakov. Other major works by Stravinsky include *Petrushka*, *The Rite of Spring*, *The Soldier's Tale*, *The Rake's Progress*, and *Song of the Nightingale*.

Unit 2: Composition

By the time he was in his late twenties, a professional orchestra had played only one piece by Stravinsky. Luckily for him, a successful concert promoter was at that concert and remembered the Stravinsky name because of Igor's famous father. A few months later, the concert promoter, Serge Diaghilev, needed a composer to write the music for a fairy tale ballet he was going to produce in Paris the next summer. He asked Stravinsky if he could compose a complete ballet in about six months. It was a huge challenge for any composer, but particularly a challenge for a young and untried composer like Stravinsky. He began composing *The Firebird Suite* in 1909 and completed it in time for the first performance on June 25, 1910, at the Paris Opéra. *The Firebird Suite* immediately established Stravinsky on the international musical scene and established an association with Diaghilev that lasted until Stravinsky's death. The work's reception immediately led Stravinsky to prepare a concert version in 1911, retaining the extravagant scoring of the complete ballet. In 1919, he arranged another suite, with somewhat different contents and a more normal orchestration; this 1919 arrangement remains the score's most popular incarnation.

The Firebird Suite is the story of a brave young prince who, with the help of the magic Firebird, destroys an evil wizard, thereby freeing the princesses that the wizard's magic had turned to stone. Probably the best-known part of *The Firebird Suite* is its conclusion, "Berceuse and Finale," the part of the ballet when the princesses slowly come back to life after having been turned to stone. A *berceuse* is a lullaby, and Stravinsky's starts slowly, softly, and magically. It increases in intensity and then suddenly explodes into rays of luminous fire as the finale.

Unit 3: Historical Perspective

Few cultural manifestations of the twentieth century can compare with the explosion that Russian impresario Serge Diaghilev set off by importing Russian music and theater to Paris beginning in 1907. At first the emphasis was on opera—for example, *Boris Godunov*—but in 1909, the *Ballets Russes* was launched. Works such as Rimsky-Korsakov's *Scheherazade* and Borodin's "Polovetsian Dances" from *Prince Igor* made an indelible impression that spread throughout the Western world.

Unit 4: Technical Considerations

The major portions of the composition are in D minor and B-flat major. There are, however, many chromatic scale patterns required of the full ensemble. There are important solos for bassoon, oboe, and French horn that lie within the normal playing range of each instrument. The flute and oboe parts have sustained triplet tonguing at quarter note = 172 for a few measures. First and second violin require altered harmonic fingerings. First violin requires fifth position, and second violin requires third position. Occasionally, all string sections have *divisi* parts.

Unit 5: Stylistic Considerations

Sudden tempo changes are required to achieve the high dramatic forces needed in this piece. Extreme dynamic changes within a few measures are necessary to gain the full impact of the piece. Muted strings must play near the fingerboard with a flautato bow stroke. The addition of a harp will make a significant change in the desired effect written in the upper woodwinds and strings. Exposed brass sections require careful balancing of chords. The last *tutti* chord requires precise articulation and intense tonal support at a *pp* level having just played *ffff* on the penultimate chord.

Unit 6: Musical Elements

The piece begins in the key of D minor with exposed instrumentation. The main theme is repeated three times with significant accompaniment changes the third time. The second major theme is introduced in B-flat major. After a brief statement in C major, the second theme returns to B-flat major and remains there. There are several shifting meter changes throughout the piece. One section written in 7/4 changes from 3–2–2 to 2–2–3. A syncopated bass line in the low woodwinds, tuba, timpani, and double bass is independent of the thematic material in the 7/4 section. Rhythmic changes, varying orchestrations, and the use of augmentation gives the impression that the final section is in a theme and variation form.

Unit 7: Form and Structure

SECTION	REHEARSAL NO.	EVENT AND SCORING
Opening		Introduction, two measures; harp, viola, and cello
Theme 1A	1	Smooth, flowing melody in D minor played by bassoon solo with continuation of harp and string accompaniment
Theme 1B		Oboe solo response with addition of upper strings
Theme 1A	2	Played again by bassoon with added violin accompaniment
Theme 1B	3	Oboe solo with extended thematic material
Theme 1B	4	Augmented with woodwind chromatic accompaniment
Theme 1B	5	Repeated with added upper woodwinds playing melody in octaves
Theme 1A	6	Repeated with upper string chromatic accompaniment

SECTION	REHEARSAL NO.	EVENT AND SCORING
Theme 1B	8	Repeated with harmonic violin accompaniment
Transition	9	Tremolo string modulation from D minor to B-flat major
Theme 2	11	Cantabile melody in B-flat major played by French horn solo with string tremolo accompaniment
Theme 2	12	Played by violin with clarinet ascending chromatic accompaniment
Theme 2	13	Played by flute and violin with string and woodwind accompaniment, gradually adding French horn and low woodwinds with increased dynamic level
Theme 2	14	Full orchestral entrance *ff* with marked, separated style in a contrasting manner
Transition	15	Chromatic material from theme 1B with increased tempo in strings in contrary motion
Theme 2	17	Played by trumpets and trombones in a detached, separated style accompanied by tremolo strings and flute
Theme 2	18	C major; played by trumpet and trombone with flute accompaniment in triplets
Theme 2	19	Continues in C major; played by entire orchestra in a separate style at *fff*
Theme 2	20	B-flat major; played by entire orchestra at half the tempo in a fanfare style using only quarter notes with countermelody in lower voices
Ending	21	B-flat in octave unison in woodwinds and strings with brass chromatic thematic material that leads to final B-flat major chord

Unit 8: Suggested Listening

Igor Stravinsky:
> *The Firebird Suite*
> *Petrushka*
> *The Rite of Spring*

Unit 9: Additional References and Resources

Stravinsky, Igor. *Chronicles of my Life*. Paris, 1935, transcribed, London: Victor Gollancz, 1936.

Stravinsky, Vera, and Robert Craft. *Stravinsky in Pictures and Documents*. New York: Simon and Schuster, 1978.

Tansman, Alexandre. *Igor Stravinsky, The Man and His Music*. New York: G. P. Putnam's Son, 1949.

Contributed by:

E. Daniel Long
Director of Orchestras
Slauson Middle School, Ann Arbor Public Schools
Ann Arbor, Michigan

Teacher Resource Guide

Carmen Suite No. 1

Georges Bizet
(1838–1875)

FULL ORCHESTRA

Unit 1: Composer

Georges Bizet was born into a musical family in 1838 and showed an early aptitude for musical achievement. He received his first music lessons from his mother, who was an excellent pianist. His father was an opera conductor. Bizet was blessed with absolute pitch, which promoted his excellence in harmony, and he began to write music at an early age. He composed his Symphony in C Major, a fresh and delightful work, at the age of seventeen. While a student at the Paris Conservatoire, he won the *Prix de Rome* at nineteen and spent four years studying composition in Rome.

Although he was a gifted composer and an accomplished pianist, Bizet encountered difficulty making a living with his music after his return to Paris. There was limited demand for chamber music or French symphonies; opera was what the public wanted. The two opera houses of Paris insisted on the narrow conventions of the time, allowing him little scope for his creative talents. By the time he wrote *Carmen*, his last and greatest opera, Bizet was not well. Unfortunately for the world of music, he died three months after *Carmen's* premiere; he was only thirty-seven.

Unit 2: Composition

The two suites from *Carmen* were extracted after the composer's death. They contain orchestral settings of some of the opera's most famous pieces. Suite No. 1 contains six movements and takes approximately seventeen minutes to perform. It begins with the Prélude to the opera and presents its ominous "fate" motive that gives a foreshadowing of the tale of tragedy to come. The

Prélude leads directly to the Aragonaise, the prelude to Act IV of the opera. With its engaging Spanish rhythm, complete with tambourine accompaniment, this movement sets toes to tapping. The third movement, "Intermezzo," is a lovely, lyrical tune that is used to open Act III in the opera. "Seguedille," the fourth movement, is from the first act and is a traditional Spanish dance. It is the song Carmen sings to beguile Don José into letting her escape after being arrested. The prelude to Act II, "Les dragons d'Alcala," sets a military mood in a reference to Don José's profession. This fifth movement to the suite adds a quiet, mysterious tone to the collection. The final movement is the famous "Les Toréadors," from the introduction to Act I of the opera. To many people, this movement *is Carmen,* an exciting, brilliant piece with driving rhythms followed by the well-known, flowing melody of the Toreador Song, sung in Act II by Escamillo, the bullfighter.

Unit 3: Historical Perspective

Bizet composed his most famous opera, *Carmen,* in 1875, the last year of his life. Its first performance in Paris on March 3, 1875, was not a success. The grim realism of the story and the depiction of persons from a low class of society shocked the audience at its first performance. But today, even though the first audience rejected *Carmen,* it has become one of the most popular and frequently performed works in all of opera literature. Two reasons for its popularity are the fresh lyricism of its tunes and the exciting, exotic rhythm of the Spanish dances. *Carmen* was ahead of its time in the world of opera, but through its ultimate success, it redefined the role of the *opéra comique* and initiated a new style of writing and subject matter that would come to flower in *opera verismo* later in the century.

Unit 4: Technical Considerations

The six movements of Suite No. 1 employ varying instrumentation, as is often the case in pieces drawn from opera. The largest number of instruments calls for, in addition to the usual strings, woodwinds in pairs (with piccolo doubling one flute and English horn doubling one oboe), full brass (except tuba), harp, and a battery of percussion, including timpani, snare drum, bass drum, cymbals, triangle, and tambourine. Transposed parts for clarinet, trumpet, and horn, and parts in modern clefs for trombone are available, but the bassoon and cello parts include a considerable amount of tenor clef writing. Woodwind parts contain many exposed solo lines, duets, and other ensemble parts, which present intonation and balance challenges to the ensemble. The third movement relies extensively on harp to accompany the melodic lines. The violin range is extended, going up to G and once to B-flat far above the treble staff. The various movements of the work employ contrasting styles of playing to set the contrasting moods. Ensemble balance, style, and intonation

challenges prevail. Sustained, lyrical playing is required in "Intermezzo," while very soft accompaniment parts appear throughout "Seguedille" and "Les dragons d'Alcala."

Unit 5: Stylistic Considerations

Carmen was written in the nineteenth century during the romantic period. It portrays the gamut of emotion as the stark realism of the drama unfolds. The different characters bring additional contrast to the music as different styles are used to depict their personalities. The dramatic music and contrasting moods of Suite No. 1 demand the entire range of stylistic interpretation. Complex rhythmic and melodic imitation as well as solo and duet writing give the pieces their character. Incorporation of Spanish rhythms and song-like melodies help to impart the dramatic impact of each movement. Without a word having been said about the opera, this composition can still be identified as a work for the stage by its varied styles and exotic expression.

Unit 6: Musical Elements

The somber keys of A minor, D minor, and G minor dominate the suite. Only the tender and melodious "Intermezzo" and the brilliant and virtuosic "Les Toréadors" are written in major keys. Players can work to achieve full command of chromatic alterations to accommodate both the minor modes and the numerous key modulations in the music.

All playing styles from crisp, saucy staccato to tender and tuneful legato are employed at one time or another. The many exposed duet and ensemble passages require the players to match their styles of articulation to one another and gauge everything in the musical context of the piece. At times, slurred notes and staccato articulations occur in close proximity, and the strings and woodwinds pass a figure back and forth. Players can imitate each other's articulation to accomplish an impeccable balance of inflection.

Extremes of dynamic contrast are needed to portray the drama of the work while allowing the exposed solo lines to be heard over the accompaniment figures. Practice at both ends of the dynamic range will help to develop these skills. The players must also pay careful attention to the dynamic markings in the music to make the most of its dramatic impact. Auxiliary percussion parts take on a special significance in an effort to characterize the Spanish flavor of the dances using the tambourine, the military precision of marching using the snare drum, or the excitement of the bullring using the cymbals. The specific mood of each piece is also reflected in its instrumentation.

Movement 6 employs the full instrumentation, with all of the instruments playing until the famous theme of the "Toreador Song" enters, and then again at the end. Movement 1 is scored for full ensemble but uses the instruments more independently as melody line, chordal background, and percussive motive. Movement 2 begins with the full ensemble, but quickly reduces instrumentation to strings, harp, tambourine, and oboe solo with a phrase-ending commentary from piccolo and clarinet. The other instruments make only brief entrances for the rest of the movement, which ends softly and with reduced instrumentation. Movement 4 does not use the harp and makes only very sparing use of the brass, although it ends loudly with all the players employed. Movement 3 uses solo instruments extensively: strings, harp, two flutes, oboe and English horn, pairs of clarinets, and bassoon, adding occasional chords from the horns and dramatic underscoring from the timpani. Movement 5 calls for the smallest instrumentation of all. It begins with strings, snare drum, and bassoon, adding flute, clarinet, and oboe only in the second theme section.

Unit 7: Form and Structure

As an operatic suite, the different movements of Suite No. 1 were chosen for their contrasting styles and the pleasing way they flow from one another. As they come from parts of the opera that are widely separated, they do not narrate the story nor do they appear in chronological order.

Movement 1: "Prélude"
> Through-composed, this movement is intended to set a dramatic tone and lead to the next movement. The "fate" theme is announced in clarinet, bassoon, trumpet, and cello over a chordal accompaniment of ominous tremolo in the strings, punctuated by two D's in bass, harp, horn, and timpani. Building tension with *crescendo* and *diminuendo* effects, Movement 1 builds to a suspenseful climax in a loud staccato chord that leads directly to the next movement.

Movement 2: "Aragonaise"
> The prelude to Act IV of the opera, this movement is a sprightly Spanish dance from Aragón, as the title implies. It is patterned after the Jota, the most common dance form from the region, and retains many of the traditional characteristics of the dance. It consists of a rhythmic introduction in triple meter followed by the phrases of melody. There are two phrases for solo oboe with an answering motive in piccolo and clarinet, two phrases for antiphonal woodwinds and strings, and two phrases of other material, which eventually lead back to the original melodic material with solo oboe. The coda is made of quotations from the last group of phrases and fades out to a quiet ending.

Movement 3: "Intermezzo"
> Movement 3 is a gentle song-like movement based on a single thematic idea. First stated in solo flute with harp arpeggio accompaniment, it is embellished by countermelodies and imitative entrances in other instruments. As complexity increases, the dynamic level builds until the

movement fades into a quiet close by fragmenting the melodic line between various woodwind instruments.

Movement 4: "Seguedille"

This movement is derived from Act I of the opera and is performed by Carmen. It is a dance in fast triple meter performed to the accompaniment of a song. Solo oboe and solo trumpet take the part of Carmen in this setting, singing the melody in the opening section. As the momentum builds, the full woodwind section shares the melody. The movement ends with two loud *tutti* chords.

Movement 5: "Les Dragons d'Alcala"

Movement 5 sets a military tone with the addition of the snare drum. The form is ABA with a coda. Bassoon plays the first theme with rhythmic accompaniment in the pizzicato strings and the snare drum. A short second theme employs antiphonal effects between flute and clarinet and the strings with a chromatic passage leading back to the reprise of the first melodic idea. Clarinet plays the original theme this time, while bassoon plays a chromatic countermelody. The strings join to accompany, and a fragmented version of the theme is passed from one woodwind voice to the next until the very quiet three final chords.

Movement 6: Les Toréadors"

The well-known melodies and virtuosic bravura of this movement make it the perfect finale for this suite. Although this movement really occurs as a prelude to Act I in the opera, it captures the spirit of the entire opera so well that it is the music most people think of when *Carmen* is mentioned. It begins with two statements of the first theme by the full orchestra. A contrasting section played by woodwinds and strings, leading back to another statement of the opening theme with all instruments, follows this first section. The famous "Toreador Song" enters first in the strings and is accompanied by short chords on the beat in trumpet and trombone. Woodwinds join at the end of this melody to answer a phrase before a scalar passage for all strings, woodwinds, and trumpets *crescendos* into the *tutti* statement of the Toreador theme. The movement finishes with a reprise of the first theme and a final flourish for a dramatic gesture with full instrumentation.

Unit 8: Suggested Listening

Georges Bizet:
> *Carmen*
> *La jolie fille de Perth* ("The Pretty Girl of Perth")
> *L'Arlésienne* Suite Nos. 1 and 2
> *Les pêcheurs de perles* ("The Pearl Fishers")
> Symphony in C

Unit 9: Additional References and Resources

Cooper, Martin. *Georges Bizet*. London, New York: Oxford University Press, 1938.

Curtiss, Mina. *Bizet and His World*. New York: Knopf, 1958.

Dean, Winston. *Bizet,* 3d edition. London: Dent, 1975.

Guin, John, and Les Stone, eds. *The St. James Opera Encyclopedia*. Detroit: Visible Ink Press, 1997.

McClary, Susan. *Bizet, Carmen*. Cambridge, New York: Cambridge University Press, 1992.

Randel, Don Michael, ed. *The Harvard Biographical Dictionary of Music*. Cambridge, MA: Belknap Press of Harvard University Press, 1996.

Sadie, Stanley, ed. *Grove Dictionary of Opera*. London: Macmillan, 1992.

Sadie, Stanley, ed. *The New Grove Dictionary of Music and Musicians*. New York: Grove's Dictionaries, 2000. Also available online at www.grovemusic.com

Scholes, Percy. *The Oxford Companion to Music*. London: Oxford University Press, 1970.

Slonimsky, Nicolas, ed. emeritus. *Baker's Biographical Dictionary of Musicians*. New York: Schirmer Books, 2001.

Contributed by:

Kristin Turner
String Music Education
Arizona State University
Tempe, Arizona

Teacher Resource Guide

Chorale Prelude: "Wachet auf, ruft uns die Stimme"

Johann Sebastian Bach
(1685–1750)

arranged by Eugene Ormandy

FULL ORCHESTRA

Unit 1: Composer

Johann Sebastian Bach was born in Eisenach, Germany, on March 21, 1685, and died in Leipzig on July 28, 1750. The greatest master of the baroque era, Bach was a teacher, composer, and conductor. He first gained prominence as court organist to Duke Wilhelm Ernst of Weimar from 1709 until 1717. In 1717, he accepted the position of music director to Prince Leopold of Anhalt in Cöthen. However, the Duke of Weimar initially refused to release Bach and had him jailed. He was finally released after a month of internment and proceeded to Cöthen, where he was extremely productive. He wrote the Brandenburg Concertos, the first volume of the *Well-Tempered Clavier*, and many purely instrumental works. In 1723, Bach was elected to the post of Cantor in Leipzig, where he focused on his greatest sacred works, *St. John Passion*, Mass in B Minor, and *Christmas Oratorio*.

Unit 2: Composition

The church cantata BWV 140, "Wachet auf, ruft uns die Stimme," was written in 1731. "Wachet auf" ("wake up") is known as "Sleepers Awake" in the United States. The main theme in the cantata was taken from a Lutheran hymn. It is also used in an organ prelude of the same name (BWV 645), arranged for modern orchestra by Eugene Ormandy, who was conductor of the

Philadelphia Orchestra from 1938 until 1980.

An organ prelude is a polyphonic elaboration of a Protestant hymn that is used as a prelude to a congregational chorale. Bach wrote more than 140 organ chorales, and they are considered to be the pinnacle of the form. This arrangement lasts approximately four minutes and thirty seconds.

Unit 3: Historical Perspective

Music of the baroque era culminates in the work of J. S. Bach. The late baroque style is marked by large, formal patterns such as the ritornello form in the concerto. Other prominent composers of this period include George Frideric Handel, Georg Philipp Telemann, and Antonio Vivaldi. The musical developments of the baroque period abandoned the more moderate *bel canto* style in favor of insistent, rhythmic motives and the strict orderly fashion of the fugue. The chorale preludes are reminiscent of the *stile antico*, maintained for religious music and some instrumental works of the period. Chorale Prelude: "Wachet auf" was written in 1731 during Bach's tenure in Leipzig. While in Leipzig, Bach composed primarily sacred works. As director of church music, he was responsible for the care of the musicians for four churches. He was also responsible for preparing music for performance at two of those churches, the Thomaskirche and Nicolaikirche. He taught at the Thomasschüle, where he founded the Collegium Musicum, an ensemble comprised of professional musicians and university students that gave weekly concerts.

Unit 4: Technical Considerations

The composition is firmly in the key of E-flat major and its related keys. The use of extensions and some alternate finger patterns will be necessary for the strings. The use of unisons and octave doublings in the orchestration will need particular attention, especially because the arranger uses extreme dynamic levels ranging from *pp* to *fff*. The tessitura demands are not extreme, although some position work will be required in the first violin and bass parts. The arranger uses the deep sonorities of the lower strings throughout the work. The piece is arranged for standard orchestration with the addition of English horn doubled in the second oboe part. The clarinets are in B-flat, and the trumpets are in C. Timpani and tam-tam are the only percussion instruments needed. Rhythmically there are few challenges—mainly syncopated entrances on the weak part of the beat.

Unit 5: Stylistic Considerations

Legato style is used throughout the piece. The arranger makes use of slurs throughout, and the conductor may need to mark bowings in the string parts. Although facilitated somewhat by orchestration, dynamics are extreme, ranging from *pp* to *fff*. The piece gradually increases in volume throughout, with some slight ebb and flow, until it ends with a flourish. Timpani and tam-tam

are used to accentuate the *fff* dynamic marking. Rich, deep sonority is needed throughout the work from all instruments. Balance needs to be maintained between the melody, countermelody, and bass line while taking the dynamic level into consideration. The tempo is steady throughout, but some liberties could be taken by the conductor to facilitate the musical line.

Unit 6: Musical Elements

Major tonality is prevalent in this work with a small excursion to minor. The melodic line contains two motives that form an antecedent-consequent relationship. The first two times the melody is presented in E-flat major. The third time the melody is in B-flat, and the fourth time it modulates to C minor. The fifth and final time the melody is presented in the tonic key of E-flat. The harmony is consonant with slight dissonance in passing notes only. The piece is strophic with slight variation at the end. As with most baroque works, the melodic material is diatonic with small leaps. The meter does not change. The melodic line uses eighth notes and long lines of sixteenth notes, while the accompaniment uses quarter notes and eighth notes.

Unit 7: Form and Structure

Form: strophic

A	A′	:‖ A′	a	A
E-flat major	E-flat major	B-flat major	C minor	E-flat major
Beginning to #2	#2	#3	#4	#5

Unit 8: Suggested Listening

Johann Sebastian Bach:
    Brandenburg Concertos
    Cantata No. 140: "Wachet auf, ruft uns die Stimme"
    Orchestral Suites 1–4
Johann Sebastian Bach/arr. Stokowski, Toccata and Fugue in D Minor

Unit 9: Additional References and Resources

Downes, Edward. *Guide to Symphonic Music*. New York: Walker and Company, 1976.

Headington, Christopher. *Johann Sebastian Bach: An Essential Guide to His Life and Works*. London, Great Britain: Pavillion Books Limited, 1997.

Kennedy, Michael, ed. *The Oxford Dictionary of Music*. 2d edition. Oxford: Oxford University Press, 1994.

Slonimsky, Nicolas, ed. emeritus. *Baker's Biographical Dictionary of Musicians*. New York: Schirmer Books, 2001.

Contributed by:

Jeffrey Bishop
Division Coordinator of Fine Arts and Director of Orchestras
Shawnee Mission Northwest High School
Shawnee Mission, Kansas

Teacher Resource Guide

Concerto Grosso No. 1 in G Major, Op. 6

George Frideric Handel
(1685–1759)

STRING ORCHESTRA

Unit 1: Composer

George Frideric Handel was born in Halle on February 23, 1685, into a family with no musicians. Handel's father reluctantly recognized his son's talent and allowed him to study with Friedrich Wilhelm Zachow, a local composer, organist, and church music director. Zachow taught young Handel organ and harpsichord, and introduced him to composition.

Handel moved to Hamburg in 1703 and then traveled in Italy from 1706 to 1710. In 1710 at the age of twenty-five, he was appointed as the Kapellmeister of the electoral court of Hanover. He almost immediately took two lengthy leaves of absence to go to London. During the second absence, his master, the elector of Hanover, was crowned King George I of England. Handel remained in London for the rest of his life. In 1727, he became a British subject and Anglicized his name.

Handel, one of the greatest composers of the baroque period, received international recognition even during his lifetime for his operas, oratorios, cantatas, sacred music, and instrumental music. His instrumental compositions include concerti grossi; harpsichord suites; organ concerti; chamber music for strings, winds, and keyboard; and large orchestral works. Handel died in London on April 14, 1759, and was laid to rest in Westminster Abby.

Unit 2: Composition

Handel composed his twelve Concerti Grossi, Op. 6, in the fall of 1739 in one month's time. He originally intended that they should be used as instrumental interludes between the choral works at the theatre. The composition was advertised in the *London Daily Post* as "Twelve Grand Concertos, in Seven Parts for Four Violins, a Tenor, a Violoncello, with a Thorough-Bass for the Harpsichord." Handel received a Royal Privilege of Copyright for the work, and his agent, John Walsh, opened a subscription for their publication.

Unit 3: Historical Perspective
Two forms of the concerto, the solo concerto and the concerto grosso, were typical in the baroque period. The solo concerto uses a single instrument as a soloist, and the concerto grosso uses a group of soloists (concertino), usually three, in contrast to the larger orchestra (ripieno). The thematic material is usually presented by the full orchestra and is then developed by the soloists, the purpose being development rather than as a display of virtuosity. Another set of concerti grossi was already well-known by the time Handel wrote his "Grand Concertos." This set by Arcangelo Corelli, whom Handel had met in Italy, was published posthumously in 1714. Corelli's set of concerti grossi was also Opus 6.

Unit 4: Technical Considerations
Preliminary work with scales in the keys of G major and E minor will prepare musicians for this composition. Both simple and compound meters with separate and hooked bowings should be practiced with rhythms that include dotted-eighth and sixteenth notes. Separate string-crossing exercises, particularly with the use of octaves, will be especially helpful for the violinists. The violin, viola, and cello parts are playable within first, second, and third position. The bass part encompasses the first four positions. An introductory explanation of baroque instruments will help the musicians understand the technical and stylistic differences between early and modern instruments.

Unit 5: Stylistic Considerations
This work should be performed in a traditional baroque style. The bowing should be controlled and on the string, with separation between the notes. Parts should be balanced with violinists, working for smooth and precise transitions connecting the sixteenth note passages. Dynamic contrast should be distinct. Trills begin on the auxiliary note.

Unit 6: Musical Elements
Contrast in this composition is achieved between the movements by the changes in tempo, meter, and key. Additional contrast is achieved through the use of the solo and concertino parts. Dynamic markings include only *forte*, *piano*, and *pianissimo*. The elegant first movement is marked "A tempo giusto," which indicates simply a precise or an appropriate tempo for the work. Four of the five movements are in G major with an occasional modulation to G

minor or D major. The third movement, "Adagio," is in E minor. The first, second, and fourth movements are in 4/4 time. The third movement is in 3/4, and the final, dance-like movement is in 6/8. The concertino parts are developmental rather than virtuosic.

Unit 7: Form and Structure

The complete Concerto Grosso No. 1 is approximately twelve minutes in length. The concertino parts and the ripieno parts are usually identical except for the solo passages. Occasionally, the parts function separately.

Movement 1: "A tempo giusto"
G major with a brief modulation to G minor; moderate tempo with an emphasis on precision; unifying rhythm pattern of quarter note/dotted-eighth and sixteenth notes/quarter note; ends on the dominant that leads into the second movement.

Movement 2: "Allegro"
4/4; G major; last two measures traditionally done at a slower tempo.

Movement 3: "Adagio"
3/4; E minor; opens with soloists; ends on the dominant that leads into movement four.

Movement 4: "Allegro"
4/4; G major; fugal style with independent parts.

Movement 5: "Allegro"
6/8; two repeated sections; G major; second section begins in D and modulates to G major; the movement, a giga, is characterized by fluid sixteenth note passage work between first and second violin.

Unit 8: Suggested Listening

Johann Sebastian Bach, Six Brandenburg Concertos
Arcangelo Corelli, Concerto Grosso, Op. 6
George Frideric Handel:
    Concerti Grossi, Op. 6, Nos. 1–12
    Concerti Grossi, Op. 3, Nos. 1–6
    Water Music

Unit 9: Additional References and Resources

Brown, Howard Mayer, and Stanley Sadie, eds. *Performance Practice: Music after 1600*. New York: W. W. Norton & Company, 1989.

Donington, Robert. *The Interpretation of Early Music*. New revised edition. New York: W. W. Norton & Company, 1992.

Grout, Donald Jay, and Claude V. Palisca. *A History of Western Music*. 6th edition. New York: W. W. Norton & Company, 2001.

Hutchings, Arthur. *The Baroque Concerto*. New York: Charles Scribner's Sons, 1978.

Randall, Don Michael, ed. *The Harvard Biographical Dictionary of Music*. Cambridge: Harvard University Press, 1996.

Randall, Don Michael, ed. *The New Harvard Dictionary of Music*. Cambridge: Harvard University Press, 1986.

Sadie, Stanley, ed. *The New Grove Dictionary of Music and Musicians*. New York: Grove's Dictionaries, 2000. Also available online at www.grovemusic.com

Slonimsky, Nicolas, ed. emeritus. *Baker's Biographical Dictionary of Music and Musicians*. New York: Schirmer Books, 2001.

Contributed by:

Mary Lou Jones
Director of Orchestras
Shawnee Mission South High School
Shawnee Mission, Kansas

Teacher Resource Guide

Concerto Grosso, Op. 6, No. 8 ("Christmas Concerto")

Arcangelo Corelli
(1653–1713)

STRING ORCHESTRA

Unit 1: Composer

Arcangelo Corelli was born in 1653 in the little town of Fusignano, between Bologna and Ravenna. After initial studies with a local parish priest, he was sent to Bologna, a principal center of violin playing in seventeenth century Italy, the most notable figures being G. B. Vitali and later Giuseppe Tartini. He moved to Rome in 1675 and accepted a variety of positions there as a freelance performer and conductor. He quickly established himself as a composer and received the patronage of the nobility, both sacred and secular. He published five sets of sonatas for violin between 1681 and 1700. Although the concerti grossi of Op. 6 were not published until 1714, the year after his death, individual works are now believed to have been composed as early as 1682. They were certainly in circulation among musicians in the late seventeenth century, for Corelli was greatly respected and widely imitated throughout Europe. He retired as an active player in 1708 and spent his years before he died in 1713 revising his concerti grossi and preparing them for publication.

Unit 2: Composition

The Concerto Grosso in G Minor, Op. 6, No. 8, is the last in the set (of twelve concerti) to be a *concerto da chiesa*, composed in the church style. Nos. 9 through 12 are in the *concerto da camera* (chamber) style, with movements given dance names. Corelli added an inscription in the score "Concerto fatto per la notte di Natale" (Concerto composed for Christmas Eve). It may have been composed as early as 1690 for one of his patrons, Cardinal Ottoboni. In

Italy at this time, it was traditional for shepherds to bring their flocks into the towns on Christmas Eve, playing tunes on their pipes or flutes as they went. The incorporation of a "Pastorale" movement evidently entitled the composer to designate his work as a "Christmas Concerto." Giuseppe Tartini, Francesco Manfredini, Johann David Heinichen, and Georg Philip Telemann composed similar works.

Unit 3: Historical Perspective
Corelli was a pivotal figure in the middle baroque period. Not only is he credited with defining the concerto grosso form, but his harmonic structure solidified the major/minor tonal system and functional harmony, and left behind the modal system that had organized European music for hundreds of years. Corelli was unusual for his time in that all of his published works were orchestrated for strings only—five sets of sonatas for violin and one set of concerti grossi. His sonatas of Op. 5 were orchestrated by Francesco Geminiani and enjoyed considerable popularity. In addition to the composers listed above, Antonio Vivaldi, Giuseppe Torelli, Benedetto Marcello, and Tomasso Albinoni in Italy, as well as George Frideric Handel, Willem de Fesch, Georg Muffat, and Johann Gottfried Walther in northern Europe carried on and developed the form. The Brandenburg Concertos of J. S. Bach are perhaps the final flowering of the concerto grosso; its logical heirs would include the *Sinfonie Concertante* of Haydn and his generation.

Unit 4: Technical Considerations
Although the concertino parts are more demanding and more exposed, the entire ensemble must be completely comfortable in G minor and its related keys. The violin parts do not go above third position, and cello does not go beyond fourth position. Scale and arpeggio figurations are common, and cadential formulas in the lower strings call for clean string crossing. The rhythms are very basic, but the suspensions and quick interjections by the ripieno call for careful counting.

Unit 5: Stylistic Considerations
Much has been written about the baroque style of bowing, baroque bows themselves, and the characteristic sound of unwrapped gut strings on instruments set up in the baroque manner. For our purposes, let us be satisfied with achieving a clean, articulate détaché and a liquid, flowing legato sound from the ensemble. At its loudest, the tone of the ensemble should sound robust but not forced and, conversely, gentle but not weak. Accents, especially in the long series of suspensions, should be sounded like bells, with a firm attack and a slight *decrescendo* so that the entering or moving voice can be heard clearly. The athletic jumps in the cello and bass line are best articulated with a slight staccato but without heavy attacks or accents.

Unit 6: Musical Elements

The interplay of the voices, not only between the concertino and ripieno but also within each group, may be described as dialog, echo, or reinforcement. In the first movement, for example, each voice enters into the conversation of suspension and resolution, with the concertino and ripieno playing together. In the second movement, the concertino violins continue the suspension dialog over a running bass line in the concertino cello. The ripieno adds reinforcement to the concertino lines in echoing passages and provides emphasis at cadences. These techniques form the basic structure of the entire concerto. Corelli's harmonic language never strays too far from the tonality of G minor and its related keys except in the third movement (see below), where the outer sections are in E-flat major and the middle section is in C minor. The final movement changes the robust nature of what has gone before—both harmonically and rhythmically—to a flowing and sunny G major tonality.

Unit 7: Form and Structure

When new tempos are indicated in baroque music, it usually signifies a separate movement. There are nine indications of tempo in the "Christmas Concerto," but some of these separate sections are very short—only a few measures long. Grouping some of them together makes more musical sense and provides contrast within a unified structure.

Movement 1: "Vivace–Grave"
>   The fanfare-like, seven-measure Vivace leads into a sostenuto Grave, which is a thirteen-measure string of suspensions very typical of the slow movements in Corelli's sonatas.

Movement 2: "Allegro"
>   A large AB form; the running bass line in the concertino cello supports more suspensions in the concertino violin, with echoes, responses, and cadences reinforced by the ripieno.

Movement 3: "Adagio–Allegro–Adagio"
>   ABA form; the concertino converses with arpeggios with support from the ripieno in the outer sections of this movement; in the Allegro section, the concertino and ripieno play together, first violin bustling along with sixteenth notes and second violin playing the melody.

Movement 4: "Vivace"
>   Another binary movement, this is a pleasant minuet, with the concertino carrying the melodic interest and being answered and reinforced at cadences by the ripieno.

Movement 5: "Allegro"
>   This is the longest binary movement of the concerto, continuing the dialog

between the concertino and ripieno with imitative entrances.

Movement 6: "Pastorale"

This is the most extended movement of the concerto, in a gently rocking 12/8 meter; at times the ripieno supports the concertino with little more than a drone, giving a bagpipe-like effect, completely in character with the tradition of the pastorale form; although both the concertino and ripieno have assertive moments, they draw together for a quiet and serene ending.

Unit 8: Suggested Listening

The "Christmas Concerto" of Corelli is one of the most recorded works in the repertoire. Interesting comparisons can be made between recordings done in the modern orchestral style and those made by ensembles dedicated to historically informed performance in the baroque style. Excellent performances are available in both styles.

Arcangelo Corelli, Concerti Grossi, Op. 6
George Frideric Handel, Concerti Grossi, Op. 6
Johann Heinichen:
    Concerto No. 8 in C Major
    Pastorale in A Major
Vincenzo Manfredini:
    Concerto in D Major, Op. 2, No. 12
    Concerto in C Major, Op. 3, No. 12
Giuseppe Tartini, Sinfonia Pastorale in D Major

Unit 9: Additional References and Resources

Bukofzer, Manfred F. *Music in the Baroque Era*. New York: W. W. Norton & Company, 1947.

Donington, Robert. *String Playing in Baroque Music*. New York: Charles Scribner's Sons, 1977.

Dorian, Frederick. *The History of Music in Performance*. New York: W. W. Norton & Company, 1942.

Palisca, Claude V. Edited by H. Wiley Hitchcock. *Music in the Baroque Era*. Englewood Cliffs: Prentice-Hall, Inc., 1968.

Sadie, Stanley, ed. *The New Grove Dictionary of Music and Musicians*. "Arcangelo Corelli" by Michael Talbot. New York: Grove's Dictionaries, 2000. Also available online at www.grovemusic.com

Contributed by:
Harry Fisher
Retired Educator, Composer/Arranger
Cherry Hill, New Jersey

Teacher Resource Guide

Concerto in D Minor

Johann Sebastian Bach
(1685–1750)

arranged by Merle Isaac

STRING ORCHESTRA

Unit 1: Composer/Arranger

Johann Sebastian Bach was born in Eisenach, Germany, on March 21, 1685. Both parents were musicians but died before Johann was ten years of age. Bach lived with his older brother, Johann Christoph, who taught him to play harpsichord and clavichord. He studied music until 1703, when he joined an orchestra in Weimar as a violinist. Bach served as organist at churches in Arnstadt and Mühlhausen (1703–08) and returned to Weimar in 1708 to work in the court of the Duke of Saxe-Weimar as court organist and chamber musician. From 1717 to 1723, he served Prince Leopold of Anhalt-Cöthen as director of music. He moved to Leipzig in 1723 to become director of music for St. Thomas's School and Church. In 1729, he became director of the Collegium Musicum of Leipzig.

Bach was Lutheran, and many of his choral and instrumental compositions were written for the church services. He had a large family—seven children from his first wife, his cousin Maria Barbara, and thirteen from his second wife, Anna Magdalena, a professional singer—but only nine children were living at the time of his death in 1750. Four of his sons had distinguished careers as composers: Wilhelm Friedemann (1710–84), Carl Philipp Emanuel (1714–88), Johann Christoph Friedrich (1732–95), and Johann Christian (1735–82).

Bach was recognized as an organist during his lifetime. Of the approximately sixty volumes of work, only nine or ten of Bach's compositions were

published while he was living. His reputation as a composer was not established until about 1829 when Mendelssohn revived his *Passion According to St. Matthew*.

Merle Isaac was born on October 12, 1898, in the rural community of Pioneer, Ohio. His family moved to Chicago when he was in fourth grade. Merle had instruction on piano and organ, and taught himself to play flute. He began his music career both as a church organist and a theater organist for silent films. When talkies began to replace the silent films, a new career was necessary. Isaac took violin and trumpet lessons plus counterpoint and orchestration. He took and passed the Chicago Board of Education Examination, and in 1929 Isaac was assigned to John Marshall High School in Chicago. In his fourteen years as the head of the Department of Instrumental Music, he developed an exemplary music program with a ninety-piece orchestra that took first place honors in city, state, and national competitions.

To further his knowledge of instruments and teaching, Isaac took classes at VanderCook College of Music and private lessons on all the string instruments, played in the band, and taught piano. Isaac's writing for orchestra began when he discovered there was a shortage of music suitable for school orchestras. He edited, arranged, and wrote music for his own groups, writing a new piece for each concert. The *Merle Isaac String Method* was written to meet the needs of his high school groups. Isaac remained active as a composer and arranger during his twenty-one years as principal of Talcott Elementary School, after his retirement in 1964, and continuing until his death on March 11, 1996.

Isaac was a forerunner in writing compositions and arrangements for the school orchestra that were both challenging and playable. Isaac was active as a clinician, as an adjudicator at all levels, and as a guest conductor. He lectured extensively at music conferences and contributed articles to many music publications. He was active in the American String Teachers Association, the National School Orchestra Association, the Music Educators National Conference, and other professional organizations. He received the ASTA Distinguished Service Award in 1970 and the Midwest International Band and Orchestra Clinic Medal of Honor in 1981. Also, National School Orchestra Association created a Lifetime Award in his honor, for which he was the first recipient in 1993. In 1996, Isaac was posthumously inducted into the Music Educators National Conference Hall of Fame.

Unit 2: Composition

J. S. Bach originally wrote the Concerto in D Minor for harpsichord solo with chamber orchestra accompaniment. It was composed between 1731–33 in Leipzig, where Bach was Cantor at St. Thomas Church, probably to be performed at the weekly concerts of the Collegium Musicum of Leipzig. Much of his work during this period was transcriptions or adaptations of concertos written by him or other composers for other instruments. This was the first time that the harpsichord was treated as a solo instrument in concerto form with orchestra accompaniment. The source of the D minor concerto cannot be traced but is generally thought to be from a violin concerto from another composer. Other concertos for one, two, three, and four harpsichords were written during this period. The Concerto in D Minor was written in baroque style with three movements (Allegro, Adagio, Allegro), but only the first movement is used in this arrangement. It is set in a somber, driving mood with strong accents and syncopation with all three movements in the minor key. It contains fugal episodes and modulates regularly to different keys. Isaac has adapted the first movement of the concerto by eliminating the harpsichord solo and using the orchestra opening, ending, and interludes to create this two-minute abridged version. Because of the flats and finger extensions as well as the skips over strings, the piece is a Grade 3–4 in difficulty.

Unit 3: Historical Perspective

The Concerto in D Minor was among the first concertos of a new genre to be written for keyboard with orchestra accompaniment in the fourth period of Bach's writing (1723–45). Bach was a devout Lutheran and, through his position as Cantor of St. Thomas Church, was the person in charge of music for all the churches in Leipzig. Many of his works were cantatas and instrumental music used in the churches and the St. Thomas School. During this period of writing, Bach had more time to devote to secular writing because St. Thomas was undergoing extensive renovation. He wrote and transcribed music for the Collegium Musicum of Leipzig. This society provided students an opportunity to perform and listen to music that was performed in weekly concerts. Bach experimented with various instrumental solo combinations in the baroque concerto and concerto grosso style. It was common for him to use whole pieces or themes in various settings. The first movement of the Concerto in D Minor was used as the introduction to Cantata No. 146 (1731), and the first and second movements were used later with modifications in Cantata No. 146 (1740). Baroque-style bowing is used throughout with accents and syncopation marked with space and separation. There is almost constant movement throughout the work. Bach was a master of counterpoint and the fugue. The Concerto in D Minor begins and ends in unison, with fugue variations and a section of fugal motifs in two-measure segments in the development.

Isaac's arrangement of the D minor concerto was published in 1985 after he had retired from his teaching career. It maintains the essence of the orchestra parts and combines them into a whole in a way that is complete without the solo part. All strings have interesting parts. Dynamics are typically baroque: thematic solo parts and unisons are *forte*; background parts are *piano*. Variations are *p*, *mf*, and *f* with no *crescendos* or *decrescendos*. The

counterpoint and the basso continuo are always scored softer than the theme.

Unit 4: Technical Considerations

The scales of D minor, A minor, and G minor are required for all parts. Two-measure motifs are played in C minor, F major, B-flat major, E-flat major, and A major for violin and viola. It is helpful to practice scales and thirds in each key. The thirds can be practiced first in eighth notes (quarter note = 60 and gradually increasing to half note = 92). Rhythmic variations can be used. Scales can be practiced in canon style a third apart, and thirds can be practiced in canon style starting every fifth note. Violin and viola stay within first position. Cello must use brief periods of second, third, and fourth positions, and backward and forward extensions. Bass players use half, second, and third positions. Bass and cello parts are simplified to make descending scale passages rather than the unison thirds of violin and viola. There is a second cello part that is in unison with the bass part and can be used for less-accomplished players. Rhythmic demands are basic with half, quarter, and eighth notes written in 2/2 time. Half notes and quarter notes need to be spaced. Eighth notes are détaché. There is a syncopated fugal theme in the inner parts that needs to be addressed.

Unit 5: Stylistic Considerations

The martelé style of baroque bowing should be maintained throughout the piece whether the part is melody or accompaniment. Melodic line must always project, especially with each fugal entrance. Movement must be precise and together in the unisons with uniform spacing of notes across the orchestra. The mood of D minor is somber and needs to be played with sonority. There is a relentless drive in the first movement that reaches a final resolution in the final unison statement of the opening ritornello. The basso continuo enhances the drive with its steady rhythm and dissonances.

Unit 6: Musical Elements

The main theme begins with a unison *tutti* in D minor. This theme—ritornel-lo—occurs again in the tonic key and then is heard in the dominant and subdominant. Contrast of timbre occurs through alternation of the parts playing the theme or fugal episodes, the syncopated counterpoint played a third above the theme, and a basso continuo. First violin begins the theme in each key, with other parts beginning one measure later. Compositional devices include motivic interplay of parts with rapid succession of modulations driving to the final resolution of D minor. The theme is basically composed of chord notes combined with both scales and descending thirds.

Unit 7: Form and Structure

SECTION	EVENT AND SCORING
Theme 1	Twelve-measure unison *tutti* in D minor; bass part simplified in mm. 3–8, then unison again in mm. 11–12
Theme 1 repeated	First violin repeats in mm. 13–22
Fugal variation 1	All other parts begin one measure later at m. 14; cello and bass begin the motif on the tonic; second violin and viola begin a third above continuing with counterpoint syncopation in m. 15 that becomes a fugue in m. 16 two beats after first violin; *tutti* unison in mm. 22–24 modulates to the dominant key of A minor
Theme 1 dominant	First violin repeats theme up a fifth in A minor in mm. 25–34
Fugal variation 2	In m. 35 cello/bass have a basso continuo part; second violin is a third above the theme with the same progression as fugal variation 1; viola begins motif on tonic with the same style of counterpoint that cello/bass played in variation 1; unison *tutti* in mm. 35–36 modulates to G minor
Theme 1 subdominant	First violin has theme in mm. 37–45 in G minor; other parts start in m. 38 with a one-measure theme motif (second violin a sixth below first violin; viola, cello, bass on tonic) that becomes a counterpoint to the theme; unison *tutti* in mm. 46–47 modulates to D minor
Fugal motive	Two-measure motifs alternate between first and second violin/viola (mm. 49–62) beginning in D minor and modulating in a pattern of keys each a fourth above the last (D minor, G minor, C minor, F, B-flat minor, E-flat, A) and leading back from dominant to tonic of D minor in m. 63; harmony alternates with the melody while the cello/bass act as basso continuo throughout
Theme 1 repeated	Scored same as beginning (mm. 63–74 parallels mm. 1–12) in D minor
Fugal variation 1 repeated	Measures 75–83 parallel mm. 13–22 in D minor
Tutti ending	Unison ending mm. 85–88; final cadence of ii°–V–I

Unit 8: Suggested Listening

Johann Sebastian Bach:
>   Brandenburg Concertos, Nos. 1–6
>   Concerto in D Minor for Harpsichord and Orchestra
>   Concerto in D Minor for Two Violins and Orchestra
>   Fugue in F
>   *Italian Concerto*

Antonio Vivaldi, *The Four Seasons*

Unit 9: Additional References and Resources

Encyclopedia Britannica. *Concerto.* Accessed 22 May 2000. Available from
   http://www.britannica.com/bcom/eb/article/4/0/5716,
   118784+4+4+10136,00.html: Internet.

Harley, Frances. Merle, Master Musician. *The American String Teacher* 46,
   No. 2 (1997: 25-31).

Paul, Steven S. Album notes from *Anthony Newman Plays and Conducts Bach
   Concerto in D Minor.* BMV1052, Quadraphonic. New York: Columbia
   Records MQ32300.

Sadie, Stanley, ed. *The New Grove Dictionary of Music and Musicians.* "J. S.
   Bach." New York: Grove's Dictionaries, 2000. Also available online at
   www.grovemusic.com

Contributed by:

Janet E. Elliott
Adjunct Professor of Music Education (Violin, Viola)
Friends University
Wichita, Kansas

Teacher Resource Guide

Dance of Iscariot

Kirt Mosier
(b. 1962)

STRING ORCHESTRA

Unit 1: Composer

Kirt Mosier is currently Director of Orchestras at Lee's Summit High School and Pleasant Lee Junior High in Lee's Summit, Missouri. He is also an adjunct professor with Baker University and a professional pianist who has played for such groups as The Drifters, Del Shannon, and The Fifth Dimension. He holds a Bachelor's of Music Education and a Masters of Music in Composition from the University of Missouri Conservatory of Music in Kansas City. Winner of the 1993 National School Orchestra Association Composition Contest for *Baltic Dance*, Mosier is an active guest clinician and school music composer. His other string orchestra compositions include Allegro from Telemann's Sonata No. 1, *Overture to the Wind*, and *Funky Fingers*.

Unit 2: Composition

Dance of Iscariot, written in 1997, is a rousing, energetic work set in ABA form. The opening section in E minor has a heavily accented staccato melody accompanied by spiccato double-stops and descending chromatic scales. Three fugal statements of a contrasting legato style and a modulation to B minor comprise the middle section. An *accelerando* to presto and a shift to E major interrupt the return of the opening section. Lasting two minutes and thirty seconds and written for Grade 4 string orchestra, this composition provides an opportunity to introduce a wide range of advanced bow techniques and minor tonalities within a context that is both appealing and satisfying.

Unit 3: Historical Perspective

In the last fifteen years, school orchestras have experienced a bold resurgence both in quantity and quality. Concurrent with this growth, an increasing number of composers have turned to writing specifically for the educational setting. Individuals such as Francis Feese, William Hofeldt, Richard Meyer, and Carold Nuñez are among the many whom have chosen to specialize in this genre. Mosier's *Dance of Iscariot* is another outstanding example of high-quality original music for young players. An excellent teaching and performance piece, it provides intermediate level string students a chance to explore contemporary harmonies, style, and the relationship of minor and major keys.

Unit 4: Technical Considerations

Dance of Iscariot poses several intonation challenges for the entire ensemble. Descending chromatic scales, non-divided double-stops, extension fingerings, and a shift to the parallel major will all require special attention to ensure accurate tuning. Set in E minor with a brief foray into B melodic minor, the piece also calls for fluency in third position for violin and viola, and half position for cello and bass. Despite simple rhythms and meter, the brisk tempo, quarter note = 148 with an *accelerando* to presto at the end, will likely need a slow, meticulous approach in early rehearsals to secure a steady and precise tempo.

Unit 5: Stylistic Considerations

The composition begins with percussive spiccato double-stops that gradually build in intensity. Three contrasting bow styles (legato, staccato, and spiccato) characterize the opening and closing sections. Students will not only need to be familiar with these styles but comfortable moving between them quickly. Due to the brisk tempo, articulation, particularly staccato, must remain light and buoyant. Rapid and repeated lift bows with a *subito p* and a *crescendo* to *f* challenge all players to execute a controlled recovery in the correct part of the bow. The B section requires a full, rich, legato sound and careful attention to the balance among the three fugal statements. Pieces in this style also demand meticulous attention to dynamics, both in terms of range as well as sudden contrasts.

Unit 6: Musical Elements

MEASURES	EVENT AND SCORING
Beginning–28	Double-stops in open fourths and fifths outline the key of E minor; descending chromatic scales in the low strings provide the harmony; motive of E–D-sharp–E (eighth–eighth–quarter) in first violin begins at m. 7 and is used throughout the melody in the A section

MEASURES	EVENT AND SCORING
29–40	Countermelody, using the same rhythm and intervals as the motive, stated in violin and viola
52–58	B theme stated in E minor by second violin and viola
59–66	B theme restated in B minor by first violin with a countermelody in second violin and viola
67–75	Key shift back to E minor; a third melody added in cello and bass
76–83	A theme restated using question and answer between first violin and lower strings
89–end	Key shift to E major

Unit 7: Form and Structure

SECTION	MEASURES
Introduction	1
A	7
A^1	29
Transition	40
B	52
B^1	59
B^2	67
A^2	76
Codetta	85

Unit 8: Suggested Listening

George Bizet, *L'Arlésienne* Suite No. 2
Francis Feese, *Saison de Cordes*
Percy Fletcher, *Folk Tune and Fiddle Dance*
Richard Meyer, *Mantras*
Kirt Mosier:
    Baltic Dance
    Funky Fingers
Camille Saint-Saëns, "Bacchanale" from *Samson and Delilah*
Peter Warlock, *Capriol Suite*

Unit 9: Additional References and Resources

Green, Elizabeth A. H. *Orchestral Bowings and Routines*, 2d edition. Ann Arbor, MI: Campus Publishers, 1978.

Contributed by:

Kirt Mosier
Director of Orchestras
Lee's Summit High School and Pleasant Lee Junior High
Lee's Summit, Missouri

Teacher Resource Guide

Don Quixote Suite

Georg Philipp Telemann
(1681–1767)

STRING ORCHESTRA

Unit 1: Composer

Georg Philipp Telemann was born in Magdeburg, Germany, in 1681, and died in Hamburg in 1767. He was a leading German composer in the early to mid-eighteenth century, composing many works in sacred and secular genres in late baroque and early classical styles. His mother, from an upper-middle-class family, raised Telemann. He was educated with the expectation that he study law or continue in the career of his deceased father, a deacon in the church parish. Musicians were considered by some people during this time to encourage unseemly behavior and perpetuate many social ills.

The young Telemann was discouraged from music as a child, even though he showed great talent and interest in musical study. At age thirteen, Telemann was sent away to study the sciences and classical languages and hopefully be distracted from his musical interests. Unknown to his mother, the professor she had selected for him as a scholar in theology, history, and mathematics had an interest in the relationship between music and mathematics. Telemann received a thorough grounding in the theoretical study of music through his teenage years. He entered the University of Leipzig in 1701, at the age of twenty, to study law. However, his musical abilities were quickly recognized, and he became known as the new talent in the musical society in Leipzig. He was awarded a regular paid contract to provide music for the church. He held church and court positions throughout Germany for most of his life, producing a great number of operas, cantatas, and instrumental works.

Through his encouragement of public concerts and the prolific publication of music, Telemann made music available to a larger segment of the

population than previously had access to performances or printed music. He was a strong advocate for student involvement in the musical culture of the cities where he lived and worked, and had great influence on musical style through his concern with stylistic innovation.

Unit 2: Composition

The *Don Quixote* Suite is an eight-movement work, written in 1721, and based on Cervantes's humorous novel, *Don Quixote*. The novel, published in two parts in 1605 and 1615, was immensely popular and began to have great influence on the musical and literary worlds. Each movement in Telemann's suite provides the performer or listener a vivid picture of an adventure from the book. Originally written with basso continuo throughout, the work is playable by strings alone or with keyboard accompaniment, by a small chamber ensemble or larger orchestra. The short, contrasting movements describe adventures from the colorful and humorous story of Don Quixote's life. He was a self-styled knight-errant, or knight in shining armor in modern parlance. His ideals of chivalry came from the many books he had read on the subject, not from any direct experience of training. He took these books very seriously, and many of his misadventures stem from his vivid imagination and literal interpretation of instructions in the books.

Unit 3: Historical Perspective

The *Don Quixote* Suite was composed in Hamburg during the baroque period. Telemann's sense of humor and lightness in the piece, as well as technically accessible style, made this a work that had broad appeal. Printed music was still rather difficult to obtain in eighteenth century Germany, and Telemann's eagerness to publish made his compositions extremely popular. Telemann was a great advocate of the Collegium Musicum, a group of students and town citizens who performed public concerts. He encountered considerable resistance from the musical establishment in several cities where he sponsored such groups but was determined to continue this valuable educational activity. Such a group in Hamburg could have performed the *Don Quixote* Suite.

Unit 4: Technical Considerations

Sixteenth note scales in G major and D major, with quarter note = 110–120, are required for all instruments, remaining in first position except for bass. Viola and cello parts are playable in first position with few exceptions. The first violin part will require brief use of third position in "The Attack on Windmills" and "Don Quixote at Rest." Bass parts require more shifting. Rhythmic requirements include dotted-eighth and sixteenth note combinations and dotted-quarter and eighth notes with hooked bowings. Some slow movements contain thirty-second note subdivisions. Quick staccato articulation is necessary in fast movements, and students must be able to play staccato notes lightly and gracefully. In the baroque style, staccato passages are not to be played off the string. However, many young orchestras will not achieve a pleasing sound with their bows stuck on the string. Experimentation with a light, brushed staccato in rehearsal may help to bring about the correct concept of articulation.

Unit 5: Stylistic Considerations

Basic knowledge of early eighteenth century stringed instruments and bows is helpful in understanding the articulation and sound quality that Telemann would have expected in the performance of his compositions. Modern student instruments are built on patterns developed from the instruments of the baroque; the original physical setup and gut strings, however, created a much softer sound than modern high-tension steel strings. Tourte developed the modern bow in the latter half of the eighteenth century, so players in Telemann's day would have been performing with bows under much less tension than modern players' bows. Articulations should be followed precisely, in a restrained manner. Staccato quarter notes are lightly separated and played on the string. The Overture is a French overture form, implying that the dotted-quarter/eighth rhythms should be played as double-dotted quarters and sixteenths. Students should subdivide to the smallest note value in the texture. Staccato eighth notes in fast movements are played on the string in late baroque style. Nevertheless, some groups may be able to achieve a lighter, more delicate sound if the bow is allowed to come off the string slightly.

Unit 6: Musical Elements

The tonal center of the suite is G major, with sections modulating to the dominant, subdominant, and supertonic. Dissonances only occur as passing tones and fall predictably within the chord structure. The tonality of this work is very familiar to students and lends itself readily to chordal analysis when one considers all parts together with the basso continuo line. The melodic line consists of many scales, patterns, and sequences, and is primarily in the first violin part with sections of imitation in the other parts. The lower string parts and keyboard outline the chord structure. Repeated rhythmic patterns are prevalent throughout the work.

Unit 7: Form and Structure

Overture: G major
French overture: Largo, Allegro, Largo

Largo	Common time; dignified introduction, with the characteristic rhythm of hooked dotted-eighths and sixteenths, which give the introduction a feeling of lightness

| Allegro | 2/4 time; four-measure phrase in violin imitated in other voices |
| Largo | Sixteen-measure return similar to the beginning |

"His Attack on Windmills"
Binary (AB) form, G major, Allegro

| ‖ : G major | D major : ‖ |
| m.1 | m. 12 |

| ‖ : D major | G major : ‖ |
| m. 13 | m. 30 |

Two primary motives: motive 1 appears in mm. 1, 13, 21; motive 2 appears in mm. 6, 27

Unit 8:Suggested Listening
Richard Strauss, *Don Quixote*
 Many recordings available; this is the most widely known instrumental work based on Cervantes's novel
Georg Phillip Telemann, *Don Quixote*

Unit 9: Additional References and Resources
Dart, Thurston. *The Interpretation of Music.* New York: Harper & Row, 1963.

de Cervantes, Miguel. *The Adventures of Don Quixote, Man of La Mancha.* Many English translations are available.

Donnington, Robert. *Baroque Music: Style and Performance.* New York: W. W. Norton & Company, 1982.

Flynn, Susan Jane. *The Presence of Don Quixote in Music.* Ph.D. diss., University of Tennessee, Knoxville, 1984.

Grout, Donald Jay, and Claude V. Palisca. *A History of Western Music.* 6th edition. New York: W. W. Norton & Company, 2001.

Petzoldt, Richard. *Georg Philipp Telemann.* Trans. Horace Fitzpatrick. New York: Oxford University Press, 1974.

Sadie, Stanley, ed. *The New Grove Dictionary of Music and Musicians.* "Georg Philipp Telemann" by Martin Ruhnke. New York: Grove's Dictionaries, 2000. Also available online at www.grovemusic.com

Contributed by:

Amy Fear-Bishop
Orchestra Director, Prairie Star Middle School
Leawood, Kansas
String Specialist, Prairie Star Middle School and Stanley Elementary
Shawnee Mission, Kansas

Teacher Resource Guide

Eight Pieces for String Orchestra, Op. 44, No. 3 ("Acht Stücke")

Paul Hindemith
(1895–1963)

STRING ORCHESTRA

Unit 1: Composer

Paul Hindemith was born in 1895 in Hanau, Germany, near Frankfurt. During the course of his life, he developed a reputation as a great composer, teacher, violist, and conductor. The eldest of three children, he began studying the violin at age nine and became noted for his proficiency at many instruments. He held positions at Hochschule fur Music in Berlin, Yale University, and University of Zurich as Professor of Composition. Known as one of the main innovators of musical modernism, Hindemith's interests included the early church, medieval philosophy and, of course, musical topics.

While he is best known for his neo-baroque style, which pays homage to the work of Bach, Hindemith's works can be divided into three stylistic periods: 1918–23, when he was experimenting with a variety of musical styles; 1924–33, when he wrote in a mature neo-baroque style; and 1934–63, when he adapted his neo-baroque music to more traditional forms and genres. In his later years, Hindemith focused primarily on conducting and undertook several major concert tours.

Unit 2: Composition

Hindemith composed Eight Pieces for String Orchestra ("Acht Stücke") in 1927 as part of his *Educational Music for Instrumental Ensemble Playing* (Schulwerk für Instrumental Zusammenspiel), Op. 44. In addition to Eight

Pieces, the work includes Nine Pieces in First Position for two groups of beginning violins, Eight Canons in First Position for two groups of slightly more advanced violins with an accompaniment part for less-advanced violinists or violists, and Five Pieces in First Position for String Orchestra for advanced players. Hindemith designates Eight Pieces as being written for "moderately advanced players." Written in eight movements, this work contains many elements of Hindemith's neo-baroque style and bears the subtitle "Partitur" or partita, reminiscent of the multi-movement works of Bach and other baroque composers. While Hindemith doesn't follow the standard four-dance movements of a traditional German partita, he does utilize many similar elements, including an opening movement resembling a praeludium, a gigue, a sarabande, and several other dance-like movements.

Unit 3: Historical Perspective

Hindemith composed Eight Pieces in 1927, the year that he accepted his post at one of Berlin's state music schools, Staatliche Hochschule für Musik. While teaching there, Hindemith became increasingly aware that there was very little modern music for young people. He noted that a shortage existed of music that took the technical capabilities of student musicians into consideration. As a result, he designed a new type of music literature, which he eventually named "Music to Sing and Play," to be used for teaching purposes and to provide quality material for those interested in modern music.

During this time, Hindemith continued to develop and define his feelings regarding musical composition. He became increasingly aware of the divergence between his philosophies and those of his noted contemporary, Arnold Schönberg. In Hindemith's opinion, Schönberg's twelve-tone system restricted the composer and did not encourage tonal and intervallic relationships, thus hindering the composer and the listener. Much of Hindemith's music of this period possessed many of the neo-baroque qualities of his later years, including clarity of form and texture, a firm tonal basis, and many contrapuntal elements.

While Hindemith's compositional theories were not published until 1937 in his book, *The Craft of Musical Composition*, he developed many of the ideas put forth in this book during his years at the Berlin Hochschule. During the same period, Igor Stravinsky explored neo-classical musical ideas, focusing primarily on the work of Mozart rather than Bach, as Hindemith did. Other influential composers of the time include Béla Bartók and Anton Webern.

Unit 4: Technical Considerations

Hindemith designed Eight Pieces to be performed in its entirety in first position by all sections of the orchestra. Nevertheless, there are some passages where shifting may be employed. Each of the eight movements of this work is written with no key signature. None of the movements employ a tonal center of C or related tonalities, and there are numerous chromatic passages throughout the work. Therefore, students must be adept at reading and playing accidentals. Additionally, students must be familiar with the chromatic scale in first position. Keen intonation is of prime importance throughout the work. There are a variety of time signatures from movement to movement, and students must adjust quickly between 4/4, 2/4, 3/8, 6/8, and 3/4. The time signature never changes within a movement. This work is rhythmically accessible as compared to other literature of comparable difficulty level. It consists of primarily quarter/eighth note patterns and very little syncopation. Nevertheless, it does require each section of the orchestra to be significantly rhythmically independent.

Unit 5: Stylistic Considerations

As this work falls into the category of neo-baroque, many baroque musical styles may be employed. Therefore, much of the bowing should be in a detached style as in baroque practice. Close attention should be paid to terraced dynamics and accents, as well as written and implied *crescendos* and *diminuendos*. Additionally, careful attention must be paid to proper balance of the ensemble throughout the work. As with any baroque work, careful attention must be paid to intonation at all times.

Unit 6: Musical Elements

While this is not an atonal work, the melodies and harmonies do not follow traditional tonal patterns. Many melodic and supporting lines are chromatic in nature. Additionally, Hindemith employs twentieth century techniques in both homophony and polyphony. All sections of the orchestra are given ample melodic material and must be aware of their role at all times; therefore, students must be made aware of melodic lines and figures versus supporting elements in the work. While numerous chromatic passages exist within the work, an overriding sense of tonal center firmly bonds each movement together.

Unit 7: Form and Structure

SECTION	MEASURES	EVENT AND SCORING
Movement 1 (moderately fast)		
A	1	
A´	10	Melody in violin I; homophonic harmony
Movement 2 (fast)		
A	1–6	Developed
	7–16	
A´	17–18	Melody in violin I

SECTION	MEASURES	EVENT AND SCORING
	19–23	Developed
A˝	24–29	

Movement 3 (moderately fast; some fugal concepts used)

	1–8	Theme introduced in violin I
	5	Reappears in viola, cello, and bass
	15	Violin I
	28	Violin I
	36	Violin II
	39	Violin I
	48	Violin I

Movement 4 (comical; moderately fast)

	1–16	Theme introduced
	17–26	Developed
	27–33	In dominant
	33–36	
	37–53	Coda

Movement 5 (fast)

	1–13	Theme introduced (repeated)
	31	Viola
	38	Violin I

Movement 6 (moderately fast)

	1–8	Theme introduced in violin I
	17	Viola
	24–53	Fugal passage
	61	Theme in violin II

Movement 7 (lively)

A	1–32	Contrapuntal interplay
B	33–58	Legato melody in viola, cello, and bass
A´	59–83	Returns to A theme with a march-like quality

Movement 8 (moderately fast; awake)

A	1–9	Introduction of theme
	10–17	Theme in violin I with more complex countermelody in violin II and viola
B	17–34	Contrapuntal figures between viola and violin I
A´		Return to original theme
Coda	48–61	Utilizing material from original theme

Unit 8: Suggested Listening

Johann Sebastian Bach, Brandenburg Concertos
Ernest Bloch, Concerto Grosso
Paul Hindemith:
    Concerto for Orchestra
    Kammermusik No.4
    Kammermusik No.5
Igor Stravinsky, *Oedipus Rex*

Unit 9: Additional References and Resources

Grout, Donald Jay, and Claude V. Palisca. *A History of Western Music*. 6th edition. New York: W. W. Norton & Company, 2001.

Neumeyer, David. *The Music of Paul Hindemith*. New Haven: Yale University Press, 1986.

Sadie, Stanley, ed. *The New Grove Dictionary of Music and Musicians*, "Hindemith," by Ian Kemp. New York: Grove's Dictionaries, 2000. Also available online at www.grovemusic.com

Skelton, Geoffrey. *Paul Hindemith: The Man Behind the Music*. London: Victor Gollancz Ltd., 1975.

Contributed by:

Scott Laird
Director of Orchestras
Eleanor Roosevelt High School
Greenbelt, Maryland

Teacher Resource Guide

Festique

M. L. Daniels
(b. 1931)

FULL ORCHESTRA

Unit 1: Composer

M. L. Daniels was born in Cleburne, Texas, in 1931. He studied music at Abilene Christian University and the University of North Texas. He became a music faculty member at Abilene Christian in 1959 and held that position until his retirement in 1993. He has contributed several string and full orchestra compositions to the school orchestra literature, including String Quartet No. 1, *Celebration*, *Fanfare and Arrayment*, and *Festique* for full orchestra; and *Air and Dance*, *Pendleton Suite*, *Interlude*, *Cello Rondo*, *Bold Venture*, and *Night Beat* for string orchestra. Daniels has also published music for choir, band, solo instrument, and solo voice.

Unit 2: Composition

Festique won the National School Orchestra Association's composition contest in 1970; it was written specifically for that contest. A six-minute piece in one movement, this work uses compound ternary form and combines quartal harmonies and clusters with traditional tertian harmonies, often using upper and lower voices in a mirroring fashion. The music also includes canonic imitation and ostinato.

Unit 3: Historical Perspective

After World War II, as school orchestras began to grow in the United States, there came a need for music written specifically for school groups that were generally unable to perform much of the difficult traditional orchestra repertoire. Contests were held to encourage the writing of school orchestra music,

and much of the music written in the late part of the twentieth century was the result of those contests. The style, like that of *Festique,* is generally a combination of contemporary and classical styles, making use of contemporary harmonies but retaining traditional forms.

Unit 4: Technical Considerations

Key signatures of one flat and one sharp primarily represent minor or modal tonalities. A large number of accidentals are found in the piece because of the manipulation of the minor scales and the construction of quartal and cluster harmonies. The main theme is syncopated, and the development of that theme throughout the composition will require a secure understanding of syncopation. In the last section, all upper woodwinds have trills, primarily the flutes. In some cases, the trills are to altered notes; otherwise, the rhythms consist mostly of quarter, eighth, and sixteenth notes in a traditional fashion.

Unit 5: Stylistic Considerations

The first and last sections of *Festique* require precise articulation because of the accents in the syncopated sections. In these sections, all the winds will need precise tonguing and a very slight separation after the accents. String players will need a brief stopping of the bow after the accents and should avoid any legato playing. In contrast, the slow middle section will require legato bowing, making each bow as long as possible, and the winds should use legato tonguing. The many nuances marked in the slow section, some of which are subtle, should all be observed carefully because it is marked "with feeling." In the fast outer sections are some rather sudden *crescendos,* which add much to the drama of the piece and must be observed by everyone in the orchestra. Near the end, the *ff* marking should be played with the fullest possible tone without losing control.

Unit 6: Musical Elements

A lot of the harmony in *Festique* is a result of contrary motion that exists between the upper and lower parts (e.g., the first few measures at measure 73 of the condensed score). In addition, there is sometimes quartal and quintal harmony (e.g., notes D, A, E in measures 62–64, and woodwind parts in measures 80–83). The chords built in fifths invert to chords built in fourths and tend to sound quite similar. This harmony was new to the twentieth century and gives *Festique* its unique flavor. The music is often homophonic, but there are many instances of canonic imitation with the theme chasing itself in contrasting voices (e.g., measures 23–38). Modal and minor melodic structure predominates.

Unit 7: Form and Structure

The main theme is stated forcefully after the brief introduction and undergoes frequent development throughout the composition. The theme is developed through canonic imitation at measure 23, mirroring at measure 39, more imitation at measure 46, and melodic mirroring at measure 59. Even the slow middle section at measure 73 is loosely based on the first three notes of the syncopated main theme. The form of the piece is compound ternary, with the slow middle section acting as the contrasting section of the three-part form. The return to the faster, main theme at measure 101 is not literal, but begins to make use of thematic material in a slightly jazzy style. At measure 118, an unusual feature occurs: a return of a portion of the slow theme from the middle section finds itself being played faster and in counterpoint to melodic fragments from the main, syncopated theme. At measure 114, an ostinato appears in cello and viola, and while it switches to violin in measure 136, it continues for thirty measures, becoming the motivation for the music, driving it toward the final section. A twenty-one measure codetta begins at measure 146 with a powerful *tutti* statement of the original theme. From there until the dramatic ending, the full orchestra plays aggressively and intensely.

Unit 8: Suggested Listening

M. L. Daniels:
> *Bold Venture*
> *Celebration*
> *Pendleton Suite*
> *Sunfest*

Unit 9: Additional References and Resources

Dallin, Leon. *Twentieth Century Composition*. Dubuque, IA: Wm. C. Brown Company Publishers, 1977.

Contributed by:

M. L. Daniels
Professor Emeritus of Music, Abilene Christian University
Abilene, Texas
Composer
Austin, Texas

Teacher Resource Guide

Finlandia, Op. 26, No. 7

Jean Sibelius
(1865–1957)

FULL ORCHESTRA

Unit 1: Composer

Jean Sibelius was born in Hameenlinna, Finland, in 1865. His early musical studies were at the Helsinki Conservatory. From 1889 until 1892, he studied in Berlin and Vienna. In 1897, he was awarded a lifetime stipend by the Finnish government, which eventually enabled him to spend his time composing, unencumbered by financial worries. His considerable musical output includes seven symphonies and many large and small symphonic poems, of which *Finlandia* is one of the best known.

Much of Sibelius's music is inspired by Finland's epic poem, *Kalevala*. Through his music, Sibelius awakened great pride and patriotic fervor in the Finnish people. He achieved the prominence of a national hero and was greatly revered by all Finns. Sibelius's music shows a development from the romantic style of his teachers to increasingly fragmented, motivic, and dissonant music in his later works. In 1929, Sibelius stopped composing completely, stating his dislike for the new trends and his unwillingness to write in the modern style. He died in 1957, still a hero in his homeland despite not having composed a note in almost thirty years.

Unit 2: Composition

Finlandia is one of a group of nationalist pieces composed in 1900, while Finland was still under oppressive Russian rule. From its very first performance, it stirred the fires of Finnish nationalism to such a degree that the work became the anthem of the Finnish independence movement. After its foreboding introduction, the work launches into ABA form. The two main themes capture the spirit of unrest as well as the hopefulness of the oppressed people. The piece ends in a triumph capable of stirring any audience. The composer uses the varied characters of the instruments and choirs or the orchestra to great advantage in a brilliant orchestration.

Unit 3: Historical Perspective

Finland, which until the 1920s was ruled by foreign powers, saw the rise of intense nationalism in the early 1900s. The young, immensely talented Sibelius, fresh from study in Berlin and Vienna, became involved in the nationalist movement. Composed during a time of great political instability throughout northern and eastern Europe, the miniature tone poem *Finlandia* rocketed Sibelius to hero status in his homeland. Although he was drawn to Finnish folklore for inspiration, he consistently denied being a folk composer. Indeed, most of his works are founded on skilled use of nineteenth century harmonic devices, forms, and orchestration, which Sibelius used in such a striking and consistent manner that we have come to identify Finland with his music. If one compares *Finlandia* to later, more mature works by Sibelius, his growth in style and depth is quite striking.

Unit 4: Technical Considerations

The work is structured in the keys of F minor and A-flat major, and presents few departures to other tonalities. The ranges are not extreme for any instrument, and all of the instruments are treated in an idiomatic manner. No string parts advance beyond fifth position. Three percussionists are required. Capability of a wide range of dynamic and tonal control is required. Wind instruments are used as sectional choirs rather than soloistically. There are currently three readily available editions of this work. The standard edition from Kalmus supplies parts for three trumpets in F, but the Carl Fischer edition, arranged by Henry Sopkin, solves this problem. The Sopkin edition also clarifies bowings and fingerings in the string parts, provides a piano reduction as well as some cross-cuing in other instruments, but changes no notes from the original. The cross-cuing enables this version to be played with double woodwinds, two horns, two trumpets, three trombones, and percussion as the minimum necessary for successful performance. Groups without two oboes and two bassoons should consider the Belwin arrangement by Owen Goldsmith, which maintains the character of the original while reducing the woodwind requirements.

Unit 5: Stylistic Considerations

At times intensely dramatic, at other times warmly subdued and singing, this work presents many contrasts of style and sonority. The powerful, romantic brass must blend as a choir with tonal range from softly supportive to full-blown power. Woodwinds must be able to produce an expressive, organ-like blend. The strings use many different tonal techniques, including multiple bows and double-stops. Clear rhythmic articulation is important, and special attention must be given to releases of phrases.

Unit 6: Musical Elements

Foremost is the contrast between major and minor. The minor sections express tension and foreboding anticipation. The major sections have a victorious air about them and call for a bright, rich sound. The hymn-like theme in the center of the piece has an ardent, inspirational character requiring a warm, rich tone. Sibelius's themes are diatonic and are often so short as to be not much more than fragments. He also relies heavily on rhythmic motifs using repeated notes or very short patterns. Contrast between fast and slow tempos are achieved by changing note durations within the same meter rather than by actually indicating a tempo change.

Unit 7: Form and Structure

A tone poem, this work is a through-composed fantasy, but it loosely resembles an ABA form with introduction.

SECTION	EVENT AND SCORING
Opening	Introduction; brass fanfare; answered and expanded by woodwinds and strings in F minor
Letter B	Part 2 of introduction; new theme area in woodwinds and strings
Letter D	Part 3 of introduction; material from Part 1; new tempo; unstable harmony
Letter F	New section; theme A in A-flat major
Letter I	Theme B in A-flat major; woodwinds; repeated in strings at letter L
Letter M	Return of theme A; extension to include fragment of theme B as coda

Unit 8: Suggested listening

Franz Lizst, *Orpheus*
Jean Sibelius:
　　The Swan of Tuonela
　　Symphony No. 2 in D
Bedřich Smetana, *The Moldau*

Unit 9: Additional References and Resources

Brockway, Wallace, and Herbert Weinstock. *Men of Music*. New York: Simon and Schuster, 1958.

Ewen, David, ed. *The Complete Book of Twentieth Century Music*. Englewood Cliffs: Prentice-Hall, 1959.

Grout, Donald Jay, and Claude V. Palisca. *A History of Western Music*. 6th edition. New York: W. W. Norton & Company, 2001.

Layton, Robert. *Sibelius*. New York: Schirmer Books, 1993.

Sadie, Stanley, ed. *The New Grove Dictionary: Turn-of-the-Century Masters*. New York: W. W. Norton & Company, 1985.

Contributed by:

Ian Edlund
Retired Music Director/Conductor
Olympia, Washington

Teacher Resource Guide

L'Arlésienne Suite No. 1

Georges Bizet
(1838–1875)

FULL ORCHESTRA

Unit 1: Composer

Georges Bizet was born in Paris on October 26, 1838, to Adolphe Bizet, a vocal instructor and gardener, and Aimée Bizet, a sophisticated and accomplished pianist. Georges demonstrated musical talent at an early age, as well as a deep interest in literature. His parents oversaw his early musical training and actually hid books from him to encourage more practice. At age ten, he entered the Conservatoire, where he studied with Marmontel, Halévy, and Gounod. He became a virtuoso pianist praised by many, including Berlioz and Liszt. He was able to sight-read full scores, a skill that would serve him well as a composer of opera. He wrote the Symphony in C at age seventeen, which was not performed until its discovery in 1935. His studies at the Conservatoire culminated in winning the coveted *Prix de Rome* in 1857.

Bizet returned from Italy in 1860 and began a career teaching piano, writing arrangements for publishers, and composing. He wrote a number of operas produced by the Paris Opéra-Comique, including *Don Procopio*, *The Pearl Fishers*, and *The Fair Maid of Perth*. Although Bizet occasionally received critical acclaim, he struggled to make ends meet in his twenties, as his productions were not very successful. In 1869, Bizet married Geneviève Halévy, daughter of his composition teacher, who brought him much happiness. Despite previous disappointments, Bizet was artistically respected and continually invited to compose.

His thirties saw some moderately successful performances of piano and orchestral music, including those of *Jeux d'enfants*, the *Petite Suite d'Orchestre*, and the *Patrie* Overture. Bizet also continued to write for the stage, which culminated in Chouden's production of *Carmen* in 1875. The opening performance was both a critical and public failure. Severely depressed, Bizet retreated to the countryside for a vacation. His state of mind may have aggravated his lifelong affliction of angina, which was the suspected cause of his death on June 3, 1875.

Unit 2: Composition

Bizet was invited by Léon Carvalho to write incidental music for Alphonse Daudet's play *L'Arlésienne* in 1872. The resulting *mélodrame* utilized an orchestra of only twenty-six musicians and was first performed on October 1 for an unappreciative audience. Although reviews were mixed, some critics applauded the music and encouraged young composers to study its score. Jules Pasdeloup, conductor of a popular orchestral series, was a champion of contemporary French composers. He invited Bizet to arrange a suite of pieces from the then-closed *mélodrame*. The resulting work was the *L'Arlésienne* Suite No. 1, which premiered on November 10, 1872. This time the performance was well received, with the Minuetto being encored. Bizet's friend and colleague, Ernest Guiraud, arranged a second suite after Bizet's death. Both works have since remained in the standard repertoire for orchestra.

Unit 3: Historical Perspective

L'Arlésienne is set in Provençe, the southernmost region of France along the Mediterranean Sea. It is characterized by a contrast of cosmopolitan and rural surroundings. It would seem quite foreign to a northern Frenchman like Bizet, although he had visited the region as a young man. The story is of two peasant brothers, Fréderi and L'Innocent. Fréderi is in love with *L'Arlésienne* (a girl from Arles), who is unfaithful to him—and never actually appears in the play. He settles instead for Vivette, but his grief over his lost love eventually causes his suicide. L'Innocent is his mentally backward brother who supports Fréderi throughout with his simple kindness, then eventually gains maturity as a result of his brother's death. *L'Arlésienne* was noteworthy because of the lowly social status of its characters, its realistic dialogue, and its somewhat tragic ending. Writing for a *mélodrame* was difficult because the spoken dialog sometimes distracted from the music, and vice versa, thereby undermining the effectiveness of both, which may explain why the music is now heard only in the concert hall.

Unit 4: Technical Considerations

Overall, *L'Arlésienne* is quite accessible to most ensembles. The orchestration is elegant and doesn't require large numbers of musicians. There are, however, many prominent solos that require strong players, including those for flute, oboe, English horn, clarinet, harp, and especially alto saxophone. Bizet must have had access to strong bassoon players, for his parts often use the highest part of its range. The percussion parts call only for timpani throughout and a snare drum in the first movement. A full string section is needed for balance, yet only the first violin and cello parts utilize the upper positions. Some parts provide cues for doubling and instrument unavailability.

Movement 1, "Overture," begins in unison and then features the wood-winds in the first variation. The strings have a challenging countermelody in the second variation, which initiates the important *crescendos*. The horns and cellos are prominent in the third variation, with the cello parts utilizing upper positions written in tenor clef. In addition, the bassoons have an important triplet accompaniment. The alto saxophone is featured on the second theme, which requires thoughtful phrasing and sensitivity. The harp has an exposed part here, also. The violins are prominent at the end and need a full, sustained tone to soar over the orchestra with the dramatic third theme.

The first violins carry the melody throughout Movement 2, "Minuetto," with the flutes being featured in the trio. Both parts require the use of their upper registers, especially the flutes. Balance is important in the second half of the trio, where the winds and strings employ call and response. The first clarinet and alto saxophone are featured in the trio, and the legato style requires firm breath control and solid phrasing. The first violin part is exposed in the transition back to the minuet, and the bassoons have a demanding part in measures 67–76.

Movement 3, "Adagietto," is written only for the violins, violas, and cellos. Bow control, vibrato, and solid intonation are all necessary to perform the movement effectively. The tempo is quite slow and the phrases are long, which requires a concentrated effort on bow placement and speed. The first violins carry the melody throughout and reach up to fifth position at the climax of the piece in measures 19–25.

The horns and harp are then featured on an ostinato, which sustains throughout the A sections of Movement 4, "Carillon." The second violins also play the ostinato at the beginning, using a snap style of pizzicato to imitate the clap of the bells. The middle section has a number of exposed woodwind solos, including the flute (measures 61–105), the oboe (measures 72–98), and the alto saxophone (measures 85–98). The horns reintroduce the ostinato in the transition back to the A section in measures 92–107 and must perform the rhythms accurately to make it effective.

Unit 5: Stylistic Considerations

Bizet's early compositions were criticized for being too complex for the genre for which he was writing, namely opera. He, therefore, made a deliberate effort with *L'Arlésienne* to write in a clear and concise manner, while maintaining musical sophistication. The resulting style is an effective blend of Mozart's melodic sense and Berlioz's dramatic orchestration. Careful thought should be given to how the sections of the theme and variations in Movement 1 relate to each other. Also, many themes of the piece represent particular characters or scenes from the play, and their moods should be considered when defining styles and phrasing. For example, Movement 3 accompanies a scene where two long-lost lovers are reunited as they relish the overwhelming joy of the fleeting moment. Comparisons to other works of incidental music, as well as movie music, can make powerful connections for better understanding of the characteristics of the work.

Unit 6: Musical Elements

Bizet attempted to capture the Provençal scenery in the music with its clarity. He also used three traditional folk melodies of Provençe that he found in a collection by musician Vidal of Aix, two of which are found in Suite No. 1. "Marcho dei Rei" is used for the theme and variations that begin Movement 1, and the beautiful "Er dou Guet" represents L'Innocent's theme, which follows the variations in Movement 1. Comparisons to other pieces using theme and variation, as well as French overtures, could demonstrate how romantic composers were expanding the forms of their predecessors.

Movement 2 is classical in form, with a light and buoyant style followed by a beautifully flowing trio. Yet Bizet makes it his own with clever transitions and by using a more serious C-sharp minor tonality.

Movement 3 is hauntingly gorgeous and portends Barber's Adagio for Strings with its powerful and skillful harmonization.

The last movement is somewhat anticlimactic, but is better appreciated by taking the setting of the *mélodrame* into consideration.

The piece suggests the sound of the carillon, a musical instrument popular in France between the fifteenth and eighteenth centuries, utilizing a set of bells controlled by a keyboard. Bizet captures its triumphant timbre in both the ostinato and the overlying theme. A listening unit of a recording or concert of carillon music could enhance the students' appreciation for the finale.

Unit 7: Form and Structure

SECTION	MEASURES	EVENT AND SCORING
Movement 1: "Overture"		
"Allegro" (march), theme and variations +		
Theme 1	1–16	"Marcho dei Rei"; stated in unison; C minor
Variation 1	16–32	Clarinet theme; legato woodwinds
Variation 2	32–48	Winds theme; strings tremolo
Variation 3	49–64	"Andantino"; cello and horn theme; C major
Variation 4	64–80	"Tempo Primo"; upper instruments theme; *ff* march accompaniment; C minor

SECTION	MEASURES	EVENT AND SCORING
Transition	80–88	Theme fragments; ends with sustained i chords
Theme 2	89–111	"Andante Molto"; alto saxophone theme (L'Innocent); violin accompaniment; A-flat major
Theme 3	112–136	"Un Poco Meno lento"; strings theme (Fréderi); bass and trombone counter; dramatic; G^7
Coda	137–143	*Crescendo* to flat-VII chord; ends *pp*; G major

Movement 2: "Minuetto"
Form: rounded binary

A	1–8 repeats	C minor; violin Theme 1; i–III
B	9–24 repeats	Winds Theme 2; strings imitate; violin Theme 1; trio; V–i
Introduction	25–28	Woodwinds, horn, strings accompaniment; III
A	29–44	Alto saxophone and clarinet theme; violin countermelody; sustained A-flat chord underneath; III
A	45–60	First violin and cello theme; woodwind and harp countermelody; III
B	61–76	Flute theme (2x); alto saxophone countermelody; waltz-like string accompaniment; i–V; i–III
A	77–91	Violin and cello theme; woodwind and harp countermelody; III
Transition	92–107	Oboe and first violin theme excerpts, leading back to the minuet; C minor
A	108–115	Violin Theme 1; i–V
B	116–129	Winds Theme 2; strings imitate; flute and clarinet Theme 1; $V–i^6_4$
Coda	130–137	Flute and clarinet alternate with violin; V–i

Movement 3: "Adagietto"

		Violin, viola, and cello only; F major
Introduction	1–2	Viola pedal tone
Theme 1	3–6	First violin theme throughout; others sustained harmony; I–V
Theme 2	7–10	V

SECTION	MEASURES	EVENT AND SCORING
Theme 1	11–14	I–V
Theme 3	15–18	Theme 2x; viola countermelodies at cadences; I–IV; II–V^7
Theme 4	19–25	Long *crescendo* to cadenza-like cadence; I–I$^6_4$
Theme 1	26–28	Final statement of theme; *pp*; I–I
Coda	29–34	Theme excerpts; sustained chords at end; I

Movement 4: "Carillon"
"Allegro moderato," E major

Introduction	1–4	Horn, second violin, viola ostinato; second violin "snap" pizzicato
Theme 1	5–12	First violin theme; others scherzo-like accompaniment; I
Theme 1	13–20	Same; I
Theme 2	21–28	Violin theme; legato; *pp* with *crescendo*; V
Theme 1	29–50	Violin and flute extended theme; builds to strong cadence; I
Transition	51–60	Dramatic chords as ostinato ends; I–III^7
Theme 3	61–71	"Andantino"; flute theme; violin and viola accompaniment; *pp*; C-sharp minor
Theme 3	72–84	Oboe joins theme; vi
Theme 3	85–97	First violin theme; alto saxophone and cello countermelody; full accompaniment; vi
Transition	98–105	Flute and violin theme excerpts; horns gradually reintroduce ostinato; I–III^7
Theme 1	106–113	Oboe theme; string accompaniment; I
Theme 2	114–121	Violin theme; legato; *pp* with *crescendo*; V
Theme 1	122–148	Violin and flute extended theme; builds to strong cadence; I

Unit 8: Suggested Listening

Georges Bizet:
> *Carmen Suite* Nos. 1 and 2
> *L'Arlésienne Suite* Nos. 1 and 2
> Overture to *Patrie*
> Symphony in C

Edvard Grieg, Incidental Music to *Peer Gynt* (Henrik Isben) (1875)

Felix Mendelssohn, Incidental Music to *A Midsummer Night's Dream*
> (William Shakespeare) (1826)

Henry Purcell, Incidental Music to *Oedipus* (Sophocles) (1692)

Unit 9: Additional References and Resources

Scores:

Bizet, Georges. Fritz Hoffmann, ed. *L'Arlésienne: Orchestersuite zu A. Daudets gleichnamigem Drama*. Leipzig: Breitkopf & Härtel, 1872.

Books:

Bizet, Georges. Claude Glayman, ed. *Lettres*. Paris: Calmann-Lévy, 1989.

Curtiss, Mina. *Bizet and His World*. New York: Alfred A. Knopf, 1958.

Dean, Winton. *Bizet*. New York: Crowell-Collier Publishing Company, 1948.

Parker, Douglas Charles. *George Bizet: His Life and Works*. Freeport, NY: Books for Libraries Press, 1926.

Pigot, Charles. *Georges Bizet et son oeuvre*. Paris: Dentu Publishers, 1886.

Web sites:
> http://www.classical.net/music/comp.lst/bizet.html
> http://www.optonline.com/comptons/ceo/00566_A.html
> http://www.philclas.polygram.nl/class/ca-b/bizet.htm

Contributed by:

Robert Gardner
Doctoral Student
Eastman School of Music
University of Rochester
Rochester, New York

Teacher Resource Guide

Legend

David O'Fallon
(b. 1950)

STRING ORCHESTRA

Unit 1: Composer

David O'Fallon, born in 1950 and a native of Oak Park, Illinois, has been composing and arranging music since the age of ten. Before attending college, he studied composition, music theory, and orchestration with Jan Bach and Easley Blackwood. At Northern Illinois University, where he received degrees in Elementary Education and Music Theory and Composition, he was the staff arranger for the legendary NIU Jazz Ensemble. He has been a member of the Chicago Civic Orchestra as a percussionist and violist, and he has also been a member of the bass section of the Chicago Symphony Chorus. O'Fallon is a frequently called extra and substitute percussionist with the Chicago Symphony Orchestra, with whom he has made numerous recordings and toured extensively. He has been the recipient of four commissions from the Chicago chapter of the American String Association's Teacher-Composer Alliance to write contemporary music specifically suited to younger musicians. *Legend* was the result of the first ASTA commission.

Unit 2: Composition

Legend takes its cue from the ever-expanding stylistic repertoire of the modern string quartet. Pulsating rhythms and gritty harmonies generally associated with contemporary rock are contrasted with a lyrical middle section. The piece was first performed in 1995 by the Avoca West Chamber Orchestra, Eugenia Meltzer, Director. *Legend* consists of 146 measures and takes approximately four minutes to perform.

Unit 3: Historical Perspective

Although for centuries the strings have had a rich and varied history of playing dance music of the day, as well as music derived from dance forms, their place and influence in the popular, jazz, and rock styles in the latter part of the twentieth century has tended to be outside of the mainstream. Beginning in the 1980s, groups like the Kronos Quartet and the Turtle Island String Quartet have been extremely influential in demonstrating to string players and listeners alike how versatile the modern string ensemble can be, while in the musical world at large, boundaries between art music and more popular styles continue to become blurred.

Unit 4: Technical Considerations

Based as it is on the rhythms found in rock music, it is important for the piece to groove. The musicians should think in terms of constant eighth notes, especially in measures that do not have written constant eighth notes (measures 1–14, the theme at measure 20, and measures 142–144, for example). Eighth notes that are not marked with a slur should be played off the string. Beats two and four—otherwise known in pop music as the back beat—form the basis of the first theme. These measures must be played heavily, with lots of bow. Two effects that may be new to younger musicians are learning to control dynamics within a tremolo (measures 37–42 and measures 134–137) and, for the violins, learning to hit a high pitch very hard and sliding it down the E string (measures 130–133). This effect alternates quickly between first and second violin, and the *glissandi* should overlap slightly.

Unit 5: Stylistic Considerations

Most of the piece can be thought of in terms of raucous eighth note-based rock. The places marked *f* and *ff* should be dug into with plenty of grit. The lyrical middle section (measures 72–127) can be approached as a graceful and legato contrast to the first theme and the coda. The transition between the raucous and the lyrical (measures 68–70 in particular) may need some attention, especially in second violin. The steady eighth notes, which until now have been played off the string, should gradually move to a brush stroke as the tempo relaxes.

Unit 6: Musical Elements

Legend is essentially in G minor, although no key signature is indicated because of the free usage of the blues scale and the Dorian mode. Accidentals are marked in the music as they occur. Melodically, the piece is a development of a single interval, the minor third. The harmonies are based on both major and minor thirds, although dissonances using diminished fifths as well as seconds, sevenths, and ninths in the middle section tend to obscure a prominent tonal center. The note values of the middle section are generally longer and

played with less gruffness than elsewhere in the piece. Textural contrast can be found in the use of unisons (monophony), melody with accompaniment (homophony), and melody with countermelody (polyphony). Timbral variety can be found in the use of tremolo, pizzicato, *glissando*, and a wide dynamic range.

Unit 7: Form and Structure

The form of *Legend* is ABA with an introduction and a coda.

SECTION	MEASURES	EVENT AND SCORING
Introduction		Fast and energetic; 4/4; quarter note = 140+; four pitches (G, B-flat, C, D-flat) are used, suggestive of the blues in G minor; minimal pitch content helps to emphasize the rhythmic gestures
A	1–19	G minor; theme presented in violin thickened through the use of *divisi* and simple double-stops; at m. 37, violin sustains an E-flat triad tremolo as introductory material is restated in the lower strings; varied repeat of the theme takes place at m. 46
Transition	20–58	E-flat triad in the lower strings is sustained against eighth notes gradually getting quieter in violin; tempo is relaxed slightly, and the meter changes to 3/4
B	59–71	Second theme presented by first violin alone, then in octaves with viola while a countermelody is added in the other strings; the theme is harmonized at m. 89 and played again at m. 108 in close canon; the lower strings begin to suggest the introductory material
Transition	72–127	Underneath a high trill by solo violin, strings, in unisons and octaves, return to the opening tempo and style, except that they remain *piano*; there is a D.S. back to the varied repeat of A
A	128–129	Return to the varied repeat of the first theme

Section	Measures	Event and Scoring
Coda	130–146	In this repeat of material from mm. 43–53, first and second violin alternate *glissandi*, sliding downward from high B-flat and high G, respectively, while the lower strings hammer out eighth notes on G in unison and octaves; at m. 134, the four pitches of the introduction are played tremolo with *tutta forza* accents by the entire ensemble; pitch D is added to the mix at m. 138; it is important for the ensemble to think in eighth notes during the one-measure rest in m. 142 and during the rests in mm. 143–144; the piece ends with material borrowed from mm. 5–6

Unit 8: Suggested Listening

Rachel Barton:
> *Storming the Citadel*
> Stringendo String Trio

Jimi Hendrix, *Purple Haze*

Turtle Island String Quartet, *Art of the Groove*

Unit 9: Additional References and Resources

Bernstein, Leonard. *The Infinite Variety of Music.* "Jazz in Serious Music." New York: Doubleday, 1993.

Larkin, Colin, ed. *The Encyclopedia of Popular Music.* 3d edition. New York: Muze UK, 1998. S.v. "Kronos Quartet" http://www.kronosquartet.org and "Turtle Island String Quartet."

Randel, Don, ed. *The New Harvard Dictionary of Music.* Cambridge, MA: Belknap/Harvard University Press, 1986. S.v. "Popular Music," "Rock," and "Rock 'n' Roll" by Charles Hamm.

Contributed by:

David O'Fallon
Composer and Percussion Teacher
Wheaton, Illinois

Teacher Resource Guide

Mantras

Richard Meyer
(b. 1957)

STRING ORCHESTRA

Unit 1: Composer

Richard Meyer received his Bachelor of Arts degree from California State University–Los Angeles and has taught middle school and high school instrumental music for over sixteen years. He conducts the Pasadena Youth Symphony Orchestra, a ninety-piece honor group composed of seventh, eighth, and ninth grade students. He has a variety of works published for band and orchestra, including *Celebration,* which won the 1989 National School Orchestra Association composition contest. More recently, his string orchestra suite, *Geometric Dances,* won the Texas Orchestra Directors Association composition contest. Meyer lives in Arcadia, California, and is a composer for Alfred Publishing Company.

Unit 2: Composition

Mantras are chanted syllables or phrases used in the Hindu and Buddhist religions. Buddhism believes mantras to be sounds inherent in the human body and the essence of cosmic forces. Humans are able to commune with these forces through the repetition of mantras. In Hinduism, mantras are believed to embody the essence of divine power. Mantras provide structure and harmony to the cosmos. This composition contains small musical phrases that are repeated and layered. This creates a mesmerizing effect that is interrupted by the composer's use of mixed meters. It is in A–B–A form (fast–slow–fast) and is approximately four minutes and thirty seconds long.

Unit 3: Historical Perspective

This contemporary piece was published in 1997. Its driving rhythms and use of mixed meters brings to mind other recently published string orchestra pieces: *Dance Parhelia* by William Hofeldt (Grade 4), *Palladio* by Karl Jenkins (Grade 3), and *Baltic Dance* by Kurt Mosier (Grade 4). Meyer's use of modalism and driving syncopation is also characteristic of *Geometric Dances*, which was published for string orchestra in 1996.

Unit 4: Technical Considerations

The scales of F major and D minor are required for this piece. The ensemble will need instruction in marcato, spiccato, pizzicato, and accents. A wide range of dynamics is needed. First violins have limited use of third position, and a violin soloist is featured for seven measures. Second violin and viola parts are integrated into the melody and require work on syncopated rhythms. The lower strings will be challenged to maintain a metronomically precise spiccato. The lively sections of the piece should have a buoyant feeling to the pulse.

Unit 5: Stylistic Considerations

Between a vigorous opening and closing is a legato middle section with staggered chordal entrances. This section requires a rich tone quality and intense dynamics to create the introspective atmosphere desired. The enclosing fast sections rely on the use of syncopation and accents in all dynamic levels. Repeated eighth notes in the fast sections require use of a brushed bow stroke rather than a true spiccato.

Unit 6: Musical Elements

Three related syncopated themes are used in the fast sections of this piece. All are in D minor and are most prominent in first violin. The main theme of the slow section seems to start over and over, as though a mantra is being tentatively repeated. Students should be directed to note the use of rests, repetition, and lengthening of note values to slow the melody down from measures 43–51. In the slow section, the composer uses very little bass through the first third of the section to give a light, unresolved harmonic feeling that climaxes at measure 72, in D major, and then quickly leads back into D minor. A major timbre change occurs at measure 97 when all instruments play pizzicato. Students need to emphasize the dynamic phrasing within each two-measure fragment. Throughout this percussive piece, accents must be emphasized. This is especially important in the inner voices, as they play afterbeats. This is illustrated at measure 10 and is used throughout.

Unit 7: Form and Structure

MEASURES	EVENT AND SCORING
Opening	Allegro introduction by cello of soft, repetitious rhythm
4–9	Quiet, syncopated violin melody placed over cello rhythm
10–15	Violin melody restated louder; octave higher
16–22	Percussive melody introduced in violin; syncopated support in other sections
22–23	*Subito p*; syncopated transition *crescendos* to *forte* melody in m. 24
24–31	Marcato; *f*; four-measure melody repeated with first violin in thirds
32–36	Transition brings dynamics back to *p*; chords in upper strings foreshadow middle section while rhythm of cello and bass reminds listener of opening statement
37–43	Restatement of ideas in mm. 4–9
43–52	Tapering off of rhythmic drive leading into B section of piece
52–88	Largo lamentoso, middle section of piece; staggered chordal entrances and mixed meter give section feeling of ethereal instability; section builds to climax in m. 72 in D major then modulates and diminishes to fermata in m. 88
89–96	Restatement of material from mm. 16–22
97–104	New pizzicato theme introduced; 3/4 used exclusively until m. 120
104–111	Solo violin melody is loose inversion of melody at mm. 24–31 placed over continuing pizzicato theme in all sections
111–118	First violin echoes solo violin melody in thirds
118–119	Syncopated transition measures
120–131	Second violin and viola state melody from m. 4 while *divisi* first violin section staggers long notes; cello and bass play the driving opening rhythm
132–139	Ends *ff*, using rhythms previously stated

Unit 8: Suggested Listening

Benjamin Britten, *Simple Symphony*
Gustav Holst, *The Planets*
John Williams, *Star Wars*

Unit 9: Additional References and Resources

"Central Asian Arts." Chicago: *The New Encyclopaedia Britannica*, 15th edition, 1998.

Contributed by:

Mary Rudzinski
Orchestra Director
Marie Murphy School
Wilmette, Illinois

Teacher Resource Guide

Millennium

Richard Meyer
(b. 1957)

FULL ORCHESTRA

Unit 1: Composer
Richard Meyer is a public school instrumental teacher with many award-winning compositions to his credit, including *Celebration*, winner of the National School Orchestra Association (NSOA) composition contest, and *Geometric Dances*, winner of the Texas Orchestra Directors contest. He received the 1994 Outstanding Music Educator Award from the Pasadena Area Youth Music Council and was the 1999 winner of the Pasadena Arts Council Gold Crown Award for Performing Arts.

Unit 2: Composition
Millennium was the winner of the 1998 NSOA composition contest. The All Southern California Junior High Orchestra commissioned the piece for 1997–98 in celebration of the sixtieth anniversary of the Southern California School Band and Orchestra Association. The three sections of this contemporary overture-style piece are introduced by a foreboding short melody played first by a solo trumpet and later joined by the rest of the brass instruments.

The first section, "Alla Marcia," features the trumpets and trombones in a heroic theme with pulsing marcato rhythms and percussive accompaniment by the rest of the orchestra.

The second section, "Andante Tranquillo," introduces a lovely theme in 3/4 time that begins with a cello soli and builds through the addition of instruments to a beautifully orchestrated climax with effective use of percussion instruments. The second section ends quietly.

The third section, "Alla Marcia," begins abruptly with the percussion section in a one-measure *crescendo* leading to an energetic march with polyphonic overtones as the brass, woodwinds, and strings each have separate melodies and countermelodies underscored by driving rhythmic accompaniments. The composition concludes with a restatement of the opening theme, marked "Molto Maestoso." Every section of the orchestra is featured in a fully orchestrated, exciting composition. The duration of the composition is approximately seven minutes.

Unit 3: Historical Perspective

This composition reflects the contemporary film music style of composers such as John Williams, as illustrated by the *Star Wars* trilogy and *E.T.* This style of writing includes heroic themes, pulsing rhythmic accompaniment, and effective use of the percussion battery. There are also elements of twentieth century British compositional techniques as practiced by Gustav Holst, Ralph Vaughan Williams, and William Walton that include lush orchestration underscoring simple melodies.

Unit 4: Technical Considerations

The tonality of the composition revolves around the keys of G, C, and D major. There are brief episodes of modulations to flat keys, with accidentals being used rather than key signatures. Special techniques for strings include artificial harmonics, tremolo, marcato bow strokes, *divisi* parts, and dramatic dynamic changes, all of which are accessible and stimulating for the junior high age group for which this piece was composed. The melodic and harmonic elements are well distributed across the sections, which should cover for any one section that might be weak, with the possible exception of the trumpets in a particular ensemble. The composition is also suitable for community orchestras. The wind and brass parts are well within the tessitura of young players. The percussion parts include snare and bass drums, crash and suspended cymbals, bells, triangle, tambourine, and three timpani. Technically, the most challenging aspects concern rhythmic accompaniments that include duple and triplet figures and some syncopated sections. All of these are accessible counting challenges. The string parts are exceptionally well bowed.

Unit 5: Stylistic Considerations

This composition primarily reflects the compositional style found in contemporary adventure films, with heroic themes and pulsing rhythmic accompaniment counterbalanced by simple and lovely melodic interludes. Most contemporary orchestral film scoring language is directly modeled upon and can be traced back to the late nineteenth and early twentieth century British and German/Austrian romantics. Much of the orchestration features a melody often played in unison among different families of instruments, which is accompanied by pulsing and dynamic rhythmic figures played by the rest of the orchestra. In the case of the second section, lush chords as well as arpeggiated, repeated rhythmic figures are used to accompany the melody. The effective use of dynamics and tempo changes are exceptional features throughout the composition.

Unit 6: Musical Elements

The composition revolves around major tonalities with brief excursions into parallel or related keys through the use of accidentals. Each of the three main melodies starts with an upward skip of a fourth or fifth generally followed by descending patterns in steps or with modest interval jumps. The harmonic construction is almost exclusively triadic. There are some rapid, arpeggiated rhythmic accompaniments in both strings and winds in the third section that will provide excellent educational and musical challenges. A few modest meter changes, mostly a 2/4 measure interjected to expand the melodic line, are interjected in the first and third sections. In general, there are few melodic leaps, with the most significant challenges left to solving repeated rhythmic figures. While not liberally used, accidentals do play a part in melodic and harmonic construction.

Unit 7: Form and Structure

SECTION	MEASURES
Introduction:	
Pedal	1
Solo theme	3
Section 1: "Alla Marcia"	
Introduction	12
A	18
A development	22
B	26
B development	30
A^1	34
A in canon	44
Development:	
A^2	52
A^1	63
Codetta	67
	73
Section 2: "Andante Tranquillo"	
Introduction	79
A	81

SECTION	MEASURES
A^1	89
A	97
A	105
B	113
B^1	117
A	125
A^1	133
A	136

Section 3: "Alla Marcia"

A	144
A	152
Coda, Section 1, A	161
Section 1, A^1	165
Codetta	169

"Molto maestoso"

Unit 8: Suggested Listening

Gustav Holst:
    The Planets
    Second Suite in F
Ralph Vaughan Williams, *English Folk Song Suite*
William Walton, *Crown Imperial*
John Williams:
    E.T.
    Star Wars

Unit 9: Additional References and Resources

Karlin, Fred. *Listening to Movies, The Film Lover's Guide to Film Music*. New York: Schirmer Books, 1994.

Karlin, Fred, and Ron Tilford. *Jerry Goldsmith from Film Music Masters*. Hillsboro, OR: Karlin/Tilford Productions, Inc., 1995.

Contributed by:

Victor Ellsworth
Chairperson, Division of Performance Studies
Music Department and Theatre Arts/Dance Department
University of Arkansas at Little Rock
Little Rock, Arkansas

Teacher Resource Guide

Overture from Music for the Royal Fireworks

George Frideric Handel
(1685–1759)

arranged by Thor Johnson

FULL ORCHESTRA

Unit 1: Composer

George Frideric Handel was of German birth but was a naturalized Englishman. He was born in Halle on February 23, 1685, and died in London on April 14, 1759. His father was a barber-surgeon. Handel was born when his father was sixty-three years old and had married for the second time. His education began with grammar school at age seven; he received a broad education that included music.

While traveling with his father, he had the opportunity to play the chapel organ at Weissenfels. The Duke heard the young Handel play and was so impressed that he asked his father to see that the child received special education in music; Handel soon began lessons with the organist Zachau at Halle. These lessons included counterpoint and harmony, the organ, harpsichord, violin, and oboe.

At age seventeen, Handel received his first appointment as an organist but stayed only one year. He left for Hamburg to play violin and harpsichord at the opera house. He received invitations to Italy and traveled there extensively. In 1710, he was appointed Kapellmeister in Hanover. He returned to Germany to take the appointment with the condition that he be allowed to travel to London. Handel made a number of trips to London and later made it his home. Handel composed in all the musical forms of the time, including

opera and oratorio. His most celebrated pieces include *Messiah* and *Water Music*.

Unit 2: Composition

The Overture from *Music for the Royal Fireworks* is one of five movements. The other movements are dances, such as a bourrée and a menuet. A French overture followed by dance movements was common; the term "overture" was sometimes given to the entire composition because of the length and grandeur of the first movement. Master baroque composers such as Bach and Telemann also used this form. The original overture has three sections: slow–fast–slow, with the Grave being permeated by dotted rhythms and the fast section in fugal style. Johnson's arrangement does not include the return to the slow section. Both the original and this arrangement are in D major.

Unit 3: Historical Perspective

The original work was written to celebrate the peace signing of Aix-la-Chappelle in October 1748. King George II wanted to celebrate the event with a fireworks display in Green Park, by St. James's, London, on April 27, 1749. King George II commissioned Handel to write music for this event. This music is from the late baroque period; other composers from this time include Bach, Telemann, and Vivaldi. The four orchestral suites of Bach are comparable to this work. Johnson edited and bowed this arrangement in 1961.

Unit 4: Technical Considerations

This arrangement, as in the original, has much doubling of wind parts with the strings, and there are no exposed wind solos. Brass play the fanfares alone. The string playing does require shifting in all parts, but not beyond third position. Cello and bass parts are the same, as was the tradition in the baroque period, and have running sixteenth note scale and arpeggio patterns. The string parts are equal in difficulty, with everyone getting melodic opportunities. The bassoon parts double the cello and bass lines. The woodwind and brass ranges are not extreme, except that the first trumpet part does require E (concert D) above the staff. Most of the instrumental parts are in D major; however, the B-flat clarinet parts are in E major. Trumpets in B-flat and horns in F are without key signatures; accidentals are added.

Unit 5: Stylistic Considerations

Johnson arranged Handel's work in 1961, before the impact of the early or original instrument groups. Bowings and articulations are good and functional but are not consistent with original notation. Careful understanding of baroque articulations is required. Johnson uses both staccato and tenuto marks in the opening, slow section. In the closing allegro, staccato marks are placed on eighth notes for the proper baroque separations. These articulations are

consistent in the string and wind parts. Dynamics used are modern markings, including *crescendos* and *diminuendos* with much use of *mp* and *mf*.

Unit 6: Musical Elements

The harmony of this work is tonal. In the style of the baroque suite, the entire piece stays in D major. There are neither extended modulations nor fugues. The piece is primarily antiphonal, with the echo effect between sections used in both sections, especially in the Allegro. The concertino of the solo players being answered by the *tutti* is used here as in the original. This arrangement uses the single dotted-quarter note followed by an eighth note, but double dotting may be employed at the discretion of the conductor.

Unit 7: Form and Structure

The original Overture by Handel is in the form of the French overture. Lully originated this form for ballet overtures. These overtures begin with a slow opening section with dotted rhythms followed by a more lively section, often fugal, with a return to the opening slow section. Johnson omits this return to the slow section. The form of the piece is now in two large sections. One is marked "Maestoso," the other "Allegro." There is a two-measure transition between sections marked "Adagio."

SECTION	EVENT AND SCORING
Maestoso	Timpani two-beat introduction; prideful melody; full orchestra
A	Strings alone, followed by antiphonal brass
B	Woodwinds respond
C	Full forces close out this section
Adagio	Two measures; low woodwinds, low brass, low strings
Allegro	Military-style fanfare in trumpet and timpani answered by strings and woodwinds
D	Chordal section with violin 1 lyrical melody
E	Antiphonal section led by violin I with full orchestra response; followed by running D major scales and arpeggios
F	Return of the military fanfare in the horns; strings and woodwinds answer
G	French horn and trumpet in fanfare
H	Return of scale and arpeggio section to the end

Unit 8: Suggested Listening
Johann Sebastian Bach, Four Orchestral Suites
George Frideric Handel:
    Messiah
    Water Music

Unit 9: Additional References and Resources
Donnington, Robert. *Baroque Music, Style and Performance: A Handbook.*
    New York: W. W. Norton & Company, 1982.

Grout, Donald Jay, and Claude V. Palisca. *A History of Western Music.* 6th
    edition. New York: W. W. Norton & Company, 2001.

Contributed by:
Jonathan D. Lane
Orchestra Director
Shawnee Mission East High School
Indian Hills Middle School
Shawnee Mission, Kansas

Teacher Resource Guide

Short Overture for Strings

Jean Berger
(b. 1909)

STRING ORCHESTRA

Unit 1: Composer

A German-born American composer, choral conductor, and pianist, Jean Berger studied music theory at the University of Vienna and the University of Heidelberg, where he earned a Ph.D. Following composition studies with Louis Aubert in Paris, he toured Europe and the Near East, and taught and conducted in Rio de Janeiro. He emigrated to the United States in 1941 and became a citizen in 1943. He has taught at Middlebury College, University of Illinois, and University of Colorado. Since 1970, he has served as a visiting professor at various conservatories and universities. The Westminster Choir, Illinois Wesleyan Concert Choir, University of Texas, Ohio Music Education Association, and the Linn Choir of Glasgow, Scotland, have commissioned some of his works. Berger's *Caribbean Concerto for Harmonica*, the first of its kind, was performed by the Saint Louis Symphony Orchestra. Berger writes primarily for voice and choral ensembles.

Unit 2: Composition

Short Overture was composed in 1958 while Berger was on the faculty of Middlebury College in Vermont. It is dedicated to Alan Carter. The approximate performance time is four minutes and thirty seconds.

Unit 3: Historical Perspective

Berger's music has been characterized as melodious and pragmatic.[1] Similar to Copland's *Fanfare for the Common Man*, the opening melodic material moves primarily by leaps and provides a sense of openness and optimism to the work.

Unit 4: Technical Considerations

Short Overture offers rhythm, intonation, articulation, and ensemble challenges. Specific features include changing meters and tempos; rapid, continuous eighths notes; modulation through keys with multiple sharps and flats; playing in higher positions—fifth position in first violin and high third position in cello; quick changes between on- and off-the-string bow strokes (measure 30); rhythmic precision and matching articulation (measures 27, 30, 157, 181); flying spiccato (measures 30, 57, 157); and repeated quarter note accents that match in intensity (measures 66, 165). To aid with ensemble clarity, the flying spiccato may be removed and the first note of the printed slurs played down-bow. At measure 181, the conductor may indicate to retake the bow following the eighth rests and play the two notes following the slur up-bow.

Unit 5: Stylistic Considerations

Quick and frequently changing tempos (Allegro ma non troppo, Molto più mosso, and Molto meno mosso) coupled with rapid eighth note passages make this an effective piece for the beginning of a program. Similar to late Renaissance music for brass ensemble, the instruments form two groups, in this case upper and lower strings. These groups frequently engage in question-and-answer dialog, often at contrasting dynamic levels. The rhythm in measures 16–17, repeated throughout the A sections, contributes to the fanfare-like quality of the piece.

Unit 6: Musical Elements

The A section of the piece consists of three short melodic figures that are developed throughout the section: (1) a fanfare-like ascending quarter note figure that ends with a dotted-quarter note/eighth note/quarter note figure in measures 16–17; (2) an eighth note answer in measures 17–18 and 21–23; and (3) a descending line with ties over the bar line in measures 40 and 62. The melodic material in the B section beginning at measure 74 is more legato and lyrical. Short Overture is written in C major with areas in G major, A minor, and E-flat major. Written primarily in 4/4 with the B section in 2/4, Berger also includes short sections in 3/4.

Unit 7: Form and Structure

This piece is in ternary form. Sections are delineated by changes in tempo.

SECTION	MEASURES	EVENT AND SCORING
A		
Introduction	1–15	Allegro ma non troppo; C major

SECTION	MEASURES	EVENT AND SCORING
A	16–45	G major; question-and-answer dialog between upper and lower strings using melodic figures one and two described above; running eighth note passage that begins in m. 32 leads to the third melodic fragment in m. 40
a´	45–69	G major modulating to A major; continued question-and-answer dialog; extension of the second melodic fragment leads to a dynamic *fff* climax and extended presentation of the third melodic fragment with accents and multiple *descrescendos*
B		
a	70–89	Molto più mosso; A minor; lyrical melody is played twice by first violin, the second time *divisi* an octave higher; melody is accompanied by running eighth notes; dynamics build throughout the B section from *mp* to *ff*
b	90–105	Melody is played twice by viola and cello, the second time in thirds with cello in high third position
a´	106–117	Melody is played once by *divisi* violins
Transition	118–130	Molto meno mosso; modulation from A to C major through the use of melodic fragments from the A section; accelerando in the last four measures leads to the new tempo
A´		
Introduction	131–146	Allegro ma non troppo; C major; repeat of mm. 1–15
a´´	146–161	Modulation from C to E-flat major; question-and-answer dialog returns followed by staggered, eighth note entrances in m. 157 by violin and viola

SECTION	MEASURES	EVENT AND SCORING
a‴	161–180	Modulation from E-flat to C major; continued question-and-answer dialog, including an accented *tutti* question in m. 165; similar to the A section, the third melodic fragment material is used for the section climax that quickly tapers
Coda	181–198	Staggered spiccato entrances of the second melodic fragment outlining a C major chord build to a final accented C, unison, *fff*

Unit 8: Suggested Listening

Jean Berger:
    Canticle of the Sun
    Magnificat (soprano, flute, percussion, and chorus)
    The Pied Piper (vocal groups and orchestra)

Unit 9: Additional References and Resources

Shuman, Philip. Dissertation, *A Stylistic Analysis of Selected Solo and Vocal Works of Jean Berger*. University of Northern Colorado, 1989.

Smith, Kenyard Earl. Dissertation, *The Choral Music of Jean Berger*. University of Iowa, 1972.

Contributed by:

Margaret Haefner Berg
University of Colorado
Boulder, Colorado

---

1 Slonimsky, Nicolas, ed. emeritus. *Baker's Biographical Dictionary of Musicians*. New York: Schirmer Books, 2001.

Teacher Resource Guide

Variations on a Well-Known Sea Chantey

Richard Stephan
(b. 1929)

STRING ORCHESTRA

Unit 1: Composer

Richard Albert Stephan was born in Buffalo, New York, in 1929. He earned degrees in music education from the State University of New York at Fredonia and the Eastman School of Music, with further study at the University of Buffalo and Brigham Young University. After a two-year tour of duty with the U.S. Army, where he served as an arranger-bandsman, Stephan began his teaching career in Buffalo, New York, followed by a position as Coordinator of Music in the Hamburg, New York public schools. In 1968, he became a member of the faculty of the Crane School of Music, State University of New York at Potsdam, until his retirement in 2000.

Throughout his career, Stephan has been active as a teacher, conductor, clinician, composer, and performing musician in both the symphonic and jazz areas. In 1984, he was honored with a Fulbright Senior Scholar Award to Australia. In 1986, his *Fanfare and Frippery* won the National School Orchestra Association competition. Other notable works by Stephan include *Fantasia on a 17th Century Tune*, Dance in D, *Adirondack Sleighride*, *Australian Folk Suite*, *Vanguard Overture*, and *Fanfare and Frippery* No. 2.

Unit 2: Composition

Variations on a Well-Known Sea Chantey consists of an introduction, theme, and eleven variations on "The Drunken Sailor." Stephan wrote:

> Always a favorite of mine since childhood, I had wanted to write something using this tune for sometime. Finally in 1989, I put my

ideas on score paper and the *Variations* was published two years later. The Suzuki Institute Orchestra gave the first performance from manuscript parts in Logan, Utah, the summer of 1990. As always, I tried to give all the instruments a variation or two of their own or at least an interesting line. An interlude was included to set the mood for the more legato variations that follow. I chose the title in an effort to minimize the advertisement of inebriation to young students.

Unit 3: Historical Perspective

The original tune is English in origin and probably dates back to the seventeenth century. It has been part of America's folk heritage since the first English seamen set foot in the New World. Folk music has been a major factor in world music both in and of itself and, as here, as a basis for embellishment and variation. Another traditional tune, "The Sailor's Hornpipe," sets a nautical mood as it provides the material for the introduction.

Unit 4: Technical Considerations

Second violin and viola play entirely in the first position while first violin has several measures that require third position. An octave harmonic is found in both the bass and cello parts. The bass also has two variations that require second and third position. All instruments utilize the D and E Dorian scales and arpeggios within these key centers. The meters of 2/2, 3/2, and 4/4 are used. Rhythms are basically straightforward with only a few sixteenths and some syncopated accents that may offer a challenge. A good mix of bowing styles is required, including détaché, martelé, and spiccato.

Unit 5: Stylistic Considerations

The primary challenge offered by the variation form is the ability to switch styles quickly from one variation to the next. The variations here encompass a wide range of dynamics from *pp* to *ff*. Articulation demands vary from energetic and powerful, to light and playful, to rich and legato. The tempo is steady throughout the introduction and first four variations. Variation 5 sets a lighter, easier-going pace until the calmness of the interlude takes over. After the completion of Variation 9, the original tempo returns and drives to the triumphant finale.

Unit 6: Musical Elements

The texture is generally homophonic with a bit of canonic imitation in Variations 3 and 10. The harmony is quite conventional except for the employment of unrelated parallel triads in Variations 8 and 9. One measure of pyramiding fourths appears in the ending. All melodic development is within the Dorian mode. Phrase length is generally governed by the harmonic structure of the given theme. Augmentation is used in Variation 10 and diminution in Variations 6 and 7. Much of the development is rhythmic in nature, which perhaps accounts for its popularity with young players.

Unit 7: Form and Structure

Section	Measures	Event and Scoring
Introduction	1–27	D Dorian; 2/2, 3/2
Theme	28	2/2
Four variations	44	2/2
Three variations	100	4/4
Interlude	132	4/4
Two variations	142	4/4
Interlude	161	Modulation to E Dorian; 2/2
One variation	169	Extended; 2/2
Finale	193	Theme reharmonized; 4/4
Codetta	208	4/4

Unit 8: Suggested Listening
Johannes Brahms, *Variations on a Theme by Haydn*
Benjamin Britten:
    Variations on a Theme by Frank Bridge
    Young Person's Guide to the Orchestra
Edward Elgar, *Enigma Variations*
Sergei Rachmaninoff, *Rhapsody on a Theme by Paganini*

Contributed by:
Richard Stephan
Crane School of Music
State University of New York at Potsdam
Potsdam, New York

Grade Five

Teacher Resource Guide

"Andante Cantabile" from String Quartet No. 1, Op. 11

Peter Tchaikovsky
(1840-1893)

STRING ORCHESTRA

Unit 1: Composer

Peter Il'yich Tchaikovsky, born in 1840 in Kamsko-Votkinsk, Russia, showed a musical sensitivity from a young age. He began studying piano at the age of five, but he didn't dedicate his life to music until the time of his mother's death in 1854. After studying law for a short period of time in his early twenties, Tchaikovsky entered St. Petersburg Conservatory in 1863 as a full-time composition student. Noted and often criticized for his personal struggles and eclectic compositional tastes, he is most identified with the romantic tradition of composition. While he always maintained that his essential nature was Russian, Tchaikovsky is not strongly associated with the Russian nationalist movement of his day. He is more strongly associated with Western attitudes and compositional techniques largely due to his conservatory training. Best known for his symphonies, Tchaikovsky employed the use of folk tunes, programmatic features, lovely orchestration, inherent tunefulness, and a rare emotional sensitivity in his work. He is recognized as one of the greatest talents in nineteenth century Russian music.

Unit 2: Composition

"Andante Cantabile" is the second movement of Tchaikovsky's String Quartet No. 1, Op. 11. It is based on a folk tune entitled "Sidel Vanya," which Tchaikovsky first heard in Kamenka in 1869. The movement attained immense popularity following the premiere of his Quartet No. 1. Transcribed for solo violin and string orchestra, it soon was regularly performed as a separate work. This popularity both pleased and exasperated Tchaikovsky. On one hand, this beautiful tune stirred the emotions of many people, yet on the other hand, Tchaikovsky often felt that his audiences wanted to hear nothing else. Critics regard the movement as musically uninteresting but praise the beauty of the folk tune and the work's overall harmonic simplicity and purity. The tune, while beautiful, is associated with the following text:

> Upon the divan Vanya sat and filled a glass with rum:
> Before he'd poured out half a tot, he ordered Katenka to come.

This text is often noted for its pedestrian nature and does not accurately reflect the true beauty of the folk song on which "Andante Cantabile" is based.

Unit 3: Historical Perspective

Completed in 1871, "Andante Cantabile" is the second movement of Tchaikovsky's String Quartet No. 1, Op. 11. This work was composed rapidly in the early months of the year to be premiered as part of a concert of Tchaikovsky's works to make him some much-needed money and to keep his name among those of serious composers of that day. To draw public interest in the concert, Tchaikovsky enlisted the help of popular performers and felt it would be advantageous to perform a new work. Premiering on March 28, 1871, the quartet met with great success, primarily because of the second movement. Many regard this quartet in its entirety as Tchaikovsky's finest chamber work. While this was the first major quartet by a Russian composer, Tchaikovsky tried to avoid the nationalistic tendencies of his contemporaries in this work without sacrificing his own musical identity. During this period in his life, Tchaikovsky also completed *Romeo and Juliet,* his piano duet arrangements of *50 Russian Folksongs,* and his tragic opera, *Oprichnik.* This period also witnessed the premieres of Wagner's *Die Walküre,* Verdi's *Aida,* and Brahms's *Schicksalslied.*

Unit 4: Technical Considerations

Tchaikovsky presents the famous melody in B-flat, modulating to D-flat in the middle of the work, and returning to B-flat at the work's completion. While the work is in 2/4 time, there are some measures of 3/4 time within the movement. Only first violin and double bass require the performers to leave first position based on the range of pitches in the work, but all of the parts require the players to be proficient in shifting between first and third positions. First violin must be proficient in first through fifth position. Double bass must have a range up to F above the staff. Rhythmic considerations for this work are fairly basic, but the nature of the work requires an ensemble that plays musically and watches the conductor closely, allowing for the natural push and pull of the phrases. There is an exposed four-measure syncopated figure in second violin at the transition from the first theme to the second. As with many slow works, "Andante Cantabile" requires a musically mature ensemble for successful performance.

Unit 5: Stylistic Considerations

Concepts in phrasing hold the greatest importance in performing this work. Long, legato phrases with both subtle and extreme dynamic changes abound. This work requires a mature legato bowing and warm vibrato from all sections. The markings "dolce" and "espressivo" appear in many sections. All sections within the orchestra must also achieve a true *pp* within the dynamic structure of the work and simultaneously continue the musical line. Additionally, an extended pizzicato ostinato section in the cello and double bass in the middle of the work requires players with the maturity to successfully maintain a steady tempo and provide a musically interesting and vibrant line.

Unit 6: Musical Elements

Tchaikovsky presents the main theme of this movement in B-flat major with a basic homophonic harmonization. The second statement of the same theme in first violin is imitated in a fugal style one measure later by viola while the rest of the orchestra continues the homophonic accompaniment. The second theme occurs in D-flat in first violin while cello and bass provide a pizzicato ostinato passage. The original theme then returns in B-flat with violin and viola in unison over a legato bass line in cello and bass. The second theme briefly returns over a pizzicato accompaniment followed by a brief coda.

Unit 7: Form and Structure

SECTION	MEASURES	EVENT AND SCORING
Theme 1	1–49	Appears first in violin 1 in B-flat major; some imitation in viola section on second appearance of the theme in m. 18; homophonic harmonization in all other parts
Transition	50–55	Second violin syncopated figure sets up static modulation
Theme 2	56–97	Appears first in violin 1 in D-flat major; brief unison violin 1 and 2; ends in violin 1; pizzicato ostinato figure in cello and bass; violin and viola arco accompaniment
Theme 1	98–137	Violin and viola unison melody in B-flat major; cello and bass, and later viola, provide harmonization

371

SECTION	MEASURES	EVENT AND SCORING
Theme 2	138–162	Violin 1 melody in B-flat major over pizzicato accompaniment in all other sections
Coda	163–185	Violin 1 melody with arco accompaniment in all other sections

Unit 8: Suggested Listening

Johannes Brahms, String Sextet in B-flat, Op. 18
Antonín Dvořák, String Quartet in E-flat Major, Op. 51
Felix Mendelssohn-Bartholdy, String Quartet in E-flat, Op. 12
Franz Schubert, String Quartet in E-flat Major, D. 87
Peter Tchaikovsky:
> *50 Russian Folksongs*
> *Romeo and Juliet Fantasy-Overture*
> String Quartet No. 1, Op. 11
> String Quartet No. 2, Op. 22

Unit 9: Additional References and Resources

Abraham, Gerald. *The Music of Tchaikovsky.* "Tchaikovsky, Pyotr Il'yich," by David Brown. New York: W. W. Norton & Company, 1946.

Brown, David. *Tchaikovsky: The Early Years 1840–1874.* New York: W. W. Norton & Company, 1978.

Grout, Donald Jay, and Claude V. Palisca. *A History of Western Music.* 6th edition. New York: W. W. Norton & Company, 2001.

Rosenstiel, Leonie, ed. *Schirmer History of Music. The Romantic and Post-Romantic Eras,* by L. Michael Griffel. New York: Schirmer Books, 1982.

Sadie, Stanley, ed. *The New Grove Dictionary of Music and Musicians.* New York: Grove's Dictionaries, 2000. Also available online at www.grovemusic.com

Contributed by:

Scott D. Laird
Director of Orchestras
Eleanor Roosevelt High School
Greenbelt, Maryland

Teacher Resource Guide

Brandenburg Concerto No. 3 in G Major

Johann Sebastian Bach
(1685–1750)

STRING ORCHESTRA

Unit 1: Composer

Johann Sebastian Bach was born in Eisenach, Germany, on March 21, 1685. He lived to the age of 65 and struggled with near blindness the last years of his life, dying of a stroke in 1750. Music was an important part of Bach's youth. He studied clavichord and harpsichord (both ancestors of the modern piano) and excelled on violin. His first professional job as a musician was as a violinist in the orchestra at Weimar. Bach was later hired as a church organist at Arnstadt and then at Mühlhausen. He married his cousin, Maria Barbara, in 1707; they had a family of seven children before she died in 1720. A year later he married Anna Magdalena Wilcken, and together they had thirteen children. Bach worked as a court organist and composed an astonishing number of works for Lutheran religious services as well as secular instrumental works. His compositions summarized the baroque era with works such as the *Passion According to St. Matthew*, the Toccata and Fugue in D minor, the Six Sonatas and Partitas for Solo Violin, and the *Well-Tempered Clavier*.

Unit 2: Composition

The six Brandenburg Concertos were written in 1721 at Cöthen, a period of instrumental composition for Bach. The Concertos were dedicated to the Margrave Christian Ludwig of Brandenburg. Bach had met the prince while on a trip to buy a harpsichord two years earlier in Berlin. The six concertos proved too difficult for the court orchestra, so they were not performed for the Margrave. The Brandenburg Concerto No. 3, BWV 1048, is a favorite of students and a significant challenge for advanced performers and conductors. The opening motive of two sixteenth notes/eighth note begins one of the most well-known themes of baroque music. The Brandenburg Concerto No. 3 possesses inherent aesthetic qualities that initially attract young people to classical music and, in that regard, makes it a composition well worth rehearsing and performing. The work has two fast movements separated by an Adagio that provides an opportunity for improvisation within its one printed measure.

Unit 3: Historical Perspective

The six Brandenburg Concertos were all composed for different groupings of instruments and, except for the third concerto, feature solos within the compositional structure. Bach composed the Brandenburg Concertos in the Italian style of a concerto grosso. This compositional technique used groupings of instruments to create a contrast between the large group and a solo or smaller group. The third concerto does not have solo players, but Bach composed the music with unison and contrapuntal writing for three groupings of instruments—Violin I, II, III; Viola I, II, III; and Violoncello I, II, III—with double bass on the continuo line. The weaving of the melodic motive with unison and canonic entrances spread out over the orchestra creates a work of great architectural interest and aesthetic satisfaction. This concerto is a summary artistic work. It presents both the simplicity and complexity of eighteenth century music. The historical context of the individual in relationship to the state and the church was also one of simplicity midst complexity. The birth roles of social relationships were simple and highly structured but about to give way to a revolution for individual freedom in Europe and Colonial America.

Unit 4: Technical Considerations

The Brandenburg Concerto No. 3 is in G major with significant modulations to D major, C major, E minor, B minor, A minor, and G minor. All the string sections must be proficient in half position through third position. The violas and the cellos stay in their respective clefs. The primary technical challenges are string crossings and unusual fingerings necessitated by the extensive use of diminished chords. The initial statement of the theme plays easily and can create a false sense of security about the considerable technical difficulties to come if the piece is to be well played.

The rhythmic challenges are primarily contained in the entrances located throughout the measures on subdivisions of the beat. Each entrance must be strong; therefore, the conductor must have capable leadership in each section. The cello sections must be proficient in half position and extensions. The bass section serves a dual role as basso continuo and lower-octave reinforcement for the cellos. The Brandenburg Concerto No. 3 can be performed without the keyboard part, but it is worth locating a harpsichord or using an electronic harpsichord stop on a keyboard to create a complete continuo line.

Unit 5: Stylistic Considerations

The first consideration is bowing. The conductor should have multiple performances on compact disc to present to students as models of baroque performance. The length of the eighth note is of particular importance in early rehearsals, because it is often the destination note of the motive and the phrase. Bow placements in the middle of the bow that allow for the alternation of the short–short–long bowing and controlled string crossing need to be stressed with string players. The importance of an anticipatory gesture during rests preceding entrances is crucial to the rhythmic stability. Dynamics are sparingly marked in the parts. The lack of printed dynamics, however, does not mean the piece is played without dynamic contrast. The phrases flow naturally with *crescendos* on ascending notes and *decrescendos* on descending notes. Scale patterns are most effectively played if the intensity increases in the middle of the scale and not always on the highest note of the run. The tempos of the two outer movements should remain steady. Student abilities and tempos deserve careful attention in Brandenburg Concerto No. 3. It is too easy to set a fast tempo and then have it drag when the string crossings or modulations prove difficult.

Unit 6: Musical Elements

The beginning musical motive—two sixteenths/eighth note—initiates the orchestra into the genius of Bach and the richness of baroque compositional technique. Growing from the first statement of the theme, the first movement goes through intervallic inversion, repetition, sequence, modulation, rhythmic retrograde, and fragmentation so that the motive is present in almost every measure. The key of G major dominates the movement, but relative minor and parallel minor as well as the dominant key cluster makes up the important tonal centers. The harmonies are so well known that it is important to find the deceptive cadences and unexpected harmonies so that the music has a sense of the brightness those early listeners would have experienced.

The third movement requires secure knowledge of the 12/8 time signature and precision on scale passages. The sixteenth note pattern is present in all forty-eight measures except one. The absolute steadiness of the sixteenth notes is made easier by presenting the eighth notes as a metronome for the orchestra. String crossings and quick shifting, including half position work, is a necessity for this movement.

The conductor is confronted with seating choices for the orchestra, which make the music easier to play or impossible to play. Because the sections operate as both unison and counterpoint, it is important to maintain sectional integrity. Seat all of the first violins together, second violins together, and violas and cellos together. The exact configuration of first, second, and third parts within the sections may have as much to do with section size and stage size as musical consideration. However, thorough consideration needs to be made of inter- and intra-sectional placement for musical unity and clarity of conducting gestures.

Unit 7: Form and Structure

SECTION	MEASURES	EVENT AND SCORING
Movement 1: Theme 1		Motive of two sixteenth notes/eighth note creates the first theme in G major; viola, cello, and continuo serve as an eighth note rhythmic structure around the chord tones; contrapuntal style with a conversational nature to the interplay; first fragmentation of the theme takes place with a modulation to D major
	8–9	Motive is present as a musical response through the next section
	22	Retrograde version of the motive—eighth/two sixteenths—leads directly into a sequence of a sixteenth note variation; cello and bass restate the retrograde theme in C major, which is then combined with the return of the sixteenth note variation in the upper strings
	47	New theme appears that gives way to another subtle version in m. 58
	78	The most noble departure from the now-familiar theme is this violin entrance
	87–91	Players engage in string crossings in distantly related keys
	97	Return to the motive in its original rhythm as the music prepares to return to the A theme in G major at m. 126
Movement 2:		The second movement is just two chords and is handled in two ways: (1) improvisation by an orchestral player, usually the concertmaster or harpsichordist, over the chordal background,

SECTION	MEASURES	EVENT AND SCORING
		or (2) insertion of a short movement from some other Bach work, which is less common.
Movement 3:		The short third movement is monothematic and only forty-eight measures long; each entrance of the theme in various keys highlights the scalewise nature of this movement.

Unit 8: Suggested Listening

There are seventy-seven complete recordings of the Brandenburg Concertos available. The following versions, with conductors listed, reflect historical and modern performance practices:

Pablo Casals, Marlboro Festival Orchestra
Christopher Hogwood, Academy of Ancient Music (authentic baroque practice)
Neville Mariner, Academy of St. Martin in the Fields
Trevor Pinnock, English Concert (authentic baroque practice)

Unit 9: Additional References and Resources

Cross, Milton, and David Ewen. *New Encyclopedia of the Great Composers and Their Music*. Garden City, NY: Doubleday and Company Inc., 1969.

Ferrara, Lawrence. *Philosophy and the Analysis of Music*. New York: Greenwood Press, 1991.

Keller, Hermann, translated by Leigh Gerdine. *Phrasing and Articulation*. New York: W. W. Norton & Company Inc., 1973.

Meyer, Leonard B. *Emotion and Meaning in Music*. Chicago: The University of Chicago Press, 1961.

Schwendowius, Barbara, and Wolfgang Domling, ed. *Johann Sebastian Bach, Life, Times, Influence*. Hamburg: Bärenreiter, 1977.

Contributed by:

James D. Hainlen
Orchestra Director
Stillwater Area High School
Stillwater, Minnesota

Teacher Resource Guide

Concerto Grosso for String Orchestra with Piano Obbligato

Ernest Bloch
(1880–1959)

STRING ORCHESTRA

Unit 1: Composer

Ernest Bloch, composer, conductor, philosopher, music educator, and administrator, was born in Geneva, Switzerland, in 1880. In his teens, he studied composition with Émile Jaques-Dalcroze and violin with Louis Rey, moving from Geneva to Brussels in 1897 to continue his education studying violin with Eugène Ysaÿe and composition with Rasse. His only opera and most successful early work, *Macbeth*, premiered at the Opéra-Comique in Paris in 1910. Bloch first came to the United States in 1916 as the conductor for a dance tour. He was invited to teach at the Mannes School of Music in New York in 1917. He was director of both the Cleveland Institute of Music (1920–25) and the San Francisco Conservatory (1925–30), and then lived in Switzerland from 1930 to 1939. From 1940 to 1952, he was on the faculty of the University of California at Berkeley. He retired to Agate Beach, Oregon, where he remained until his death in 1959. Active throughout his life composing in many genres and styles, Bloch was recognized in his lifetime with awards for many of his works. Among them were the Coolidge Prize for his Viola Suite (1919) and New York Music Critics' Awards for String Quartet No. 3 and Concerto Grosso No. 2. His rhapsody for orchestra, *America* (1927), was awarded first prize in a contest sponsored by *Musical America*, and was premiered by five American orchestras in one weekend, though it was not a critical success. His best-known work is *Schelomo* (1916), a rhapsody for cello and orchestra, based on Hebrew themes.

Unit 2: Composition

Concerto Grosso No. 1 was written for the student orchestra at the Cleveland Institute, though it quickly became, and has remained, a standard in the professional repertoire. Bloch intended it to demonstrate to composition students that one could create a "modern" piece while still adhering to traditional forms and structures. The Concerto Grosso consists of four contrasting movements: Prelude, Dirge, Pastorale and Rustic Dances, and Fugue. The piece is harmonically accessible, yet it contains many traits characteristic of Bloch's compositional style: bitonal and modal writing; mixed meters in all but the final movement, cross rhythms, elements of folk music in the third movement, and a thick, broad texture throughout. The piano truly serves as an obbligato, rather than continuo or concertino, function in this work. In fact, no concertino group exists in the first movement and is used minimally in the others. The work is approximately twenty-two minutes in duration.

Unit 3: Historical Perspective

Like many of his peers bridging the nineteenth and twentieth centuries, Bloch began his career working in neoromantic style, influenced by such composers as Richard Strauss. Around 1910, he began to compose large, rhapsodic works on Hebrew themes; these dominated his output until about 1920. Even today, this period is called his "Jewish" cycle. The Concerto Grosso, premiered in the late spring of 1925, is one of several pieces that mark the beginning of a neoclassical period in Bloch's style, particularly in chamber music. Though many of these works return to seventeenth and eighteenth century forms, they contain many elements that are decidedly modern, such as the impressionistic use of tone color—likely Debussy's influence—in "Pastorale" of the Concerto Grosso, and the use of quarter tones in the string parts of the First Piano Quintet (1921–23). Several of Bloch's peers also adopted the neoclassic aesthetic, partially as a reaction to the excesses of the romantic period, writing smaller works that employed more traditional practices and forms. Examples include Stravinsky's Octet for Wind Instruments (1923) and Peter Warlock's *Capriol Suite* (1928), with which this work has much in common. The concerto grosso as a form enjoyed a revival beginning around this time, continuing well into the century by composers such as Stravinsky with his *Dumbarton Oaks* (1938), and Vaughan Williams's Concerto Grosso for Four String Orchestras (1950). Bloch himself composed a second concerto grosso in 1950.

Unit 4: Technical Considerations

The concerto is tonally centered around D, F-sharp, and F in a variety of modes. The key relationships, bitonal passages, frequent non-harmonic tones, clef changes in cello and viola parts, and chromatic passages contribute to make the piece challenging reading. The non-resonant quality for string instruments of F-sharp major can create intonation difficulties. The cello and first violin parts in the first movement are written in a high range, which presents shifting challenges; this is also the case with some of the solo concertino parts in the second and third movements. Otherwise, left-hand demands are not great. The bowing is idiomatic and presents few problems, utilizing the détaché, martelé, and spiccato strokes. The greatest rhythmic, conducting, and ensemble challenges occur in the third movement, which shifts rapidly among tempos and meters, and is polymetric in spots. This movement also requires the most independent part playing; even the fugue has a more homophonic texture. Despite the challenges, the piece is actually quite accessible technically. Bloch's expertise as a violinist is evident.

Unit 5: Stylistic Considerations

Though neoclassic in construction, the concerto is romantic in language and style, which requires that kind of performance practice. Movement 1 is bold, opening with sweeping chords and repeated down-bows. A heavy détaché bowing style interspersed with martelé on the accented notes is necessary, even in the fast passages. Movement 2 utilizes dotted rhythms, though they must not be too short to be compatible with the tenuto feel in the A section. The tranquil B section requires a legato, but light, approach and must be delicately balanced among solo and *tutti* parts to create an impressionistic effect. The Pastorale sections of the third movement also have an impressionistic texture, with *tutti* parts sometimes in harmonics contrasting with the more staccato, pesante Rustic Dance sections. The final movement requires a more baroque playing style, with light eighth notes and quarter notes that are somewhat separated in a baroque détaché. However, the dynamic contrasts are quite dramatic and more romantic in nature.

Unit 6: Musical Elements

True to the neoclassic aesthetic, Bloch utilizes many baroque compositional devices in this piece. The first movement is termed "Prelude" and has a ritornello form, both typical of the concerto grosso in Corelli's time. The ritornello is a rather short theme that begins each section; the material following is based on the ritornello. Movement 4, "Fugue," is probably the most neoclassic in conception and development. It is based on one subject with a following countersubject, and the statements of the subjects are often a fifth apart as Bach's would have been. The expositions, or groups of subject statements, are separated by an episode, in this case a short, lively theme in a major key. In the fourth exposition, Bloch utilizes augmentation of the subject (doubling the note values) as well as diminution. All but the first movement also alternate a concertino with *tutti* group, though more sparingly than in Handel's works. Bloch's musical content, though, is much more modern. Harmonically, in much of this work Bloch utilizes ninth and eleventh chords that present bitonal melodic writing. The opening of Movement 2, "Dirge," is a clear example: the dotted-rhythm melody in the upper strings is in F-sharp minor Dorian, and the cello line is in D major. This gives the music a somewhat exotic flavor and, combined with the wide spacing of voices in the Pastorale section of Movement 4 is reminiscent of Debussy. Bloch does not firmly establish modes but shifts among major, minor, and Dorian on a specific tonal center. The same is true of rhythmic elements; in the Pastorale, for example, voices often enter playing together in different meters, while the basic themes shift meters often, giving the music a rhapsodic, capricious character. Though not considered a nationalistic composer, although he is often associated with Jewish music, Bloch found fertile ground in Swiss folk dances for the melodic content of the third movement.

Unit 7: Form and Structure

SECTION	MEASURES	EVENT AND SCORING
Movement 1: "Prelude"		
Form: ritornello		
A	1	Begins in a quick tempo with a *tutti* ritornello of wide leaps and rapidly changing rhythms; in 4 +2; starting in D minor Dorian
	21	Spinning out (extension and development) of ritornello material
A´	44	Ritornello returns; in A minor Dorian; voicing changed; followed by more extension at m. 61
A	73	Ritornello returns in D minor Dorian; nearly a recapitulation of the first
Codetta	102	Ritornello material; in D Dorian; resolving in D major
Movement 2: "Dirge"		
Form: AA´BA´A (arch)		
A	1	Slow 3/4; use of dotted rhythms reminiscent of a French dance; F-sharp minor Dorian in upper strings, D major in lower parts (bitonality); three-note melodic motive of m. 3 inverted in m. 10
A´	19	Elaboration and extension of A; basically in same tonality and meter; section is repeated

381

Section	Measures	Event and Scoring
B	36	Smooth and tranquil; 4/4 time; impressionistic texture; solo piano and viola begin with slurred arpeggios; violin solo enters with high melody in C-sharp minor Dorian; tonality is F-sharp major overall, but lower strings repeat the three-note motive from m. 10 in B-flat major
A´	68	Abbreviated return of material from the earlier section; barred in 4/4, but beginning with piano solo, metric feel is 3/4; written signature changes to 3/4 in m. 72; returns to F-sharp minor Dorian
A	80	Almost a literal restating of the opening, with voicing inverted

Movement 3: "Pastorale and Rustic Dances"
Form: ABAB+coda, roughly

Pastorale	1	Solo viola introduces pastorale motive A in C Dorian; other voices are in F major; slow, rhapsodic feel; viola introduces the 6/8 dance motive b in E Dorian in m. 9; a free development with cross rhythms and meters takes place
Dances	41	Fast 6/8; violin plays motive B in D Mixolydian
	48	Violin presents modified duple, march-like theme C in G major, followed by development of material at m. 70
Pastorale	104	A and B motives layered; slow, with similar meters and tonality to opening
	114	Viola introduces theme D; 3/4; A major; "horn call" flavor
Development	126	All material, plus the three-note motive from the second movement; fast, with rapidly shifting meters and tonalities

SECTION	MEASURES	EVENT AND SCORING
Closing	184	Return to F major and almost literal statement of theme C; short coda at m. 209

Movement 4: "Fugue"

SECTION	MEASURES	EVENT AND SCORING
Exposition 1	1	Six statements of lively subject and countersubject in 4/4 and D Dorian, starting with viola
Episode 1	44	Short, dance-like transitional section beginning in A major; features concertino group
Exposition 2	56	Three statements of subject, beginning in F major
Episode 2	75	Similar to first episode, beginning in F major
Exposition 3	81	Four statements of subject; the first is accomplished by the solo first violin in g minor; last three are melodically inverted
Episode 3	115	A major
Exposition 4	119	Development of all material; use of stretto entrances, diminution, and augmentation in the subject; begins in D Dorian and moves to E minor when material from the opening ritornello in Movement 1 is quoted in m. 142
Closing	157	Recaps all material, no longer imitative, all centered in D; short coda in D major presented on the subject material beginning in m. 179, with a D pedal in the bass throughout

Unit 8: Suggested Listening

Ernest Bloch:
   Concerto Grosso No. 2
   Schelomo
Arcangelo Corelli, Concerto Grosso in G Minor, Op. 6, No. 8 ("Christmas Concerto")
Gustav Holst, *St. Paul's Suite*
Igor Stravinsky, *Dumbarton Oaks*
Ralph Vaughan Williams, Concerto Grosso for String Orchestra
Peter Warlock, *Capriol Suite*

Unit 9: Additional References and Resources

Bloch, Suzanne, and Irene Heskes. *Ernest Bloch, Creative Spirit: A Program Source Book*. New York: Jewish Music Council of the National Jewish Welfare Board, 1976.

Jones, W. M. "The Music of Ernest Bloch." Dissertation, Indiana University, 1963.

Kushner, David Z. *Ernest Bloch: A Guide to Research*. New York: Garland, 1988.

Sadie, Stanley, ed. *The New Grove Dictionary of Music and Musicians*. S.v. "Ernest Bloch" by David Z. Kushner. New York: Grove's Dictionaries, 2000. Also available online at www.grovemusic.com

Slonimsky, Nicolas, ed. emeritus. *Baker's Biographical Dictionary of Musicians*. New York: Schirmer Books, 2001.

Strassburg, Robert. *Ernest Bloch, Voice in the Wilderness: A Biographical Study*. Los Angeles: Trident Shop, California State University at Los Angeles, 1977.

Contributed by:

Judy Palac
Associate Professor of Music Education
Michigan State University
East Lansing, Michigan

Teacher Resource Guide

Concerto Grosso for String Orchestra

Ralph Vaughan Williams
(1872–1958)

STRING ORCHESTRA

Unit 1: Composer

Ralph Vaughan Williams was born in Down Ampney, Gloucestershire, on October 12, 1872. He died in London on August 26, 1958. His father was a clergyman—an important influence on Vaughan Williams's interest in religious music—who died when Ralph was a child. He studied violin and piano while living at his maternal grandfather's residence in Surrey.

In 1887, he enrolled at Charterhouse School in London, where he played violin and viola in the school orchestra. He studied composition with Hubert Parry from 1890 to 1892 at the Royal College of Music in London, and with Max Bruch in Berlin in 1897. Vaughan Williams then went on to Trinity College, Cambridge, where he received his Doctor of Music in 1901. He sought advice from Maurice Ravel in Paris in 1908 concerning modern orchestration techniques that emphasized orchestral color. During the first decade of the 1900s, he collected English folk songs, which would be of paramount importance in his compositions.

Vaughan Williams was an artillery officer in World War I, and then a professor of composition at the Royal College of Music in London from 1919 to 1939. After the death of his first wife, he married for a second time at the age of 80, and then gave a lecture tour at several universities in the United States, a tribute to the vitality of his old age. He continued composing until his death at age 85.

Unit 2: Composition

The Rural Music Schools Association of Great Britain commissioned Vaughan Williams to write the Concerto Grosso for String Orchestra to celebrate the twenty-first anniversary of the movement. The first performance, by four hundred adults and young people from the Rural Music Schools Association, took place in Royal Albert Hall on November 18, 1950. Sir Adrian Boult was the conductor and shared Vaughan Williams's obligation to and delight in music for amateurs.

The orchestra is divided into four groups, as detailed in the preface to the score:

1. Concertino, consisting of about 6.6.4.4.2 skilled players
2. *Tutti*, for all those who can play in the third position and can play simple double-stops
3. *Ad lib.* parts for less-experienced players: two such parts for violin and one each for viola and cello
4. *Ad lib.* open strings parts for violin, viola, cello, and bass for those players who prefer to use only open strings

The composer thanks three people, apparently music teachers: Gertrude Collins, Edwina Palmer, and Arthur Trew "for much advice and help in preparing my score. Indeed, the *ad lib.* parts have been written entirely under their direction."

The composition lasts approximately seventeen minutes and is divided into five movements:

Movement 1: "Intrada" (Largo)
Movement 2: "Burlesca Ostinata" (Allegro moderato)
Movement 3: "Sarabande" (Lento)
Movement 4: "Scherzo" (Allegro—tempo di valse)
Movement 5: "March and Reprise" (Alla marcia)

The Reprise is an exact repeat of the Intrada.

Unit 3: Historical Perspective

The Concerto Grosso for String Orchestra is one of the earliest examples of "educational music" that is extant in the repertoire, although this work by Vaughan Williams ranks in the upper echelon of music written specifically for beginning and intermediate students. The music is never trite or condescending. Until 1950, string students played material from the existing method books as well as arrangements—often by Merle Isaac—of the standard orchestral repertoire. The availability of educational music written specifically to further technical advancement and to provide enjoyment for young people was much less prevalent in 1950.

Unit 4: Technical Considerations

The Concerto Grosso presents the modal harmonic language intrinsic to the English sound of Vaughan Williams. The melody and harmony of the five movements use both the Dorian scale based on D and the D-natural minor scale, a tonal center chosen because of the open string parts for beginners. The concertino parts require the use of the upper positions—up to high F-sharp in first violin and high D in thumb position in cello—and frequently call for rapid string crossings. The concertino is more complex rhythmically than the other parts, although the *tutti* is often in unison with the concertino. The *tutti* first violins infrequently employ third position. The difficulty in the open strings part for beginners lies not in playing the notes, but in playing the rhythms—often on afterbeats—and counting rests and empty measures. The open strings parts would best be played by at least an intermediate student; they can be omitted with no detriment to the work. Meter, tempo, and stylistic changes are plentiful in the second, fourth, and fifth movements.

Unit 5: Stylistic Considerations

Sudden dynamic changes and shadings of the phrases necessitate a high level of musicianship. Performers must have the ability to pull a huge sound from their instruments in Movement 1, which is a stunning opening and closing movement. Lyricism abounds in sections of all the movements. Spiccato is required of the concertino and *tutti* in Movement 4 and Movement 5. All violinists must use hooked bowing for the crisp dotted rhythms that lead back to Movement 1.

Unit 6: Musical Elements

The harmony is derived from modal as well as traditional major and minor scale structures. Although many of the thematic ideas are based on the use of the open string pitches, Vaughan Williams's genius skillfully keeps interest alive for both player and audience. There are numerous key or modality changes throughout the piece, and many sudden meter and stylistic changes, which can be a challenge to amateurs.

Unit 7: Form and Structure

Section	Event and Scoring
Movement 1: "Intrada"	
1	Beginning; D Dorian
2	#1; D major; slightly more active rhythmically
3	#2; C major but immediately modulating and incorporating melodic and rhythmic ideas from the first two sections

Section	Event and Scoring
4	#3; D major; begins *ff*, *diminuendos* and then builds to a mighty climax

Movement 2: "Burlesca Ostinata"

A theme	Beginning; D minor; theme cleverly built entirely of pitches of the open strings
A, Variation 1	#1; open string theme embellished with neighboring tones to create a flowing, sinuous line
A, Variation 2	#2; theme in violin similar to that at #1, but a new thematic idea with a one eighth/two sixteenth note rhythm (R) is added in second violin, viola, and cello; syncopation in the *tutti* parts
A, Variation 3	#3; thematic idea from Variation 2 continues; first violin plays a sixteenth note angular variation or embellishment on (R)
A, Variation 4	#4; new thematic idea with dotted rhythm introduced (DR); rhythmic activity subsides somewhat; rhythm of (R) remains, but more subtle
A, Variation 5	Opening material boldly proclaimed by first violin against (DR) and (R)
B	Four measures after #6; 3/4; D Mixolydian; tranquil, flowing melody in first violin against complicated accompaniment in viola and cello
C	#8; 4/4; D-natural minor; six measures, which are repeated
A	Four measures before #9; used as a bridge section to D
D	#9; D major; entirely new lyrical theme that lasts only eight measures
A, Variation 2	Vivace after #9; 2/4; D Mixolydian with pedal C; not a repeat of A, but further development of the (R) idea from Variation 2
B Variation 1	Four measures before #11; 3/4; G major; accompaniment different from previous B section
Coda	#12; ending in open fifths on D; series of chords with the concertino playing harmonics

Movement 3: Sarabande"

First half	G Phrygian at beginning; binary dance form with repeated first section; triplets against two eighth notes add to the rhythmic complexity of the flowing melody and accompaniment

SECTION	EVENT AND SCORING
Second half	Six measures before #2; recapitulation of material from the first half, though quite changed, occurs two measures before #3; codetta lasts for four measures

Movement 4: "Scherzo"

Introduction	Beginning; unison G; two measures in length
A	m. 3; C minor; *pp* concertino section followed by *fortissimo* section using the entire orchestra
B	#2; A minor; with new thematic idea at #4 that acts as a bridge to a *fortissimo* replay of the material at #2, but expanded in tessitura and with the accompaniment changed
C	2/4 before #10; C Dorian; parallel fifths between viola and cello
Coda	Presto before #12; replaces the traditional *da capo* to the beginning of a scherzo; 3/4; C minor ending in C major; based on B

Movement 5: "March and Reprise"

1	Beginning; A theme displays ambiguity between D major and B minor; entire orchestra varies the opening material at #1
	#2; B theme appears; B minor
	#4; D major emerges and A and B themes are in counterpoint; an important dotted-rhythm motive appears four measures before #6; derived from the rhythm of the opening material
2	#6; A-natural minor; first played by the concertino, then the *tutti* is added; similar to the unequal forces structure at the beginning
3	3/4 before #8; new thematic material permeated by the previous dotted-rhythm motive
4	2/4 before #9; tonal ambiguity of D major/B minor; short reprise of A with dotted-rhythm accompaniment
Coda	#10; 3/4; concertino and *tutti* entirely in dotted rhythms; acts as a bridge to Movement 1, which is repeated in its entirety

Unit 8: Suggested Listening

Edward Elgar:
    Introduction and Allegro (string quartet and string orchestra)
    Serenade in E Minor (string orchestra)
Gerald Finzi:
    Prelude for String Orchestra
    Romance for String Orchestra
Gustav Holst:
    Brook Green Suite (string orchestra)
    St. Paul's Suite (string orchestra)
C. Hubert H. Parry, *English Suite* (string orchestra)
Ralph Vaughan Williams:
    English Folk Song Suite
    Fantasia on a Theme of Thomas Tallis (string orchestra)
    "Fantasia on Greensleeves" from the opera *Sir John in Love*
    Five Variants of "Dives and Lazarus" (string orchestra)
    The Lark Ascending (with violin solo)
    A London Symphony
    Rhosymedre

Unit 9: Additional References and Resources

Day, James. *Vaughan Williams*. London: Oxford University Press, 1998.

Foss, Hubert. *Ralph Vaughan Williams: A Study*. London: Harrap, 1950.

Howes, Frank. *The Music of Ralph Vaughan Williams*. London: Oxford University Press, 1954.

Mayer, F.R., ed. *The String Orchestra Super List*. Reston, VA: Music Educators National Conference, 1993.

Slonimsky, Nicolas, ed. emeritus. *Baker's Biographical Dictionary of Musicians*. New York: Schirmer Books, 2001.

Contributed by:

David Littrell
Professor of Music
Kansas State University
Manhattan, Kansas

Teacher Resource Guide

Concerto Grosso in D Minor, Op. 3, No. 11

Antonio Vivaldi
(1678–1741)

STRING ORCHESTRA

Unit 1: Composer

Born in 1678, Antonio Lucio Vivaldi was ordained as a priest in 1703, and because of his distinctive red hair, he came to be known as "The Red Priest." Vivaldi was an excellent violinist and as such was appointed violin master at the Ospedale della Pietà, a church-run orphanage for female foundlings that was located in Venice. The females of the school were musically trained and those with talent were assigned to the choir and orchestra. The performance of these ensembles helped to support the institution through donations. Vivaldi's earliest musical compositions coincide with his first years at the Pietà, where many of the compositions were written for his students. Much of Vivaldi's career revolved around the Pietà: as violin master (1703–09, 1711–15), as director of instrumental music (1716–17, 1735–38), and as a paid composer of compositions for the Pietà (1723–29, 1739–40). Vivaldi also composed in other mediums, including vocal sacred music and opera. His instrumental works alone total 554 compositions. Perhaps his most important contribution was the standardization of the solo concerto into a three-movement formula of fast–slow–fast. Although once prosperous, Vivaldi died a pauper while on a trip to Vienna in 1741.

Unit 2: Composition

Opus 3, known as *L'estro armonico* and translated as "The Harmonious Fancy," was an important collection of twelve concertos known for the uniqueness of the compositions and the emotional character of the music. Written during a time when Vivaldi was free of obligations to the Pietà, this work was one of the largest collections of concertos to be written in Italy. In 1711, *L'estro armonico* was published by the Amsterdam music publishing firm of Estienne Roger. This collection of concertos secured Vivaldi's fame throughout Europe and paved the way for the sale of future compositions; however, only Opus 8, which includes "The Four Seasons," met with the same success as *L'estro armonico*. The Concerto Grosso in D Minor, Op. 3, No. 11, includes a concertino of two violins and one violoncello contrasted with a ripieno of string orchestra and continuo. The melodies are distinct in their rhythmic vitality, drive, and personal expression. The first movement begins with an impetuous canonic melody in the *concertanti* violins followed by the entrance of the solo cello with continuo, which leads to a three-measure Adagio Spiccato e Tutti that is followed by a fugue in *concertante* style. The second movement, "Largo e Spiccato," is a siciliano whose melody is dominated by the first solo violin. The third movement consists of a concertante Allegro that is reminiscent of the nature of the first movement.

Unit 3: Historical Perspective

The principal orchestral music of the baroque era, c.1600–c.1750, was the concerto grosso, an instrumental composition based on the opposition of dissimilar groups. A small group of instruments, the *concertino*, was contrasted with a large group of instruments, variously known as the *concerto grosso*, *tutti*, or *ripieno*. These compositions reflected major currents of the baroque period, namely thorough-bass, improvisation, emergence of the major-minor tonal system, the doctrine of the affections, unflagging rhythm, continuous melody, harmonic counterpoint, terraced dynamics, virtuosity, instrumental color, and a growing importance of the orchestra. The social function of the concerto grosso was stated in 1701 by Muffat:

> These concertos…suited neither to the church (because of the ballet airs and airs of other sorts which they include) nor for dancing (because of other interwoven conceits, now slow and serious, now gay and nimble, and composed only for the express refreshment of the ear), may be performed most appropriately in connection with entertainments given by great princes and lords, for receptions of distinguished guests, and at state banquets, serenades, and assemblies of musical amateurs and virtuosi.
>
> (as translated in Oliver Strunk's Source Readings in Music History, W. W. Norton & Company, Inc., New York, 1950, p. 449)

The concerto grosso reached its height with George Frideric Handel's Opus 6 of 1740 and was supplanted by the solo concerto. Composers such as Igor Stravinsky and Henry Cowell revived the form in the twentieth century.

Unit 4: Technical Considerations

The solo writing in the Concerto Grosso in D Minor is an idiomatic and effective melding of style with technical considerations. D minor is the predominant tonal center throughout, and students should learn the D minor scale in both the natural and melodic forms. Rhythms do not exceed quarter note = 120, with the highest division of the beat being sixteenth notes. The ripieno parts are relatively easy compared to the concertino with the exception of the fugue. The violins of the concertino do not extend past third position, and the solo cello is required to leave first position only once. The first violins of the ripieno are the only section required to leave the first position, with the rare exception of the contrabass. The difficulty does not lie so much in the position work as it does in the speed of the sixteenth notes. Facile technique will be required to play at the correct tempo. The bowing has important technical considerations for the execution of proper style. Students must have good control of bow weight, speed, and placement for accurate accentuation of the terraced dynamics. In addition, détaché and martelé bow strokes will predominate in the faster movements.

Unit 5: Stylistic Considerations

The baroque style of the Concerto Grosso in D Minor is largely achieved through the use of proper bowing styles with contrasting legato sixteenth notes and articulated and detached eighth notes in fast movements. The slow, three-measure introduction to the fugue in the first movement is a circle of fifths chord progression that ends on the dominant and serves as a preparation for the return of D minor. Entrances of the statement within the fugue should be balanced against other sections that are playing. The baroque style was to arouse emotional states by appealing to the senses. The fast movements excite the senses, and the slow second movement is a contrasting pastorale to its surrounding movements. Because of its pastorale nature, this movement requires the most legato and expressive playing of any of the movements. Throughout the composition, the terraced dynamics should be observed to accentuate the baroque desire for contrast and competing elements. The rhythm should remain constant in each movement and be energetic in the fast movements to bring out the virtuosic writing for the concertino.

Unit 6: Musical Elements

Tonality is established throughout by frequent cadences, use of arpeggiated chords in the melody, and pedal point that is established either through a sustained note or the rhythmic repetition of a single pitch. Chain suspensions with circle of fifths chord progressions that allow for sequenced melodic material are one means of brief forays into other tonal centers. After these brief modulations, there is always a drive to the return of D minor. Chain suspensions with circle of fifth chord progressions are typical of Vivaldi's style and are found in all movements of the Concerto Grosso in D Minor. The second movement outer sections are in D minor, while the solo violin section modulates briefly into the keys of A major, G major, and F minor. These are the main key center modulations used throughout the Concerto Grosso.

Homophony is pervasive throughout with the exception of the harmonic counterpoint of the four-voice fugue, which contains a full exposition with both a subject and countersubject, followed by episodic melodic fragments based on these subjects. The melodic material outlines the tonality through arpeggiated figures and scale runs, which reinforces the baroque predilection for major-minor tonality over modal writing of the Renaissance. Melodic repetition and sequence are pervasive throughout, and it is a stylistic feature used particularly at the beginning of the third movement. The fast movements have an unrelenting drive and rhythm that is established through the intense concentration of rhythmic figuration. In the second movement, the 12/8 meter with dotted rhythms in the melody and the flattened supertonic is characteristic of a siciliana. The designation of spiccato before 1750 means detached or separated as opposed to legato. Vivaldi, himself a violinist, composed solo parts that are virtuosic in nature and highly idiomatic.

Unit 7: Form and Structure

SECTION	MEASURES	EVENT AND SCORING
Movement 1:		
Allegro (sectional)		
A	1	Allegro; canonic writing between violin I and II in concertino with rhythmic pedal tone D minor tonality
	20	Concertino cello and continuo with circle of fifths chord progressions
Adagio Spiccato e Tutti		
	32	Three-measure Adagio; circle of fifths chord progression ending on the dominant of D minor
Allegro (fugue)		
	35	Exposition
	51	Episode
Movement 2:		
Largo e Spiccato (simple ritornello form)		
A	105	*Tutti*
B	107	Violin solo with upper string accompaniment

SECTION	MEASURES	EVENT AND SCORING
A´	121	*Tutti*

Movement 3:
Allegro (ritornello form)

A	125	
B	131	
B^1	147	
C	159	
D	167	
A	177	
B´	183	

Unit 8: Suggested Listening

Arcangelo Corelli, Concerti Grossi, Op. 6, Nos. 1–12
George Frideric Handel, Concerti Grossi, Op. 6, Nos. 1–12
Antonio Vivaldi:
   Concerti Grossi, Op. 3, Nos. 1–12
   Concerti Grossi, Op. 8, Nos. 1–5

Unit 9: Additional References and Resources

Hutchings, Arthur. *The Baroque Concerto.* Revised edition. New York:
   C. Scribner's Sons, 1979.

Kolneder, Walter. *Antonio Vivaldi: His Life and Work.* Berkley and Los
   Angeles: University of California Press, 1970.

Landon, H. C. Robbins. *Vivaldi: Voice of the Baroque.* New York: Thames
   and Hudson, 1993.

Pincherle, Marc. *Vivaldi: Genius of the Baroque.* New York: W. W. Norton &
   Company, 1957.

Talbot, Michael. *Antonio Vivaldi: A Guide to Research.* New York: Garland,
   1988.

Talbot, Michael. *Vivaldi.* London: Dent, 1993.

Contributed by:

C. Gregory Hurley
Associate Professor of Music, Music Education Chair,
   and String Pedagogy
University of Northern Colorado
Greeley, Colorado

Teacher Resource Guide

Divertimenti, K. 136–138

Wolfgang Amadeus Mozart
(1756–1791)

STRING ORCHESTRA

Unit 1: Composer

Wolfgang Amadeus Mozart was born in Salzburg in 1756 and died in Vienna in 1791 at age thirty-six. He is the best-known Mozart, from a family of south German and Austrian composers and musicians that left the world a musical legacy. W. A. Mozart showed his musical talent as a small child, learning the same piano pieces that his father, Leopold Mozart, taught to his sister who was four years older. Leopold Mozart was a respected violinist and composer, who taught his children music and the other subjects at home.

The young Mozart wrote his first composition and performed for the first time in public at age five, where he was said to have played the clavier amazingly well. He and his sister were famous as child prodigies and spent three years touring Europe with their father, performing for wealthy and influential people wherever they went. Mozart's first major opera was performed in Milan just before his fifteenth birthday.

Mozart spent the majority of his adult life in Vienna, working as a freelance composer. He was one of the first musicians who lived and worked independently of a wealthy patron, church, or court. He was successful for a time but was plagued with financial difficulties. He was often thought to be fond of lavish spending and to have difficulty managing money. Despite his fame and enduring success as a composer, upon his death in 1791 Mozart was buried in an unmarked public grave.

Unit 2: Composition

The string quartets K.136–138 that Mozart wrote in Salzburg in early 1772 were some of his earliest works for string quartet. The title "Divertimenti" was not added until later. Mozart wrote these quartets when he was sixteen, during a short stay at home in Salzburg before his third journey to Italy. The three quartets, K. 136–138, are three-movement works in the keys of D major, B-flat major, and F major. They are not yet fully developed string quartets but show evidence of features that are present in many of his later works. Mozart's tempo markings for K. 136 and 138 are "Allegro, Andante, Presto"; K. 137 opens "Andante," followed by "Allegro molto" and "Allegro assai."

Unit 3: Historical Perspective

Mozart composed the three quartets, K. 136–138, in Salzburg in the early months of 1772. They are in the classical style but are much lighter and simpler than his later string quartets. Mozart's works from this time show the influence of Michael Haydn and Bach as well as his father, who still held great influence over his professional and personal life. Franz Joseph Haydn, who was twenty-four years older than Mozart, and Christoph Willibald Gluck, famous for his operatic compositions, were also important figures in musical society.

Unit 4: Technical Considerations

The two movements of primary discussion in this article are the Presto from K. 136 and the Allegro from K. 138. Other movements have similar technical requirements. The final movement of K. 136, "Presto," is in D major. Both violin parts contain sixteenth note scale figures in D and closely related keys. All parts, but primarily viola and cello, contain repeated eighth notes to be played off the string, requiring the ability to produce a controlled spiccato. Students must be able to stay in the correct part of the bow and change to bowing on the string for slurred sections. The first violin part requires use of third and fifth position. Other parts are playable in first position, even though there may be more desirable fingerings that use higher positions. There are several trills in the violin parts. Double-stops are playable in first position, most with one open string. The Allegro from K. 138 is in F major and modulates to closely related keys. There are brief sixteenth note scale patterns in the violin parts. The first violin part requires shifting to third and fifth position. The second violin part contains several sections that are easier to play in third position than first. Bowing requirements are similar to those in the Presto from K. 136.

Unit 5: Stylistic Considerations

Performance of literature from the classical period requires a precise, controlled approach to articulation and dynamics. Staccato eighth notes should be taken off the string, but with a stroke that is brushed rather than percussive. Students should be careful to remain in the correct part of the bow to achieve the control necessary for correct articulation. The opening eighths in the Presto of K. 136 may be played up-bow to encourage light staccatos within the *piano* dynamic. The dotted-eighth/sixteenth figure in the Allegro of K. 138 must be subdivided in sixteenths to keep them from being played as triplets. All of the movements have a constant pulse, of which the students must be constantly aware. Cellists must be aware of their role in providing the tonal and rhythmic support for the structure of the piece.

Unit 6: Musical Elements

The works of Mozart contain many distinct melodic ideas. The opening of the Presto of K. 136 begins with a two-measure rhythmic motive followed by a lyrical one. The melodic ideas presented early in the composition reappear throughout the movement. The tonal structure is a predictable classical binary form, modulating to the dominant at the end of the first section and exploring the closely related keys while modulating back to the tonic for the return. The chordal structure is fairly easy for experienced students to analyze. Modulations move to closely related keys, and cadences are easy to identify in this style.

Unit 7: Form and Structure

"Presto," K. 136
Binary (AB) form, D major
||: D major   A major :||
m. 1   cadence mm. 57–58
Motives repeated in antecedent/consequent pairs
||: D major through related keys back to D major, cadence in D major
mm. 59, 70   B theme canonic for two measures :||

"Allegro," K. 138
Binary (AB) form, F major
||: F major   C major :||
m. 1   cadence m. 35
Antecedent/consequent pairs in phrase groupings
||: C major through related keys to F major, cadence in F major :||

Unit 8: Suggested Listening

Franz Joseph Haydn, early string quartets (e.g., Op. 20)
Wolfgang Amadeus Mozart:
  string quartets (including *Eine Kleine Nachtmusik*, K. 525)
  Symphony No. 25 in G Minor
  Symphony No. 40 in G Minor
  Symphony No. 41 in C Major ("Jupiter")
  Three Divertimenti, K. 136–138

Unit 9: Additional References and Resources

Dart, Thurston. *The Interpretation of Music*. New York: Harper, 1963.

Erich, Otto. *Mozart: A Documentary Biography*. Eric Blom, Peter Branscombe, Jeremy Noble, trans. London: Black, 1966.

Kenneson, Claude. *Musical Prodigies: Perilous Journeys, Remarkable Lives*. Portland: Amadeus Press, 1998.

Mozart, W.A. *The Letters of Mozart and His Family*. Emily Anderson, ed. and trans. New York: W. W. Norton & Company, 1985.

Sadie, Stanley, ed. *The New Grove Dictionary of Music and Musicians*. "Wolfgang Amadeus Mozart." New York: Grove's Dictionaries, 2000. 12:680–752. Also available online at www.grovemusic.com

Slonimsky, Nicolas, ed emeritus. *Baker's Biographical Dictionary of Musicians*. New York: Schirmer Books, 2001.

Soloman, Maynard. *Mozart: A Life*. New York: Harper Collins Publishers, 1995.

Contributed by:

Amy Fear-Bishop
Orchestra Director, Prairie Star Middle School
Leawood, Kansas
String Specialist, Prairie Star Middle School and Stanley Elementary
Shawnee Mission, Kansas

Teacher Resource Guide

Fugue in G Minor ("The Little"), BWV 578

Johann Sebastian Bach
(1685–1750)

arranged by Lucien Cailliet

FULL ORCHESTRA

Unit 1: Composer/Arranger

German baroque composer and performer Johann Sebastian Bach remains one of the most influential musicians of all time through his large output of works and uniquely creative compositional genius. Bach's compositional talents were so integral in the historical development of the fugue that the *Harvard Dictionary of Music* includes the phrase "brought to perfection by J. S. Bach" in the very definition of "fugue." Bach gained fame as a virtuoso violinist and organist, and composed over one thousand secular and sacred works.

Arranger Lucien Cailliet was born in France and came to the United States in the 1920s. He joined the Philadelphia Orchestra, serving as clarinetist, saxophonist, and staff arranger during the tenures of Leopold Stokowski and Eugene Ormandy. In fact, some of the famous Bach-Stokowski and Wagner-Stokowski orchestral arrangements were done by Cailliet, then performed and recorded (with Cailliet's permission) under Stokowski's name. Cailliet's career included teaching on numerous prestigious music faculties, guest conducting major symphony orchestras, and publishing over 140 compositions and arrangements in various idioms.

Unit 2: Composition

Composed originally for organ, "The Little" nickname is attached to this fugue to distinguish it from Bach's more fully developed "great" fugue in the same key, which was composed later. Despite being one of Bach's more simply constructed early fugues, "The Little" Fugue is one of his most widely known and frequently performed. The beauty and melodic balance of the subject, along with the youthful spontaneity of the work, contribute to its enduring popularity. The work has a performance time of approximately four minutes.

Unit 3: Historical Perspective

"The Little" Fugue was likely composed prior to 1707, when Bach was under the age of twenty-two. During this early period, Bach held organist positions in Arnstadt and Mühlhausen. At this point, Bach was already forging his own musical path, but his compositions were still dependent on traditional German and Italian models. The great German organist and composer Dietrich Buxtehude (c.1637–1707), whom Bach admired greatly, exerted a strong musical influence on the young organist's playing and composition. Bach also forged a relationship with Georg Philipp Telemann (1681–1767) during this time. Other contemporary composers included a young George Frideric Handel (1685–1759) moving from Hamburg to Venice, François Couperin (1668–1733) in Paris, an aging Arcangelo Corelli (1653–1713) in Rome, and Antonio Vivaldi (1678–1741) who had just begun teaching at the Pietà in Venice.

Unit 4: Technical Considerations

Cailliet's transcription is for full orchestra, including piccolo, English horn, bass clarinet, contra-bassoon, full brass section, harp, and five percussionists. Contra-bassoon and harp parts are clearly optional, and essential lines are conveniently doubled or cross-cued to allow for incomplete instrumentation. All instruments are actively featured in subjects and counterpoint. A solo clarinet (Cailliet's major instrument) begins the fugue with the opening subject. Brass ranges are reasonable, with horn playing G on top of the staff and first trumpet reaching only A. The percussionists play only in the climactic final seven measures. First violin must be comfortable through fifth and sixth positions, and second violin requires third position. Viola, cello, and bass shift minimally. The string bass section has the option of using an E-string extension or tuning down in the final measures to facilitate a more cohesive final statement of the subject. Though Cailliet wrote a *tremolo* for strings on the final note, conductors may prefer to create more of a pure organ sound by sustaining it with two or more bows. The second violin part has one error, lacking the F-sharp accidental five measures from the end. (The score is correct.)

Unit 5: Stylistic Considerations

Though the orchestration is worthy of nineteenth century grandeur, contrapuntal sixteenth notes and eighth notes can be played in the style of a baroque concerto grosso, with light sixteenth notes and a slight separation between eighth notes. Cailliet writes accents to highlight the first three notes of each subject or answer, more likely with the intention of asserting importance than articulating heavily. Cailliet's orchestration and attention to individual dynamic markings provide excellent balance for the subjects and answers. Conductors should be certain to alert students to these individual dynamics and their significance.

Unit 6: Musical Elements

The subject and answer must always be performed melodically, with attention to the three parts of the phrase. The first part is framed by a broken tonic triad (G–D–B-flat) and the dominant triad (F-sharp–A–D), and should lead the listener toward the B-flat and F-sharp of those triads, respectively. The short second part of the phrase leads to the B-flat in a simple statement of repeated tonic and dominant harmonies. The third part is an extension of the second that seems to gain confidence through the upward octave leap that launches the more assertive sixteenth notes. Students should play their subjects simultaneously in rehearsal to compare and match articulation and phrase direction. Performers should take care to gently stress harmonically and melodically significant "goal" notes in the sixteenth note passages, and to choose and sustain a moderate tempo that allows for such subtle phrasing. Cailliet recommended a metronome marking of quarter note = 108, but most performances by organ or orchestra are closer to quarter note = 78.

Unit 7: Form and Structure

While completely true to Bach's notes and rhythms, originally written in a continuous common time signature, Cailliet wisely chose to strategically place five single measures of 2/4 time to allow subjects, answers, episodes, and rehearsal numbers to align conveniently on bar lines. The formal and harmonic structure is listed below, noting the instruments for only the initial subject, answer, and countersubject. Only the first countersubject is listed below; note that it appears opposite all subjects and answers except for the very first.

SECTION	EVENT AND SCORING
Beginning	Subject; G minor; clarinet 1
1	Answer in English horn/clarinet 2; D minor; countersubject in flute/clarinet
2 1/2 mm. before 2	Bridge

SECTION	EVENT AND SCORING
2	Subject; G minor
3	Answer; D minor
4	Episode; d–g–c–F–B-flat–E-flat–a–D; dominated by circle of fifths; sequence
5	Subject; G minor
6	Subject; B-flat major
7	Subject; B-flat major
8	Episode; B-flat–c–F–B-flat–E-flat–A-flat–d°–G^7–c–f–G^7; dominated by circle of fifths; sequence
9	Subject; C minor
10	Episode; c–F–B-flat–E-flat–a-flat$°^7$–D^7; dominated by circle of fifths; sequence
11	Episode continued; g–D^3_7x–g–F–B-flat–G^7–C–A^7–D–g–c^7–F–B-flat–E-flat–a°–D^7; dominated by circle of fifths; sequence
12	Final subject; G minor

At first glance, the passage at 5 appears to be an example of *stretto* (two over-lapping subjects), but the first statement in the low woodwinds is merely a single measure of the subject followed by the countersubject to the oboe/trumpet subject. Bach's typical sustained pedal tones on the dominant pitch appear during the subjects and answers after 3, 5, 6, 7, 9, and 12. Cailliet usually places these pedal tones in either a low, middle, or high grouping of instruments until the final phrase. Here, where an organist would generally choose to "pull out all the stops," he/she sustains the pedal in the timpani, horns, English horn, and piccolo, while the final subject appears in three powerful, adjacent low octaves.

Unit 8: Suggested Listening

Johann Sebastian Bach:
   Fugue in G Minor ("The Little") BWV 587, Canadian Brass "Great Baroque Music"
   Fugue in G Minor ("The Little") BWV 587, organ recordings
   Toccata and Fugue in D Minor, BWV 565, Canadian Brass "Great Baroque Music"
   Toccata and Fugue in D Minor, BWV 565, organ recordings
Johann Sebastian Bach/arr. Stokowski, Toccata and Fugue in D Minor, BWV 565 (Disney's original *Fantasia*)
Arcangelo Corelli, Concerto Grosso, Op. 6, No. 1, Movement 3 ("Fugue")

George Frideric Handel:
    Concerto Grosso Op. 6, Nos. 1, 2, 4, 5, 6, 7, 9, 12,
      (Fugue Movements 2, 4, 5)
    Messiah, Fugues in Overture and final "Amen"
Antonio Vivaldi, Concerto, Op. 3, No. 11, Movement II ("Fugue")

Unit 9: Additional References and Resources

Fisher, Larry. "Lucien Cailliet: His Contributions to the Symphonic Band,
    Orchestra, and Ensemble Literature," *Journal of Band Research*, Vol. 18,
    No. 2 (Spring 1983).

Grace, Harvey. *The Organ Works of Bach*. New York: H. W. Gray, 1922.

Hitchcock, H. Wiley, and Stanley Sadie. *The New Grove Dictionary of
    American Music*. London: Macmillan, 1986.

Keller, Hermann. *The Organ Works of Bach: A Contribution to Their History,
    Form, Interpretation and Performance*. New York: C. F. Peters, 1967.

Randel, Don, ed. *The New Harvard Dictionary of Music*. Cambridge, MA:
    Harvard University Press, 1986.

Sadie, Stanley, ed. *The New Grove Dictionary of Music and Musicians*. New
    York: Grove's Dictionaries, 2000. Also available online at
    www.grovemusic.com

Widor, Charles-Marie, and Albert Schweitzer. *Johann Sebastian Bach
    Complete Organ Works, Vol. 2: Preludes and Fugues of the First Master-
    Period*. New York: Schirmer, 1940.

Contributed by:

Ray E. Ostwald
Director of Orchestras
York Community High School
Elmhurst, Illinois

Teacher Resource Guide

"Hoe Down" from Rodeo
Aaron Copland
(1900–1990)

STRING ORCHESTRA AND FULL ORCHESTRA

Unit 1: Composer

Aaron Copland, born November 14, 1900, in Brooklyn, New York, the youngest of five children, died December 2, 1990, in North Tarrytown, New York, after a long illness. His career as pianist, composer, conductor, and teacher spanned fifty years, earning him the title of "Dean of American Composers." Early influences included Nadia Boulanger, Igor Stravinsky, popular music, and European nationalists. Notable works are *Billy the Kid*, *A Lincoln Portrait*, the Pulitzer Prize-winning *Appalachian Spring*, *Fanfare for the Common Man*, and the Oscar-winning film score, *The Heiress*. Copland lectured at Harvard University and taught at Berkshire Music Center in Tanglewood for twenty-five years. He was an ardent advocate for new music and one of the most honored cultural figures in United States history.

Unit 2: Composition

The Ballet Russe de Monte Carlo commissioned choreographer Agnes de Mille (niece to Cecil B. de Mille) and Aaron Copland to collaborate on a western ballet for its 1942–43 season. *Rodeo* was the resulting work. Copland subsequently extracted an orchestral suite for concert performance titled "Four Episodes" from *Rodeo*. "Hoe Down" is the fourth movement, using as a principal theme the square dance tune "Bonyparte." The movement is marked "Allegro" and is approximately three minutes in length.

Unit 3: Historical Perspective

"Hoe Down" is one of the staples of contemporary American symphonic literature, conveying Copland's artistry with simple folk melodies and popular tunes. The ballet received twenty-two curtain calls at its premiere. The main theme has been arranged for elementary band and orchestra, and the entire work has been played in concert halls around the world, even in television commercials. While purely Copland, it conveys America in simpler times. As de Mille described it:

> ...Often, on the more isolated ranches, the rodeo is done for an audience that consists only of a handful of fellow-workers, women-folk, and those nearest neighbors who can make the eighty or so mile run-over. The afternoon's exhibition is usually followed by a Saturday night dance at the Ranch House.

In furious *tutti* sixteenth note passages, the two principal motives convey the spirit of the individual cowboy and the teamwork of cowhands. The orchestral suite was premiered by the New York Philharmonic Symphony in July 1943.

Unit 4: Technical Consideration

Set at a non-stop allegro, students in every section must have full mastery of the technical demands of their instrument. The full orchestra score requires full winds and brass, including English horn, bass clarinet, bass trombone, full percussion, and piano. Both full and string orchestra arrangements are in the key of D major. The comfortable key provides only limited relief for the strings, as *tutti* first violin, second violin, and viola use harmonics, third and fifth positions throughout, with brief exceptions at solo sections. Viola moves into treble clef regularly. Cello and double bass use extended positions, including fourth position, octave leaps, and harmonics. In the full orchestra, the solo trumpet must cleanly hit high A, and first oboe and first clarinet must single tongue sixteenth note scale passages in D major ranging an octave and a fifth. The 2/4 rhythmic considerations are easily understood and passed between sections. Slurred sixteenth note grace notes are easily memorized and fingered. Entrances on the second sixteenth note of the passage require both technical mastery and memorization. The sheer joy of performing this selection tends to inspire students to achieve the necessary skills.

Unit 5: Stylistic Considerations

Bowings and articulations require authority and precision. Détaché, staccato, and marcato must be used with facility in the allegro tempo. Dynamic contrasts require focused preparation and instant execution as the motives race past. Clean contrast between staccato and legato, *p* and *ff*, is necessary to convey the high spiritedness of this work. As in virtually all of Copland's works, intonation between fifths and octaves is essential within sections and between sections. Irresistible color is provided through double-stops, octave harmonics, pizzicato and, in the full orchestra arrangement, hard mallets on cymbal and xylophone, rim shots, and a delicious *ritardando molto* descending chromatically and melting into a fermata with celesta.

Unit 6: Musical Elements

Throughout the approximate three minutes of this selection, the limited musical elements must be precise. Thirty-three measures of triplet sixteenth notes dance among sections. Triple-stopped string pizzicatos add weight to the barnyard clucking and calls. As if all the participants have finally gathered, the main theme then takes off in furious passages of scales and arpeggios. Eighth notes must be clean and crisp. Syncopation must be powerful, and accented offbeats require care to avoid disturbing the forward momentum. Brief, exposed solo passages must be balanced carefully with the *tutti* first violin responses. Control of the dynamics for *mezzo piano* and *piano* must be achieved to avoid repetitiveness of the principal theme.

Unit 7: Form and Structure

Form: ABA

SECTION	MEASURES	EVENT AND SCORING
Introduction		Sets up main motives in mm. 1–4 and 14–17; hovering, slurred triplet sixteenth notes
	5–13	Clucking eighth notes
	19–38	Off-balance walking bass motive
A	39–62	Principal theme, "Bonyparte"
	63–78	Violin and viola contrasting theme, two octaves apart
	79–88	Bonyparte theme resumed, then transition to B
B	97–121	Contrasting theme; presented in solo trumpet, oboe, clarinet, violin, *tutti* upper strings
	121–141	Furious development to dramatic false ending in dominant
	142–158	Resume clucking eighth note motive; to fermata on E-flat
A	159–182	Return of furious principal theme; recapitulation of motives; a kicker cadence in tonic

Isolating each motive with the emotion it brings provides a valuable approach to teaching this work comprehensively instead of measure to measure.

Unit 8: Suggested Listening
Aaron Copland:
>   *Appalachian Suite*
>   *Fanfare for the Common Man*
>   "Four Dance Episodes" from *Rodeo*
>   *A Lincoln Portrait*
>   *Music for the Theatre*
>   *An Outdoor Overture*
>   Symphony No. 3 ("Bonyparte") (traditional fiddle tune)

Unit 9: Additional References and Resources

Copland, Aaron, and Vivian Perlis. *Aaron Copland Since 1943*. New York: St. Martin's Press, 1989.

Copland, Aaron. Sites on World Wide Web, particularly those of Boosey & Hawkes.

Copland, Aaron. *What to Listen for in Music*. New York: New American Library, 1985.

Pollack, Howard. *Aaron Copland: The Life and Work of an Uncommon Man*. Urbana, IL: Henry Holt & Co., 2000.

Contributed by:
Arlene Witte
Music Coordinator
Atlanta Public Schools
Atlanta, Georgia

Teacher Resource Guide

Holberg Suite, Op. 40
Edvard Grieg
(1843–1907)

STRING ORCHESTRA

Unit 1: Composer

Edvard Grieg is regarded as one of Norway's greatest cultural heroes and the founder of a distinctly Norwegian musical style. His musical promise at age fifteen was evident to virtuoso violinist Ole Bull, who recommended Grieg for study at the Leipzig Conservatory. Grieg remained in Leipzig for four years, immersed in the German musical influences of Wagner and Schumann. Upon his return to Norway, Grieg and other like-minded artists began to craft what they hoped would be works reflecting the unique aspects of their native culture. His compositional techniques influenced the Impressionism of Debussy and Ravel, and his use of folk materials preceded, and perhaps inspired, the research and composition of Bartók.

Unit 2: Composition

Aus Holbergs Zeit was written in late 1884 for the celebration of the bicentennial of the birth of Ludvig Holberg (1684–1754). Referred to on the title page of the score as "the Molière of the Northerners," Holberg was a prolific writer, poet, political satirist, historian, and dramatist whose works firmly established modern Danish as a literary language. Grieg's *Suite* was first written for piano and dedicated to Erika Lie Nissen, one of the first prominent Norwegian women pianists. Grieg performed the *Suite* in Bergen on December 7, 1884. Perhaps to promote sales of the work in Germany, his publisher, Peters, decided to release the string orchestra version first and to promote it as an original string composition rather than a rework of a piano piece. The string orchestra version was first performed on March 12, 1885, in Bergen.

Unit 3: Historical Perspective

Grieg's *Suite* can be considered alongside other compositions that, in various ways, attempt to evoke or imitate music of a bygone era. In this case, the model is the seventeenth and eighteenth century dance suite typified by the instrumental works of J. S. Bach and others; the standard format presents a prelude and a number of stylized dances in binary form. The sarabande perhaps originated in Mexico and was widely popular throughout Europe by way of Spain. The gavotte, musette, and rigaudon originated in France. The musette, a dance associated with the countryside, prominently imitates the drones of a small bagpipe, also known as a musette. The air, or aria, emphasizes the production of vocal, song-like expression. Rather than trying to exactly duplicate the so-called old style, Grieg adopts the rhythmic and formal traditions of the dance suite while maintaining his unique compositional voice.

Unit 4: Technical Considerations

Grieg's string writing is demanding technically and in its artistic expression. The keys of G, C, D, and F-sharp major and B, G, D, and E minor are prominent, as well as chromatic alterations within these key areas. Register is not a particular concern, although the first violin part requires a B-flat on the fifth ledger line, as in measures 26–27 of the third movement. The cello part remains below the octave harmonic on the A string, with only a brief passage notated in tenor clef.

Perhaps the most obvious challenges are those of tempo: the viola parts in particular and upper strings in general contain passages that require good fingerings and plenty of practice to be executed precisely at the appropriate tempo. See, for example, measures 19–29 of the first movement and measures 12–15 of the third movement. The second and fourth movements offer many opportunities to enhance the expression through judicious variation in the width, speed, and intensity of the vibrato. The chromatic passages permit the exploration of the tempering of intervals, such as at letter G in the second movement. The score is rich with expressive markings that demand a variety of bowings and articulations. The full range of on- and off-the-string strokes can be found, from the smoothest legato détaché (as in measures 1–8 of the second movement), to a brisk spiccato (such as found at letter L of the third movement), to everything in between: slightly articulated détaché in the accompaniment eighth notes in the fourth movement, balanced and relaxed shuffle bowing in the upper strings throughout the first movement, or more vigorous accents and martelé (measures 68–71 of the first movement). Slurred and separate string crossings present a challenge. Control of bow speed both in rapid and sustained playing is a necessity.

Unit 5: Stylistic Considerations

Particular attention should be paid throughout to the consistent interpretation of *fp*, *ffp*, and accents at various dynamic levels. In spite of the busy scoring in the faster movements, the overall goal should be to reveal large structures and phrases—for example, in the Prelude, the beginning to letter A represents a single gesture. The rhythmic pulse of the Sarabande can be played with a slight emphasis on the second beat of each measure. The double nature of the composition presents interesting interpretive choices. On the one hand, a clear and refined period style will provide coherence and intelligibility of balance and form. On the other hand, this is a work from the 1880s, and a case could be made for the romantic approach to attacks, vibrato, and an overall rich approach to tone production. Perhaps the most rewarding solution is a judicious mixture of the two—for example, the repeated sections in the Sarabande and Air can reveal two different aspects of the same musical idea.

Unit 6: Musical Elements

Grieg's musical language is firmly rooted in common eighteenth century practice, with a few more modern elements. Phrase lengths and harmonies are fairly straightforward and adhere to the tonic–dominant–tonic patterns of the traditional dances. In places, phrases are extended and harmonies enriched, particularly through the use of secondary dominant chords such as found in measure 40 of the first movement, as well as pedal points in measure 24 of the second movement and measures 1–4 of the fifth movement. The textures are predominantly homophonic with a single, clear melodic voice, although the scoring makes extensive use of *divisi* and doublings that are definitely not of Holberg's time, such as in the Musette of the third movement.

Unit 7: Form and Structure

SECTION	MEASURES
Movement 1: "Prelude"	
Form: sonata	
A: Theme 1	1
Theme 2	9
B: development	19
A′: recapitulation,	
Theme 1	42
Theme 2	55
Movement 2, "Sarabande"	
Form: rounded binary, AABA′	
A	1
B	9

SECTION	MEASURES
A′	25

Movement 3: "Gavotte"
Form: overall ternary, Gavotte–Musette–Gavotte; rondo ABACA plus ternary DDED

Section	Measure
A	1
B	9
A	15
C	24
A	32
D	41
E	49
D	61

Movement 4: "Air"
Form: rounded binary, AABA′

Section	Measure
A: Theme 1	1
Theme 2	9
B	16
A′: Theme 1 (in cello)	40
Theme 2 (in violin I)	48

Movement 5: "Rigaudon"
Form: ternary, Rigaudon–trio–Rigaudon; binary, AAB plus rounded binary trio CCDC+codetta

Section	Measure
A	1
B	8
C	41
D	48
C	57
Codetta	64

Unit 8: Suggested Listening

J. S. Bach:
    Orchestral Suites (Overtures) 1–4
    English Suites (keyboard)
Benjamin Britten, *Simple Symphony*
Edvard Grieg:
    Peer Gynt Suites 1 and 2
    Piano Concerto in A Minor
Sergei Prokofiev, *Classical Symphony*

Maurice Ravel, *Le Tombeau de Couperin*
Ottorino Respighi, *Ancient Airs and Dances*, Suite No. 3
Igor Stravinsky, *Pulcinella*

Unit 9: Additional References and Resources

Grieg, Edvard. *Aus Holbergs Zeit: Suite im alten Stil*, Op. 40.
    Ed. Einar Steen-Nøkleberg and Ernst Herttrich. Urtext piano part.
    Munich: G. Henle Verlag, 1989.

Monrad-Johansen, David. *Edvard Grieg.* Translated by Madge Robinson.
    New York: Tudor Publishing, 1938. Reprint, New York: Kraus Reprint
    Co., 1972.

Steen-Nøkleberg, Einar. *Onstage with Grieg: Interpreting His Piano Music.*
    Translated by William H. Halverson. Bloomington, IN: Indiana
    University Press, 1997.

Contributed by:

Bret P. Smith
Lecturer, Music Education (Strings)
University of Maryland
College Park, Maryland

Teacher Resource Guide

Molly on the Shore
Percy Grainger
(1882–1961)

STRING ORCHESTRA

Unit 1: Composer

The son of an architect, Australian pianist and composer Percy Grainger was born in 1882 in Brighton, Victoria, Australia. As a youth, he was considered a precocious young pianist, and revenues from his early performances supported his studies in Germany. Following this training, Grainger began a career as a concert pianist, giving recitals throughout Europe; he settled in London in 1901. While in England, he gained a keen interest in collecting and arranging folk music, with a particular interest in British folk music and its authentic performance. His associations with Delius and Grieg fueled this passion.

With the outbreak of World War I, Grainger came to the United States and enlisted as an army bandsman, becoming a U.S. citizen after the war. However, throughout his life, he claimed his roots in Australia. He later was the head of the Music Department at New York University, and throughout his life was viewed as a bit of an eccentric. He composed and arranged works for a wide variety of instruments and ensembles, and in doing so gained much popularity both in his lifetime and thereafter. He died in White Plains, New York, in 1961.

Unit 2: Composition

Molly on the Shore is an Irish reel that Grainger arranged with elastic scoring for a number of instrumental combinations: piano, violin and piano, and military band, string quartet, and orchestra among them. Grainger wrote (August 6, 1959):

414

In setting *Molly on the Shore* I strove to imbue the accompanying parts that made up the harmonic texture with a melodic character not too unlike that of the underlying reel tune. Melody seems to me to provide music with an initiative, whereas rhythm appears to me to exert an enslaving influence. For that reason I have tried to avoid rhythmic domination in my music—always excepting irregular rhythms, such as those of Gregorian chant, which seem to me to make for freedom. Equally with melody, I prize discordant harmony, because of the emotional and compassionate sway it exerts.

Unit 3: Historical Perspective

Grainger's arrangements and compositions reflect the musical experimentation of his era but in an interestingly personal manner. His interest in nationalism, folk music, and what today would be called "world music" becomes the essence for much of his sonoric creativity. While still a student in Germany, he proposed to study Chinese music in China; this youthful inquisitiveness was a precursor to his later experiments in tone color. While *Molly on the Shore* may be considered musically tame in many respects, Grainger's later compositions featured use of musical glasses, marimba bars played with a cello bow, random discord, and a foray into what he called "free music," in which "reigns complete freedom from scales, complete rhythmic freedom, and complete freedom from what [he called] 'harmonic morality.'" Grainger is noted for his use of English, as opposed to Italian, dynamic and speed descriptors, a practice that now appears to many to be amusingly quaint.

Unit 4: Technical Considerations

Molly on the Shore demands advanced technical skills, both right and left hands, if it is to be played at speed. Shifting requirements are minimal—first violin: sixth position; second violin: extension into fourth position; viola: third position (treble clef); cello: thumb position (treble clef); bass: fifth position. Significant ability to vary articulations is necessary given sudden accents and *sforzandos*. Spiccato bowing is also required. Rhythmic demands are not complex, with very few syncopations; however, accurate counting may prove challenging for students. Triplets and shuffled eighths serve as ornaments and may be difficult to master at speed. Repetition of phrases throughout the piece makes the thematic material quite accessible. All sections function as the "lead" voice at some time during the piece.

Unit 5: Stylistic Considerations

It is fitting that *Molly on the Shore* be performed with an eye and ear toward the Celtic origins of the melody. As music, Irish reels in "the field" are extraordinarily functional, at first meant to inspire and propel dancers. Thus, the rhythmic vitality and structural clarity of *Molly on the Shore* should not be diminished. The tempo is described simply as "Fast (half note = 112–132)." When the dynamic markings are properly observed, the inherent melodic interplay among sections of the ensemble will be audible; care must be taken to underplay the accompanying parts. Grainger uses common articulation markings (i.e., accents and staccato markings); when executed, they will yield a crisp and light feel to the tune. However, by interpreting *Molly on the Shore* with more folk-like articulations and characteristics (i.e., shuffle-bowing patterns, emphasis on the back-beat, slides into the notes), the arrangement may sound even more "Irish." This actually may be more in keeping with Grainger's intention given his interest in musical authenticity.

Unit 6: Musical Elements

Molly on the Shore is written primarily in G major and related key areas. The tune is in five parts, providing all of the melodic content of the piece. The accompaniment is filled with countermelodies (measures 78–85) as well as drones (measures 126–128), ostinatos (measures 26–32) and rhythmic figures (measures 51–61) that emulate folk instruments. Grainger inserts one particularly extended area of chromaticism and discordant harmonies (measures 86–110) that serves to offer interesting variety. This section of the piece briefly implies a G minor tonal area in a legato setting. It is in contrast to what precedes and follows it, and thus serves as the centerpiece to an over-arching ABA form for the work.

Unit 7: Form and Structure

Molly on the Shore is constructed in an over-arching tripartite form. Within that form, as with most fiddle tunes, the piece is constructed in a series of repeated, evenly measured phrases. Grainger chose to transcribe this tune in eighth notes, thereby making the phrases four-measure phrases. The tune could have as easily been written in quarter notes, forming eight-measure phrases, which is currently a more common way to transcribe fiddle reels.

MEASURES	EVENT AND SCORING
1	The piece begins with two measures of *piano* pizzicato arpeggios that serve as introduction to and then ongoing accompaniment for the initial statement of the first section (A) of the theme; presented *pp* in viola
10–17	Viola then repeats the A theme and continues with the second section of the tune (B) and its repeat
18	Cellos take over with the third section of the tune (C) and its repeat, now with a very rhythmic and chordal on/off beat accompaniment in the other instruments

MEASURES	EVENT AND SCORING
26–41	As the piece continuously "loudens" (Grainger's directions in the score), second violin then reiterates A and B, now an octave higher than the initial statement
42–45	The fourth section (D) of the repeated tune is presented by first violin; this part of the tune implies a contrasting A minor tonal area
46–53	First violin continues with a closely related fifth section, E, with all other sections continuing a rhythmic/chordal accompaniment related to that which accompanied C previously
54–61	First violin begins the A tune again and with ever-louder dynamics
62–69	First two sections of the tune then appear again, now in violin, with each section repeated (AA in mm. 54–61, BB in mm. 62–69); this presentation is an octave higher than was heard in the viola statement of the theme at the beginning of the piece in mm. 3–17; this time includes a gradual *crescendo* throughout, with Grainger's directions to "louden bit by bit."
70–77	Cellos present a slight variant of C with hints of chromaticism entering the rhythmic accompaniment
78–93	Violins restate A and then C an octave higher, ending the first large portion of the work
94	The piece then enters a quieter, less-active, contrasting section marked by more dissonant harmonies and chromaticism in the accompanying voices; D and E parts of the tune are played twice each in second violin (D–E–D–E) over gently undulating chromatic movement in first violin and viola, and a drone in the lower strings
126	A legato recapitulation of A in viola marks the beginning of the third, final section of this work
129–130	This line is taken over by first violin, continued into the B theme in higher octaves (mm. 130–141) and louder
142–149	Restated by second violin and viola in octaves A; accompaniments in this section are variants of previous accompaniments to these themes
150–158	Violas continue alone with C with sustained accompaniment, including a conspicuous drone in the lower strings
158–173	This more subdued accompaniment continues with second violin and viola restating D and E

MEASURES	EVENT AND SCORING
174–185	The piece becomes increasingly more *piano*, with slightly varied restatements of A by viola and first violin
190	An abbreviated restatement of B in second violin, with diminuendo chordal accompaniment, is a precursor to a surprise final *ffff* chord in all instruments

Unit 8: Suggested Listening

Country Gardens. Eastman Rochester Pops Orchestra/London Pops Orchestra, Frederick Fennell, conductor. New York: Mercury Living Presence, 1990
Publisher's Number: CD 434 330-2

The Grainger Edition, v. 3. Works for Chorus and Orchestra. City of London Sinfonia, Richard Hickox, conductor. New York: Chandros, 1991
Publisher's Number: CHAN 9499 (Grainger Edition v. 3)

Grainger on the Shore. English Sinfonia, Neville Dilkes, conductor. His Master's Voice p1979
Publisher's Number: ASD 3651 (1 disc. 12 in. 33 1/3 rpm. stereo)

Molly on the Shore. The Greene String Quartet, 1988. Carthage Records, Inc., HNCD 1333

Peer Gynt (includes recording of *Molly on the Shore*). Tokyo Kosei Wind Orchestra; Frederick Fennell, conductor. Tokyo: Kosei, p1990
Publisher's Number: KOCD-3566 (1 sound disc: digital)

Pioneer Gold. Pioneer High School (Ann Arbor, MI) Symphony Orchestra, Marijean Quigley-Young, conductor. Ann Arbor, MI: Brookwood Studios, Inc., 1997

Youthful Rapture: Chamber Music of Percy Grainger. Joel Smirnoff, violin and viola; Joel Moerschel, violoncello; Stephen Drury, piano. Boston, MA: Northeastern Records, 1987
Publisher's Number: NR 228-CD (1 sound disc: digital, stereo)

Unit 9: Additional References and Resources

Balough, Teresa. *A Complete Catalogue of the Works of Percy Grainger*. Nedlands, Western Australia: University of Western Australia, 1975.

Bird, John. *Percy Grainger*. New York: Oxford University Press, 1999.

Dorum, Eileen. *Percy Grainger: The Man Behind the Music*. Hawthorne, Victoria, Australia: IC & EE Dorum, 1986.

Grainger, Percy. *The Farthest North of Humanness: Letters of Percy Grainger 1901–14*. London: Macmillan, 1985.

Lewis Foreman, ed. *The Percy Grainger Companion*. London: Thames, 1981.

Lowe, Rachel. *A Descriptive Catalogue with Checklist of the Letters and Related Documents in the Delius Collection of the Grainger Museum, University of Melbourne, Australia*. London: Delius Trust, 1981.

Tall, David Orme. *Percy Grainger: A Catalogue of the Music*. London: Schott, 1982.

Web site:
http://www.bardic-music.com/grainger.htm

The Percy Grainger Society was founded in June 1978 in London. It has nearly five hundred members worldwide. Membership is open to all by payment of an annual subscription. For this, members receive two journals a year and the newsletter *Random Round*, which keeps them informed of international activities in performance and scholarship.

Contributed by:

Andrew H. Dabczynski
Professor of Music Education
Brigham Young University
Provo, Utah

Teacher Resource Guide

Rhosymedre ("Prelude on a Welsh Hymn Tune")

Ralph Vaughan Williams
(1872–1958)

arranged by Arnold Foster

STRING ORCHESTRA AND FULL ORCHESTRA

Unit 1: Composer

Ralph Vaughan Williams was born in 1872 at Down Ampney, Gloucestershire, England. He received a Doctor in Music from Trinity College, Cambridge, and studied with German composer Max Bruch and French composer Maurice Ravel. Vaughan Williams was highly active in preserving English folk songs and editing the English Hymnal. A majority of Vaughan Williams's compositions were based on English folk tunes and hymns, making him a nationalist composer. *Rhosymedre* is just one example of his many nationalist compositions. Others include *Fantasia on a Theme by Thomas Tallis* and *Fantasia on Greensleeves*. Vaughan Williams died in 1958 at the age of eighty-five.

Unit 2: Composition

Rhosymedre was first written for organ by Vaughan Williams and then orchestrated later by Arnold Foster. J. D. Edwards (1805–85) wrote the hymn tune. It still appears in hymnals, often under the title of "My Song Is Love Unknown." Vaughan Williams weaves beautiful polyphonic countermelodies around the theme, with every string part having a beautiful and interesting line. This piece, approximately four minutes long, serves as an introduction to the turn of the century English music of Vaughan Williams, Holst, Delius,

420

Grainger, and Elgar. The piece may be played with strings only or with the addition of the following winds: two flutes, one oboe, two clarinets, two bassoons, two horns, and one trumpet.

Unit 3: Historical Perspective

A unique Welsh musical and religious tradition is to gather people together, often on hilltops, and sing hymns. While singing, people improvise harmonies around the melodies of the hymns. This Welsh tradition is known as Gymanfa Ganu and is still practiced today. In this piece, Vaughan Williams represents this tradition by sustaining the hymn tune in one instrumental part while countermelodies sound simultaneously in other parts. This composition technique gives the impression of improvisatory lines around the hymn tune. This peaceful work was written in 1940–41, a time when England was undergoing the trials of war.

Unit 4: Technical Considerations

Rhosymedre is in G major and does not modulate. The main technical challenge is reading and playing rhythms in 4/2 time. This challenge is augmented by independent polyphonic lines, which requires all players to be very independent in their rhythmic skills. The piece will demand time spent on all the rhythmic combinations of 4/2 time. Each part has rhythmic challenges and yet must fit into all the other parts interlacing around it. Because the viola part has the hymn tune when first stated, a strong viola section is needed. Also, all parts except the double bass have some *divisi* parts. Only the top violin and cello parts must shift occasionally into upper positions. The conductor might consider reversing the bowings indicated in both violin parts. By starting down-bow instead of up-bow, the phrasing of the lines is made easier.

Unit 5: Stylistic Considerations

The entire piece is in a legato style with smooth, connecting bow strokes. There are many times in the violin parts where small, light pauses are inherent in the phrase. An example would be after the first quarter note in measures 2–5 in the first violin part. Because the hymn tune is first stated in viola, the dynamics need to be restrained in the other parts while the violas play with a rich, resonant tone. When the theme is restated in first violin, all dynamics can be raised to a beautiful *forte*. A major challenge to the musicians is to make each independent line have an ebb and flow of its own as well as supporting the line of the hymn tune.

Unit 6: Musical Elements

Using an improvisatory style, Vaughan Williams surrounds the hymn tune with a rhythmically complex set of parts. These parts have moving melodic lines of their own yet still support the melody. This polyphonic texture is at the heart of the music. The melody and harmony are quite simple, allowing the rhythm to flow easily. Because the countermelody is presented first and then the hymn tune is hidden in the viola part, it is easy for the listener to think the countermelody is in the main theme. Much attention is needed to balance the orchestra so the hymn tune is clearly heard. The conductor may choose to introduce the piece by teaching the hymn tune by rote with no music. Each individual student may then simultaneously improvise harmony parts to the theme. After handing out the setting of the hymn tune from a hymnal, have the students read it in homophonic style, with the violas reading treble clef. Finally, hand out the music and have the students discover the hymn tune and how Vaughan Williams developed the harmony parts.

Unit 7: Form and Structure

SECTION	MEASURES	EVENT AND SCORING
Introduction	1–8	Introduces countermelody in first violin before main theme is played
Theme I	8–24	Letter A; the main theme is the hymn tune, which is played by viola; first violin continues with the main countermelody
Theme I	25–40	Letter C; the main theme is now played in octaves by first violin; all other string parts have moving, weaving lines around the theme
Extension	41–45	A five-measure extension that starts at the end of the repetition of the theme and connects the end of the theme to the coda
Coda	46–end	Letter D; the coda is exactly the same as the introduction; the main theme is not played, and the focus returns to the main countermelody

Unit 8: Suggested Listening
Aaron Copland, "Variations on a Shaker Melody" from *Appalachian Spring*
Percy Grainger:
   Irish Tune from County Derry
   Molly on the Shore
Gustav Holst:
   First Suite in E-flat Major
   St. Paul's Suite

Vachav Nelhybel, *A Mighty Fortress*
Ralph Vaughan Williams:
   English Folk Song Suite
   Fantasia on a Theme by Thomas Tallis
   Fantasia on Greensleeves
   Three Preludes on Welsh Hymn Tunes for Organ
   Two Organ Preludes

Unit 9: Additional References and Resources

Dickinson, A. E. F. *An Introduction to the Music of Ralph Vaughan Williams*. Oxford: Oxford University Press, 1928.

Kennedy, Michael. *The Works of Ralph Vaughan Williams*. 2d edition. Oxford: Oxford University Press, 1980.

Vaughan Williams, Ralph. *National Music and other Essays*. "A Musical Autobiography," Oxford: Oxford University Press, 2d edition, 1987.

Vaughan Williams, Ursula. *Ralph Vaughan Williams: A Biography*. Oxford: Oxford University Press, 1964.

Web sites:
   http://www.cs.qub.ac.uk/~J.Collis/RVW.html
   http://w3.rz-berlin.mpg.de/cmp/classmus.html

Contributed by:

Gary Wolfman
Director of Orchestras
Appleton North and West High Schools
Appleton, Wisconsin

Teacher Resource Guide

Rounds

David Diamond
(b. 1915)

STRING ORCHESTRA

Unit 1: Composer

David Lee Diamond was born in Rochester, New York, in 1915. He studied composition with American composer Roger Sessions in New York City. He also studied with Nadia Boulanger in Paris, where the music of Ravel and Stravinsky influenced him. Diamond has taught at the Juilliard School from 1973 to the present. He requires students to be firmly grounded in traditional compositional techniques. He has written eight symphonies, chamber music, and music for ballet, theater, and film.

Unit 2: Composition

Rounds for string orchestra was composed in 1944 and dedicated to Dimitri Mitropoulos. The composition uses diatonic and modal harmonies. The three movements to be played without pauses are "Allegro molto vivace," "Adagio," and "Allegro Vigoroso." Performance time is twelve minutes.

Unit 3: Historical Perspective

Dimitri Mitropoulos asked Diamond to write a happy composition. "These are distressing times, most of the music I play is distressing. Make me happy." *Rounds* was a refreshing contrast to the new music from the twelve-tone school, which dominated the contemporary music scene. *Rounds* is one of Diamond's most-performed works and resounds with joy and laughter. The original themes are folk-like and distinctly American.

Unit 4: Technical Considerations

Rounds is technically challenging for all sections of the string orchestra. The players must execute scales and arpeggios in the major keys of G, D, A, E, F, B-flat, E-flat, and A-flat, and the minor keys of A, D, and F. Tempos in the first and third movements require agility, with quarter note = 132. All styles of bowing are required, from legato to détaché, martelé, spiccato, and sautillé. Ranges cover the entire instrument and go into the upper registers for first and second violin and double bass. Grace notes, pizzicato, snapped pizzicato, natural and artificial harmonics, double-stops, and glissandos are techniques required in the performance of *Rounds*.

Unit 5: Stylistic Considerations

The first movement is to be performed with intensity and energy. Fiddle-like ostinatos, accents, syncopation, and contrasting legato lines are written with dynamics ranging from *p* to *fff*. The second movement begins with five solo violins setting the mood of the movement in polytonal chords. It is a slow, legato movement with hints of impressionism in its melody and harmony. A quartet of soloists appears briefly in the middle of the movement. Dynamic contrasts are dramatic. The third movement is similar in style to the first. The style is a bit more aggressive than the first movement with snapping pizzicatos, prominent *glissandi,* and rowdy double-stops in the low strings.

Unit 6: Musical Elements

Melody in the first and third movements consists of short figures and motives that are cleverly interwoven through contrapuntal compositional techniques. Melody in the second movement is rich with a perfect balance of scalewise and intervalic movement. Harmonies are diatonic, model, and polytonal, and bitonality is prevalent in the first and third movements. Harmonies in the second movement are polytonal in the introduction. The melodic sections of the movement feature fourths and fifths of the linear and vertical lines, creating an impressionistic effect. The time signature in the first movement is 2/4, with some instances of triple meter. In the second movement, the quarter note is the beat, with the introduction in four and the melodic sections in three. The final movement is mainly in 4/4 with some meter changes to 3/4 and 5/4.

Unit 7: Form and Structure

SECTION	MEASURES	EVENT AND SCORING
Movement 1: "Allegro molto vivace"		
Form: through-composed		
A		Ostinato theme
B	10	Syncopated theme

SECTION	MEASURES	EVENT AND SCORING
C	19	Staccato figure

The three ideas are combined and interwoven throughout the movement using contrapuntal compositional techniques.

Movement 2: "Adagio"
Form: ABA

Introduction		Chordal; polytonal
Theme A	1	D-flat
Theme B	15	B-flat/E-flat
Theme A	35	D-flat
Chordal ending	48	Polytonal

Movement 3: "Allegro Vigoroso"
Form: through-composed

A	1	Syncopated theme
B	19	Ostinato theme
C	30	Heavily accented figure

These three themes are quite similar to those of the first movement and treated in a similar fashion.

D	84	Legato theme

Unit 8: Suggested Listening
David Diamond:
> *Romeo and Juliet*
> *Rounds*
> Symphony No. 2
> *The Tempest*
> *Timon of Athens*
> *The World of Paul Klee*

Unit 9: Additional References and Resources
Austin, William W. *Music in the 20th Century*. New York: W. W. Norton & Company, 1966.

Benjamin, Thomas, Michael Horvit, and Robert Nelson. *Techniques and Materials of Tonal Music with an Introduction to Twentieth Century Techniques*. Boston: Houghton Mifflin, 1986.

Goetschius, Percy. *Lessons in Music Form*. Bryn Mawr, PA: Oliver Ditson, 1982.

Web sites:
www.americancomposers.org
www.etext.org/Zines/ASCII/CosmikDebris/february97.txt

Contributed by:

Ida Steadman
Orchestra Conductor
Morehead Middle School/Coronado High School
El Paso, Texas

Teacher Resource Guide

Simple Symphony
Benjamin Britten
(1913–1976)

STRING ORCHESTRA

Unit 1: Composer

Benjamin Britten was born in Lowestoft, England, in 1913, into a moderately prosperous family. His father was an orthodontist, and his mother was an amateur singer. He began his composition studies at age thirteen with English composer Frank Bridge. In 1930, he entered the Royal College of Music in London, where he studied composition with John Ireland. He wrote his first composition in 1934, titled *Sinfonietta*. Britten founded the Aldeburgh Opera Festival in 1948.

Although he is known primarily for his operatic works, Britten also wrote symphonies, chamber music, concertos, and music for the theater and cinema. He received several awards for his compositions; among these were the Companion of Honour in 1952, the Aspen Award in 1964, and the Order of Merit in 1965. Queen Elizabeth also made him a life peer of Great Britain in 1976. Britten died in Aldeburgh, England, in 1976.

Unit 2: Composition

Simple Symphony was written in 1934, a year after Britten graduated from the Royal College of Music. He based the composition on material from works he wrote between the ages of nine and twelve: "Boisterous Bourrée" comes from Suite No. 1 for piano written in 1926; "Playful Pizzicato" comes from the Scherzo for Piano written in 1924; "Sentimental Saraband" comes from Suite No. 3 for piano written in 1925; and "Frolicsome Finale" comes from Piano Sonata No. 9 written in 1926. It is set in the style of a baroque dance suite and makes use of binary and ternary forms.

Unit 3: Historical Perspective

Britten was the outstanding figure among the generation of English composers prior to the outbreak of World War II in 1939. His opera *Peter Grimes*, premiered in 1945, laid the foundation for the revival of English opera in the 1950s and 60s. He also played an important role in the creation of a body of modern English songs and music for amateurs and children. He was considered to be the most important English composer since Henry Purcell. His symphonies are set in a chamber music format and make use of baroque compositional forms and mild diatonic dissonance. *Simple Symphony* contains many of the elements that are found in his later instrumental works such as tarantella-like themes and the resonant sound of double- and triple-stopped open string chords.

Unit 4: Technical Considerations

The scales of D minor and G minor, and the major scales of C, G, D, F, and B-flat, are required for the entire ensemble. There are also numerous chromatic passages that require a facile left-hand technique. The challenge of precise ensemble pizzicatos is presented in Movement 2. In addition, Movement 3 presents a bow control problem because of the lento tempo and tied notes. Shifts to third position are found in all the parts, as well as one shift to fifth position at the end of Movement 4. Because of the numerous left-hand technical demands at fast tempos, this piece is best suited for an advanced high school string orchestra.

Unit 5: Stylistic Considerations

Movement 1 should be performed in a rollicking manner similar to a lively baroque dance. Stylistic contrasts should be made between the accented, marcato passages in the A sections and the lyrical, cantabile melody in the B sections. Careful attention should be paid to the dynamic contrasts in Movement 2 to highlight its playful character. Movement 3 should stand apart from the other movements and be performed in an expressive style that contrasts the serious mood of the A sections with the lighter mood of the B sections. The last movement should drive relentlessly forward to convey its frolicsome character.

Unit 6: Musical Elements

Although chromatic alterations occur in all four movements, the harmony is essentially tonal with well-defined key centers. The fast–fast–slow–fast movement pattern is similar to that of a modified baroque dance suite. The third movement, in particular, is reminiscent of Bach's Orchestral Suite in D with its lyrical slow movement. The thematic imitation in the A section of the first movement is similar to that found in seventeenth century ricercare.

Unit 7: Form and Structure

This work contains four movements set in the style of a baroque dance suite.

SECTION	MEASURES	EVENT AND SCORING

Movement 1: "Boisterous Bourrée" (*alla breve*, Allegro)
Form: binary

A	1–33	Moves between D minor and D major; two themes set in imitative fashion
B	33–68	F major, D major, F major; new lyrical melody set against chordal pedal point
A	69–125	D minor to D major
B	126–155	Key change to D major
Coda	156–171	Keys of D minor to D major; A theme; ends with D major chords

Movement 2: "Playful Pizzicato" (Presto, 6/8, tarantella rhythm)
Form: ternary

A	1–61	F major; eighth note theme moves from voice to voice
B	62–99	Trio; C major; new melody accompanied by strummed chords
A	1–60	F major; jump to m.100
Coda	100–120	F major; B melody plus strummed chords; *diminuendo* followed by final loud pizzicato chord

Movement 3: "Sentimental Saraband" (Lento, 3/2)
Form: binary

A	1–57	G minor; melody in first violin; chordal accompaniment pesante style
B	58–90	B-flat major; "tranquillo"; lyrical melody in viola and cello
A	91–125	G minor; "più agitato"
B	126–150	B-flat major; "tranquillo"; m. 135 louré-style connected chords

Movement 4: "Frolicsome Finale" (*alla breve*, "Prestissimo")
Form: binary

A	1–47	G minor; staccato theme set in imitative fashion in different voices
B	48–96	F major; cantabile theme
A	97–160	Several keys: A minor, C major, D major; staccato theme

SECTION	MEASURES	EVENT AND SCORING
B	161–190	D major; cantabile theme
Coda	191–214	Presto; D major; A theme; all voices together on D at end

Unit 8: Suggested Listening

Benjamin Britten:
    "Four Sea Interludes" from *Peter Grimes*
    Mont Juic
    Prelude and Fugue
    Simple Symphony
    Sinfonia da requiem
    Sinfonietta
    Soirées musicales
    Suite on English Folk Tunes
    Variations on a Theme of Frank Bridge
    The Young Person's Guide to the Orchestra

Unit 9: Additional References and Resources

Cooke, Mervyn. *The Cambridge Companion to Benjamin Britten*. Cambridge: Cambridge University Press, 1999.

Evans, Peter. *The Music of Benjamin Britten*. Minneapolis: University of Minnesota Press, 1979.

Palmer, Christopher, ed. *The Britten Companion*. Cambridge: Cambridge University Press, 1984.

Contributed by:

Camille Smith
Associate Professor of Music
University of Florida–Gainesville
Gainesville, Florida

Teacher Resource Guide

Sospiri, Op. 70

Edward Elgar
(1857–1934)

STRING ORCHESTRA

Unit 1: Composer

Sir Edward Elgar's story is one of immense acclaim and intense personal struggle. Born in Broadheath, England, in 1857, Elgar was the son of a piano tuner and music shop owner. Except for a few violin lessons, he was essentially self-taught, absorbing much of his musical education in the shop, in cathedral services, and at music societies. From the age of sixteen onward, he worked as a freelance violinist, organist, bassoonist, conductor, and teacher, never holding a regular, secure post. As a composer, he drew his language from English culture and landscape, and his craft from studying other composers, successfully combining nobility and spirituality with a popular style. By any measure, Elgar ranks high among romantic composers and at the peak of British music of his time. His contribution to the string and orchestral repertoire was immeasurable and lasting. Elgar received the Order of Merit in 1911; he died near his birthplace in 1934.

Unit 2: Composition

Throughout his career, Elgar was interested in the possibility of mechanically recording sound; the composition of *Sospiri* in 1914 was, indirectly at least, a result of that interest in technology. In 1913, orchestral recording was still quite a crude process: the acoustic horn could capture only sounds made close to it, so the prospect of recording orchestral music seemed completely impractical. As an alternative, Elgar was contracted to write two short and light pieces, and "two thirds of net royalties received in respect of mechanical instrument reproduction [were] to be paid to the Composer." This was significant both for recording rights and marketing because the idea was to record the new pieces before their publication so as to have records in the shops when the music appeared. The first piece was written and almost immediately recorded, but sketches for the second expressed a depth of feeling unsuited for the required "light" quality of the project. Written initially as a violin solo, Elgar subsequently set the work for strings, harp, and harmonium and arranged for its separate publication by Breitkopf & Härtel with the title *Sospiri*. The contract was fulfilled several months later.

Unit 3: Historical Perspective

Sospiri is the Italian word for "sighs." Though premiered shortly after the outbreak of World War I, it is unlikely that *Sospiri* is an emotional response to the prospect of war. It may have expressed Elgar's personal sorrow for the death of a friend, but to at least one Elgar biographer "the brooding tragedy of the music, its Mahlerian intensity, suggests that these 'sighs' are for something known only to Elgar. It is…a major work of grave beauty, an epitome of Elgar's ability to express nostalgic regret" (Kennedy, 1982).

In terms of Elgar's other best-known string and orchestral output, this work follows *Serenade for Strings* (1892), *"Enigma" Variations* (Op. 36, 1898–99), four of the five *Pomp and Circumstance* marches (1901, D major and A minor; 1904, C minor; 1907, G major), the *Introduction and Allegro* for string quartet and string orchestra (1901), the *Elegy* for Strings (1909), and the Violin Concerto (1909–10). Compositionally and expressively, *Sospiri* looks ahead to the Cello Concerto of 1919.

Unit 4: Technical Considerations

Bow distribution and sostenuto control are important in all parts. Violin 1 requires fifth position, portato shifts, and a wide range of dynamic control. The upper part of the divided second violin requires fifth position for only two and one-half measures, as well as chromatic alterations and tremolo control; the lower part is playable in first position except for a two and one-half measure *divisi* section that puts the top part in third position. Both parts of the divided viola part are playable in first position and have chromatic alterations, augmented seconds, and tremolo; both are melodically interesting. About half of the upper cello part is written in tenor clef and requires thumb position; chromaticism also presents a challenge. The lower part is relatively easy, with only one and one-half measures in tenor clef. Chromaticism and octaves present intonation challenges, and both cello parts have a reasonable amount of melodic interest. The bass part is playable in first position with only two exceptions and has limited melodic interest.

The harp part is not particularly difficult and would be quite playable for a high school intermediate level harpist. It primarily involves two-hand rolled chords, which only occasionally reach beyond an octave span for either hand.

There are few pedal changes, and the part could be adapted for lever harp with only slight modifications. As the score indicates, piano may be substituted for harp—and *should* be used, if necessary. Only the harmonium (a bellows, or pump organ) or organ part is *ad libitum*.

Unit 5: Stylistic Considerations

Sospiri is a thoroughly romantic work in which Elgar uses a recitative style. Rubato is extremely important, and care must be taken to balance the voices to preserve the basically homophonic texture. At its most elemental, this piece is about breathing: it challenges string players to approach phrasing and ensemble vocally.

Unit 6: Musical Elements

Theme 1 is essentially diatonic, with extensive use of syncopation in the melodic line. All voices except Violin 1 are muted. Theme 2 is built on a broken octave motive, adding more melodic movement in all voices and more extensive chromaticism. Mutes are off until just before the return to the first theme. This return is marked *"sonoramente"* and features extensive tremolo and *fp* dynamic contrasts. The concluding statement of Theme 2 is in the context of a *ritard al fine*, diminishing to *pppp*.

Unit 7: Form and Structure

SECTION	MEASURES	EVENT AND SCORING
Introduction	2 mm.	Establishes D minor
Theme 1	8 mm.	Rehearsal 1; melody in Violin 1
Theme 2	4 mm.	Rehearsal 2; F major
	5 mm.	Rehearsal 3; B-flat major
Theme 1	8 mm.	Rehearsal 4; D minor
Theme 2	7 mm.	Rehearsal 5; F major

Unit 8: Suggested Listening

Edward Elgar:
    Cello Concerto, Op. 85 (also arranged for viola by Lionel Tertis)
    Elegy for Strings, Op. 58
    Enigma Variations, Op. 36
    Introduction and Allegro, Op. 47
    Pomp and Circumstance
    Serenade for Strings, Op. 20
    Violin Concerto, Op. 61

Unit 9: Additional References and Resources

Anderson, Robert. *The Master Musicians: Elgar.* New York: Schirmer Books, 1993.

Hurd, Michael. *The Great Composers: Elgar.* London: Faber & Faber, 1969.

Kennedy, Michael. *Portrait of Elgar.* London: Oxford University Press, 1982.

Longyear, Rey M. *Nineteenth-Century Romanticism in Music.* Englewood Cliffs, NJ: Prentice Hall, 1973.

Monk, Raymond, ed. *Elgar Studies.* Aldershot, England: Scolar Press, Gower Publishing, 1990.

Sadie, Stanley, ed. *The New Grove Dictionary of Music and Musicians.* New York: Grove's Dictionaries, 2000. Also available online at www.grovemusic.com

Contributed by:

Janet L. Jensen
Associate Professor of String Pedagogy
University of Wisconsin–Madison
Madison, Wisconsin

Teacher Resource Guide

St. Paul's Suite

Gustav Holst
(1874–1934)

String Orchestra

Unit 1: Composer

Gustavus Theodore von Holst was born in Cheltenham, Gloucestershire, England, to a musical family in 1874. He shortened his first name and dropped the "von" at an early age. His father was a composer and, when piano did not seem feasible because of neuritis in his hands, Gustav took up composition. His first teacher described him as "hardworking, not brilliant." In his studies at the Royal Academy in London, he began by imitating Wagner and later, upon befriending Vaughan Williams, became interested in folk tunes. Ravel and Stravinsky influenced him to consider more freedom in his composing. He started teaching at the St. Paul School in 1905 and wrote *St. Paul's Suite* for the students in 1912–13. Other famous works include *The Planets* (1918) and First Suite in E-flat for band (1909). He died in London in 1934.

Unit 2: Composition

St. Paul's Suite is a good example of the use of folk tunes and modal melodies in Holst's music. It is also characterized by a lack of fundamental harmonies, but ostinatos and rhythm are used to create larger forms. The first movement is a jig marked "Vivace." Dances such as jigs have no set form, so Holst is allowed freedom in his writing while maintaining the spirit of a jig. The second movement, "Ostinato," contains a relentless pattern in second violin at a "Presto" tempo, given only temporarily to first violin and changing meter once. The third movement, "Intermezzo," is a study in contrast with a somber, slow section contrasting to a spirited Vivace section tending toward major with both sections then repeated. The finale is a lilting tune called

436

"Dargason," which means dwarf (information found in Playford's book), but is an eight-measure circular tune with no conclusion. At allegro tempo, the most notable aspect is a pairing of the "Dargason" with "Greensleeves," which occurs twice in the work. Throughout the movement the "Dargason" is a continuous, circular tune. The work takes approximately nine minutes to play.

Unit 3: Historical Perspective
St. Paul's Suite was composed in a period that is described as the Renaissance of English music. Composers such as Vaughan Williams and Gordon Jacob looked to earlier musical forms and folk tunes to distinguish their writing. Holst wrote this for the students in the school and took into account their technical abilities. Another influence on Holst at the time was the study of Hindu literature. Another piece for the "Sanskrit period" of 1908–12 is the opera *Savitri*. *The Planets* followed in 1918.

Unit 4: Technical Considerations
This is a lengthy work that is lyrical and, in some sections, difficult to play. One difficulty comes in the first movement, nineteen measures after Rehearsal 8. This passage is a decorated C-sharp Mixolydian scale in two octaves with a difficult shift in tonality at the top from E-sharp to F-natural in fifth position; the ear wants a resolution to F-sharp. The only difficulty in the second movement is concentration and stamina for the ostinato. In the third movement, the challenge is catching the abrupt tempo changes. The finale swings along but requires clear conducting to keep the two melodies together at Rehearsal 3 and 9. Cellos have tenor clef in one section of the "Greensleeves" tune. The coda is difficult to coordinate the solo violin and bass.

Unit 5: Stylistic Considerations
The movements are dance-like, with lilting or legato styles required. Dynamic contrasts are also very important to help delineate the form. The third movement alternates between legato and marcato. A lyrical style and strong tone are helpful throughout. The full sound of this work is a result of the many double-stops and chords in the parts.

Unit 6: Musical Element
The piece is modal, which places restrictions on melody and harmony. Functional harmony with leading tones and full cadences is not used. Patterns and ostinatos define the direction and structure. Meters shift between sections and tonal centers shift, both abruptly. In the first movement, the main theme returns in the same tonality, but several other modes are used with abrupt shifts rather than modulations. Another compositional technique used in this movement is augmentation of the theme. The second movement is in C major, but circles around without cadences. There is a stepwise second theme

that ends with the F scale returning to the first theme in C. The third move-ment opens in E Dorian mode, shifts to D harmonic minor, and leads into A major in the contrasting Vivace section. The second time this happens, the vivace shift goes into F major. The piece ends with the modal, slow material based on E, but the final note of bass and cello is a pizzicato A, leading one to believe that A is the tonal center. The final movement is consistently in C major except for a chromatic buildup leading to the final double statement of the "Dargason" and "Greensleeves."

Unit 7: Form and Structure

SECTION	MEASURES	EVENT AND SCORING
Movement 1: "Jig" (Vivace)		
A	1–Rehearsal 3	Includes three statements of the theme in original key and extensive cadential material
B	Rehearsal 3–Rehearsal 5	Two simple statements of second theme
Development	Rehearsal 5–Rehearsal 7	Development material of B augmented and A themes
A	Rehearsal 7–Rehearsal 9	*ff* multi-stopped chords with statement in original key and unusual C-sharp Mixolydian buildup to ending material
Coda	Rehearsal 9–end	Includes brief statement of B theme
Movement 2: "Ostinato"		
A	1–Rehearsal 1	Lyrical first theme first outlined in pizzicato, then slurred in violin
B	Rehearsal 1–Rehearsal 4	Scale-type theme
A	Rehearsal 4–Rehearsal 5	Brief return to A theme
Coda	Rehearsal 5–end	
Movement 3: "Intermezzo"		
A	1–Rehearsal 2	Slow E Dorian theme in solo violin
B	Rehearsal 2–Tempo I after Rehearsal 3	Lively A major theme
A	Tempo I after Rehearsal 3–Rehearsal 5	Beginning with *ff tutti* and then restated in solo violin and viola

SECTION	MEASURES	EVENT AND SCORING
B	Rehearsal 5 to Tempo I after Rehearsal 6	
Coda		Final adagio; solo string quartet using first theme

Movement 4: "Finale" (Variation on the "Dargason")

A	1–Rehearsal 3	Theme in violin only with a thin orchestral texture
A1	Rehearsal 3– Rehearsal 4	Coupled softly with "Greensleeves"
A2	Rehearsal 4– Rehearsal 9	Variations marked by tremendous growth of dynamic and thick texture
A3	Rehearsal 9– Rehearsal 10	Coupled loudly with "Greensleeves"
A4, Coda	Rehearsal 10– end	Fading away to solo violin and bass in contrary motion scale line to *tutti* C major final chord

Unit 8: Suggested Listening

Gustav Holst:
  Brook Green Suite
  First Suite in E-flat
Ralph Vaughan Williams, *English Folk Song Suite*

Unit 9: Additional References and Resources

Holst, Imogen. *Holst: A Biography.* London: Oxford University Press, 1969.

Holst, Imogen, *Music of Gustav Holst.* London: Oxford University Press, 1968.

Playford, John. *English Dancing Master.* A facsimile reprint from 1651. London: Schott, 1957.

Sadie, Stanley, ed. *The New Grove Dictionary of Music and Musicians.* New York: Grove's Dictionaries, 2000. Also available online at www.grovemusic.com

Short, Michael. *Holst—Man and His Music.* London: Oxford University Press, 1990.

Contributed by:

Joanne Erwin
Associate Professor, Director of Music Education
Oberlin College
Oberlin, Ohio

Teacher Resource Guide

Symphony No. 8 in B Minor ("Unfinished")

Franz Peter Schubert
(1797–1828)

FULL ORCHESTRA

Unit 1: Composer

Franz Peter Schubert was born on January 31, 1797, in a suburb of Vienna, Austria. He began studying the piano with his older brother, Ignaz, while his father gave him his first lessons on the violin. In 1808, he was accepted as a choirboy in the imperial court chapel. This led to studies in music theory and composition with the Court Kapellmeister, Antonio Salieri, beginning in 1812. As Schubert progressed on the violin, he eventually assisted in conducting the student orchestra. Schubert is well known for his orchestral, piano, and chamber music works, as well as more than six hundred songs. Schubert died on November 19, 1828, of "nervous fever" probably associated with syphilis that he contracted in late 1822, the same time he was working on Symphony No. 8.

Unit 2: Composition

Schubert may have composed Symphony No. 8, dated October 30, 1822, as an offering to the Styrian Musical Society of Graz, which was considering presenting Schubert with an honorary membership. Schubert gave this symphony to his friend, Anselm Hüttenbrenner. Hüttenbrenner kept the work in his care until 1865 when he was persuaded to release the score for performance. The first performance of the work took place on December 17, 1865, more than forty-three years after it was composed. The "Unfinished" Symphony is so named because Schubert completed only two movements rather than the usual four. Sketches for the first nine measures of the third movement were also found, and attempts have been made by various composers to finish the symphony in the style of Schubert. The two movements include the "Allegro moderato in B minor" and the "Andante con moto in E major." Evident in both movements is Schubert's great gift of melody and his seamless transitions from one theme to the next.

Unit 3: Historical Perspective

Schubert composed Symphony No. 8 at the end of 1822. During this time, composers such as Beethoven were stretching the boundaries of the classical style of composition toward the larger, freer romantic style. If we consider Beethoven as the composer who bridges the classical and romantic periods of music, then we must recognize Schubert as the first major composer of the romantic era. His songs demonstrate the unique ability to depict the meaning of the text in the musical accompaniment. Works for chamber ensembles, including string quartets, are sometimes based on existing songs, thus demonstrating Schubert's ability to use his melodic material in diverse forms. The symphonies are excellent examples of Schubert's sensitivity to orchestration as yet another means of achieving musical effect.

Unit 4: Technical Considerations

The first movement is predominantly in B minor; therefore, students must be able to read accidentals, including E-sharp and A-sharp. First violins must play up to B6; second violins have short sections in third position; cellos have a short section at measure 291 in tenor clef, but the highest note is only G-sharp4 (above middle C). Woodwind parts are well within normal ranges, but the score calls for clarinets in A, horns in D (also in E for the second movement), trumpets in E, and first and second trombone parts in alto clef. Other technical considerations in the first movement include tuning and balance of the woodwind parts, articulations and bowings, several passages of sixteenth notes in upper strings, and a section at measure 202 for all strings that includes fast grace notes of D major and E major scales. Syncopation occurs when a section is used as accompaniment; otherwise, the first movement is relatively straightforward.

The second movement is in 3/8 time and in the key of E major, which presents greater problems in negotiating additional sharps and accidentals as well as more difficult syncopations. Dominant seventh chord arpeggios should be practiced in preparation for this movement. Scale drills in C-sharp minor and E minor would also prepare the thirty-second note sections at measures 103–111 and 244–252.

Unit 5: Stylistic Considerations

Symphony No. 8 still possesses many of the characteristics of the classical era. Attention to bowing style, using slightly detached articulations in détaché sections, and playing within a controlled range of dynamics is appropriate to this work. At the same time, the dynamics can be expanded from those of a Mozart symphony, which allows greater latitude in interpretation. Effective performances of Schubert works always focus the listener to the attractive melodic material inherent in the composition. Rubato should not be overused for early romantic pieces. Rhythmic control and precision is necessary in all parts, melodic and accompaniment.

Unit 6: Musical Elements

The first movement opens with a short theme in the low strings followed by a sixteenth note accompaniment figure in the upper strings. The first main theme is heard in oboe and clarinet, and creates a type of polyphonic texture to open the movement. The genius of Schubert lies in his ability to make even the accompaniment parts very tuneful and melodic. The movement follows the standard sonata-allegro form of exposition–development–recapitulation.

The second movement is a theme and variations form that has a lot in common with the second movement of Beethoven's Symphony No. 5. Both are in triple meter and variations have similarities in instrumentation and rhythmic alterations.

Unit 7: Form and Structure

SECTION	MEASURES	EVENT AND SCORING

The first movement follows a standard sonata-allegro form.

Introduction	1	
Exposition		
Theme 1	13	Theme in oboe and clarinet
Theme 2	44	Theme in cello
Theme 3	73	Short theme between violin and viola/cello
Development	110	
Recapitulation	218	

The second movement is a form of theme and variations with three themes, two of which are subject to short sections that are varied in mode, orchestration, or texture.

Theme 1	1	Theme introduced in horn and completed in violin
Theme 1, variation 1	18	Theme in E minor, then G major; completed in E major
Theme 1, variation 2	33	Theme in winds altered rhythmically; texture change
Theme 2	66	Theme in clarinet in C-sharp minor

Section	Measures	Event and Scoring
Theme 2, variation 1	84	Theme in oboe in D-flat major
Theme 2, variation 2	96	Rhythmically altered; *fortissimo* dynamic
Theme 2, variation 3	103	Rhythm from variation 2 present; accompaniment changed
Theme 3	112	Alternating between low strings and upper strings
Theme 1	142	
Theme 1, variation 1	159	
Theme 1, variation 2	173	
Theme 2	207	Theme in oboe in A minor
Theme 2, variation 1	225	Theme in clarinet in A major
Theme 2, variation 2	236	Theme in low strings
Theme 2, variation 3	244	
Coda	268	Based on Theme 1

Unit 8: Suggested Listening
Ludwig van Beethoven, Symphony No. 5 in C Minor, Movement 2
Franz Schubert:
> Symphony No. 8 in B Minor ("Unfinished")
> Symphony No. 9 in C Major
> Various Lieder (songs)

Unit 9: Additional References and Resources
Chusid, Martin, ed. *Symphony in B Minor* ("Unfinished"). New York: W. W. Norton & Company, 1971.

McKay, Elizabeth Norman. *Franz Schubert: A Biography*. New York: Clarendon Press, 1996.

Contributed by:
Phil Peters
Orchestra Director
Valley High School
West Des Moines, Iowa

Teacher Resource Guide

"Variations on a Shaker Melody" from Appalachian Spring

Aaron Copland
(1900–1990)

FULL ORCHESTRA

Unit 1: Composer

Aaron Copland was born and educated in Brooklyn, New York. There he studied piano and composition privately as a young student. After graduating from Boy's High School in 1918, he studied composition in Paris with Nadia Boulanger and Paul Vidal from 1920 to 1924. He studied further in Europe during visits in 1926, 1927, and 1929, and organized with Roger Sessions the Copland-Sessions Concerts from 1928 to 1931. He taught a modern music course for the New School for Social Research in New York from 1927 to 1937. He founded the American Composer's Alliance in 1937, and served as head of the composition department from 1940 to 1965.

During Copland's career, he was a recipient of a Guggenheim Fellowship (1925–27), the Pulitzer Prize and New York Music Critic's Circle Award for *Appalachian Spring* in 1945, the RCA Victor Award for *Dance Symphony*, the New York Critics Circle Award for Symphony No. 3 in 1947, an Academy Award for *The Heiress* in 1950, and the Presidential Medal of Freedom in 1964. Copland was awarded numerous honorary doctorates and international awards for his musical contributions.

Unit 2: Composition

"Variations on a Shaker Melody" is a four-minute excerpt from the end of Copland's ballet, *Appalachian Spring*. The original ballet was composed in

1943–44 for Martha Graham and was performed by Graham's company in 1944. The original scoring for the ballet called for thirteen instruments. The current arrangement for symphony orchestra was originally copyrighted in 1960 and was intended for performance by school and community orchestras. The Shaker melody on which the "Variations" are based is titled "Simple Gifts," a favorite song of the Shaker sect from 1837–47. The full ballet depicts the life of a young couple living in the wilderness of pioneer Pennsylvania. The theme and variations of "Simple Gifts" depict the couple settling down into a simple life after the boisterousness of early love. Copland's treatment of "Simple Gifts" is not so simple; he begins variations layered in canonic form almost from the beginning. When the hymn finally appears unaltered in homophonic form 125 measures into the piece, the result is a feeling of resolution and peace.

Unit 3: Historical Perspective

Composers rendering their own works to be more accessible to less-mature performers is not an entirely new concept. Bach provided his pupils with arrangements of compositions at a less-demanding technical level. When the composer arranges his work for a nascent performer, then it can be said that his original intent for the work survives. Alteration by a third party, such as an arranger, may lead to changes in the historical style, texture, or other musical elements of the composition. When the original composer arranges the work, his or her unique intent for the work is preserved. One layer of interpretation in an arrangement that could exist between the original composer and the performer is eliminated.

Copland regularly provided original works, arrangements of his own works, and adaptations of his works so young people and amateur orchestras could perform his music. Excerpts from his ballet and suite *Billy the Kid* (1938); *An Outdoor Overture* (1938); *Prairie Journal* (1937, 1968); excerpts from *Rodeo* (1942), including the ubiquitous "Hoe Down"; *The Red Pony* (1948); and *Fanfare for the Common Man* (1942) are but a few works often performed by school groups with great success.

Unit 4: Technical Considerations

The piece is composed in the keys of F, E-flat, and A major. Clarinet and trumpet need to negotiate long tones in the transposed key of B major from measure 75 until the end, but the trumpet part is written with all chromatics indicated note by note in the part. Most student players easily negotiate all instrumental ranges, with violinists venturing into extensions and fifth position after measure 85 until measure 109. Woodwinds enjoy exposed writing throughout. Clarinet receives solo treatment at the opening and close of the piece. Oboe and bassoon double each other at measure 28, supported only by sustained writing in trumpet. Horn receives exposed and characteristic melodic treatment at measure 3 and throughout. A short transitional section from measures 71–75 requires woodwinds and strings to coordinate bird calls reminiscent of those found in Beethoven's "Pastoral" Symphony. The rapid trumpet and trombone mirror passages from measures 77–109 require precision and balance. The timpani part is basic. The harp and piano parts add fullness and character to the texture but are doubled in other parts, offering some interesting substitution possibilities for understaffed school groups.

Unit 5: Stylistic Considerations

This piece is a model because of the breadth of creativity employed using a simple melody within a short time span. Tone, orchestral balance, precision, and dynamic contrast are especially exploitable elements of music for the conductor. Stylistically, Copland draws from contrapuntal and homophonic styles from the past but weaves them into an art form that is a synthesis of European past practice and American ingenuity. There is nothing naive about this seemingly simple gift from Copland.

Unit 6: Musical Elements

The piece is tonal throughout, combining contrapuntal and homophonic writing. The meter is either in two or in one, though the section in one can be conducted in four, reflecting four eight-measure phrases, or perhaps eight half phrases. The violins sound the "Simple Gifts" theme first in the Variations and are almost immediately followed by horn, viola, and then flute. A lone clarinet then plays the theme *alla breve*. From that moment on, the variations gain speed, the ensemble increases in size, and the contrapuntal sophistication increases toward the *tutti* statement in the middle. Trombone and viola share the melody during the thick contrapuntal section in measures 44–71. The trumpet and trombone variation follows demonstrating mirroring, with flurries of supporting string scale passages driving toward the concluding statement that appears in long homophonic tones. The tranquil coda is like a prayer that is intended to leave the couple from the ballet quiet and strong in their new home.

Unit 7: Form and Structure

The theme and variations technique employed is not a model for its rigid adherence to statement, variations, and a return of the original statement. Copland begins his variations before three measures have passed.

SECTION	MEASURES	EVENT AND SCORING
Introduction	1–9	Theme stated in violin, but additive technique employed in other instruments, that is, instruments enter in layers to thicken the texture and add sonic volume

SECTION	MEASURES	EVENT AND SCORING
Theme	9–25	In clarinet
Transition	26–27	Modulation to E-flat
Variation	28–44	
Variation	44–71	
Transition	71–77	Modulation to A major
Variation	77–109	
Variation	109–125	
Theme	125–139	Original melody
Coda	140	

Unit 8: Suggested Listening

Aaron Copland:

Appalachian Spring

Billy the Kid

Down a Country Lane

El Salón México

"Four Dance Episodes" from *Rodeo*

Our Town (film score)

An Outdoor Overture

Quiet City

The Red Pony

Symphony Nos. 1–3

The Tender Land

Unit 9: Additional References and Resources

Copland, Aaron. "Variations on a Shaker Melody" from *Appalachian Spring*. New York: Boosey & Hawkes, 1967.

Copland, Aaron, and Vivian Perlis. *Copland: 1900 through 1942*. New York: St. Martin's Press, 1984.

Copland, Aaron, and Vivian Perlis. *Copland: Since 1943*. New York: St. Martin's Press, 1989.

Hodeir, André. *The Forms of Music*. New York: Walker and Company, 1951.

Holloman, D. Kern. *Evenings with the Orchestra: A Norton Companion for Concertgoers*. New York: W. W. Norton & Company, 1992.

Mordden, Ethan. *A Guide to Orchestral Music: The Handbook for Non-musicians*. New York: Oxford University Press, 1980.

Perlis, Vivian. *A Guide to the Music of Aaron Copland*. New York: Boosey & Hawkes, 1998.

Contributed by:
Michael Allard
Orchestra Conductor, Porterville Unified School District
Adjunct Professor, Porterville Community College
Porterville, California

Grade Six

Teacher Resource Guide

Academic Festival Overture, Op. 80

Johannes Brahms
(1833–1897)

FULL ORCHESTRA

Unit 1: Composer

Johannes Brahms was born in Hamburg, Germany, on May 7, 1833, and died in Vienna, Austria, on April 3, 1897. Brahms's father was a double bassist who sought to have the young man schooled in music. He was trained in piano performance and first premiered as a soloist in 1848. Brahms earned his living teaching and playing the piano from the time he was thirteen years of age. His composition career began when his friend, the famous violinist Joseph Joachim, introduced him to Liszt and Schumann. Schumann immediately hailed his work to be that of a genius and took an active role in promoting the young man as a pianist and composer. Brahms's first compositions were not well received critically, and his first real success did not come until 1857 with the *German Requiem*. Brahms distanced himself from what he called the new music of Franz Liszt and Richard Wagner and wrote strictly within classical forms, albeit with a highly romantic style. Brahms was a highly prolific composer, having written four symphonies, four concertos, numerous choral works, hundreds of songs, and a tremendous output of chamber music, most of which are still considered to be masterpieces today.

Unit 2: Composition

The *Academic Festival Overture*, Op. 80, was written in 1880 in response to the University of Breslau conferring upon Brahms an honorary doctorate degree. "A jolly potpourri of student songs à la Suppé" was how Brahms described his work (Downes). Written in strict first-movement sonata allegro form, the thematic material consists of four student songs popular at that time. Although he was not a university man, Brahms drew upon his memories as a young man in the university town of Göttingen to create a piece that was at once both nostalgic and celebratory. At the time of the composition of this work, Brahms began work on a companion piece that would balance the carefree nature of the *Academic Festival Overture* with something darker, even melancholy. The resulting work was the *Tragic Overture*, Op. 81. Both pieces were premiered in 1881.

Unit 3: Historical Perspective

Brahms composed the *Academic Festival Overture* while he was firmly established as a great composer throughout Europe. His works were being premiered throughout the continent, and he was enjoying a sense of self-sufficiency that allowed him to concentrate further on his compositions. At that time there appeared two distinct schools of thought regarding composition. The works of opera composer Richard Wagner, with their continuous streams of music that flowed without a sense of form at times, stood in stark contrast to the works of Brahms, who modeled his works using the forms of such classicists as Mozart and Beethoven. Composers such as Liszt and Hugo Wolff were in the Wagner camp, while Antonín Dvořák, whom Brahms tirelessly promoted, was safely on the classical side.

Unit 4: Technical Considerations

The tonal centers of C minor, C major, and G major are explored throughout the work. The time signature also changes within the form of the work from *alla breve* to 4/4 to 2/4 to 3/4. All parts require a high level of technical proficiency. Players will need to pay attention to the highly syncopated rhythms in the introduction. Brahms uses a diatonic language, and he also utilizes many arpeggiated figures in the strings and woodwinds. Legato, marcato, and staccato articulations and bowings are used in the piece. There are exposed sections throughout the work, including a brass choir in measures 64–87, and a bassoon duet in measures 157–173, which will need special attention from the conductor. A special demand is made of the upper strings, with lengthy sections of running sixteenth and thirty-second notes. Tempo will need to be a consideration in balancing the stylistic elements with the technical proficiency of the string players. The orchestration calls for a large orchestra that includes piccolo, two flutes, two oboes, two clarinets, two bassoons, contrabassoon, four horns, three trumpets, three trombones, tuba, timpani, bass drum, cymbals, triangle, and strings.

Unit 5: Stylistic Considerations

The contrasting styles of legato, marcato, and staccato are used throughout the work. Dynamic levels, like that of so many late romantic compositions, are extreme, ranging from *pp sempre e sotto voce* to *ff*. *Sforzandos* and accents punctuate the heavier sections, while it is not uncommon to see "espressivo" and "dolce" written above single melodic lines in the other sections. The introduction needs a feeling of anticipation that builds up to the first theme. The first theme in the exposition should be played with a singing style, while the second theme, introduced by a rollicking bassoon duet, should be more comical in character. The majestic coda requires a full, sonorous sound from all players with care not to overplay the instruments.

Unit 6: Musical Elements

The introduction is a brooding C minor that builds through a transition to C major. The first theme of the exposition begins in C major with a slight diversion to E major, which then transitions to the second theme. The second theme stays within the bounds of G major. The development returns to C minor, using the previous thematic material to build to the recapitulation. The recapitulation and coda are firmly in C major. Four university songs provide the thematic material for the piece. Although not always quoted in their entirety, the songs are used as thematic material and recur in the development section along with new melodies used by Brahms as transitional material. The piece is marked by the lush sonority of the late romantic era as exemplified in the coda—a glorious rendition of the college song "Gaudeamus igitur" played by the brass and woodwind choirs accompanied by soaring violin scales.

Unit 7: Form and Structure

Form: sonata allegro

SECTION	MEASURES	EVENT AND SCORING
Introduction	1–87	
Exposition	88–240	
Theme 1	88–156	"Wir hatten gebauet ein stattliches Haus" and "Der Landesvater"
Theme 2	157–240	"Was kommt dort von der Höhe"
Development	241–289	
Recapitulation	290–378	
Coda	379–401	"Gaudeamus igitur"

Unit 8: Suggested Listening

Johannes Brahms:
    Concerto for Violin in D Major
    Hungarian Dances (originally for piano, later orchestrated)
    Symphony Nos. 1–4
    Tragic Overture
    Variations on a Theme by Haydn

Antonín Dvořák:
   Slavonic Dances
   Symphony No. 9 ("From the New World")

Unit 9: Additional References and Resources

Botstein, Leon, ed. *The Compleat Brahms: A Guide to the Musical Works of Johannes Brahms*. New York: W. W. Norton & Company, 1999.

Downes, Edward. *Guide to Symphonic Music*. New York: Walker and Company, 1976.

Kennedy, Michael, ed. *The Oxford Dictionary of Music*. 2d edition. Oxford: Oxford University Press, 1994.

Slonimsky, Nicolas, ed. emeritus. *Baker's Biographical Dictionary of Musicians*. New York: Schirmer Books, 2001.

Contributed by:

Jeffrey S. Bishop
Director of Orchestras
Shawnee Mission Northwest High School
Shawnee Mission, Kansas

Teacher Resource Guide

"Adagietto" from Symphony No. 5

Gustav Mahler
(1860–1911)

STRING ORCHESTRA

Unit 1: Composer

Gustav Mahler was born in Kalischt, Bohemia, in 1860. He entered the Vienna Conservatory in 1875, where he studied piano, harmony, and composition. His first conducting position was in Hall, Upper Austria, in 1880 at the Operetta Theater. Within a few years, Mahler was offered a position as music director of the Vienna court opera. To take this post, Mahler was forced to change his religion from Judaism to Catholicism. He conducted the Vienna Philharmonic from 1898–1901 and moved to New York to conduct the Metropolitan Opera in 1907. In 1909, Mahler was appointed conductor of the New York Philharmonic, a position that he kept until shortly before his death in 1911. As a composer, Mahler is best known for his very personal, introspective, and philosophical approach to composition. Mahler did not assign programs to his pieces, encouraging listeners to create their own programs based on their response to the music.

Unit 2: Composition

Mahler composed the Fifth Symphony in 1901–02 and conducted its premiere in Cologne on October 18, 1904. The symphony is divided into three parts. The first and second movements are linked together as part 1. The third movement, "Scherzo," is part 2. The Adagietto is linked with the Rondo: Finale as part 3. The scoring of the Adagietto for strings and harp is similar to that of the four Rückert songs that Mahler composed in 1901, specifically "Ich bin der Welt abhanden gekommen," and several of the *Kindertotenlieder*. There has been a

great deal of debate on the correct tempo of the Adagietto. Recorded performances vary in length from seven minutes to over thirteen minutes, indicating the variety of interpretation common with works of the romantic period.

Unit 3: Historical Perspective

Although the symphony received critical acclaim, the Adagietto was thought to be the weakest movement because of its sentimentality. Nevertheless, audiences enjoyed the Adagietto more than any other movement. The chronology of the composition indicates that Mahler composed the Adagietto at about the same time that he met and fell in love with his future wife, Alma Schindler. A note in a score used by the conductor, Willem Mengelberg, informs us that Mahler used this Adagietto instead of a letter as a declaration of love for Alma. Mahler conducted the Adagietto as a separate work in Rome in 1907. Leonard Bernstein conducted the Adagietto at the funeral of Sen. Robert Kennedy in 1968.

Unit 4: Technical Considerations

This composition uses the key signatures of F, G-flat, E, and D major, although extensive use of chromaticism typical of late romantic style requires performers to play through some very difficult modulations. The work consists of long phrases requiring great bow control to perform a wide range of dynamic and expressive markings. Subtle changes in tempo demand excellent communication between conductor and performers. First violins are required to play up to C-flat7 (five ledger lines and a space above the staff) and cellos up to A4. The work requires a harpist with excellent rhythmic skills. Rhythmically difficult passages are found where triplet eighth notes proceed to sixteenths. The slow tempo of this work makes these rhythmic transitions harder to feel for some student musicians. Knowledge of German or access to a good German/English dictionary is necessary to interpret performance directions in the score.

Unit 5: Stylistic Considerations

Long, lyrical phrases offer great opportunity to explore contour and shaping through the use of bowing, vibrato, and dynamics. Typical of late romantic style, the Adagietto incorporates extreme dynamic markings from *ppppp* to *ff* with the additional notation of "viel Ton!" (big sound). Mahler's dynamic markings, tempo markings, and other performance directions are abundant and detailed. If one has in mind the similarity of this Adagietto to a wordless song, tempo choices can be guided by capabilities of a human voice to sustain phrases over a period of time.

Unit 6: Musical Elements

The themes used in the Adagietto are closely related rhythmically through the use of three pickup notes followed by longer notes that suspend the melodic motion. This creates harmonic tension that is released with the resolution of suspensions. The harmonic structure is typical of late romantic songs that use extensive chromaticism during modulations. Key development moves from F major to G-flat major followed by a brief three-measure section in E major. A nine-measure passage in B minor leads back to F major and a restatement of the first two themes to conclude the work.

Unit 7: Form and Structure

The form of the Adagietto has been compared to "a wordless Rückert song for orchestra alone,"[1] thus drawing a comparison between this movement of the Fifth Symphony and a set of songs composed by Mahler in June/August 1901. Thematically the work contains four themes, each closely related due to rhythmic structure and phrase length:

SECTION	MEASURES	EVENT AND SCORING
Theme 1	2	Stated in first violin
Theme 1 repeated	10	Stated in viola using rhythmic augmentation
Theme 2	23	Stated in first violin
Theme 3	39	Developed from motive in cello part in mm. 19–21
Theme 4	47	New theme features melodic material from previous themes
Quote	61	From the gaze motif in Wagner's *Tristan und Isolde*
Theme 1 return	73	
Theme 2 return	86	

Unit 8: Suggested Listening

Gustav Mahler:
    "Ich bin der Welt abhanden gekommen" (I Have Slipped Away
        from This World)
    Symphony No. 5, Adagietto
Richard Wagner, *Tristan und Isolde*, Prelude to Act I

Unit 9: Additional References and Resources

Floros, Constantin. *Gustav Mahler: The Symphonies*. Portland, Oregon: Amadeus Press, 1993.

Mitchell, Donald, and Andrew Nicholson, eds. *The Mahler Companion*. New York: Oxford University Press, 1999.

Contributed by:
Phil Peters
Orchestra Director
Valley High School
West Des Moines, Iowa

1   Mitchell, Donald. "Eternity or Nothingness? Mahler's Fifth Symphony," *The Mahler Companion*. Donald Mitchell and Andrew Nicholson, eds. New York: Oxford University Press, 1999, 312.

Teacher Resource Guide

Adagio for Strings, Op. 11
Samuel Barber
(1910–1981)

STRING ORCHESTRA

Unit 1: Composer

Samuel Barber was born in West Chester, Pennsylvania, in 1910. He studied piano from childhood, wrote a juvenile opera and many songs, led a high school orchestra, and was an organist at a local church. Coming from a musical family, Barber entered the Curtis Institute when it opened in 1924, studying composition, piano, conducting, and voice. Barber received his B.M. in 1934. During his student years, he wrote the well-known *Dover Beach* for tenor and string quartet (1931), the Cello Sonata (1932), and songs and works for piano. By the time he left Curtis, his works had already been performed in New York and Philadelphia.

Barber's overture, *The School for Scandal*, was awarded the Bearns Prize in 1933 and was premiered by the Philadelphia Orchestra. Barber began a lifelong friendship with the composer, Menotti, while traveling in Europe in 1933. The two met Toscanini soon after, who premiered Barber's Adagio for Strings and his *Essay for Orchestra* with the NBC Symphony in New York in 1938.

Barber continued to compose in his lyric style for many years, though his works after 1939 became increasingly more dissonant. Composing for most classical music performing media, including opera, Barber was awarded the New York Critic's Circle Award in 1962 for his Piano Concerto. He died in 1981.

Unit 2: Composition

Adagio for Strings is an arrangement for string orchestra of the second movement of Barber's String Quartet No. 1. Barber found inspiration for the work from Vergil's *Georgics*. He envisioned a small stream that grows into a large river. The work was popularized and recorded by Toscanini. Barber casts a series of sequences from a single, meandering melody that moves along mostly in quarter note values. The melodic melodic contour is mostly diatonically stepwise and supported by a chordal accompaniment. The melody begins first in violin, then is passed downward to viola and cello until each instrumental voice has been exploited. Every upward rise is answered by a subsequent fall. In the center section, basses rest as the treble instruments participate in a bright climax. The climax is dissipated when bass return in a sequence of cadences. A true recapitulation reverses course, settles in the home key, then dies away. The resulting music results in quiet, spiritual reflection.

Unit 3: Historical Perspective

It is possible to classify this work as neoromantic because of Barber's tonal and lyric approach, and the work's emotional impact. Barber's Bach-like *Fortspinnung* approach to the single theme hints at a hybrid approach with neoclassic tendencies. The singular nature of this work and its established place as a pinnacle of compositional achievement make it unique within established musical practice. It is impossible to overstate the power of this work and its effect upon listeners at the time of its premiere and today. Clearly, Barber synthesized the past with his own creative forces to compose this work at a time when "serious" composers were moving away from tonal music toward dodecaphonic music, an expanded use of dissonance, expressionism, realism, and other rejections of romantic practice.

Unit 4: Technical Considerations

The piece is written in B-flat minor. It exploits the full and extreme range of dynamics for stringed instruments. The melodic writing is primarily by step, though some large leaps occur. The playing is sustained, requiring exceptional bow control and stamina. Clean bow placement is valuable throughout to ensure solid entrances, particularly in quiet passages. Precise intonation is a necessity due to exposed writing, octaves between parts, and high positions. The viola part splits into two in measures 27–57, written in alto and treble clefs. The cello part is written in bass, tenor, and treble clefs. Mutes are required at measure 57, and there is an advantage in using slide-on orchestral mutes to avoid unnecessary noise during the rest. All parts, save the string bass, present the melody. Critical thinking and creative interpretation opportunities are present, particularly at the *ad lib.* at measure 4, the 6/2 at measure 15, the 5/2 at measure 31, and the 5/2 at measure 60. The extra pulses in these measures merely add expressive breadth.

Unit 5: Stylistic Considerations

A mature orchestra will explore the far ranges of its lyrical expression through performance of Adagio for Strings. Sustained legato and expressive playing will need attention in rehearsal. Rhythmic precision between string sections is necessary for vertical harmonies to line up properly. An exploration of the sounding point or "point of contact" of the bow on the string will enhance the orchestra's ability to alter dynamics to the extremes called for in this piece. Within the sustained phrases, an opportunity exists to explore bowing choices depending upon the maturity of the orchestra and the musical interpretation of the conductor. This piece offers an opportunity to explore breath control and its relationship to string playing.

Unit 6: Musical Elements

The music is tonal, beginning and finishing in B-flat minor. The melodic structure is diatonic, with a few leaps. Neoromantic, neoclassic, and original style elements are present. Legato, expressive, and sustained writing appears throughout. Dynamics range from *pp* to *ff* and are mostly prepared changes through *crescendos* and *decrescendos*, though after the *ff* climax the change to *pp* is quite sudden. This writing demonstrates the use of sequence for variation. Normally, composers employ this simple device sparingly. Barber spins an entire work from it. Stress, tension, and release are the product of this type of writing.

Unit 7: Form and Structure

SECTION	EVENT AND SCORING
Beginning	Melody in first violin in B-flat minor
#1	Melody in viola; first violin continues with second half of lengthy theme as a countermelody to first half of melody played by viola
#2	New melodic idea in first violin over the continuation of the original theme in viola; double bass drops out
#3	Theme in cello; harmony provided by lengthy notes of non-thematic nature
#4	Continuation of theme in cello; first violin restates original theme in E-flat minor; second violin and viola play lengthy fragments of theme as countermelody to cello and first violin; climax on enharmonic equivalent of E major chord
#5	Three-measure transition harmonic progression dissipates the energy from the climax; double bass returns
Tempo I	First violin and viola restate original theme
#6	Continuation of theme, which then fragments and is augmented rhythmically to conclude the piece on the dominant (F) of B-flat minor

Unit 8: Suggested Listening
Aaron Copland, *Quiet City*
Edward Elgar, Serenade for Strings in C Minor, Op. 20
Edvard Grieg, "Åse's Death" from *Peer Gynt Suite* No. 1, Op. 46
Alan Hovhaness:
    Alleluia and Fugue
    Psalm and Fugue
Gustav Mahler, "Adagietto: Sehr langsam" from Symphony No. 5
Pietro Mascagni, "Intermezzo" from *Cavalleria rusticana*
Peter Tchaikovsky, "Elegy: Larghetto elegiaco" from Serenade for Strings in
    C Major, Op. 48

Unit 9: Additional References and Resources
Heyman, Barbara B. *Samuel Barber: The Composer and His Music*. New York:
    Oxford University Press, 1994.

Holoman, D. Kern. *Evenings with the Orchestra: A Norton Companion Guide
    for Concertgoers*. New York: W. W. Norton & Company, 1992.

Mordden, Ethan. *A Guide to Orchestral Music: The Handbook for Non-
    musicians*. New York: Oxford University Press, 1980.

Randel, Don Michael, ed. *The Harvard Biographical Dictionary of Music*.
    Cambridge, MA: The Belknap Press of Harvard University Press, 1996.

Contributed by:
Michael Allard
Orchestra Conductor, Porterville Unified School District
Adjunct Professor, Porterville Community College
Porterville, California

Teacher Resource Guide

Egmont Overture, Op. 84

Ludwig van Beethoven
(1770–1827)

FULL ORCHESTRA

Unit 1: Composer

Ludwig van Beethoven was born in the German city of Bonn in 1770 and remains to this day one of the most well-known composers of the orchestral repertoire. Beethoven's life spanned two of the more important stylistic epochs of musical history, the classic and romantic eras, during a time when the arts and Western Europe were particularly influenced by the American and French Revolutions of the late eighteenth century.

Beethoven came from a family of court singers, but his early family life was rather unhappy because of the abuse from an alcoholic father and the need for Beethoven at an early age to take on the role of caregiver to his mother and two younger brothers. In his early teen years, he was already working as a chapel organist, and at the age of seventeen, he traveled to Vienna to play for Mozart. Beethoven's talents continued to evolve, and by the age of twenty-two, Beethoven decided to permanently move to Vienna and study with Haydn. His career in Vienna demonstrated his great talent as a solo pianist and included an additional commitment to composition. He was welcomed into the homes of the music-loving aristocracy of Vienna, and through the influences of those wealthy patrons, Beethoven was able to receive support and commissions from a series of counts and princes, many of whom received dedications in Beethoven's compositions. By his early thirties, Beethoven had achieved fame as a serious and successful composer with several publishers competing for his compositions.

As his success continued to grow, Beethoven was inflicted with a loss of hearing. His middle and late years were dedicated to the challenges of life in

an environment filled with the politics of a new democracy in Europe, his own physical and psychological frustrations brought on by his increasing deafness, and the drive to create an expressive and emotional ideal unique in the history of music.

Unit 2: Composition

Overture to *Egmont* is the opening composition for incidental music Beethoven composed to accompany the tragic play about the story of Egmont, written by Johann Wolfgang Goethe (1749–1832), German poet, dramatist, novelist, and scientist whose genius embraced most fields of human endeavor. The story of Egmont describes the final years of Count Lamoral Egmont (1522–68), the Flemish general and statesman who was executed by the Spanish. Egmont was born in Hainaut (now in Belgium). As a general of the Habsburg Emperor Charles V, Egmont had won victories over the French, which made him a popular hero. Charles's son, Philip II, King of Spain, appointed him governor of Flanders and Artois. Egmont protested against the infringement of Flemish liberties and the introduction of the Inquisition into the Netherlands; but when insurrections arose, Egmont supported Philip. When the Duke of Alva arrived in 1567 to restore order in the country, Egmont was imprisoned, condemned to death, and beheaded. The story and music of *Egmont* speaks to Beethoven's commitment to democracy, freedom, and the battle against tyranny.

The overture is in F minor, is in one movement, and lasts approximately eight minutes and thirty seconds to nine minutes. The overture has three sections: an opening slow section in 3/2 meter, Sostenuto ma non troppo; a middle section, Allegro, in 3/4; and the final 4/4 section, Allegro con brio.

Unit 3: Historical Perspective

The music for *Egmont* comes from Beethoven's middle period, which was his most successfully creative period. Beethoven's middle period was one in which he was past the immaturity of his youth and not yet so overcome by the impending gloom of his late period. His works from this period, approximately 1800–15, include Symphony Nos. 3–8; his only opera, *Fidelio*; the Op. 59 Razumovsky string quartets; and fourteen piano sonatas, including *Moonlight*, *Waldstein*, and *Appasionata*. During this middle period, sometimes referred to as the "period of invasion" because of the French conquest of Austria and entry into Vienna during these years, Beethoven experimented with melodic and formal aspects of his compositions, and he expanded upon the classical sonata forms he inherited from Mozart and Haydn. In addition, the technical challenges Beethoven brought to his players raised the level of virtuosity of the performers of his day.

Unit 4: Technical Considerations

Familiarity with F minor scales and arpeggios may become a technical focus for the entire ensemble during rehearsals of this work. Various technical routines should be incorporated into the daily rehearsal routines. In addition, some of the faster technical passages in the Allegro, 3/4 section will require the string players to become technically adept at some of the more advanced string techniques and routines: spiccato, détaché, marcato, and martelé. Likewise, the wind players will need to synchronize basic issues of style and length with the string players. The conductor may want to coordinate various bowing and rhythmic exercises along with the scales and arpeggio routines to achieve more efficiency.

Finally, Beethoven's compositional style includes an advanced approach to the notion of *subito* dynamic changes, which provides a challenge for the listeners who are unprepared for the changing dynamics. There is also a technical challenge for the players who, even at a more experienced level, need encouragement to maximize the dynamic changes required in the score. Various creative exercises can be invented for the players to address the two basic *subito* dynamic changes: the *subito f* or *ff*, prepared by a *diminuendo*, and the *subito p* or *pp*, prepared by a *crescendo*. The ensemble can also be drilled to acquire a more mature approach to dynamics by addressing the *fp* and *sforzando* dynamics, being careful to ensure that a clear distinction is made between those two dynamics.

Unit 5: Stylistic Considerations

Beethoven's *Egmont* music comes during his middle period, at the beginning of the nineteenth century. There are several important stylistic considerations for the conductor to include in the preparation of the Overture. They include an awareness of the conventions that should be carried over from the classical period and the influences from Mozart and Haydn's later works.

SEATING:
The violins should be divided, with the first and second violins sitting on either side of the conductor facing each other. This common practice seating was the expected seating throughout much of the nineteenth century and is an important practice sometimes ignored by contemporary conductors. The trumpets and timpani should be seated close together. The woodwinds should be seated in the traditional center grouping of two rows.

INSTRUMENTAL CONSIDERATIONS:
During Beethoven's time, the horn and trumpet players played natural instruments without pistons; these natural horns limited players to the notes available in the overtone series. The timpani player played on two different drums, tuned to the tonic and dominant keys of the composition. The timpani sticks were rather hard and the heads of the timpani were of animal hide. The

timpani player should be encouraged to investigate sonic compensations for the original instruments given that the more modern instruments cannot adequately duplicate the original instruments of Beethoven's day. The conductor may want to investigate further the dynamic and sonic implications of the tone quality and sound blend of such instruments and adjust the printed dynamics appropriately. Beethoven and his contemporaries still approached the notation of dynamics with a verticality of convenience, that is, the same dynamic notation was vertically notated in each instrument in the score without regard for the technical abilities or limitations of individual instruments.

The string instruments of Beethoven's time are regarded today as having had a smaller, lighter sound when compared to modern string instruments. The classical era string instruments would have made exclusive use of gut strings, with a tone quality markedly different from contemporary instruments that possess a tone quality affected by the modern steel string. The classical era bows would have also been somewhat shorter, and players did not enjoy the strength experienced by players who use the more modern sticks. To help compensate for these changes, the conductor may want to experiment with having the string players hold their bows a little higher on the stick, loosen the tension of the bow hair, and minimize their left-hand vibrato usage.

TEMPO AND METER:
Arguably, the most challenging aspect of the performance of pre-metronomic compositions in this common practice period is a correct approach in deciding on tempo, speed, and character. Frequently abused misinterpretations for this aspect of performance by today's conductors are often heard when specific notations for meters seem to be generally ignored. Some of the more common misinterpretations include the *alla breve*, which in slow introductions is often ignored and over-subdivided by the conductor, ultimately leading to a loss of musical flow. Additional misreadings affecting the flow of the music come from the frequent lack of distinction between 3/8 and 3/4, with important agogic stresses incorrectly performed. The Overture's introduction (3/2 Sostenuto) should be conducted in a slow three at half note = ca. 42. The middle section (3/4 Allegro) should be conducted in a one pattern at the speed of dotted-half note = ca. 56 or quarter note = 168. To help the ensemble at the beginning of the 3/4 Allegro, the conductor may want to begin in a fast three pattern for the first four measures and then conduct in one by measure 5 of the Allegro. The final coda (4/4 Allegro con brio) section can best be accomplished at the L'istesso tempo of the middle (3/4 Allegro) section with quarter = 168 or half note = 84. This final section can be started in four and, at the ninth measure of the Allegro con brio, can be conducted in two until the end.

Unit 6: Musical Elements

HARMONY:

The first two main sections of the composition are in the key of F minor. The final Allegro con brio section is in the key of F major. The second section of the Overture is the lengthy 3/4 Allegro, which functions very similarly to a sonata form with its own exposition with a second theme or key area beginning at Letter B, a development, and a condensed recapitulation. The first time the second theme appears, it is in the key of A-flat major; the second time it appears, it is in the key of D-flat major.

MELODY:

It is by no means accidental that a detail such as the key areas of the main 3/4 section outlines the D-flat triad. Beethoven's preoccupation in melodic construction included what may be regarded as an obsession with scales and arpeggios. The opening 3/2 Sostenuto and 3/4 Allegro sections both develop a melodic cell of the scale by the interval of the second. The final 4/4 Allegro con brio melody is made up of the outlining of the F major arpeggio in first inversion, superimposed over an ostinato double pedal point that repeats the interval C–B in the low strings.

RHYTHM:

The ensemble will have to address the challenge of being able to think and perform half and quarter note pulse and rhythmic subdivisions accurately in the 3/2 Sostenuto. Furthermore, the players will also need to track the next level of division of eighth note pickups in this introduction. The 3/4 Allegro second theme, five measures after letter B, features a motto rhythmic figure of two quarter notes/eighth rest/eighth note pickup. In addition, the 3/4 Allegro makes frequent use of the dotted-quarter followed by three eighth notes in a rising scale pattern. The strings and winds will need to provide for the unanimous release of the dotted-quarter and for the placement of an accent on the middle eighth note to help clarify the distinction of a 3/4 feeling from a 6/8 feeling. The placement of the accent on the middle eighth note is helpful in achieving this metric clarification.

Unit 7: Form and Structure

The Overture to *Egmont* is in a three-part form; the middle section, being the longest of the three, takes on characteristics of a condensed three-part form of its own. The large, middle section (Allegro) includes two themes, a short development/transition, and a recapitulation of themes, all of which appear before the final third section, which functions like a coda for the entire Overture.

SECTION	MEASURES
Introduction	1
Allegro/Theme A	25
Theme B	82
Development	124
Recapitulation/	
Theme A	193
Theme B	225
Coda	287

Unit 8: Suggested Listening
Ludwig van Beethoven:
   Coriolan
   Fidelio
   King Stephen
   Leonore No. 3
   Symphony Nos. 1–9
Franz Joseph Haydn, Symphony Nos. 88, 92, 100, 102, 104
Wolfgang Amadeus Mozart, Symphony Nos. 39–41

Unit 9: Additional References and Resources
The bibliography available for the life and music of Beethoven is extensive. The reader may want to further investigate more of the available sources. The following represents a limited, general, and highly selective sampling of the available resources.

Carse, Adam. *The Orchestra from Beethoven to Berlioz*. New York: Broude, 1948.

Carse, Adam. *The Orchestra in the XVIII Century*. Cambridge: W. Heffer & Sons, Ltd., 1940.

Del Mar, Norman. *Conducting Beethoven. Volume 2: Overtures, Concertos, Missa Solemnis*. London: Oxford University Press, 1989.

Kolisch, Rudolf. "Tempo and Character in Beethoven's Music." *Musical Quarterly*, April 1943.

Leinsdorf, Erich. *The Composer's Advocate*. New Haven, CT: Yale University Press, 1974.

Marty, Jean-Pierre. *The Tempo Indications of Mozart*. New Haven, CT: Yale University Press, 1988.

Rudolf, Max. "The Metronome Indications in Beethoven's Symphonies." *The Journal of the Conductor's Guild*, Vol. I, No. 1: Spring 1980.

Weingartner, Felix. *On the Performance of the Beethoven Symphonies.* (English edition by Dover, 1968.) Leipzig: 1928.

Zaslaw, Neal. *Mozart's Symphonies: Context, Performance Practice, Reception.* Oxford: Clarendon Press, 1989.

Contributed by:

Glenn Block
Director of Orchestras and Opera, and Professor of Conducting
Illinois State University
Bloomington, Illinois

Teacher Resource Guide

Five Variants
of Dives and Lazarus
Ralph Vaughan Williams
(1872–1958)

STRING ORCHESTRA

Unit 1: Composer

Ralph Vaughan Williams was born in Ampney, Gloucestershire, England, in 1872. He studied English folk songs and was convinced that the feeling of folk music should permeate classical composition. His interest in English folk music was so thorough that he joined the Folk Song Society and also edited a book of English hymn music. He was commissioned to write the coronation music for Queen Elizabeth II in 1953. His best-known orchestral works include *Fantasia on a Theme by Thomas Tallis*, *The Lark Ascending*, and *Fantasia on Greensleeves*. Vaughan Williams studied with Ravel in Paris and returned to England as one the country's most prominent composers. He died in 1958, but provided a link between the nationalism of the romantic era and contemporary music.

Unit 2: Composition

The British Council commissioned the *Five Variants of Dives and Lazarus* (pronounced like "dives" in swimming) to represent the music of England in 1939 at the World's Fair in America. The literal reference to Dives and Lazarus is Biblical and recalls the story of Lazarus in poverty being ignored by the wealthy Dives. Aesthetically, this is a composition that contrasts simplicity of notes (poverty) with a prolixity of notes (wealth). The musical genesis of the work is not one folk song with five variations. Rather, it is as Vaughan Williams states, "These variants are not exact *replicas* of traditional tunes but rather reminiscences of various versions in my own collection and those of others."

The music for *Dives and Lazarus* dates back to the sixteenth century in

England and was a ballad entitled either "Murder in the Red Barn" or "Murder of Maria Marten." Both this folk song and the theme for the fifth variant, "The Star of the County Down," are available on compact disc for illustrating the historical antecedents to the composition (see Unit 8). The A theme begins with a soft Adagio, after which the music is divided into the five variants, easily seen by headings in the parts. *Five Variants of Dives and Lazarus* appears simple to students when they look at the printed music. The conductor, however, can ill afford to ignore the considerable difficulties of three against two, the range of the first violin part, the clef reading for cello, the time signature relationships, and the need for strong soloists on violin, cello, and harp. The piece must be rehearsed carefully and performed several times for the students to feel the musical nuances.

Unit 3: Historical Perspective

Five Variants was first performed in 1939 and made available for public performance in 1940. One does not sense in the music any of the historical disruption that was going on in England from World War II. Rather, the performers and listeners are transported to another England, an earlier time when folk music represented the life of the community. Songs were used in work, in worship, in telling stories, in remembering events, and in binding a group of people together within a common aesthetic tradition. The music is transparent at many points but becomes dense in Variant V, as if Vaughan Williams is presenting a choice of complexity versus simplicity for the listener. The final cello solo followed by the ascending harp arpeggios raises the same questions as Copland's *Quiet City*. What quality of life do we choose in the modern world? The metaphor of poverty and wealth is juxtaposed over the tranquil and the urbane.

Unit 4: Technical Considerations

The key signatures of B minor, D major, D minor, F minor, C minor, and some modal variations are required for *Five Variants*. First violin ranges up to B, five ledger lines above the staff, with several significant unprepared leaps of an octave and a third or an octave and a fourth on consecutive notes. The viola part stays in alto clef; a strong viola section can provide great harmonic stability in this work. The cello part changes frequently into tenor clef and ranges up to C above middle C. The harp part requires two harpists to play all of the notes or editing of the part to perform the essential notes by one harp player. The low octaves can prove to be a difficult stretch for players with small hands, and care is necessary to avoid injuries. Letter H presents an extended section of three against two, and conductors can develop exercises to make the rhythms accessible before the rhythm is combined with the pitches. Variant III requires rhythmic precision between the solo violin and the harp. The variation ends with hemiolas that lead directly to a 2/4 section of

overlapping melodies. Variant IV is the most complex in rhythmic conception. The lower strings play a counterpoint line against the upper strings, who are performing a rhythm that is off by one sixteenth note from matching the low voices. This rhythmic complexity alternates between the sections, leading to a dramatic unison at the end of the variation. Variant V requires excellent solo playing in violin, cello, and harp.

Unit 5: Stylistic Considerations

Five Variants of Dives and Lazarus demands multiple bowing skills. The parts from the publisher are sparsely marked for bowings. Because it is rental music, there can be several conductors' ideas marked in the parts. The conductor is advised to mark in specific bowings by looking directly at the parts, not the score. The stylistic interpretation must be based on a folk song sense that the music remains transparent. Dynamics are thoughtfully marked, and the softer dynamics contribute to an understated sense of singing the music. The piece is conceptually closer to Vaughan Williams's vocal works, and the importance and independence of each line is crucial. The conductor is responsible for several difficult tempo changes. These changes happen at the beginning of each of the Variants and require, as Daniel Barenboim said, "knowledge at the beginning of the end and knowledge at the end of the beginning and awareness in the middle of the beginning and the end."

Unit 6: Musical Elements

Unison strings in the opening Adagio state the main theme. It is a lush melody with a sense that it is being played in the distance. The B minor quality and the placement on the G string for violin and the A string for cello make the unison quality exquisite. Lower and upper strings alternate presenting the musical material in a waltz tempo in Variant I. A clear harmonic structure is outlined in the harp. Variant II moves into one beat per measure to enable the three against two to develop with strength and clarity. The tension that is created in this movement by the rhythmic devices is a high point of the music. Variant III presents three modulations that propel the music forward to a transparent 2/4 ending of sixteen measures. Variant IV feels jumpy and off beat. The use of tied notes over bar lines and beat divisions along with dotted-eighth/sixteenth rhythms create a jerky musical line quite in contrast to anything in the rest of the music. Variant V separates first violin, second violin, and cello into divided sections and further divides those players with a *divisi* for upper and lower notes. The modulation back to B minor and the introduction of a new theme enhances the cantabile effect and provides a satisfying ending to this music.

474

Unit 7: Form and Structure

SECTION	EVENT AND SCORING
Introduction	Two-measure introduction in low strings and harp; unison strings play the first folk song, "Murder in the Red Barn"; at letter A viola and cello play the theme; the theme is then fragmented into the initial eighth note statement and played in imitative style with the descending notes predominating
Variant 1	Changes into a waltz and also changes the destination notes into ascending arpeggios and interval leaps with descending resolutions
Variant 2	Must be conducted in one to establish the tension of the three against two; meter change seven measures after L deserves close attention by the conductor and players
Variant 3	Solo violin and solo harp provide a slower variation in a return to 3/4 time; underlying eighth note accompaniment is constant in the harp and at P in the strings
Variant 4	With a feeling in one, viola enters with a variation far different from the A theme: ascending in nature and soon turns into a complex dotted rhythm with a fugue-like nature
Variant 5	The final variant is a new folk song in 4/4, with a sense of developing from earlier material although it is entirely new music; theme is stated one time and then ends with a cello solo accompanied by a violin quartet; from W to the end, there is a strong sense of ascending as the chord structures move upward through inversions

Unit 8: Suggested Listening

There are eight recordings available of this work; it seems to be increasing in popularity in live performances and play time on classical music stations.

Five Variants of Dives and Lazarus, Marriner, Academy of St. Martin in the Fields

Five Variants of Dives and Lazarus, Thomson, London Philharmonic Orchestra

Patrick Ball, *From a Distant Time*, Patrick Ball, celtic harp, Vol. 2, Track 12, "The Star of County Down"

Aaron Copland, *Quiet City* for trumpet, English horn, and orchestra

Charles Ives, Variations on "America" for Organ

Virgil Thompson, *The Plow that Broke the Plains*

Troubadours of British Folk, Vol. 2, Track 2, "Murder of Maria Marten"
Ralph Vaughan Williams:
  Fantasia on a Theme by Thomas Tallis
  The Lark Ascending

Unit 9: Additional References and Resources

Day, James. *Vaughan Williams*. London: Oxford University Press, 1998.

Foss, Hubert. *Ralph Vaughan Williams: A Study*. London: Harrap, 1950.

Gerle, Robert. *The Art of Bowing Practice*. London: Stainer & Bell, 1991.

Gerle, Robert. *The Art of Practicing the Violin*. London: Stainer & Bell, 1983.

Howes, Frank. *The Music of Ralph Vaughan Williams*. London: Oxford University Press, 1954.

Storr, Anthony. *Music and the Mind*. New York: Ballantine Books, 1992.

Contributed by:

James D. Hainlen
Orchestra Director
Stillwater Area High School
Stillwater, Minnesota

Teacher Resource Guide

Serenade in C
for Strings, Op. 48

Peter Ilyich Tchaikovsky
(1840–1893)

STRING ORCHESTRA

Unit 1: Composer

Peter Ilyich Tchaikovsky was born in Votkinsk, Russia, on May 7, 1840. His father, a mining inspector, moved the family to St. Petersburg, where Tchaikovsky graduated from preparatory school and the School of Jurisprudence. He worked for three years as a clerk in the Ministry of Justice. He became increasingly interested in music, and in 1862 gave up his government post to attend the newly established St. Petersburg Conservatory. After graduation, he became professor of harmony at the Moscow Conservatory.

Tchaikovsky lived a tormented personal life. In 1877, he married a high-strung, neurotic music student, hoping to silence rumors of his homosexuality, and the marriage was such a disaster that he attempted suicide. Failing that, he deserted his wife and spent a year traveling around Europe. About this same time, he began a curious relationship with a wealthy woman, Nadezhda von Meck, who became his confidante and patroness. The stipend Tchaikovsky received from her enabled him to compose and be financially independent. She provided him with the impetus to compose most of his greatest works. As he grew older, his chronic melancholia became deep depression. He died of cholera on November 6, 1893.

Unit 2: Composition

Tchaikovsky was inspired only by personal desire to compose the Serenade for Strings. He expressed his hope to create a work of art; the result was an extensive, four-movement work. In a letter to his patroness, Mme. von Meck,

Tchaikovsky acknowledged his indebtedness to Mozart and stated that he intended the opening movement as a tribute to the classical master. The second movement is a flowing, melodic waltz with subdued Spanish rhythmic influences. The third movement is an elegy, with two alternating themes of doleful, shamelessly expressive character. The finale arrives from an ethereal beginning that becomes a lively dance. Thematic material for the finale comes from two Russian folk songs, the only nationalistic element in this composition. To conclude the work, the opening of the first movement returns to become the coda of the last movement, a device also employed by Dvořák in his string Serenade written five years earlier.

Unit 3: Historical Perspective

The pure romanticism of nineteenth century Europe never really arrived in Russia. Composers in Russia used the technical advances of the romantic era to compose a vast body of nationalistic music, making use of folk tales, songs, and dances indigenous to Russia. Tchaikovsky was the only Russian composer who embodied an almost pure romantic style. He lived in an era of heightening Russian awareness of the arts in relation to their own cultural heritage and that of the rest of Europe. Tchaikovsky, almost alone among Russian composers, traveled widely in Europe and assimilated his cultural experiences into his music. Tchaikovsky composed the Serenade in Italy in 1880 during an extended stay, which also saw completion of *Capriccio Italien* and the famous *Overture 1812*, two vividly descriptive pieces in contrast to the abstract formality of the Serenade.

Unit 4: Technical Considerations

This is a standard repertoire work that makes significant technical and musical demands of the players. Players of all instruments need facility to fifth position within a wide variety of keys. Although the work uses mostly the keys of C, G, D, and E-flat major, there are many short forays into other keys via accidentals. Technical fluency in both scales and arpeggios is required. In addition, a mature grasp of stylistic playing is necessary for successful presentation. Although most of the rhythms employed are fairly straightforward, cross-rhythms occur frequently, especially in the third movement. A wide variety of bowing styles is called for in each of the movements.

Unit 5: Stylistic Considerations

The Serenade is a wonderful example of the romantic style, demonstrating many of the musical and compositional techniques that characterize the music of Tchaikovsky. Attention must be paid to the shape of the melodic lines, whether the notes are very slow or very fast. Dynamic shadings of larger phrases, smaller figures, and individual notes are of great importance, as is the attainment of the many musical contrasts imbedded in the work. Off-string bowings must be cleanly executed, and lines must be passed easily from one section to another. Although the Waltz looks less complicated and shorter than the others, it is, in fact, the most difficult movement to perform successfully. The facile waltz style is difficult to achieve with student orchestras. The other three movements each stand alone well and work well in combination.

Unit 6: Musical Elements

Traditional major/minor harmony is employed throughout. The keys of C and G major are most prevalent, although a large portion of the Finale is in E-flat major. Sequential phrases are often employed; Tchaikovsky uses this technique for harmonic development and to extend musical ideas. Each movement presents two contrasting themes, and in each, the two themes are combined in some fashion during the development. Pedal point appears on several occasions to solidify the harmonic direction of extended passages. Every section has the opportunity to play soloistically, and lyrically, as well as in a virtuoso style.

Unit 7: Form and Structure

SECTION	MEASURES	EVENT AND SCORING
Movement 1:		
Form: sonatina		
Introduction	1–36	C major
Theme A	37–90	C major
Theme B	91–145	Predominantly G major; developmental mm. 106–145
Codetta	146–155	G major
Literal repeat of both themes	156–274	C major throughout
Coda	275–end	Restatement of opening; C major
Movement 2:		
Form: three-part song (A A´ A´´–B–A A´ A´´)		
Theme A, part 1	1–20	G major
Transition	22–33	
Part 2	34–52	G major
Part 1´	52–72	G major
Theme B	73–114	B minor
Theme A, literal return	114–189	G major
Coda	190–end	Derived from both A and B themes; G major

SECTION	MEASURES	EVENT AND SCORING
Movement 3:		
Form: three-part (A–B B´–A)		
Theme A	1–20	D major
Theme B, part 1	21–42	D major
Part 2	43–69	A major
Part 1´	70–89	D major
Transition,		
recitative	90–108	Modulatory
Theme A	109–137	D major
Coda	138–end	D major
Movement 4:		
Form: sonata		
Introduction	1–43	G major (V of C)
Theme A	44–83	C major
Theme B	84–123	E-flat major
Codetta	124–167	
Development	167–231	
Retransition	232–264	C major
Theme A	264–295	C major
Theme B	296–336	C major
Transition	336–385	
Coda	386–end	Begins with restatement of first movement introduction; accelerating to the coda derived from Theme A

Unit 8: Suggested Listening
Antonín Dvořák, Serenade in E for Strings
Peter Tchaikovsky:
  Sleeping Beauty (ballet music)
  Symphony No. 2
  Symphony No. 4

Unit 9: Additional References and Resources

Abraham, Gerald, ed. *The Music of Tchaikovsky.* New York: W. W. Norton & Company, 1978.

Bowen, Catherine: *Beloved Friend—The Story of Tchaikovsky and Nadejda von Meck.* New York: Random House, 1937.

Brown, David: *Tchaikovsky.* New York: W. W. Norton & Company, 1978.

Evans, Edwin. *Tchaikovsky.* New York: Pellegrini and Cudahy, 1949.

Ewen, David, ed. *The Complete Book of Classical Music*. Englewood Cliffs, NJ: Prentice-Hall, Inc., 1965.

Holden, Anthony. *Tchaikovsky—A Biography*. New York: Random House, 1966.

Poznansky, Alexander, ed. *Tchaikovsky Through Others' Eyes*. Bloomington: Indiana University Press, 1999.

Contributed by:
Ian Edlund
Orchestra Director
North Thurston High School
Lacey, Washington

Teacher Resource Guide

Serenade, Movement 1 ("Eine Kleine Nachtmusik"), K. 525

Wolfgang Amadeus Mozart
(1756–1791)

STRING ORCHESTRA

Unit 1: Composer

Wolfgang Amadeus Mozart was born January 27, 1756, in Salzburg, Austria. His older sister, nicknamed Nannerl, took harpsichord lessons from her father, Leopold. The young Mozart, being greatly influenced by these sounds from birth, also took harpsichord as well as violin lessons. Leopold soon began concert tours all over Europe with his progeny, visiting Munich, Vienna, Frankfurt, Paris, London—where J. C. Bach befriended them—Rome, and numerous other cities. He encountered the music of Haydn in Vienna in 1773, a style that had a lasting influence on Mozart, as his own music later had an influence on Haydn. Haydn later said to Leopold, "Before God and as an honest man I tell you that your son is the greatest composer known to me either in person or by name."

In 1781, Mozart lost his position with the Archbishop of Salzburg and so moved to Vienna. He married Constanze Weber in 1782 and began a family, which added to his financial concerns. He composed his greatest works over the next nine years: *The Marriage of Figaro*, *Don Giovanni*, *Cosí fan tutte*, Symphony Nos. 35–41, the Clarinet Concerto, several string quartets, and the *Requiem*. He died at the age of 35 on December 5, 1791. Numerous romantic myths arose almost immediately concerning his death, all of which have been disproved: (1) that Salieri confessed to poisoning him, (2) that a snowstorm prevented the family from attending his burial—his body was removed from its original resting place because no one paid the mandatory fees, and (3) that the Masons and Jews had murdered Mozart, a story that readily appealed to the Nazis.

Unit 2: Composition
"Eine Kleine Nachtmusik" ("A Little Night Music") is one of the most endearing pieces in the repertoire. Mozart wrote this serenade in August 1787 while he was composing Act II of *Don Giovanni*. Originally a second minuet appeared between the first and second movements, which was standard for the eighteenth century serenade, but the autograph score has no such minuet.

Unit 3: Historical Perspective
After 1780, entertainment music included the genres of serenades, divertimentos, cassations, and notturnos, that is, background music for celebrations and often performed outside. Thousands of these works were written in the latter half of the 1700s; indeed, Mozart wrote twelve in this genre, as well as several marches. Works in this category have numerous movements and often include two or more minuets. Before 1780, the term "divertimento" could be applied to what we now consider serious music, that is, string quartets and keyboard sonatas.

Unit 4: Technical Considerations
Pianist Arthur Rubinstein once stated that "Mozart is easy enough for children to play, and too difficult for adults." Young people in string orchestras indeed love to play "Eine Kleine Nachtmusik" and eagerly accept the technical and stylistic challenges. Technical difficulties include (1) spiccato bowing and the lightness that Mozart's style requires; (2) an abundance of ornamentation, especially in the Romanze; (3) frequent chromatic lines, a trait that differentiates Mozart from Haydn; (4) complicated figurations in the accompanimental voices; and (5) a delicateness of tone for certain passages interspersed with vigorous sections that cannot exceed the bounds of eighteenth century taste.

Unit 5: Stylistic Considerations
There are numerous dynamic changes between antecedent and consequent phrases, typical of Mozart's form on a small scale. Performers must have excellent bow control for the lightness needed for spiccato and for playing and phrasing with good taste. Care must be taken to bring out the difference between strong and weak beats; amateurs often give equal weight to each beat, which gives a ponderous and unimaginative interpretation.

Unit 6: Musical Elements

The harmonic language is that of the late eighteenth century, that is, of the common practice period. Modulations occur mostly between closely related keys. In the first movement's development section, there are sudden harmonic shifts that make this the most interesting section of the movement. The second movement has numerous chromatic neighboring and passing tones, and modal shift from C major to C minor.

Unit 7: Form and Structure

SECTION	MEASURES	EVENT AND SCORING
Movement 1: "Allegro"		
Form: sonata		
A	1	Exposition; principal theme in G major
B	28	Second theme (letter A) in D major
Development	56	Short modulatory section
A	76	Recapitulation; principal theme (letter C) in G major
B	101	Second theme (letter D) in G major
Coda	124	Letter E in G major
Movement 2: "Romanza: Andante"		
Form: five-part rondo (ABACA)		
A	1	Rondo theme in C major
B	16	In G major
A	30	Middle of m. 30; letter A in C major
C	38	Middle of m. 38; in C minor
A	50	Middle of m. 50; letter B in C major
A´	66	Variant of "A" that extends into a coda in middle of m. 66 in C major
Movement 3: "Menuetto: Allegretto"		
Form: minuet–trio		
Minuet	1	a; G major
	9	b
	13	a´
Trio	17	c; D major
	25	d
	29	c´
Movement 4: "Rondo: Allegro"		
Form: sonata–rondo		
A	1	G major
B	17	D major

Section	Measures	Event and Scoring
A´	33	D major; extended section
A´	58	E-flat; functions as a short development section
B	85	G major
A	100	G major
Coda	131	G major

Unit 8: Suggested Listening

Wolfgang Amadeus Mozart:
    Serenades (complete)
    String Quartets, K. 387 and later
    String Quintets
    Symphony Nos. 1–41, especially Nos. 35–41

Unit 9: Additional References and Resources

Heartz, Daniel. *Haydn, Mozart, and the Viennese School.* New York: W. W. Norton & Company, 1995.

Randel, Don. ed. *The New Harvard Dictionary of Music.* Cambridge, MA: Harvard University Press, 1986.

Rosen, Charles. *The Classical Style: Haydn, Mozart, Beethoven.* New York: Viking, 1971.

Sadie, Stanley, ed. *The New Grove Dictionary of Music and Musicians.* New York: Grove's Dictionaries, 2000. Also available online at www.grovemusic.com

Slonimsky, Nicolas, ed. emeritus. *Baker's Biographical Dictionary of Musicians.* New York: Schirmer Books, 2001.

Todd, R. Larry, and Peter Williams, eds. *Perspectives on Mozart Performance.* New York: Cambridge University Press, 1991.

Valentin, Erich. *Mozart and His World.* New York: Viking, 1959, 1970.

Venezia, Mike. *Wolfgang Amadeus Mozart.* Illustr. Mike Venezia. Chicago: Children's Press, 1995. (Juvenile Literature)

Contributed by:

David Littrell
Professor of Music
Kansas State University
Manhattan, Kansas

Teacher Resource Guide

Serenade in E for String Orchestra, Op. 22

Antonín Dvořák
(1841–1904)

STRING ORCHESTRA

Unit 1: Composer

Antonín Dvořák was born on September 8, 1841, in Nolahozeves in what is now the Czech Republic. His origins were humble because his father worked as an innkeeper and a butcher. At first, it seemed as if the young Dvořák would follow his father in that profession. Nevertheless, when his talent for music attracted the attention of his first teacher, in spite of their modest means his family saw to it that he was able to pursue music. In 1857, Dvořák went to study at the Organ School in Prague. Upon graduation, he played viola under the baton of Smetana in the orchestra of the Bohemian Provisional Theater for eleven years and later became organist of the church of St. Adalbert. He wrote many songs, overtures, and symphonies while serving as organist, but his first successful work was *Hymnus*, with a text by Halek, which was well received at its first performance in 1873.

Soon, Dvořák began to enjoy the acclaim of other musicians. He met Brahms, who greatly influenced his later work. Brahms was one of a committee that awarded Dvořák the Austrian State Prize in 1875 and again in 1877. Revenue from that grant enabled him to write many more pieces in the next two years. By 1878, his fame had spread to other countries, and he began to be a successful and acclaimed composer. He traveled to America in 1892 and was appointed the director of the National Conservatory of Music in New York. His impressions of America inspired several compositions. In 1901, he was appointed director of the Prague Conservatory.

Among his many compositions were nine symphonies; several symphonic poems; a concerto each for violin, piano, and cello; ten operas; and numerous chamber works and songs. Dvořák, together with Smetana, who influenced his early years, and Josef Suk, his pupil at the Prague Conservatory (and, later, his son-in-law), exemplified the Nationalistic Czech style of composition. Dvořák died on May 1, 1904.

Unit 2: Composition

Serenade for Strings, Op. 22, was composed in just two weeks during May 1873. It was first performed in Prague on December 10, 1876. This work was written for strings only and today is considered one of the major works in the string orchestra repertoire. It joins other serenades by such composers as Tchaikovsky and Grieg. The piece is in five movements that pattern a graceful and elegant expression of lyrical beauty, a striking characteristic of Dvořák's youthful works. An instant success, the Serenade was acclaimed for its admirable writing for strings and the direct and unpretentious expression of joy and tenderness it displays. Although subtle hints of its Bohemian roots are audible, especially in the last movement, this work displays the elegant, drawing room style of many of its Austrian predecessors by Mozart and Haydn. It is music that was written for the audience's enjoyment.

Unit 3: Historical Perspective

A serenade was originally a vocal or instrumental work intended for performance in the evening and usually addressed to a lover, a friend, or a person of rank. By the eighteenth century, the form had evolved into a composition for instruments, often commissioned for a particular occasion. Its form was based on the typical eighteenth century standard instrumental work, a three-movement piece (fast–slow–fast) with additional march or dance movements. The tradition continued in the nineteenth century, as evidenced by Brahms's two compositions in this genre, one by Tchaikovsky and this one by Dvořák specifically for strings. The music was generally light, pleasant, and entertaining in character, with none of the fire, pathos, or angst of a symphony or a tone poem. The Serenade has five movements: Moderato; Waltz and Trio; Scherzo: vivace; Larghetto; and Finale: allegro vivace. The work is tied together by the generally cheerful and elegant expression, a pleasing and imaginative lyricism, and the cyclical use of melodic material in some of the movements.

Unit 4: Technical Considerations

Most of the technical demands of stringed instrument playing are required to play Dvořák's Serenade for Strings. All players must have command of the gamut of scales, chromatic alterations, and a wide range calling for numerous high notes. The first violin part frequently goes up to G-sharp and A in the octave above the treble staff. Cellists must be aware of the convention, common in Dvořák's time, of reading the treble clef an octave lower than it is written if the part goes directly from bass to treble clef without first passing through the tenor clef. There are many instances where the cello part is so written. Cello and bass parts are independent from each other virtually throughout the work. The viola part is divided much of the time and goes into treble clef several times. Some spots require three independent cello lines, each crucial to the music's effectiveness. Second violin parts frequently carry the melodic line either alone or in some relationship to another instrument. The ensemble must consist entirely of strong, independent players who are equal to the technical and musical demands of the composition. Rapid technical passages demanding dexterity and long, sustained melodic lines requiring the limits of expressive playing appear in the work.

Unit 5: Stylistic Considerations

Dvořák lived and composed during the romantic period. Music of this period extended the limits of dynamic contrast and tempo extremes and widened the melodic range of earlier music. Thematic fragments, or thematic material developed from these fragments, often recur and tie the five movements of the Serenade together. The five movements reflect the eighteenth century serenade idea of a basic fast–slow–fast instrumental form, with the Waltz and the Scherzo forming the two additional dance movements. Most of the movements are in some type of three-part form, and most vary or develop the first material a certain amount upon the return. An additional unifying factor is provided by the frequent use of canonic imitation and sharing the melodic material between sections of the orchestra.

Unit 6: Musical Elements

Lyrical, expressive playing in the romantic style gives the lovely themes and phrases of this elegant work their life and character. Full, smooth bow strokes must be cultivated to perform the Moderato opening and the Larghetto in the appropriate manner. Short, off-the-string strokes will also be needed, as the music frequently changes character. Full group practice in achieving and matching the style and sound of off-the-string bowing will help the ensemble perform the Scherzo movement more effectively.

The melodic line is passed around frequently among various voices, making the balance between harmonic and melodic parts tricky to achieve. In many cases, the instrument with the most technically difficult part does not carry the melody and, thus, is not the most important voice. In several spots, figuration or melodic material passes from one section to another, requiring seamless precision of playing. All sections must bow similar passages the same way. The work abounds in tempo changes, *ritardando* effects, and fermata pauses. Rhythmic variety provides further contrast. Ensembles must take care to perform either vigorously or smoothly the rhythm in the contrasting sections in the Moderato and Scherzo.

Unit 7: Form and Structure

SECTION	MEASURES	EVENT AND SCORING
Movement 1: "Moderato"		
A	1–28	E major; smoothly flowing melody accompanied by slightly detached, repeated eighth notes
B	31–51	G major; angular, rhythmic motive in vigorous dotted-eighth and sixteenth notes; addition of cello obbligato on repeat, recalling earlier lyric elements
Transition	52–53	
A	54	E major, incorporates transitional material as accompaniment and features octave doublings and different instruments as a variation from the first statement
Movement 2: "Waltz and Trio"		
Waltz	1–70	C-sharp minor; graceful melody over harp-like chordal accompaniment; three melodic ideas follow one another in close succession; ends with two short, sharp chords establishing the tonality
Trio	72–197	D-flat major; slower motive becomes more emphatic and marked in style until the return of main theme; high and low strings set up an antiphonal and then a canonic treatment of melodic fragments before the *da capo*
Waltz		C-sharp minor; *da capo* with final ending; ends with C-sharp major chord
Movement 3: "Scherzo"		
A	1–60	F major; energetic melody in cello; first violin canon at the measure; canon idea and scurrying sixteenth note accompanying figures passed among various instrument combinations

SECTION	MEASURES	EVENT AND SCORING
Second theme	67–119	F major; more subdued theme also receives canonic treatment with rhythmic motives in the accompanying figures; modulates to A minor, ushering in the middle section
B	120–177	A major; angular melody with wide skips and longer note values, contrast to the previous section; theme accompanied by pulsating rhythmic motives provides contrast to smoother rhythm
False return	178	Still in A major; revisits the mood of the Scherzo; modulates over a dominant pedal with melodic fragments until the real return at m. 202
A	202–285	F major; theme is stated first in cello; themes are reworked in a slightly shorter version
Coda	286–323	F major; the quieter second theme and a hint of the original accompanying figure combine in a gentle statement before the final gesture with a motive from the original first theme is accomplished in a final rush of energy

Movement 4: "Larghetto"

SECTION	MEASURES	EVENT AND SCORING
A	1–46	A major; melody is initially stated in first violin; beginning in cello on the second statement; canonic treatment
B	47-67	C-sharp minor; short contrasting section employing a drier, staccato tune juxtaposed against a wandering arpeggiated eighth note figure in canonic style between violin and viola slips briefly into E major before the return at m. 68
A	68–101	A major; the original melody in its canonic form heralds the return but is accompanied by a little hint of rhythmic motive in viola

SECTION	MEASURES	EVENT AND SCORING
Movement 5: "Finale"		
A	1–85	C-sharp minor; a spiky, mostly staccato melody, again employs canonic treatment; motives derived from the theme fragmented and developed into accompanying figures for the skipping rhythm of the second theme in E major at m. 31
B	86–173	C-sharp minor; vigorous double-dotted rhythms and energetic sixteenth note accompaniment figures mark the contrasting section; fragments of the melody, accent displacements, and abrupt dynamic changes spin out the interlude with a mostly dominant feel up to the return
A´	174–392	E major; original theme group returns in the major mode, lapses into a brief reprise in m. 343 of Moderato theme and cadence; restatement of the opening Finale theme at m. 358; ends in E major

Unit 8: Suggested Listening

Antonín Dvořák:
    Cello Concerto
    Romance for Violin and Orchestra
    Slavonic Dances, Ops. 46 and 72
    Symphony Nos. 1–9
    Violin Concerto
Edvard Grieg, *Suite in Olden Style from Holberg's Time*
Bedřich Smetana, *Ma Vlást*
Josef Suk, Serenade for Strings
Peter Tchaikovsky, Serenade for Strings

Unit 9: Additional References and Resources

Clapham, John. *Dvořák*. New York: W. W. Norton & Company, 1979.

Fischl, Viktor. *Antonín Dvořák: His Achievement*. Westport, CT: Greenwood Press, 1970.

Hughes, Gervase. *Dvořák: his life and music*. New York: Dodd, Mead & Co., 1967.

Randel, Don Michael. *The New Harvard Dictionary of Music*. Cambridge, MA: Harvard University, 1986.

Robertson, Alec. *Dvořák*. London: J. M. Dent and Sons, Ltd., 1947.

Sadie, Stanley, ed. *The New Grove Dictionary of Music and Musicians*. New York: Grove's Dictionaries, 2000. Also available online at www.grovemusic.com

Slonimsky, Nicolas, ed. emeritus. *Baker's Biographical Dictionary of Musicians*. New York: Schirmer Books, 2001.

Sourek, Otakár. *Antonín Dvořák: his life and works*. New York: Philosophical Library, Inc., 1954.

Westrup, Jack. *Collins Encyclopedia of Music*. New York: W. W. Norton & Company, 1981.

Contributed by:
Kristin Turner
String Music Education
Arizona State University
Tempe, Arizona

Teacher Resource Guide

Symphony No. 1, Op. 21
Ludwig van Beethoven
(1770–1827)

FULL ORCHESTRA

Unit 1: Composer

Ludwig van Beethoven was born in Bonn, Germany, in 1770. He remains to this day one of the most well-known composers of orchestral repertoire. Beethoven's life transcended two of the more important stylistic epochs of musical history, the classic and romantic eras, during a time when the arts and Western Europe were particularly influenced by the American and French Revolutions of the late eighteenth century.

Beethoven came from a family of court singers, but his early family life was rather unhappy because of the abuse from an alcoholic father and the need for Beethoven at an early age to take on the role of caregiver to his mother and two younger brothers. In his early teen years he was already working as a chapel organist, and by his seventeenth year, Beethoven traveled to Vienna to play for Mozart. Beethoven's talents continued to evolve, and at seventeen, he traveled to Vienna to play for Mozart. Beethoven's talents continued to evolve, and by the age of twenty-two, he decided to move permanently to Vienna to study with Haydn.

Beethoven's career in Vienna demonstrated his great talent as a solo pianist and included an additional commitment to composition. He was welcomed into the homes of the music-loving aristocracy of Vienna, and through the influences of those wealthy patrons, Beethoven was able to receive support and commissions from a series of counts and princes, many of whom received dedications in his compositions. By his early thirties, Beethoven had achieved fame as a serious and successful composer with several publishers competing for his compositions. His success continued to grow; however, he

was afflicted with the loss of hearing. As a result, his middle and late years were dedicated to the challenges of life in an environment filled with the politics of a new democracy in Europe, his own physical and psychological frustrations brought on by his increasing deafness, and the drive to create an expressive and emotional ideal unique in the history of music.

Unit 2: Composition

Symphony No. 1 is one of Beethoven's truly pivotal compositions, coming at the turn of the century, 1799–1800. It is modeled after the mature symphonies of both Haydn and Mozart and is composed in the traditional four-movement classic symphony scheme. The first movement begins with a slow introduction (common time, "Adagio molto") and leads into the *alla breve* "Allegro con brio" main body of the movement. The key is C major for the entire first movement, with various other key areas explored in the development. The second movement, which functions as the slow movement of the symphony, is a 3/8 "Andante cantabile con moto" in the key of F major, the subdominant relationship to the C major key of the symphony. The third movement is titled "Menuetto, Allegro molto e vivace." This movement is in 3/4 in the key of C major. The fourth and final movement begins with a short, slow introduction, designated "Adagio," in 2/4 in the key of C major. It continues into the main body of the movement, the "Allegro molto e vivace," still in 2/4 and still in C major.

Unit 3: Historical Perspective

As its composition date of 1799–1800 suggests, Symphony No. 1 looks back on one century and ahead to the next. Neither the number of the forces used nor the work's formal dimensions expand on the later symphonies of Haydn. Mozart's influences may run even deeper compositionally.

There has been a melodic comparison made between the first movement of Symphony No. 1 and the opening theme of Mozart's Symphony No. 41 ("Jupiter"). Beethoven's opening chord, the C dominant seventh chord, immediately resolves to an F major chord, setting up the strong relationship to C major's subdominant keys and flat side of the home key. Likewise, Mozart's commitment to second movement key areas shows a strong pattern of subdominant keys rather than the more traditional relative minor or dominant key.

Beethoven composed this symphony during what is referred to as his "early period," which coincides with his arrival in Vienna in 1799. During this early period, Napoleon's military successes gained Beethoven's support, politically and socially, as the French Revolution was nearing ten years. Symphony No. 1 rang with the enormous optimism and talent of a young composer, newly settled in the exciting metropolis of Vienna at the beginning of a new century. It wasn't until three years later when Beethoven would experience his loss of hearing.

Unit 4: Technical Considerations

Familiarity with the C major and F major scales and arpeggios may become a technical focus for the entire ensemble during rehearsal. Various technical routines should be incorporated into the daily rehearsal routines. In addition, some of the faster technical passages in the Allegro portions of the first and last movements will require the string players to become technically adept at some of the more advanced string techniques and bowing routines: spiccato, détaché, marcato, and martelé. Likewise, the wind players will need to synchronize basic issues of style and length with the string players. The conductor may want to utilize various bowing and rhythm exercises with the scale and arpeggio routines to achieve more technical confidence.

In addition, a dominant compositional feature in Beethoven's style is frequent use of the *subito* dynamic changes that provides a challenge for the listeners who are unprepared for the changing dynamics and the players who, even at a more experienced level, need encouragement to maximize the dynamic contrasts required in the score. Various creative exercises can be invented for the players to address the two basic *subito* dynamic changes: the *subito f* or *ff* prepared by a *diminuendo*, and the *subito p* or *pp* prepared by a *crescendo*. The ensemble can also work to achieve a more mature approach to the *fp* and *sfz* dynamics, being encouraged to perform these nuances with a clear distinction made between the two dynamics.

SEATING:

The violins should be divided, with the first and second violins sitting on either side of the conductor facing each other. This seating was the common practice throughout much of the nineteenth century and is an important practice sometimes ignored by contemporary conductors. The trumpets and timpani should be seated close together. The woodwinds should be seated in the traditional center grouping of two rows.

INSTRUMENTAL CONSIDERATIONS:

During Beethoven's time, the horn and trumpet players played natural instruments without pistons; these natural horns limited players to the notes available in the overtone series. The timpani player played on two different drums, tuned to the tonic and dominant keys of the composition. The timpani sticks were rather hard, and the heads of the timpani were made of animal hide. The timpani player should be encouraged to investigate sonic compensations for the original instruments given that the more modern instruments cannot adequately duplicate the original instruments of Beethoven's day. The conductor may want to investigate further the dynamic and sonic implications of the tone quality and sound blend of such instruments and adjust the printed dynamics appropriately.

Beethoven and his contemporaries still approached the notation of dynamics with a verticality of convenience; that is, the same dynamic notation was vertically notated in each instrument in the score without regard for the technical abilities or limitations of individual instruments. The string instruments of Beethoven's time are regarded today as having had a smaller, lighter sound when compared to modern string instruments. The classical era string instruments made exclusive use of gut strings, with a tone quality markedly different from contemporary instruments that possess a tone quality affected by the modern steel string. The classical era bows were also somewhat shorter and did not enjoy the strength of more modern sticks. To help compensate for these changes, the conductor may want to experiment with having the string players hold their bows a little higher on the stick, loosen the tension of the bow hair, and minimize their left-hand vibrato usage.

Unit 5: Stylistic Considerations

Beethoven's nine symphonies traverse all three creative periods of his compositional life. The music of the early symphonies comes from his early period at the beginning of the nineteenth century. There are several important stylistic considerations for the conductor to include in the preparation of the early symphonies of Beethoven, such as an awareness of the conventions that should be carried over from the classic period and the influences from Mozart's and Haydn's later works. Choices of editions rank very high on any conductor's priority list because new musicological research and increasingly dependable scores and orchestral materials are available.

TEMPO AND METER:

Even though there are metronome indications listed for all movements, those indications came later in Beethoven's life when his physical and emotional state was far different than when he had actually composed Symphony No. 1. There is to this day an enormous controversy about the correctness and appropriateness of adhering strictly to those metronome markings; conductors must decide for themselves. Because of the existence of these metronome markings, the conductor can assume that the compositional practice of *tempi ordinari* is not appropriate in Beethoven performance practice. A perusal of the symphonies' metronome markings show that Beethoven and his other contemporaries utilized the metronome precisely to assist the performer in avoiding an approach to tempo whereby the sections and movements of a large work would have been related with a unifying pulse.

Arguably, the most challenging aspect of the performance of these early metronomic compositions in this common practice period is deciding on the correct tempo, speed, and character. Frequent misinterpretations of this aspect of performance by today's conductors are often heard when specific notations for meters are too often ignored. Some of the more common misinterpretations include *alla breve*, which in slow introductions is often ignored and over-subdivided by the conductor, ultimately leading to a loss of musical flow.

Additional misreadings affecting the flow of the music come from the frequent lack of distinction between 3/8 and 3/4, with important agogic stresses incorrectly performed. Fast 2/4 movements, such as in the last movement of this symphony with a metronome marking of half note = 88, indicate that such movements should be conducted in one.

Unit 6: Musical Elements

HARMONY:
The first movement, "Adagio molto; Allegro con brio," is in C major. The most dramatic and noteworthy feature of the opening of the symphony is the harmonic relationship that sets up the key of F so early in the introduction. A harmony that begins on the dominant seventh *on* C rather than *in* C sets up an important statement to the listeners—that their musical expectations may not always be realized. The second key area is in the traditional dominant key of G major. The development traverses the key areas of G minor, B-flat major, E minor, and G major. The recapitulation places both themes in the key of C major.

The second movement, "Andante cantabile con moto," is in the subdominant key of F major. The second theme is in the relative key of D minor. The development begins in the key of C minor, with the recapitulation's first theme returning in F major and the second theme now appearing in G major rather than the traditional F major.

The third movement, "Minuet and Trio," is perhaps the most original movement of the symphony with regard to melodic construction and pedal point harmonies. This movement is in C major. The trio's two sections are in the keys of C and G major, respectively.

The final movement, "Adagio," begins on a strong dominant fermata chord of G major, which sets the entire six-measure, slow introduction as a musical upbeat into the large, fast section that forms the body of the movement. The second theme is in the dominant key of G major. The long, extended development traverses a number of keys in a condensed circle of fifths that finishes in the dominant key area of G that sets up the recapitulation and C major return. The recapitulation of the first theme is in C major with the second theme in F major. A series of fermatas leads into the coda section that finishes in the C major key.

MELODY:
Performers will be quick to note Beethoven's preoccupation in melodic construction with scales and arpeggios. The themes for each of the movements are all constructed by rising scale cells. The opening Allegro theme of the first movement also makes use of the interval of the fourth, which allows Beethoven to explore those implied arpeggio figurations in the melodic writing of the symphony.

RHYTHM:

Beethoven frequently employs a long/short rhythmic relationship with his melodic cells, apparent in the first movement introduction and Allegro rhythms. The second, third, and fourth movements also share this rhythmic idea in their respective melodies. An important historic occurrence of rhythmic synchronization appears in the closing theme passages of the second movement. These passages are marked by an ostinato timpani figuration of dotted-sixteenth/thirty-second groupings under a sixteenth note triplet violin passage (measures 53–61, 153–161). The conductor should view this performance practice issue with some care. The practice of synchronization comes from earlier baroque traditions in which the dotted figures would be lined up with triplet melodies, and such a practice seems implied even in this Beethoven symphony. There are many musical examples that bear evidence of this practice well into the nineteenth century—even as late as some of the operas and large choral works of Verdi.

Unit 7: Form and Structure

Two of the more popular classical forms are utilized in this symphony: sonata-allegro and minuet-trio. The performance of repeat sections is critical to the symmetry of a movement's sections in this early classical period. The conductor should also note that Beethoven's approach to form altered and expanded upon the historic models. Beethoven's recapitulations, for example, in both the first and second movements alter the orchestration and dynamics when compared to the exposition scorings. The second movement recapitulation is also characterized by the incorporation of a fugal countersubject to the main theme. Also of major importance to the conductor is the formal design of the menuet/trio and the need to perform all the repeats of this movement, even on the *da capo* return of the Menuet.

SECTION   MEASURES

Movement 1: "Adagio molto, Allegro con brio"
Form: sonata–allegro

Section	Measures
Introduction	1
Allegro/Theme A	13
Theme B	53
Development	110
Recapitulation/	
Theme A	178
Theme B	206
Coda	259

SECTION   MEASURES

Movement 2: "Andante cantabile con moto"
Form: sonata–allegro
Theme A   1
Theme B   27
Closing Theme   53
Development   65
Recap/Theme A   100
Theme B   127
Closing Theme   153
Coda   162

Movement 3: "Menuetto, Allegro molto e vivace"
Form: trio–menuet–trio
Menuetto:
   Theme A   1
Theme B   9
Theme A´/
   extended   45
Trio: Theme C   80
Theme D   104
Menuetto *da capo*

Movement 4: "Adagio, Allegro molto e vivace"
Form: sonata–allegro
Introduction   1
Allegro/
   Theme A   8
Theme B   56
Development   96
Recapitulation/
   Theme A   164
Theme B   192
Coda   268

Unit 8: Suggested Listening

Ludwig van Beethoven, other "heroic" overtures:
   Coriolan
   Fidelio
   King Stephen
   Leonore No. 3
Ludwig van Beethoven, Symphony Nos. 1–9

Franz Joseph Haydn, Symphony Nos. 88, 92, 100, 102, 104
Wolfgang Amadeus Mozart, Symphony Nos. 39–41

Unit 9: Additional References and Resources

The bibliography available for the life and music of Beethoven is extensive. The reader may want to further investigate more of the available sources. The following represents a limited, general, and highly selective sampling of the available resources.

Carse, Adam. *The Orchestra from Beethoven to Berlioz*. New York: Broude, 1948.

Carse, Adam. *The Orchestra in the XVIII Century*. Cambridge: W. Heffer & Sons, Ltd., 1940.

Del Mar, Norman. *Conducting Beethoven. Volume 2: Overtures, Concertos, Missa Solemnis*. London: Oxford University Press, 1989.

Kolisch, Rudolf. "Tempo and Character in Beethoven's Music." *Musical Quarterly*, April 1943.

Leinsdorf, Erich. *The Composer's Advocate*. New Haven, CT: Yale University Press, 1974.

Marty, Jean-Pierre. *The Tempo Indications of Mozart*. New Haven, CT: Yale University Press, 1988.

Rudolf, Max. "The Metronome Indications in Beethoven's Symphonies." *The Journal of the Conductor's Guild*, Vol. I, No. 1: Spring, 1980.

Weingartner, Felix. *On the Performance of the Beethoven Symphonies*. (English edition, Dover, 1968.) Leipzig: 1928.

Zaslaw, Neal. *Mozart's Symphonies: Context, Performance Practice, Reception*. Oxford: Clarendon Press, 1989.

Contributed by:
Glenn Block
Director of Orchestras and Opera
Professor of Conducting
Illinois State University
Bloomington, Illinois

Index by Orchestration

STRING ORCHESTRA

TITLE	COMPOSER/ARRANGER	GRADE	PAGE
"Adagietto" from Symphony No. 5	Gustav Mahler	6	457
Adagio for Strings, Op. 11	Samuel Barber	6	461
Adieu	Todd Coleman	4	265
Air for Strings	Norman Dello Joio	4	269
Allegro in D	Antonio Vivaldi/arr. Steven Frackenpohl	3	165
"Andante Cantabile" from String Quartet No. 1, Op. 11	Peter Tchaikovsky	5	369
Andante Festivo	Jean Sibelius	4	273
Apollo Suite	Merle J. Isaac	1	51
Peer Gynt Suite No. 1, Op. 46, Movement 2 ("Åse's Death")	Edvard Grieg	4	277
"Bark" Gigue, A	Ralph Hultgren	3	169
"Basse Danse" and "Mattachins" from *Capriol Suite*	Peter Warlock	4	280
Brandenburg Concerto No. 3 in G Major	Johann Sebastian Bach	5	373
Brandenburg Concerto No. 3 in G Major	Johann Sebastian Bach/arr. Merle Isaac	3	173
Brandenburg Concerto No. 5, Movement 1	Johann Sebastian Bach/arr. Merle Isaac	2	89
Canyon Sunset	John Caponegro	1	56
Concerto Grosso for String Orchestra	Ralph Vaughan Williams	5	385
Concerto Grosso for String Orchestra with Piano Obbligato	Ernest Bloch	5	378
Concerto Grosso in D Minor, Op. 3, No. 11	Antonio Vivaldi	5	391
Concerto Grosso No. 1 in G Major, Op. 6	George Frideric Handel	4	300
Concerto Grosso, Op. 6, No. 8 ("Christmas Concerto")	Arcangelo Corelli	4	304
Concerto in D Minor	Johann Sebastian Bach/arr. Merle Isaac	4	309
Contredanse	Antonio Salieri/arr. Edvard Fendler	3	178
Cripple Creek	arr. Edmund Siennicki	1	59
Dance of Iscariot	Kirt Mosier	4	315
"Dance of the Tumblers" from *Snow Maiden*	Nikolai Rimsky-Korsakov/ arr. Sandra Dackow	2	95
Danny Boy	arr. Harry Alshin	2	99

* plus rhythm section

FULL ORCHESTRA

Index by
Composer/Arranger

Index by Title